ORTHODOX AND WESLEYAN SPIRITUALITY

Orthodox and Wesleyan Spirituality

edited by

S T Kimbrough, Jr

ST VLADIMIR'S SEMINARY PRESS
CRESTWOOD, NEW YORK 10707
2002

Library of Congress Cataloging-in-Publication Data

Orthodox and Wesleyan spirituality / edited by S T Kimbrough, Jr.
   p. cm.
   Includes bibliographical references.
   ISBN 0–88141–235–X
   1. Wesley, John, 1703–1791. 2. Wesley, Charles, 1707–1788. 3. Orthodox Eastern Church—Influence. 4. Spirituality—Orthodox Eastern Church. 5. Spirituality—Methodist Church—History—18th century. 6. Orthodox Eastern Church—Relations—Methodist Church—History—18th century. 7. Methodist Church—Relations—Orthodox Eastern Church—History—18th century. I. Kimbrough, S T, 1936–

BX8495.W5 O75 2002
248'.088'27—dc21

2001059156

ST VLADIMIR'S SEMINARY PRESS
575 Scarsdale Rd., Crestwood, NY 10707
1-800-204-2665

ISBN 0–88141–235–X

PRINTED IN THE UNITED STATES OF AMERICA

Contents

Foreword

Methodists and Orthodox have been moved in recent years to return to the sources of their respective traditions. Though the specific reasons for this return differ in the two churches, the basic reason for it is the same. Thinkers in both churches have been led to question theological, liturgical, spiritual, and organizational developments, because they believe that things have gone awry, that the original vision and practice of their churches have been lost, that things alien to their traditional beliefs and practices have entered their ecclesial bodies.

Difficulties in maintaining the church's original and organic tradition began among the Orthodox with the coming of Ottoman rule over most of Orthodoxy in the fifteenth century, followed by the so-called "Western captivity" of Orthodox theology, church polity, and popular piety since the seventeenth. Difficulties in the Methodist church seem to have started shortly after the passing of the Wesley brothers, especially within the peculiar conditions of Protestant America.

For the Orthodox, the return to the sources has primarily meant a "return to the church fathers." This has been for the most part a return to the Fathers whose writings have been preserved in Greek. It has necessarily included the recovery of the liturgical, spiritual, dogmatic, and canonical texts that accompany the writings and witness of these holy men. For the Methodists, the return has been almost exclusively to the works of John and Charles Wesley and their coworkers, and through them to writers of the early church. Here also the recovered resources not only have been theological and catechetical in nature, but also doxological, sacramental, social, and evangelical. In both churches the return to original sources and authoritative testimonies also has necessitated a return to the Bible, with all of the exegetical challenges that this now entails, especially in regard to a theological and spiritual reading of the text, with application to devotional and doxological as well as ethical and ecclesiastical issues.

What makes the return to the sources in Orthodoxy and Methodism particularly meaningful for their churches, and for Christianity generally, is the striking similarity between the two traditions, which perhaps best may be described by noting what they both, each in their own way, are not.

Neither Orthodoxy nor Methodism is Augustinian in the essential ways in which Roman Catholicism, Lutheranism, and Calvinism (and the ways these traditions have influenced various forms of Anglicanism) obviously are. Neither Methodism nor Orthodoxy has been much influenced by the writings of St Augustine. Neither has engaged in major disputation about predestination, free will, justification, the atonement, the operation of the sacraments, or authority in the church. Neither church has had a tradition of "scholastic" theology, though Orthodoxy has had its imported version in recent centuries, which the proponents of the "neo-patristic consensus" and

others (like the modern Russian Slavophile, sophiological, and existentialist thinkers)
have criticized and abandoned. Articulation of doctrine in neither church traditionally has depended upon a particular philosophy, certainly not that of the church
fathers or the Wesleys. The Orthodox have been accused of being Hellenistic, which
they firmly deny while affirming that their church fathers (and modern Russians
influenced by idealism and existentialism) spoke the language, used the categories,
and engaged the issues of their day. Well-known Methodist theologians in America
recently have adopted the process philosophy of Alfred North Whitehead, while others have felt compelled to follow existentialist and liberationist thinkers.

While Orthodoxy and Methodism are traditionally allergic to an Augustinian
understanding of predestination, their "synergistic" understanding of human cooperation with divine grace sometimes has drawn accusations of being "semi-Pelagian."
When assessed in the anthropological framework of the great disputations between
Augustinians and Pelagians, which neither Orthodox nor Methodist theologians seem
to accept traditionally or seem moved to clarify carefully, this accusation is understandable. Writings in this present volume shed light on this difficult subject, although
none treats it directly.

Both churches reject the claims of the modern Roman papacy, yet both surely
would be sympathetic to what was once called "monastic theology" in the Latin West
and to the spiritual, ascetical, and mystical teachings of writers like Teresa of Avila,
John of the Cross, and Jan van Ruusbroec. Neither tradition in its origins has been
particularly legalistic or juridical, moralistic, or puritanical. Both have been accused
of being pietistic, which they both have denied when the term is used pejoratively.
Both place great emphasis on corporate worship of a highly sacramental and doxological character and on private prayer and devotion in which the mind is united to
the heart.

Both traditions are rooted in the Bible as God's Word without being fundamen-
talist. Neither has been known for selecting biblical verses to proof-text peculiar, often
controversial, confessional positions. Except for some North American Methodists,
neither has found modern biblical scholarship to result in a dismantling of traditional
Christian doctrine, worship, and spiritual life. Those in both churches who have been
inspired to return to their traditional sources affirm the classical Christian dogmas of
the Tri-personal Godhead and the divinity and humanity of Jesus Christ confessed as
God's only Son and the world's only Savior. Christ crucified and glorified is the foundational "canon of faith" in both traditions that provides the key to interpreting and
applying the whole of Scripture. Both traditions see God's glory fully revealed in the
cross of Christ. Both emphasize the presence and power of the Holy Spirit working
directly in creation. Both affirm the necessity of suffering for salvation and sanctification. Both insist that participation in God's being and life is what human being and
life is about.

Whatever the influences of early Eastern Christian writers on the Wesley brothers' doctrine and hymnody (which, as every teacher knows, cannot be determined
simply by counting references in writings), the essays in this volume clearly demonstrate that what informed, instructed, and inspired the Orthodox church fathers and
their disciples and John and Charles Wesley and their companions was exactly the

same. These were men and women bound to God's Word recorded in the Bible and recapitulated in Christ crucified. They read, prayed, preached, and lived this Word, personally and in community, as called, chosen, and faithful people justified, sanctified, and glorified by the one God and Father and his only Son Jesus Christ, God's incarnate Word, and the one Holy Spirit. They were witnesses and worshippers of the Holy Trinity, one in nature and undivided.

What can be learned about Christian faith and life in the original sources and authoritative witnesses of Eastern Orthodoxy and Wesleyan Methodism is boundlessly enlightening and life-giving. We thank God for raising up Christian scholars capable of offering these theological and spiritual treasures. We also thank these scholars for accepting their calling and fulfilling it so well.

Fr Thomas Hopko, Dean
St Vladimir's Orthodox Theological Seminary
Epiphany 2002

Preface

1995 marked the 250th anniversary of the publication of John and Charles Wesley's volume *Hymns on the Lord's Supper* (1745), without question one of the most significant collections of eucharistic hymns ever published in the English language. In celebration of a commemorative facsimile reprint of the first edition of this volume by The Charles Wesley Society, the society focused the theme of its annual meeting, held that year at The Divinity School of Duke University in Durham, NC, on views of *Hymns on the Lord's Supper* from the diverse perspectives of various church traditions: Orthodox, Roman Catholic, Anglican, Methodist, Reformed, and free church traditions. The presenter from the Orthodox tradition was The Very Reverend Leonid Kishkovsky, Ecumenical Officer for the Orthodox Church in America. In discussions with him following his lecture, he commented that perhaps ecumenical discussion would be best served in the future, particularly as pertains to the Orthodox and Wesleyan traditions, by going back to the sources of the traditions and examining them for their own veracity and by moving from within the traditions outward and forward.

With this in mind discussions began between Dr S T Kimbrough, Jr of the General Board of Global Ministries of The United Methodist Church, The Very Reverend Leonid Kishkovsky, and The Very Reverend Dr Thomas Hopko, Dean of St Vladimir's Orthodox Theological Seminary in Crestwood, NY, regarding plans for the first consultation on Orthodox and Wesleyan Spirituality, which was held in January of 1999. The consultation was not intended as an "official" ecumenical consultation of Orthodox and Wesleyan tradition churches, rather it was a gathering of leading scholars, clergy, and laity to explore the roots of spirituality in both traditions. There were participants from the following traditions: Greek Orthodox Archdiocese, the Orthodox Church in America, the Russian Orthodox Church, the British Methodist Church, The United Methodist Church, The Methodist Church in Singapore, The Nazarene Church, and the Roman Catholic Church. The primary themes addressed by the presenters had to do with holiness and perfection, the impact and influence of the East in the writings of John and Charles Wesley, the founders of Methodism, and the common and foundational ground on which the Wesleys and many of the eastern Fathers stood.

All of the papers published in this volume were prepared for the 1999 consultation. The Reverend Dn John Chryssavgis, one of the scheduled presenters, was not able to attend the consultation but made his paper, included here as chapter 3, "The Practical Way of Holiness: Isaiah of Scetis and John Wesley," available to all members of the consultation when it convened. Some segments of the paper by Kathleen E. McVey, "Ephrem the Syrian: A Theologian of the Presence of God," have appeared previously in the general introduction and introductions to individual hymns and notes of her book, *Ephrem the Syrian: Hymns*, Classics of Western Spirituality (New York: Paulist, 1989). The chapter as it appears here was first published by Routledge Press in the volume *The Early Christian World*, edited by Philip F. Esler and is reprinted here by permission. Its unrevised version was first delivered as a paper at the 1999 consultation on "Orthodox and Wesleyan Spirituality."

There is a strong presence of the theology and spirituality of the early church fathers in the writings and practice of the Wesleys, as evidenced in the discussions presented here by persons from the Orthodox and Wesleyan traditions. While there is much to be done toward establishing the direct channels of influence, the discourses of this volume will serve well the cause of discovering commonalities, as well as differences, in their theology and practice. The chapters in this volume were not developed out of a specific methodology as to how to address the study of materials which are separated by hundreds of years but which share common sources of history, knowledge, and theology. They are foundational, however, to an ongoing discussion out of which the guidelines of such a methodology may emerge. Each presenter was encouraged to speak from within his or her tradition and research outward, rather than with a predisposed quest for commonalities or differences. Nevertheless, one will find here foundation stones for building bridges of understanding and the deepening of spirituality in one's journey with Christ and the church.

Deep appreciation is expressed to the executive staff and faculty of St Vladimir's Orthodox Theological Seminary in Crestwood, NY for hosting the first consultation on "Orthodox and Wesleyan Spirituality" in January 1999, to St Vladimir's Seminary Press for publishing the papers presented at the consultation, to The Very Reverend Leonid Kishkovsky and The Very Reverend Dr Thomas Hopko for their roles in planning and leadership, and to the General Board of Global Ministries of The United Methodist Church for providing the primary funding, and to its executive staff for planning and leadership.

S T Kimbrough, Jr
Editor

Introduction

Contrary to the popular conclusion of the distinguished Wesley scholar, Albert Outler, that John Wesley relied heavily on the writers of the early church for the formation of his thought, Richard P. Heitzenrater concludes in chapter 1, "John Wesley's Reading of and References to the Early Church Fathers," that this view cannot be supported merely by the references in Wesley's writings to the works of the early church fathers. Rather Wesley's uses of their works were polemical, conservative, programmatic, aphoristic, and for the purpose of name-dropping.

Heitzenrater surveys all of the references to the early church fathers in Wesley's writings. Clearly he had read Clemens Romanus, Ignatius, Polycarp, Ephrem Syrus, and refers to at least one reading of Justin Martyr, Tertullian, Origen, Clemens Alexandrinus, and Cyprian. Nevertheless, the evidence of the references does not support the view that Wesley relied heavily on the works of the early church fathers. Most of the references are very early in his letters, journal, and diaries. He does cite them from time to time, especially to support his own doctrinal views. Heitzenrater maintains that the strength of Wesley's reliance on the early church fathers cannot be measured adequately from his citations of their works or quotations from the same.

He concludes, however: "One certainly cannot dismiss the influence of the early church in his [Wesley's] life and thought—it is evident in the shape of his theology and the details of his program. Nevertheless, it appears that a great deal more work needs to be done on the specific channels by which that thought was transmitted to Wesley."

Without question in the Wesleys one finds two eighteenth-century divines of the Church of England through whose thought the window to the East remains open. This volume explores the reality that the influence from the East is present in the writings of John and Charles Wesley. Heitzenrater is right to point scholarship to an exploration of the channels through which the influences of the early church fathers were transmitted to John Wesley. The investigations of this volume assist in that process. Even discussions of parallel theological precepts in the Wesleys and the early Fathers, while not revealing direct channels of influence, may aid the discovery of such channels and the common and foundational ground upon which these eighteenth-century Western divines and the Eastern Fathers stood.

In chapter 2, Carlton R. Young presents "A Survey of Eastern Sources in British and American Methodist Hymnals." It is one of the first substantive discussions addressing the repertory of Eastern hymnody which has made its way into the hymn books of Methodism, a primary contribution of the nineteenth-century British hymnic explosion, which resulted in the publication of *Hymns Ancient and Modern*, 1861. This is unquestionably a late appearance in Western Christianity of extremely important hymnic literature of the East.

Young highlights the appearance of Eastern hymns through the diligent work of the scholar-priest, John Mason Neale (1818–1866). Neale understood the liturgical values of the material and his translations from Latin and Greek still have a freshness and eloquence about them. He had a special gift to form centos out of rhythmical prose for both chant and rhymed metered verse. These became used both by choirs and congregations.

In addition to the hymnic texts, Young discusses the liturgical texts shared in common with the liturgies of St John Chrysostom and of St Basil the Great, including spoken and sung texts for the Eucharist, as well as canticles and prayers.

With some very helpful charts at the conclusion, Young tracks the Eastern sources in the hymnals of Methodism and some ecumenical sources.

Chapter 3, "Trinitarian Theology and Wesleyan Holiness," is by Geoffrey Wainwright, who avers that belief in the Triune God is integral to Orthodox and Wesleyan spirituality and it is the Triune God who enables holiness. Wainwright notes at the outset of this chapter what he deems to be an "accurate systematization of the scriptural record" in St Basil's work, *On the Holy Spirit,* in which he maintains "that all works of God towards us start from the Father, proceed from the Son, and are completed in the Holy Spirit; and that our grateful response begins in the Spirit and ascends through the Son to the Father" (Wainwright, p. 60).

From this vantage point Wainwright proceeds to explore the corresponding resonance in the writings of John and Charles Wesley. He begins with John Wesley's elaboration of the Creed in his *Letter to a Roman Catholic.* Here, for example, Wesley stresses that the Holy Spirit enlightens our understanding, rectifies our wills and affections, renews our natures, unites our persons with Christ, assures us of the adoption as sons, purifies and sanctifies our souls and bodies, and leads us in our actions. Wainwright also emphasizes the role of the restoration of the image of God in Orthodox and Wesleyan spirituality, which is essential for the movement of human beings toward holiness and the quest of perfection.

From the *Hymns on the Trinity* (1767) of Charles Wesley, Wainwright has illustrated the fusion of soteriology and doxology in Wesleyan theology. He has superbly shown from Charles's poetry that each person of the Trinity has a role in salvation.

In chapter 4, "The Practical Way of Holiness: Isaiah of Scetis and John Wesley," John Chryssavgis pursues parallel insights in the writings of the *Ascetic Discourses* of Abba Isaiah and those of John Wesley, both of whom are interested in the practical way of holiness and the holy calling to perfection. Abba Isaiah is seen by Chryssavgis as a *praktikos,* who focuses on a life of *ascesis* or the way of perfection and he approaches the way of perfection from an eschatological perspective.

The spirituality of Abba Isaiah like that of Wesley is radically evangelical with a strong emphasis on repentance. They share in common an inward and outward spirituality, pursuing a way of perfection and holiness. Of vital importance to contemporary ecumenism is their openness in personal relations and breadth in confessional tolerance.

Though the work *Ascetic Discourses* of Abba Isaiah and the works of John and Charles Wesley come from different times and contexts, Professor Chryssavgis has demonstrated the value of exploring parallel insights in these spheres of Orthodox and Wesleyan traditions. He does not superimpose a conceptual structure on the thought of Abba Isaiah and the Wesleys; rather he allows their writings to speak from within outward. For both of them a practical way of holiness and the high calling to perfection are vital to Christian spirituality.

In chapter 5, "Holiness in Perspective of Eucharistic Theology," Petros Vassiliadis approaches the Christian understanding of holiness from the perspective of eucharistic theology. He seeks to relate eucharistic theology and monastic spirituality rather than juxtapose them. Biblical eschatology is a major point of reference in his discussion, since the eucharistic community is an eschatological community involved in an eschatological act or celebration, i.e. the Eucharist.

This is by no means a matter unrelated to Wesleyan spirituality, since this volume clearly shows how important the exploration of the Eastern Christian heritage is for an understanding of Wesleyan spirituality. Therefore, Vassiliadis views his discussion as an "ecumenical contemporary theological reflection."

The chapter focuses on the Eucharist as the springboard of the mission of the church. When the eschatological community gathers, it is the church in mission. The author avers, "the church sanctifies and saves the world not by what she does, or by what she says, but *by what she is.*" If one understands holiness from this perspective, its goal cannot be merely one of individual perfection, rather it is directly related to the shared life of communion that is discovered in God.

The theological shifts emphasized by Vassiliadis are extremely important for contemporary theological discussion, for a grasp of Wesleyan spirituality, and for ecumenical understanding. They are as follows: from eucharistic experience to the Christian message, from eschatology to Christology and to soteriology, from the event (Kingdom of God) to the bearer and center of this event (Christ and sacrament). These theological shifts take on significance for the contemporary church, as one sees the early church Eucharist as a communion event and not merely as an act of personal devotion. In this event holiness is expressed in the soul's union with the *logos,* the Word made flesh, rather than being connected simply with the coming Kingdom. Clearly such a view is worthy of continued examination in the light of a Wesleyan document such as *Hymns on the Lord's Supper* (1745).

The section on holiness concludes with chapter 6, "The Way of Holiness," by Dimitar Popmarinov Kirov, who addresses the concept of holiness in the Holy Scriptures in relation to ethics, the Christian mind, and the church. In Kirov's view holiness issues from God and is not an acquired state, rather a way—a way of life, a way toward God. He finds a tension between the concepts of personal and social holiness and avers that, according to the Bible, holiness is primarily personal, but since it is relational, namely, to God, others, and the world, all of God's creation may become holy. Indeed, holiness is the purpose of creation. As one travels the path of spirituality toward God, one becomes holy. Kirov points out that "everything issues from the heart," however, "and moves outward, not vice versa."

Even though he maintains that "the purpose of perfection is not the society, but the person," it is precisely the relational dimension of holiness which prevents one from living in isolation, as though one could become holy without relating to God, others, and creation. Ethics, however, are not to be equated per se with the way toward holiness. There is no system of ethics which leads to holiness, yet, ethics may indeed affirm persons on their way toward God. Ethics cannot be a substitute for the mediation of holiness to all humankind through Christ. It is here that one becomes aware that God's holiness is transmitted through the mysteries of the Incarnation and the life of the church, outside of which there is no holiness. In participation in the life and sacraments of the church one becomes holy.

Kirov emphasizes the contemporaneity of holiness by pointing to the weakness of Christianity in former communist countries, where the weakness is precisely the strength of the faith. The institutions of the church are weak but God's holiness is being discovered in relationships where no one imagined it might exist or be visible.

Chapter 7, "A Testimony to Christianity as Transfiguration: The Macarian Homilies and Orthodox Spirituality," by Alexander Golitzin addresses the question of the juxtaposition of Macarius as a man of feeling or heart and Evagrius as a man of intellect and heart. He puts Macarius and his views into perspective by contrasting him with Evagrius. Golitzin's discussion is concerned first and foremost with the inner life of the human being. Subjects upon which he touches include the role and eschatological destruction of the body, *theosis, synergia,* prayer, *visio Dei,* the relationship of the church's sacraments and the liturgical assembly to the inner human being, the glory of God, and the inner church. The Eucharist is understood as the real anticipation and illustration of the Christian's eschatological transformation.

Golitzin's careful research is essential to the study and evaluation of John Wesley's appropriation of the Macarian homilies. One cannot accept, appropriate, or adequately evaluate Wesley's use of the homilies without giving careful consideration to many dimensions of Golitzin's study. His discussion of the question of authorship, "pseudo-Macarius," of the authenticity of the homilies and their role in Orthodox spirituality is essential and lays an excellent foundation for Frances Young's investigation of John Wesley's reading of Macarius.

Frances Young is concerned in chapter 8, "Inner Struggle: Some Parallels between the Spirituality of John Wesley and the Greek Fathers," with Macarius as read by John Wesley and in Wesleyan English. Wesley and "Macarius" have a common practical theology, a common drive towards perfection, but the perfection they pursue is rooted in the reality of struggle. The "common drive towards perfection" of which Young speaks is the goal of the Christian life and there can be no Christian life without struggle.

Chapter 9, "From Glory to Glory: The Renewal of All Things in Christ: Maximus the Confessor and John Wesley," by Kenneth Carveley explores also parallel reading of texts from the Orthodox and Wesleyan traditions, namely, the writings of Maximus the Confessor (sixth and seventh centuries) and the sermons of John Wesley. Carveley points out at the beginning of the discussion that there is no evidence that John Wesley ever read anything written by Maximus the Confessor. The writer succeeds, however, in constructing a dialogical conversation between them on the theme of "religion of the heart," a central focus of their theology, of their spirituality. Carveley also accents the dialogue with poignant quotations from Charles Wesley's hymns.

Through the exploration of a series of theological emphases integral to a "religion of the heart" Carveley finds mutual resonance in Maximus and the Wesleys. Maximus's stress upon deification is echoed in the Wesley's confidence in the restoration of the divine image that transpires through the Incarnation. There is also a common understanding that to love God results in the all-embracing love for others. Maximus and the Wesleys also emphasize the circumcision of the heart as a reality and that there is hope of perfect love, though Maximus stresses more the eschatological possibility of such perfection, rather than the possibility of its present reality, as in expressed in John Wesley.

A primary dimension of "religion of the heart" revealed in the dialogue between Maximus the Confessor and the Wesleys is that salvation is a universal and cosmic process. Christ redeems all creation! The Wesleys echo the affirmation of Maximus and the Scriptures that *all things* are made new in Christ. Maximus's two-fold explanation for the Incarnation—deification of human nature and the saving work of Jesus Christ for all humankind—is also in concert with Wesleyan perspectives.

Carveley does more than whet one's appetite with some quotations from here and there in the writings of Maximus and the Wesleys. He provides a broad spectrum of material from both traditions, which provide an in-depth view from the Orthodox and Wesleyan traditions.

What becomes increasingly clear, as one pursues the study of Orthodox and Wesleyan spirituality, is that both are much more *a way* of life, a way of dynamic living with, in, and through the Triune God, which is expressed in the practice of devotion, worship, and service rather than in a specific set of doctrines. It is the *way* that integrates these realities in one's daily walk with God.

Peter C. Bouteneff moves the discussion to the sphere of the Cappadocian Fathers and the Wesleys in chapter 10, "All Creation in United Thanksgiving: Gregory of Nyssa and the Wesleys on Salvation." His focus is on the universality of salvation. At the outset Bouteneff is appropriately cautious about any overdrawn conclusion, such as that of Albert Outler regarding the evidence of John Wesley's reliance on the early church fathers for much of his theological thought development.

The path Bouteneff has chosen for this discussion is one that is extremely important for contemporary ecumenical discussion. The question he addresses very clearly is—What is the relationship between apostolic themes and the Wesleys? Bouteneff is careful to give due regard to Gregory of Nyssa and the Wesleys in the contexts of their own times.

There are many parallel thoughts between Gregory of Nyssa and the Wesleys on the subject of universal salvation. There are nuances of difference as well, which Bouteneff stresses, such as, that Gregory maximizes the givenness of universal salvation, while the Wesleys maximize the call to universal salvation and the extent to which one may achieve perfection in this life. For both Gregory of Nyssa and the Wesleys' universal salvation unquestionably means restoration of the divine image. Both are also aware of the incompleteness of salvation in their own time, but stress the path toward perfection, and they aver that the closer we are to perfection, the closer we are to God.

Bouteneff has shown how one can explore the literature of the Wesleys and the early church fathers and find parallel and differing views with integrity without overstressing the idea of "reliance." The discovery of mutual "resonance" of theological ideas and practice will be of great service to ecumenism and contemporary Christian and human understanding.

In chapter 11, "The Missiology of Charles Wesley and Its Links to the Eastern Church," Tore Meistad addresses for the first time the significant linkage between the Orthodox and Wesleyan traditions regarding a theology of mission. He draws heavily on Charles Wesley's hymnic literature, St Simeon the New Theologian, and other Eastern sources emphasizing similarities, commonalties, and differences. For both traditions mission has its foundation in the Triune God. Meistad carefully shows that Charles Wesley's emphasis on the plurality of the Trinity rather than its unity reveals his dependence on the Byzantine conception of God as multifaceted and a God who intervenes.

Aside from common theological ground which Meistad finds in such concepts as universal redemption, eschatology, and love as God's presence, his discussion explores the Wesleyan and Orthodox traditions' affirmation of mission as the essence of the church and that this perspective issues from a theology of salvation. The author's extensive use of the Wesleyan hymn corpus and Eastern sources give strength and breadth to one of the first substantive discussions of mission and soteriology within the two traditions.

Ioann Ekonomtsev's discussion in chapter 12, "Charles Wesley and the Orthodox Hesychast Tradition," opens by setting the stage for the growth of the Hesychast controversy within fourteenth-century Orthodoxy. He notes the tension that emerged between Barlaam, the Calabrian monk, who viewed God as incomprehensible, and the monks of Aphon who claimed to have received grace from a personal God of the universe. Essential questions to be addressed were: What is the basis of faith? Can we *know* God? Barlaam's greatest opponent was the future Archbishop of Thessalonica, St Gregory Palamas, whose great achievement was his development of the early Father's teaching of God the Creator. It is indeed in God's creative energy that humans can and do participate, and, hence, *experience* God. The Archbishop's view that grace does not depend on human efforts is very close to the prevenient grace concept of the Wesleys. He understood that there is interaction between divine grace and human free will, the concept of *synergia* of the early Fathers of the Church.

Ekonomtsev then moves to a discussion of eighteenth-century England that he finds to be the antithesis of fourteenth-century Byzantium. Nevertheless, he views the Wesleys' response to the rationalism of the time and the quest for a true religious experience as a parallel to the response of the Aphon monks. He finds the content and spirit of Charles Wesley's poetry to be strikingly similar to that of St Symeon the New Theologian. Furthermore, the strong social-political resonance of the Wesleys' preaching and ministry was similar to the Hesychastic teachings in the East. Ekonomtsev points to what may be an important spiritual bridge between the Christian cultures of the East and West, namely participation in the divine creative energy. Creative inspiration originates in divine grace. In Charles Wesley's poetry there is a superb example of creative art issuing from divine grace. Here the parallel with the Hesychasts who seek human perfection in the image of God is obvious. In the future the dimensions of this spiritual bridge between the Christian cultures of the East and West, which Ekonomtsev effectively elucidates, should unquestionably be explored in more depth.

In chapter 13, "Ephrem the Syrian: A Theologian of the Presence of God,"

Kathleen E. McVey discusses the historical and theological significance of the foremost fourth-century (C.E.) writer in the Syriac tradition of Christianity. His historical, theological, and liturgical importance is immense. Writings attributed to Ephrem appear in Greek, Coptic, Ethiopic, Armenian, Georgian, Arabic, Latin, and Slavonic but his authentic Syriac writings are not represented well in the extensive writings attributed to him in most of the languages mentioned.

Concentrating on this literature, McVey discusses Ephrem's theology of the presence of God in the world and his approach to the historical dimensions of reality. Drawing heavily on Ephrem's *Nativity Hymns* she addresses the themes of the paradox of the Incarnation, God's ongoing presence in individuals, and *theosis*, or sanctification, and is careful to elucidate Ephrem's biblical interpretation. For example, he portrays the Samaritan woman as "an apostle, prophet, and type of the *Theotokos*." Or McVey elucidates Ephrem's understanding of the role of Mary, the mother of Jesus, and John, the beloved disciple, in the ongoing process of the Incarnation, i.e. *theosis*. They exemplify the mysteries of God's love that is now accessible to all.

In the concluding section of her paper McVey discusses the historical dimension of reality evident in Ephrem's writings. She views this from the standpoint of biblical symbols, the sacred dimension of all history, and the realm of nature. One sees the significant role typology plays in Ephrem's biblical interpretation, as he understands the events in Israel's history revealed in the Hebrew Scriptures to have religious significance for all humankind.

Ephrem's *Hymns against Julian* and his *Nisibene Hymns* reveal, however, that he views all historical events, not just those of the Scriptures, as having religious significance. Finally, his stress on the Incarnation and its role in the process of sanctification reveals the special place that human beings have in the created order. One of the extremely helpful aspects of McVey's presentation is the extensive citation of relevant texts from Ephrem's literature, especially his contributions in the Syriac language and her own eloquent translations of them.

"*Kenosis* in the Nativity Hymns of Ephrem the Syrian and Charles Wesley" is the subject of S T Kimbrough, Jr's study in chapter 14. The discussion treats twenty-eight hymns of Ephrem (including the sixteen *Hymns on the Nativity*) and forty-seven hymns of Charles Wesley (including the eighteen from his collection *Hymns for the Nativity of Our Lord* [1745]). A basic difference between the two poets' styles of writing is that Ephrem's texts are characterized by highly developed typological exegesis and those of Wesley are not. Something they share in common, however, is that some of the nativity hymns of both writers have become integrated into the liturgical and worship life of Eastern-Rite churches (Ephrem) and Western-Rite churches (Wesley).

It is in the theology of the nativity hymns of the two sacred poets that the most striking commonalties are found. For both *kenosis* (God's taking on of human nature) is the beginning point in understanding the Incarnation; and *theosis* (human beings' taking on of God's nature) is central to the human experience of moving toward holiness and perfection.

Kimbrough points to numerous instances of common theological understanding in Ephrem and Wesley as regards God's revelation in the Incarnation and its benefits for humankind and creation, such as sanctification, hope, peace, the church, sharing life with the poor, sharing in the life of Mary, and the contemplative life. Clearly for both Christian spirituality is incarnational, and one can confidently live the mystery and paradox of the Incarnation. What is extremely important in this study is that in the art and theology of these poet-priests one experiences the memory of an undivided, common tradition of the church which roots all spirituality in the Incarnation of God in Jesus Christ and we are shown what the life-posture for living, worship, and service should be. The ecumenical implications of this reality are vitally important.

Conclusion

The values of this volume are primarily twofold in nature: theological and ecumenical. While it has long been maintained that there is a strong influence of the early church fathers reflected in the theology of the Wesleys, the channels of the influence have not been extensively explored. While there is important research yet to be done in the areas of history and historical theology, this volume contributes to an understanding of common theological ground in Orthodox and Wesleyan theology, as well as differences. Voices from both traditions speak authentically without presuppositions of influence or congruencies. One finds much shared theological understanding in such concepts as *kenosis, theosis,* universal salvation, holiness, religion of the heart, the Holy Trinity, and the incarnational nature of spirituality.

Nevertheless, it is important to note that neither the Orthodox nor the Wesleyan tradition places primary emphasis on a specific set of doctrines. Rather both are *a way* of life and of participation in the divine energy of the Triune God in this world and beyond through the Incarnation of Jesus Christ. Both express themselves in specific spiritual formation and practice: devotion, worship, and service. Hence, one finds in this volume a discussion of the relationship of great apostolic themes and the theology of the Wesleys.

Unquestionably there is much to be explored in the area of methodology as to how one studies theological traditions which are hundreds of years apart but which share sources of history, knowledge, and theology. The process of the development of such exploration receives input and impetus in the studies of this volume. It is extremely important as one looks from within the traditions outward toward the primary theological and hermeneutic emphases to see where these intersect in the traditions. Thorough studies of this nature, as found here, do not control the material by imposing some predisposed posture about so-called "common ideas" one is seeking.

As regards historical research, it should be noted that Alexander Golitzin's chapter illustrates the kind of careful historical and textual work on the Macarian homilies which is imperative for an understanding of John Wesley's reading of them. Kathleen McVey provides also the kind of thorough historical and textual analysis of Ephrem the Syrian, which is foundational for an interpretation of the historical, theological, and liturgical importance of this fourth-century poet-priest.

This volume serves as a signpost for the future of ecumenical study, consultation, and understanding. It may be that one will do more for ecumenical understanding by going back to the sources of faith and faith direction than in attempting to draft contemporary ecumenical statements. One thing is very clear from these studies, namely, the exploration of the Orthodox Christian heritage is an imperative for an understanding of Christian spirituality in the West.

On the other hand, the study of Wesleyan theology serves as an important bridge in this understanding. In terms of going back to the sources of faith and faith direction as foundational for ecumenical understanding, this entire volume may be read within the context of what Professor Petros Vassiliadis calls a "contemporary ecumenical-theological reflection."

S T Kimbrough, Jr
Editor

Eastern Sources and the Wesleyan Tradition

1

John Wesley's Reading of and References to the Early Church Fathers

Richard P. Heitzenrater

For many years, now, Wesley scholars have followed the lead of Albert Outler in stressing Wesley's reliance upon the writers of the early church, especially the Eastern Church, for his view of the Church and the Christian life.[1] One might assume, therefore, that Wesley would have spent a significant amount of time reading the works of those "Fathers" throughout his life and also exhibited a significant degree of substantive content of their ideas in his own writings. My task in the following discussion is to investigate the matter of Wesley's reading of and references to the Fathers, especially of the Eastern Church. My assumption at the outset was that the results of such an investigation would provide substantial detail for the general claims of Outler and others over these last few years.

Wesley's Reading of the Early Church Writers

One of the best resources for checking anything relating to John Wesley's reading is a private bibliographical listing of Wesley's reading created by Frank Baker over his lifetime. Professor Baker noted every reference that he found in Wesley's published writings of any indication that Wesley was reading a particular work.[2] These references are primarily from Wesley's letters, journals, and sermons, but also from other treatises and miscellaneous writings. From Wesley's letters, spanning some sixty-five years, Baker lists three references to his having read particular Fathers—Augustine, Jerome, and Clement of Alexandria. Baker found four references in Wesley's fifty-six years of published journals: one to Cyprian and three to Ephrem Syrus—and they are all from the Georgia period in the 1730s. There are also ten references in other works, each mentioning single instances of reading Tertullian, Chrysostom, Clement of Rome, Justin Martyr, Origen, Basil of Caesarea, Ignatius, Polycarp, and two instances of reading Macarius.

One should remember that Wesley was a voracious reader and a person that recommended that his preachers read at least five hours every day.[3] Of the fourteen authors mentioned above, Wesley noted having read six of them during the Oxford period, which represented less than one percent of his reading list.[4] Baker's listing of Wesley's reading beyond Oxford is over eighty pages with perhaps as many as ten to twelve works cited on a page. All of this is to say that there are both absolutely and relatively very few references in Wesley's published writings to his having read the Fathers.

There are a few additional references to these readings, however, in his private diaries. In some cases, the notations are to multiple readings of a particular author over a period of time. For instance, in 1730 as a tutor at Oxford, Wesley started to read Augustine in September. There are then 127 notations of his reading Augustine's *Confessions* and the *Meditations* over the following several months, up to March 2, 1731.[5] Augustine was, of course, basic reading in the Oxford curriculum, all the masters students being required to "do their Austins," i.e., debate issues in Augustine's theology.[6] In another instance, he read from Ephrem Syrus in Georgia during fifty-seven sittings between September and December, 1736. In this case, he was reading the work with Sophie Hopkey and Ms Bovey, two of his female friends whom he was tutoring. When Ms Bovey dropped out of the activity, he continued to read to Miss Sophie and teach her French. His student was apparently more interested in other aspects of their relationship than in learning about the early Fathers, but Wesley seems to have imbibed enough of the early church teachings about purity to resist her temptations. When she threatened to marry the scoundrel William Williamson in order to maneuver Wesley into following the inclinations of his heart, he wished her happiness in such a gentlemanly way as to push her into that unfortunate matrimonial union, much to John's chagrin. Apparently he did not learn how to deal with those situations from his reading of Ephrem.

The references in Wesley's diaries (1725–41, 1782–91) to his reading the Fathers reveal several rather startling statistics: (1) he mentions reading only nine writers from the early church;[7] (2) most of those writers would not necessarily be classified as "Eastern"; (3) no writer was read on more than two occasions;[8] and (4) except for one reference to Ignatius in 1741, all the other references occur between 1726 and 1737. There are no references in the diary to reading any of the Fathers after 1741.

Wesley noted in his diary having read a number of other works that are related to the early church, though not specifically writings of the early fathers. He read William Cave's *Primitive Christianity*. He read William Beveridge on the early Canons (*Codex canonum ecclesiae primitivae*). He read Thomas Deacon's *Compleat Collection of Devotions* and other Nonjurors who were interested in the early church as a pattern of liturgy and devotion.[9] One work that I have not been able to trace is *Confessio fidei ecclesiae orientalis*, which he read for two hours in January 1734, while walking from Oxford to Stanton Harcourt. Wesley, as you know, made very good use of his time, frequently reading books while walking or riding, either on horseback or in a carriage.

In addition to notations concerning his reading of the Fathers and related materials, Wesley also noted occasions when he talked about the writers of the early church. There is no specific reference that he read the *Shepherd of Hermas*, but he did record that he had religious talk with Mr Greenway (or Greenaway) about the *Pastor Hermae*.[10] There is not enough information in the diary to indicate what he thought of the work or how familiar he was with it. In fact, we should point out that, while the manuscript diaries give us a great deal of bibliographical information about Wesley's reading, they seldom record comments that would help us know which parts he read, what topics interested him in particular, or what he thought about them. And while electronic databases of Wesley's writings allows for rapid and complete searching of particular entries, one must be careful not to make sweeping assertions on the basis of not finding a specific entry, which may be different from the reference or spelling that Wesley used.[11]

In addition to specific references to his having read the Fathers, Wesley also records purchasing and owning books, including such works. In his diaries, Wesley occasionally listed portions of his library (presumably as packing lists, etc.), and he noted in his financial accounts when he purchased or bound such items. Although one might assume that he would read these works that he owned, they do not add any names to his repertoire of early Fathers. These records indicate that he owned three works that were specifically the works of the Fathers: (1) he owned Augustine's *Meditations*, thought then to have been an authentic work; (2) he owned Justin Martyr's *Apologia*; and (3) he owned William Wake's *Genuine Epistles of the Apostolic Fathers*. Entries in his Oxford diaries specifically record his reading Ignatius and Polycarp with his pupils, probably from this latter collection.

The available data concerning Wesley's references to reading the Fathers, then, reveal a relatively slim bibliography, both in actual numbers and in relative proportion to his vast reading bibliography. Even when one includes the notations of his discussions that contain references to the Fathers, the list is not substantially enlarged.

Wesley's References to the Early Fathers

In addition to Wesley's occasional notations of reading and talking about the Fathers or purchasing their works, the most common reference to the early church leaders comes in his comments about their ideas or their significance. One particularly useful resource for studying these references is the work by Ted Campbell, one of my Ph.D. students at Southern Methodist University. His book, entitled *John Wesley and Christian Antiquity*, is based on his dissertation, "Wesley's Understanding of and Use of the Early Church Fathers."[12] I am particularly focusing here on Wesley's *use* of the Fathers.

There are 201 references in this list to the Fathers, some of which quote from a particular writing, some just a passing reference. Of these, about half (106) are to something that they wrote—if not an actual quotation, at least an illusion to an idea from a particular writing. Of those one hundred and six references, eighty-one of them are contained in three of Wesley's writings that have a special focus on the Fathers: his *Letter to the Reverend Dr Conyers Middleton* (1749),[13] his *Roman Catechism; with a Reply Thereto* (1756), and his *Farther Appeal to Men of Reason and Religion* (1745). In all three writings, of course, he is responding to other works that make frequent reference to the Fathers. Middleton's work attempts to debunk the early Fathers, in particular their ideas on miracles, so Wesley is naturally forced to provide his view of their work. The *Roman Catechism* makes heavy use of the Fathers, so Wesley is again drawn into that conversation. Fifty-three of Wesley's references to the Fathers are in his response to Middleton; nineteen in his reply to the *Roman Catechism;* nine are in his *Farther Appeal*. Those three sources, then, account for most of Wesley's references to the writings of the Fathers.

Taking both the references to specific writings of the Fathers and passing refer-

ences to them by name only, the most frequently mentioned person is Augustine—
twenty-nine times. There are also twenty-four references to Cyprian and twenty-one
references to Justin Martyr. Most likely, these three authors would be considered as
Western rather than Eastern.[14] In addition, there are twenty-one references to Origen,
fifteen to Tertullian, and thirteen to Chrysostom. These top six account for nearly half
of his references, and the proportions are about three to one, Western to Eastern. From
there on, the number of references per author gets very sparse—six or less for Irenaeus, Ignatius, Clemens Romanus, Clemens Alexandrinus, Ephrem Syrus, Macarius,
and so forth. Surprisingly, there are no references that one might expect of a person
steeped in Eastern thought to some writers such as Gregory of Nyssa (compared with
at least fifteen references to the Spanish mystic, Gregory Lopez). Gregory Nazianzus
is quoted only one time (in the reply to the *Roman Catechism*). Unfortunately, as we
sit here in the Three Hierarchs Chapel, two of those in the hierarchy are pretty much
ignored by Wesley. There is one quotation from Basil of Caesarea in the work on the
Roman Catechism, and that is more or less an aphorism. Wesley does make a few references to Chrysostom, some in passing, some more substantial.[15]

These statistics are surprisingly slim, seen in the light of the common assump-
tions about Wesley's reliance upon and admiration for the Eastern Fathers. We must
remember, therefore, that Wesley's specific quotation of the Fathers and his references
to them in his works are somewhat limited and very specifically focused in particular
directions, primarily in a very few polemical works.

Wesley's Publishing of the Early Church Fathers

As part of Wesley's ongoing effort to furnish his people with useful publications, Wesley produced a few works based on the writings of the early church. He not only published some historical works that included observations on the early church, but he
also edited and published some of the writings of the Fathers. His major collection of
primary sources for his people is found in *The Christian Library,* published in the early
1750s in fifty volumes. These volumes contained choice works from the history of
Christianity that Wesley felt were important resources for Methodists and other
Christians in the eighteenth century. Part of his effort is to demonstrate that Christian truth is one from the beginning to his own day. The first volume, therefore, con-
tains materials from the early church. His choices, in fact, represent an abridgement
of the first half of William Wake's *Genuine Epistles of the Apostolic Fathers*—extracts
from Clement of Rome, Polycarp, and Ignatius. Wesley provides prefaces for these materials but does not indicate that he has selected the prefatory material from chapter ten
of Wake as well as the having extracted the writings of the three Fathers from Wake.
To these Wesley adds some of the homilies of Macarius, apparently abridged from the
English edition published by Thomas Haywood in 1721. These four selections in that
one volume of *The Christian Library* represent the totality of Wesley's publishing of
the early Fathers' writings among the over four hundred books that he published.

Mark Kurowski, a student of mine at The Divinity School of Duke University, has
published an article on Wesley and the Macarian homilies. His primary interest is the

relationship between Macarius and Wesley's theologies on the idea of prevenient grace. He spent a summer translating some of Macarius from the Greek edition, thus producing his own English version. He then compared his version with the Haywood translation, and then both of them with the Wesley extracts. His comparative theological analysis produced some interesting conclusions. He noticed that nearly every time Macarius mentioned a typically Eastern idea, Wesley dropped it out, even though it was present, of course, in the Haywood translation. Ted Campbell generally comes to the same conclusion, as noted in his introduction. Campbell dedicates his book in memory of Albert C. Outler. He then goes on to say that he is very sorry that his own study of the Fathers did not come to the conclusion for which Albert was hoping. Campbell's research did not support the idea that Wesley's doctrine of sanctification "was in essence that of ancient Eastern Christian asceticism" transmitted to Wesley from Gregory of Nyssa by way of the Macarian homilies.[16]

Wesley's Use of the Early Fathers

In his study of Wesley and the Fathers, Professor Campbell also looks at the various ways in which Wesley used the materials from the early church in his own writings. He categorizes these uses into three groups: polemical, conservative, and programmatic. Polemical usages would be those instances where Wesley used a quotation from an early Father to contradict an argument, such as in his reply to Middleton or the *Roman Catechism*. The conservative use, as Campbell calls it, is really Wesley's apologetic use of the early church material in order to defend contemporary doctrines, structures, and procedures of the church. The programmatic use entails Wesley's references to the Fathers in order to support ideas or practices that he thinks are important for his own time, such as fasting, penitential practices, or the need to experience persecution as a mark of one's Christian calling.

Campbell sees Wesley's use of the early Fathers as primarily focused on this latter category of programmatic usage. However, some exceptions might be noted to this generalization. For one, the majority of references, as we noted above, are in three works that might easily be viewed as polemical works. In some cases, Wesley is quoting one of the Fathers against Middleton's use of one of the Fathers. The same is true in his reply to the *Roman Catechism*, where at many points Wesley's replies imitate the form of the Thomist *sed contra*: "On the contrary, St Augustine writes, 'If any one concerning Christ and his Church, or concerning any other things which belong to faith or life, I will not say if we, but (which St Paul hath added) if an angel from heaven, preach unto you besides what ye have received in the Law and Evangelical Writings, let him be accursed.'"[17]

This quotation is quite typical of Wesley's polemical use of a selection from one of the Fathers against an idea (sometimes from the same or a different Father) that has been mentioned in the work that he is refuting. The programmatic usage of the Fathers, however, is almost never accompanied by a quotation. These references almost always recall some person in the history of the early church who fasted or used penitential prayers or psalms. The same is true for most of the instances where Wesley might be seen employing a "conservative" use of the Fathers in an attempt to conserve or apologize for some particular facet of Methodism or the Church of England in his own day.

There are two other usages of the Fathers, however, that Campbell does not classify or categorize, but which I would say might be the most prevalent usages. One is the aphoristic use; the other is name-dropping. In the latter category I would put all the many times that Wesley simply lists a person or a group of people from the early church who agree with him on some particular idea. Additionally, there are many occasions when he simply provides a list of such authors that he thinks people should read. The names are fairly predictable. As a good "Church of England man" (his own tag for himself), he highly recommended in particular the Ante-Nicene Fathers. In his advice to the clergy, he perhaps betrays his own preferences when he suggests that they ask themselves, "Have I read over and over the golden remains of Clemens Romanus, of Ignatius and Polycarp; and have I given one reading, at least, to the works of Justin Martyr, Tertullian, Origen, Clemens Alexandrinus, and Cyprian?"[18] More often than not, the only thing we get from a Wesleyan reference to an early Father is his name.

When Wesley does refer to a quotation from the Fathers, the selection is usually a very familiar aphoristic saying that he uses as a punch line. A typical example is Wesley's multiple use of the phrase from Augustine: "He that made us without ourselves will not save us without ourselves."[19] Another phrase is very familiar: "Nor can he rest till he thus rests in God."[20] One seldom gets the impression that Wesley is drawing substantively from some writings of the Fathers that are resting open at his elbow. References are almost always general and in passing, or, if quotations, they are most often one-liners. And quite often these proverbial aphorisms are not accurately quoted; at times they are even misattributed by Wesley.[21]

Wesley's tendency to misquote does not necessarily mean that he did *not* read the writing in question any more than it proves that he *did* read the writing. For years I have been saying that Cyprian said, "There is no salvation outside of the Church." I have, indeed, read selections from Cyprian, but I don't remember having ever read the whole of *On the Unity of the Church*. And I have no idea if that quotation is, in fact, accurate. But almost any textbook on the history of Christianity will transmit to the reader the basic idea in question and attribute it to Cyprian. The same process is, no doubt, true for Wesley in his acquisition of knowledge about the Fathers. His day was very interested in recapturing the teachings of the early church; his own church was interested in modeling the life and thought of the early church. The ideas of the Fathers were in the air, so to speak, just as were the ideas of Richard Hooker, whose ideas Wesley followed in some very significant ways without ever referring to him or his writings.

Conclusion

The results of my survey of Wesley's reading of and references to the early church Fathers are not what I anticipated. The paucity of Wesley's direct reading, the generality of his references, the "Western" weighting of those references, and the aphoristic nature of his quotations leave one wondering about the level of his reliance upon and knowledge of the primary sources, especially of the Eastern Church. One certainly cannot dismiss the influence of the early church in his life and thought—it is evident in the shape of his theology and the details of his program. Nevertheless, it appears that a great deal more work needs to be done on the specific channels by which that thought was transmitted to Wesley. The ideas and influence of seventeenth and eighteenth century writers who were themselves plumbing the depths of primitive spirituality, polity, liturgy, and theology would need special attention. It is my suspicion that many of the early church ideas and practices passed through several filters before reaching Wesley from a number of sources. Explicit grounding in the life and thought of the early church was evident in his own Church of England during that day as well as in the holy living tradition of the English and German pietists and French mystics that he read and admired.[22] The fact that such influence was present is evident. The precise shape of the theological and spiritual genealogy that passed on such a heritage remains to be fully described.

Endnotes

[1]*John Wesley* (New York: Oxford University Press, 1964). See also "John Wesley's Interests in the Early Fathers of the Church," in *The Bulletin* (Committee on Archives and History of the United Church of Canada) 29 (1983):5–17.

[2]These include only direct references to reading, not oblique implications that he had read a particular work. These manuscript volumes are kept in the Baker Methodist Research Collection of the Divinity School Library at Duke University.

[3]See his comments in the *Minutes* of 1766, in *Minutes of the Methodist Conferences* (1862), 1:68.

[4]The bibliography of Wesley's reading during the eight years of his Oxford diaries numbers over eight hundred works.

[5]Although the particular writing is not always mentioned in the daily entry, the titles are frequently listed in his monthly summaries of reading.

[6]L. S. Sutherland, *The Eighteenth Century,* vol. 5 of *The History of the University of Oxford* (Oxford: Oxford University Press, 1986), 471.

[7]Augustine, Justin Martyr, Clement of Rome, Ignatius, Polycarp, Lactantius, Clement of Alexandria, Ephrem Syrus, and Macarius.

[8]An "occasion" in this instance might entail several successive sittings in order to finish a work, such as was noted with Augustine and Ephrem.

[9]These writers include George Hickes, Jeremy Collier, John Kettlewell, Charles Leslie, John Cosin, Thomas Ken, and Peter Gunning.

[10]MS Oxford Diary IV (Friday, March 8, 1734) [Methodist Archives, Rylands, University Library of Manchester, U.K.]

[11]My analysis of Wesley's use of the Fathers during his early years is largely based on a card file of Wesley's reading that I have kept over the years, which provides a good check against the electronic database.

[12]Appendix 2 of the published work is "References to Ancient Christian Works in John Wesley's Works" (125–34). The list, done in the pre-computer era, misses a few entries but is useful as a starting point.

[13]See *The Works of John Wesley* (Nashville: Abingdon, 1976), 11:527–38.

[14]The distinction "Eastern" and "Western" is not always clear for some writers; e.g., Irenaeus, who can be seen as fitting in both categories. Whether they wrote or published in Latin or Greek does not always seem to be the deciding factor.

[15]His own father, Samuel Wesley, had highly recommended that clergy read Chrysostom in his *Advice to a Young Curate.*

[16]Campbell, x. Campbell claims in particular that Wesley consistently left out references to "deification," perhaps the most distinctively Eastern note in the Macarian literature."

[17]*Roman Catechism,* Sect. 1, Qu. 6 (quoting Augustine, *Contr. Petil.,* l. 3, c. 6), in Wesley, *Works* (Jackson), 10:90.

[18]*Address to the Clergy* (1756), II.1, in *Works* (Jackson), 10:492.

[19]Sermon 63, "The General Spread of the Gospel," §12, quoting Augustine, Sermon 169, on Phil 3:3–16. See also Wesley's Sermon 85, "On Working Out Our Own Salvation," II.7. This saying is also included in Richard Baxter's *Aphorisms,* which Wesley abridged and published in 1745.

[20]This is his favorite allusion to Augustine, found in some form in at least seven of his sermons. See *Works,* 1:148, n.77.

[21]We need not be too critical of Wesley, of course. I was recently asked to write an article on Wesley's familiar saying, "In essentials, unity; in non-essentials, liberty; in all things, charity." It is, of course, not to be found in Wesley. Nor is it to be found in Augustine, to whom it has often been attributed. It apparently comes from Rupert Maldenius, an obscure Dutch theologian who had the fortune to be quoted by the right people at the right time, such as Richard Baxter. Attribution of such quotations to an early church father (or even a church founder) provides a good saying with even greater authority. See William Abraham and Donald Messer, *Unity Liberty and Charity: Building Bridges Under Icy Waters* (Nashville: Abingdon, 1996) chapter 1.

[22]See such expressions as, "Our Church, adopting the words of St Chrysostom, expressly affirms. . . ." Letter to Melville Horne (1762).

2

A Survey of Eastern Sources in British and American Methodist Hymnals

Carlton R. Young

I am very pleased to contribute to this discussion of Eastern and Western traditions. As we already have experienced and will continue to discover, worshipping communities in these traditions are never fully gathered until they have sung or otherwise expressed themselves musically.

My presentation is in three parts: first, a survey of some hymns, canticles, prayers, and music from Eastern sources in British and American Methodist hymnals since 1875; second, the examination of some of these metered and prose texts; third, some suggestions for incorporating Eastern texts into future consultations, including the possible publication of a collection of extant works.

Eastern worship-song is the precious link, Eric Werner called it the "sacred bridge," of Jewish and Christian traditions of Scripture song, prayer, and praise. Creating and singing hymns to teach doctrine and celebrate the Incarnation of God in Christ are a distinctive quality of Eastern church worship-song, which began in New Testament and Patristic times, culminated in the vast, elaborate, varied and complex repertory of Byzantine classic hymnody. The 1500-year proliferation, and development, as well as the expansion of this body of hymnody in the many languages of Eastern liturgies are unprecedented in Christian hymnody. Two aspects of its repertory and performance practices, i.e., Christological hymns and responsorial psalmody, were taken into early Western hymnody, and are perpetuated in that body of worship song and hymnic literature.

In the early nineteenth century Eastern hymns and liturgical texts began to be formed into English-language and British-style hymns. This development was related to a far greater number of Latin and German hymns that were translated by-products of the Oxford movement's attempts to reclaim and reform the church's liturgy and spirituality, and examine and recover its historical roots. The translation of ancient hymns in part initiated the four-decade British hymnic explosion,[1] which culminated in the publication of *Hymns Ancient and Modern* (HAM) 1861.[2] Translations comprised one half of the first edition of this extraordinary, successful parish hymnal,[3] thus fulfilling "ancient" in the collection's title. However, Eastern hymns were not included until the 1868 Appendix to the parent book.

The most important and prolific translator of Eastern hymns was scholar-priest John Mason Neale, who produced an impressive repertory of hymns from Latin and Eastern sources, for example from the Latin, "Of the Father's love begotten" (HAM/184) and from the Greek, "The day of resurrection" (HAM/303). Egon Wellesz comments that Neale approached Eastern hymns as a liturgist "who regarded these hymns as part of the liturgy, and instinctively recognized the greatness of their poetry."[4]

John Mason Neale graduated from Trinity College, Cambridge, in 1840. In spite of his evangelical upbringing he became identified with the Oxford movement and was a founder of the Cambridge Camden Society. He was ordained priest in 1842. However, chronic lung disease and his strong Anglo-Catholic leanings kept him out of the parish priesthood. In 1846 he became warden of Sackville College, East Grinstead, a home for old men. Besides researching and writing in his "leisure time,"[5] he also founded a nursing sisterhood, promoted social welfare, and expanded the ministry of Sackville College to orphans and young women. His primary publications include *Hymns of the Eastern Church*, 1862, *Mediaeval Hymns and Sequences*, 1851, 1863, and *Hymns, Chiefly Mediaeval, on the Joys and Glories of Paradise*, 1865. His many original hymns as well as translations were included in *The Hymnal Noted*, 1851, 1854.

There was precedent in British hymnody for publishing translations of Latin and German hymns, for example *Lyra Davidica*, 1708, and of course John Wesley's impressive and enduring repertory of translated German pietistic hymns which he began to develop while a missionary priest in Georgia.[6] However, in the instance of Eastern hymns and liturgical texts there was little or no precedent.

In the preface to *Hymns of the Eastern Church*, 1862, Neale comments on the general lack of interest and the marvelous ignorance in which ecclesiastical scholars are content to remain [regarding] this huge treasure of divinity . . . [and] a glorious mass of theology.[7] He also comments on the difficulty in forming a hymn from a Greek Canon:

> . . . one is all at sea. What measure shall we employ? Why this more than that? Might we attempt the rhythmical prose of the original, and design it to be chanted? Again, the great length of the Canons renders them unsuitable for our churches, as wholes. Is it better simply to form centos of the more beautiful passages: or can separate Odes, each necessarily imperfect, be employed as separate hymns? And above all, we have no pattern or example of any kind to direct our labor"[8]

And these closing remarks:

> I trust the reader will not forget the immense difficulty of an attempt so perfectly new as the present, where I have had no predecessors, and therefore could have no master.[9]

At first, Neale and his colleagues constructed literal translations of Latin or Greek texts for reading and reflection. John Julian[10] comments that in the journey from Greek to English:

> . . . the sparkling Greek freezes in our meters, and the unity, proportion of parts, compactness, and selection of allied ideas, which we demand, have no correlatives in the loose, wandering, disconnect strophes.[11]

Seeking a larger audience[12] for their work, some set translated rhythmical prose for choirs and academic congregations. Neale moved beyond this to cast his translations of individual lines into rhymed metered centos. He also formed hymns with parallel meaning to sections of larger works. Neale often deleted, compressed, or added words and expressions to make the text conform to the desired poetic foot and meter and perhaps to an existing tune. Therefore, most of his and others' Eastern hymns in translation are really adaptations which convey selected qualities of the original texts. Further, as they entered general hymnals and were set to Victorian tunes they became contextualized.

Eastern Source Texts In British and American Methodist Hymnals, 1875–1989

Including translations of German, Latin, and Greek texts in British and American Methodist hymnals was part of the process of broadening the contents of late nineteenth-century collections. For example, the 1878 American hymnal included in one format, without separate text and tune books, standard evangelical tunes of the eighteenth and early nineteenth centuries, USA fuging tunes from shaped-note song books, and Lowell Mason's tunes and his adaptations of tunes by Handel and Haydn. Folk melodies of Great Britain, Northern Europe, and the USA tunes were placed alongside the Lutheran chorale (in isometric form), Anglican chant (40 single and double chants), and "new and popular" four-part English parish hymn tunes by Dykes and Barnby.

Another result of broadening the content was the diminishing number of editions of hymns and translations by John and Charles Wesley, which had previously accounted for over one half the total number of hymns. The chart on page 41 shows the decreasing number of Charles Wesley hymns in British and American hymnals.

The chart on page 40 traces the appearance of nineteen[13] Eastern texts in British and American Methodist authorized hymnals from 1875–1989. The dates of the British collections are in bold italic. The selection number in *The United Methodist Hymnal* (UMH) is included in the left column.

Two general comments: First, there is a remarkably full range of topics and content: Eucharistic, Christian Year – Christmas/Easter – strength in conflict, prayers and praise, including the *Te Deum*, whose Eastern roots were elaborated and developed in Western traditions. Second, while there is an increase in the number of Eastern hymns in recent editions, for the most part they are nineteenth-century hymns. Neale authored in 1862, for example, the Christmas hymn, "A great and mighty wonder," which entered *Hymns and Psalms* (HAP) in 1983. An exception is the late F. Bland Tucker's paraphrase of portions of the second-century *Didache*, "Father, we thank you, who has planted," *United Methodist Hymnal* (UMH) 565, which first appeared in *The Hymnal 1940*.

The foregoing hymnals include three of Neale's best known translations, "Come, ye faithful raise the strain," "The day of resurrection," and "The day is past and over." As singable Easter and evening hymns, they were successfully introduced and assimilated into the repertory of Anglican parish worship music, and within a generation they entered British and American Methodist hymnals.

One of Neal's gifts is the ability to maintain biblical metaphors while converting their meaning into lyrical English. Appendix A and Appendix B on pages 46 and 47 allow the reader a glimpse of the task of the translator and versifier to make hymns out of prose. I have put in parallel columns a prose translation on the left by Erik Routley, and on the right, Neale's "Come, ye faithful, raise the strain," trochaic 76.76.D ABCB-DEFE, a favorite meter and rhythm scheme that easily accommodates long narrative, detailed, and thick stanzas, e.g., "The churches' one foundation." Neale translated and adapted this text from John of Damascus' first Ode of the Canon for St Thomas's Sunday (the first Sunday after Easter, in the West called "Low Sunday"), based on the first canticle Exodus 15:1–19 (see Appendix: A/B, pp. 46 and 47). Compare Routley's version of the first stanza with 37 words, to Neale's 39 words. Line 1:5–6 in Neale's paraphrase demonstrates his lyrical gift and his ability to elaborate the essential meaning:

> "who has delivered Israel from Pharaoh's bitter bondage,
> and who has led him through the depths of the sea dry-shod"

lyrically rendered and elaborated becomes:

> loosed from Pharaoh's bitter yoke
> Jacob's sons and daughters,
> led them with unmoistened foot
> through the Red Sea waters.

Note the rhyming of "daughters" and "waters."

Consider for a moment the matter of the musical settings of these hymns. As previously stated, because Neale was creating hymns for use in Anglican parishes, he had dismissed the option of setting literal, rhythmic prose translation to chant. While it is not known whether Neale suggested the tunes to which his hymns would be sung, we are aware of Victorian editors' predilections to promote prettiness to the exclusion of appropriateness.

In 1872 the operetta composer Arthur S. Sullivan composed "St Kevin" for "Come, ye faithful, raise the strain" and included it in *The Hymnary*, 1872, for which Sullivan was music editor. [A bit of hymnic trivia: in 1903, Sullivan named it "St Kevin" (Irish: *Coemgen*, 'fair begotten') after a seventh-century hermit in the Vale of Glendalough (Valley of the Two Lakes), Ireland]. It would be difficult to find a more inappropriate setting for this historic, dynamic resurrection hymn. However, hymnal editors, like parents, don't always have their way. I much prefer to sing this to *Ave Virgo Virginum*.

Let us turn to the second most popular hymn, "The day of resurrection." I have included Neale's translation on the left and Neale's iambic 87.87.87, ABCDCB hymn on the right. Neale's evening hymn, "The day is past and over," has been included in most hymnals since 1875 (see Appendix: C/D, pp. 48 and 49). It was matched to J. S. Bach's harmonization of an early melody in the 1935 American hymnal, whose editors following the British example did not include the original stanza 4:

> Lighten mine eyes, o SAVIOUR,
>   Or sleep in death shall I;
> And he, my wakeful tempter,
>   Triumphantly shall cry:
> "He could not make their darkness light,
> Nor guard them through the hours of night!"

Turn now to "Let all mortal flesh keep silence," Gerard Moultrie's well crafted hymn (see Appendix: E/F, pp. 50 and 51). Notice its rhyme scheme ABCBDB with three unrhymed lines is based on a standard nineteenth-century translation of the fourth-century Liturgy of St James. The elaboration adds powerful eucharistic metaphors. It is interesting that this hymn, which was formed in 1864, did not enter Methodist hymnals until 1935. Its first appearance in a general hymnal was in *The English Hymnal*, 1906, where Vaughan Williams skillfully set it to a traditional French melody.

Let us consider F. Bland Tucker's eucharistic hymn, "Father, we thank you who has planted." I have included a translation of those portions from the section on church orders in the second-century Didache[14] that Tucker formed into a dactylic/trochaic 98.98 ABCB hymn (see Appendix: G/H, pp. 52 and 53). One feature of one of the settings in *The United Methodist Hymnal* (UMH) is the late William Albright's tone-cluster accompaniment of a simple chant-like melody. From the standpoint of musical style this setting effectively contextualizes the hymn in the twentieth century.

Finally, let us consider the evening hymn, "O gladsome light," one of the earliest hymns in the repertory. The prose translation is by John A. McGuckin from his recent book of translations, *At the Lighting of the Lamps: Hymns of the Ancient Church*. Robert Bridges, one of the most successful translator-hymn writers since Neale, cast his hymn setting in iambic 667.667 AABCCB, which is set to the Genevan psalter tune at number 686 in the hymnal (see Appendix: I/J, pp. 54 and 55).

Eastern Source Liturgical Texts and Canticles

In approaching this part of my task, I did not tally the numerous prose and metered settings of the psalms which appear in these hymnals. However, it is my opinion that because the book of Psalms is the hymnbook of the Bible and the heart of Judeo-Christian worship and prayer, singing the psalms in various styles could be a substantial and creative aspect of Orthodox/Methodist worship and conversation.

I also have formed an accounting of prose liturgical texts with Eastern roots. This list, and I am sure it is incomplete, was formed by reading the three liturgies in common use in Orthodoxy: the Liturgy of St John Chrysostom, most frequently used, the Liturgy of St Basil, and the Liturgy of St James. When it appeared there were portions of a liturgical text, for example "the Lord's Prayer," that were included in British and American Methodist hymnals, I made a mark. I did not reference these churches' books of orders or worship that would probably include more commonly used materials.

"O Lamb of God," "*Agnus Dei*," a paraphrase of a portion of the "*Gloria in Excelsis*," the Greater Doxology, has only been included in four hymnals, three American.

"Glory be to the Father," the Lesser Doxology, is only included in American hymnals. All but one hymnal included a spoken and/or sung version of "The Lord's Prayer." The Nicene creed is included in the last two American Methodist hymnals. The "Holy, holy, holy" and "Lord, have mercy," have generally been included in these hymnals.

Canticles

I have traced the prose settings in these hymnals of canticles listed in "Codex Alexandrinus," from the fifth century. In common use are the three Lukan hymns, "Song of Mary" (*Magnificat*), "Song of Zechariah" ("*Benedictus Dominus Deus*"), "Prayer of Simeon" ("*Nunc Dimittis*"), and the "Morning Hymn," ("*Gloria In Excelsis*," the Greater Doxology). At 134–35 in *The United Methodist Hymnal* (UMH) is an interesting joining of the biblical narrative of the Exodus with an African American spiritual, "O Mary, don't you weep don't you mourn."

Prayers

The United Methodist Hymnal (UMH) includes three prayers from Eastern sources: 466, Dimitri of Rostov; 676, an Orthodox prayer; and 412, Prayer of John Chrysostom, which was also included in the previous edition.

Music

All hymnals include the Bortniansky melody, with some variants. In American Methodism it has been matched to the Charles Wesley hymn, "Thou hidden source of calm repose" 88.88.88. Russian hymnals use another harmonization of an apparently earlier version of the tune. "Byzantine Chant," UMH 485, is apparently a traditional setting of "*Kyrie*" for male voices. The tune "Russian Hymn" by Alexis F. Lvov has been included in all hymnals. It is the music of the Russian national anthem, "*Bozhe, tsarya khrani*" ("God save the Tsar") that was composed in 1833. See UMH 653. Russian Orthodox Chant, UMH 485, is apparently a traditional responsorial setting for the "*Kyrie*."

In conclusion, I suggest the compilation of hymns, chants, and prayers for use in Methodist-Orthodox consultations to extend the present repertory of hymns, prayers, canticles, and other music from Eastern sources included in the British and United Methodist hymnals. There are at least three repertories that could be included in a modest collection:

1. The four hymns not included in UMH that are in HAP, and others from the estimated 300 hymns formed from Eastern sources during the nineteenth century which were included in general hymnals of the twentieth century. For example, *The English Hymnal*, 1906, which includes 23.

2. Wesleyan Hymns that parallel some aspects of Eastern theology in their hymns and writings.[15] Frank Baker comments that John Wesley in his approach to the Eucharist made

a deliberate attempt to recapture the liturgy of the apostolic church ... even (by way of the hymns) of the epiclesis or prayer for the descent of the Holy Spirit, otherwise preserved only by the Eastern Church.[16]

Geoffrey Wainwright illustrates Baker's point in the preface to the Charles Wesley Society's facsimile of the Wesley's *Hymns on the Lord's Supper*, 1745,[17] by citing two hymns that express the epiclesis: "Come, Holy Ghost, thine influence prove" (72) and "most remarkably" in "Come, thou everlasting Spirit" (16):

1. Come, thou everlasting Spirit,
    bring to every thankful mind
all the Savior's dying merit
    all his suffering for mankind:
True recorder of his passion,
    now the living faith impart,
now reveal his great salvation,
    preach his gospel to our heart.

2. Come, thou witness of his dying,
    come, Remembrancer Divine,
let us feel thy power applying
    Christ to every soul and mind;
let us groan thine inward groaning,
    look to him we pierced, and grieve,
all receive the Grace Atoning,
    all the sprinkled blood receive.

Wainwright, in *Doxology*,[18] cites other parallels in Eastern and Wesleyan hymns, for example, rapturous praise in Christmas and Good Friday hymns. Lester Ruth[19] in a recent article "Where Heaven meets Earth (and East meets West): The Nativity Hymns of Charles Wesley" explores the mystery and paradox of the Incarnation which are paralleled in Eastern and Wesleyan hymns.

3. Additional Translations and Transcriptions of Orthodox Hymns and Liturgical Music.

Many have appeared in recent ecumenical collections, for example, *Cantate Domino*, 1964; *Global Praise 1*, 1996; *Global Praise 2*, 2000.

Some Eastern Source Liturgical Texts and Canticles in Methodist Hymnals. British edition dates in bold italic.

PROSE LITURGICAL TEXTS, SPOKEN AND SUNG	1875	1878	*1904*	1905	*1933*	1935	1966	*1983*	1989
O Lamb of God (*Agnus Dei*)					*	*	*		*30
Glory be to the Father (Lesser Doxology)		*		*	*	*	*		*71
Our Father (The Lord's Prayer)[20]		*	*	*	*	*	*	*271	
Creed (Nicene)[21]						*		*880	
Holy, holy, holy (*Sanctus*)		*		*	*	*	*		*12
Lord, have mercy (*Kyrie*)		*	*	*	*	*	*		*483
PROSE CANTICLES[22], SPOKEN AND SUNG									
1. Song of Moses (1) (Ex 15:1–19)[23]									*135
2. Song of Moses (2) (Deut 32: 1–43)		*							
3. Prayer of Hannah (1 Sam 2: 1–10)									
4. Prayer of Habbakuk (Hab 3:1–19)[24]				*					
5. Prayer of Isaiah (Is 26:9–20)									
6. Prayer of Jonah (Jon 2:3–10)									
7. Prayer of Hezekiah (Is 38:10–20)									
8. Prayer of Manasseh (Apocrypha)									
9. Prayer of Azariah (Dan [Apoc] 3:26–56)[25]				*					
10. Song of The Three Children (Dan [Apoc] 3:57–68)[26]				*	*				
11. Song of Mary (Lk 1:46–55)			*			*	*	*	*199
12. Song of Zechariah (Lk 1:68–79)[27]			*		*	*	*	*	*208
13. Prayer of Simeon (Lk 2:29–32)			*			*	*	*	*225
14. Morning Hymn (Greater Doxology)	*					*			*82

Some Hymns with Eastern Sources in Methodist Hymnals. British edition dates are in bold italic.

	1875	1878	*1904*	1905	*1933*	1935	1966	*1983*	1989
A great and mighty wonder								*	
Art thou weary, art thou languid	*		*	*	*	*	*		
Christian, doth thou see them		*	*	*	*	*			
Come, ye faithful, raise the strain		*	*	*	*	*	*	*	*315
Father, we praise you, now the night is over							*	*	*680
Father, we thank you who has planted						*	*	*	*565
Let all mortal flesh keep silent						*	*	*	*626
Lord Jesus, think on me					*		*	*	
O gladsome light (Hail gladdening light)			*		*			*	*686
O happy band of pilgrims		*	*		*				
O King enthroned on high								*	
Praise ye the Lord, ye servants								*	
Safe home, safe home in port			*		*				
Shepherd of eager youth		*		*		*	*		
Strengthen for service, Lord								*	
The day is past and over	*		*	*	*	*	*	*	*683
The day of resurrection		*	*	*	*	*	*	*	*303
The King shall come when morning dawns							*		
We praise you, O God (*Te Deum*)		*	*	*	*	*	*	*	*80

Some Hymns with Eastern Sources in Methodist Hymnals (continued)

	1875	1878	1904	1905	1933	1935	1966	1983	1989
PRAYERS									
An invitation to Christ									*466
For a new day									*676
Prayer of John Chrysostom							*		*412
MUSIC									
Bortniansky melody ST PETERSBURG	*	*	*	*	*	*	*	*	*153
Byzantine Chant									*485
Greek Air HEBER (O God, the Rock of Ages)			*		*				
Greek Amen							*		
Greek Melody ATHENS ("I think, when I read that sweet story of old")			*		*				
RUSSIAN HYMN (Alexis F. Lvov)	*	*	*	*	*	*	*	*	*653
Russian Orthodox Chant									*483

Charles Wesley Hymns

The number to the left indicates Charles Wesley (CW) hymns, the number on the right the total number of hymns.

American Methodist hymnals:
Hymns included from three Wesley collections are shown:

HLS, *Hymns on the Lord's Supper*, 1745
HNL, *Hymns for the Nativity of our Lord*, 1745
HOT, *Hymns On The Trinity*, 1767.

	1878	1905	1935	1966	1989
CW	315—1155	102—748	56—644	71—552	51—734
HLS	15	2	0	4	2
HNL	3	2	1	1	1
HOT	0	0	0	0	0

British Methodist hymnals:

	1875	1904	1933	1983
CW	558—1026	425—991	243—984	156—888

Endnotes

[1]Singing hymns, contrasted to the established practice of singing metrical psalms, was not officially sanctioned for British Anglican worship until early in the nineteenth century. The practice of singing hymns was a feature of evangelical parishes and hospital chapels. An example of the former is the Olney parish where John Newton and William Cowper produced the 1779 *Olney Hymns* (containing 281 hymns by Newton, e.g., "Amazing grace," and "Glorious things of thee are spoken"). Robin Leaver calls the collection "the everlasting testimonial to Anglican evangelical hymnody" (Raymond Glover, ed. *The Hymnal 1982 Companion*, vol. 1 [New York: Church Hymnal Corporation, 1990], 389).

[2]Erik Routley has commented: *Hymns Ancient and Modern* "gathered up the discoveries of previous [nineteenth-century] editors; combin[ed] church dogma and easily accessible musical style for parish family participation, led by the choir and organ [and] translated into parish practice the principles of the Tractarians. 1. The arrangement of the book corresponds very closely to that of the *Book of Common Prayer*, 1662, thus laying stress on the centrality of its use in liturgy; 2. It incorporated into parish worship the hymns of the ancient Offices, matched them to easily learned and sung tunes." Erik Routley, *The Music of Christian Hymnody* (London: Independent Press, 1957), 92.

[3]The musical settings in *Hymns Ancient and Modern* were almost exclusively Victorian hymn tunes, which in a generation became, and in some places remains the paradigm of British and USA congregational song. There are four qualities of this style of hymn tune:
- It is always a four-voice tune that with notable exceptions is dependent on harmony for interest;
- Its setting in Anglican parish worship where there were few trained singers meant that it had to be supported by choir and organ, the congregation singing what they could, usually melody;

- The role of the organ and choir was basically to set and maintain rhythm and pitch, but an important by-product was the smoothing out of the congregation's imperfections, a strictly musical understanding of congregational song that made the sounds of hymn singing bearable for the sensitive tastes of trained musicians;
- Its acceptability and accessibility allowed Anglo-Catholics and evangelicals to express their sometimes contrasting beliefs in a common musical style.

[4]Egon Wellesz, *History of Byzantine music and Hymnography* (London: Oxford University Press, 1949, rev. 3/1963), 14.

[5]John M. Neale, *Hymns of the Eastern Church, Translated, With Notes and An Introduction* (London: J.T. Hayes, 1862), xi.

[6]The first group appeared in *A Collection of Psalms and Hymns* 1737, Charleston.

[7]Neale, 1862, xv.

[8]Neale, 1862, xiii.

[9]Neale, 1862, xv.

[10]Roman Catholics accused Neale of deliberate deception because he modified or left out of his Latin and Eastern hymns "the honor and power ascribed to the Blessed Virgin" (Julian 1907, 466). Neale's response was that he was preparing translations for use in broad-based Anglican devotion and worship, and for the theology of that church.

[11]Julian 1907, 460.

[12]It should be noted that for various reasons relatively few of an estimated 300 hymns formed from Eastern sources during the nineteenth century were included in general hymnals. In this regard *The English Hymnal*, 1906, included the most, 23. For Methodists the inclusion of translations was a part of the broadening of contents in hymnals here and in Britain, where in previous editions Wesley hymns had accounted for more than one half the total.

[13]British hymnals include: *Wesley's Hymns and New Supplement, with Tunes*, 1875; *The Methodist Hymn Book*, 1904; *The Methodist Hymn Book*, 1933, *Hymns and Psalms*, 1983; American Methodist hymnals authorized by The Methodist Episcopal Church, 1878; The Methodist Episcopal Church, and Methodist Church, South, 1905; The Methodist Episcopal Church, Methodist Episcopal Church, South, The Methodist Church, 1935, which 1939 formed The Methodist Church in 1939; The Methodist Church, 1966, and The United Methodist Church, formed in 1968 from The Methodist Church, and The Evangelical United Brethren Church, 1989.

[14]In two sections, one a manual of moral catechism (chapters 1–5), the other a manual of Church Order (chapters 6–15). The text is believed to have originated in the Church of Antioch, Syria, perhaps as early as A.D. 110. There has been exhaustive research on its date and authorship since the only extant manuscript, dating from the middle of the eleventh century, was discovered in Constantinople in 1875 by the Greek scholar Bryennios.

[15]The Wesleys were apparently acquainted with Greek literature. In his sermons and other writings John cites Pythagoras, Socrates, and Plato, the four Greek sects: Platonic, Peripatetic, Epicurean, and Stoic. In his sermon "On a single eye" John cites Clement of Alexandria, and quotes St John Chrysostom: "Hell is paved with the souls of Christian Priests." John is also critical of the Eastern Church: "What do the Christians, so called, of the Eastern Church, dispersed throughout the Turkish dominions, know of genuine Christianity? Those of the Morea, of Circassia, Mongrelia, Georgia? Are they not the very dregs of mankind?" (Sermon 116 "Causes Of the Inefficacy of Christianity").

[16]Frank Baker, *John Wesley and The Church of England* (Nashville: Abingdon Press, 1970), 86.

[17](Madison, NJ: The Charles Wesley Society, 1995), ix.

[18]Geoffrey Wainwright, *Doxology. The Praise of God in Worship, Doctrine, and Life: A Systematic Theology* (New York: Oxford University Press, 1980), 206, 307.

[19]"Where Heaven meets Earth (and East meets West): The Nativity Hymns of Charles Wesley." *Sacramental Life*, Advent/Christmas 1998: 170–75.

[20]Full text spoken or sung by the congregation, includes, "For the kingdom and the power . . ."

[21]The "Apostles Creed" is included in all American hymnals, which during the twentieth century evolved into worship books, in contrast to British editions.

[22]Included in "Codex Alexandrinus" (fifth century). Later reduced to nine odes, and omitted these canticles: (7) Prayer of Hezekiah, Is. 38:10–20; (8) Prayer of Manasseh (Apocrypha); (12) Prayer of Simeon,

Lk 2:29–32 ("Lord, now let your servant depart in peace"; "*Nunc Dimittis*," UMH 225; metrical paraphrase at UMH 226); (14) Morning Hymn ("Glory be to God on high"; "*Gloria In Excelsis*").

[23]Those identified as canticles in Western traditions are noted in italics, e.g., "*Nunc Dimittis*." Some canticles are also included in metrical paraphrases: "Then Moses and the people of Israel sang this song to the Lord"; "*Cantemus Domino*."

[24]vv. 17–18.

[25]vv. 29–34. "Blessed art thou, O Lord"; "*Benedictus es, Domine*."

[26]vv. 35, 40–41, 45, 47, 51, 54, 56, 58, 65, 68 ("Bless the Lord, all works of the Lord"; "*Benedicite, omnia opera Domini*").

[27]"Blessed be the Lord God of Israel"; "*Benedictus Dominus Deus*." Part 2 or Ode 9; metrical paraphrase at UMH 209.

APPENDIX A

All peoples: let us sing praise to him
who has delivered Israel from Pharaoh's bitter bondage,
and who has led him through the depths
of the sea dry-shod,
by a way of victory, to his glory.

Today is the spring of souls,
for Christ, like the sun shining after dark winter,
has shone out again after three days,
driving away the winter of our sin;
we sing praise to him, to his glory.

On this royal light-bringing day of days,
the gift-bearing Queen of seasons
brings joy to the chosen people of the church,
ceaselessly praising the risen Christ.

Neither the gates of death,
nor the seals on the tomb, nor the keys of its doors,
held you back, O Christ;
but, risen, Master, you gave your Peace to your friends,
a gift which exceeds all understanding.

Translation by Erik Routley, ed., *A Panorama of Christian Hymnody*
(Collegeville, MN: The Liturgical Press, 1979).

John of Damascus, 8th century, from the first *Ode at the Canon for
St Thomas's Sunday*, based on the canticle Exodus 15:1–19.

APPENDIX B

1. Come, ye faithful, raise the strain
    of triumphant gladness;
    God hath brought us, Israel,
    into joy from sadness:
    loosed from Pharaoh's bitter yoke
    Jacob's sons and daughters,
    led them with unmoistened foot
    through the Red Sea waters.

2. 'Tis the spring of souls today:
    Christ hath burst His prison
    and from three days' sleep in death
    as a sun hath risen.
    All the winter of our sins,
    long and dark, is flying,
    from his light, to whom we give
    laud and praise undying.

3. Now the Queen of seasons, bright
    with the day of splendor,
    with the royal feast of feasts,
    comes its joy to render;
    comes to glad Jerusalem,
    who with true affection
    welcomes in unwearied strains
    Jesus' Resurrection.

4. Neither might the gates of death,
    nor the tomb's dark portal,
    nor the watchers, nor the seal
    hold thee as a mortal;
    but today amidst thine own
    thou didst stand, bestowing
    that thy peace which evermore
    passeth human knowing.

5. Alleluia now we cry
    to our King Immortal,
    who triumphant burst the bars
    of the tomb's dark portal;
    Alleluia, with the Song
    God the Father praising;
    Alleluia yet again
    to the Spirit raising.

trochaic 76.76.D
ABCBDEFE

Translation by John M. Neale, "Greek Hymnology," in the periodical *Christian Remembrancer* (London: April, 1859). Stanza 5 was first included in *Appendix* to the 1861 edition of *Hymns Ancient and Modern* (London: Novello, 1868), #292.

APPENDIX C

On the day of Resurrection
let us O people,
be clothed with gladness;
it is the Pascha, a Pascha of the Lord!
for from death to life,
and from earth to heaven,
hath Christ our Lord caused us to pass over,
singing the Hymn of Victory.

Cleanse we our souls,
and we shall behold Christ
glittering in the unapproachable light
of the Resurrection,
and we shall clearly hear him saying
"Hail!";
and singing the Hymn of Victory.

Let the heavens, as it is meet; rejoice,
and let the earth exult;
and let the whole universe,
visible and invisible, keep festival;
for Christ has arisen,
and there is eternal joy.

John of Damascus, 8th century, from the first *Ode of the Golden Canon for Easter Day.*

Translation by John M. Neale, *A History of the Holy Eastern Church,* 5 vols. (London, 1873), 1:880–885; vols. 1 and 2 were originally published in 1847. The translation is also found in Egon Wellesz, *A History of Byzantine Music and Hymnography,* 3rd revision (London: Oxford, 1963), 207–208.

APPENDIX D

1. The day of Resurrection!   iambic 76.76.D
      Earth! tell it out abroad!   ABCBDEFD
   The Passover of gladness!
      the Passover of God!
   From death to life eternal,
      from this world to the sky,
   our Christ hath brought us over
      with hymns of victory.

2. Our hearts be pure from evil,
      that we may see aright
   the Lord in rays eternal
      of Resurrection-light:
   and, listening to his accents,
      may hear so calm and plain
   his own 'All hail!' and hearing
      may raise the victor strain!

3. Now let the heavens be joyful!
      let earth her song begin!
   Let the round earth keep triumph,
      and all that is therein:
   Invisible and visible,
      their notes let all things blend
   for Christ the Lord hath risen
      our joy that hath no end.

Translation by John M. Neale, *Hymns of the Eastern Church, Translated,*
With Notes and An Introduction (London: J.T. Hayes, 1862), #42

APPENDIX E

Hymn at the "Great Entrance" of the holy gifts,
Liturgy of St James, 4th cent.

Let all mortal flesh be silent, and stand with fear and trembling, and
meditate nothing earthly within itself:

for the King of kings and Lord of lords Christ our God, comes forward to
be sacrificed, and to be given for food to the faithful;

and the bands of angels go before him with every power and dominion,

the many-eyed cherubim, and the six-winged seraphim, covering their
faces, and crying aloud the hymn, Alleluia, Alleluia, Alleluia.

Translation by William MacDonald in *Ante-Nicene Christian Library*,
24 vols., Alexander Roberts and James Donaldson, eds., vol. 24, *Early
Liturgies and Other Documents* (Edinburgh: T. and T. Clark, 1872), 24:19.

APPENDIX F

Prayer of the Cherubic Hymn   iambic 87.87.87
ABCBDB

1. Let all mortal flesh keep silence,
        and with fear and trembling stand;
   ponder nothing earthly-minded,
        for with blessing in his hand
   Christ our God to earth descendeth
        our full homage to demand.

2. King of kings, yet born of Mary,
        as of old on earth he stood,
   Lord of lords, in human vesture
        —in the Body and the Blood—
   he will give to all the faithful
        his own self for heavenly Food.

3. Rank on rank the host of heaven
        spreads its vanguard on the way,
   as the Light of light descendeth
        from the realms of endless day,
   that the powers of hell may vanish
        as the darkness clears away.

4. At his feet the six-winged Seraph:
        Cherubim with sleepless eye,
   veil their faces to the Presence,
        as with ceaseless voice they cry,
   'Alleluia! Alleluia!
        Alleluia! Lord most high.'

Translation by Gerard Moultrie in *Lyra Eucharistica, Hymns and Verses on the Holy Communion, Ancient and Modern, with Other Poems*, 2nd edition, Orby Shipley, ed. (London: Longman and Green, 1864).

APPENDIX G

The Teaching of the Lord to the Gentiles
by the Twelve Apostles (also known as DIDACHE, 2nd cent. CE)

Didache 10:2

We give Thee thanks, Holy Father,
for Thy holy name,
which Thou hast made to tabernacle in our hearts,
and for the knowledge and faith and immortality,
which Thou hast made known unto us
through Thy Son Jesus;
Thine is the glory for ever and ever.

Didache 10:3

Thou, Almighty Master,
didst create all things for Thy name's sake,
and didst give food and drink unto men for enjoyment,
that they might render thanks to Thee;
but didst bestow upon us spiritual food and drink and eternal life
through Thy Son.

Didache 10:5

Remember, Lord, Thy Church
to deliver it from all evil
and to perfect it in Thy love;
and gather it together from the four winds—
even the Church which has been sanctified—
into Thy kingdom which Thou hast prepared for it;
for Thine is the power and the glory for ever and ever.

Didache 9:4

As this broken bread was scattered upon the mountains
and being gathered together became one,
so may Thy Church be gathered together
from the ends of the earth into Thy kingdom;
for Thine is the glory and the power
through Jesus Christ for ever and ever.

Translation by Joseph B. Lightfoot in *The Apostolic Fathers*, Joseph B. Lightfoot
and J.R. Harmer, eds. (London: Macmillan, 1898), 213–242.

APPENDIX H

1. Father, we thank you, who has planted
       your holy name within our hearts.
Knowledge and faith and life immortal
       Jesus your Son to us imparts.

dactylic/trochaic
98.98   ABCB

2. Lord, you have made all for your pleasure,
       and given us food for all our days,
giving in Christ the bread eternal;
       yours is the power, be yours the praise.

3. Watch o'er your church, O Lord, in mercy,
       save it from evil, guard it still;
perfect it in your love, unite it,
       cleansed and conformed unto your will.

4. As grain, once scattered on the hillsides,
       was in this broken bread made one,
so from all lands, your church be gathered
       into your kingdom by your Son.

Translation by F. Bland Tucker, 1939, in *The Hymnal 1940* (New York: The Church Pension Fund, 1943), #195

APPENDIX I

Jesus Christ,
the Gladdening Light
of the deathless Father's
holy glory;
the heavenly,
holy, blessed one.

As the sun reclines
we see the light of evening
and sing our hymn to God,
The Father, Son, and Holy Spirit.

Worthy are you, O Son of God,
through each and every moment,
that joyful songs should hymn you.

You are the giver of our life,
and so the world gives glory.

The Greek Liturgy of the Hours, anonymous ca. 3rd century, translation by John A. McGuckin.

John A. McGuckin, *At the Lighting of the Lamps: Hymns of the Ancient Church* (Oxford: Sisters of the Love of God Press, 1995). Reprinted by permission of Morehouse Publishing, Harrisburg, PA.

APPENDIX J

1. O gladsome light, O grace   iambic 667.667
   of our Creator's face,   AABCCB
      the eternal splendor wearing;
   celestial, holy blest,
   our Savior Jesus Christ,
      joyful in your appearing!

2. As fades the day's last light
   we see the lamps of night,
      our common hymn outpouring,
   O God of might unknown,
   you, the incarnate Son,
      and Spirit blest adoring.

3. To you of right belongs
   all praise of holy songs,
      O Son of God, lifegiver.
   You, therefore, O Most High
   the world does glorify
      and shall exalt forever.

Translation by Robert S. Bridges, ed. *Yattendon Hymnal* (Oxford: Clarendon Press, 1899), #84.

Perspectives on Holiness
in Eastern Sources and the Wesleys

Trinitarian Theology and Wesleyan Holiness

Geoffrey Wainwright

Trinitarian Teaching

Trinitarian doctrine is grounded in, and proved by, an experience of salvation that finds its source and shape in the reality of the Triune God. Such is the conclusion of John Wesley in his sermon of 1775 "On the Trinity," in which he shows how "knowledge of the Three-One God is interwoven with all true Christian faith, with all vital religion":

> I know not how anyone can be a Christian believer till "he hath" (as St John speaks) "the witness in himself" [1 John 5:10]; till "the Spirit of God witnesses with his spirit that he is a child of God" [Romans 8:16]—that is, in effect, till God the Holy Ghost witnesses that God the Father has accepted him through the merits of God the Son— and having this witness he honours the Son and the blessed Spirit "even as he honours the Father" [John 5:23]. Not every Christian believer adverts to this; perhaps at first not one in twenty; but if you ask any of them a few questions, you will easily find it is implied in what he believes.[1]

The same point is made in a formal dogmatic way in Wesley's open Letter to a Roman Catholic, written in Dublin in 1749.[2] There Wesley sets out the faith of "a true Protestant" by way of an expansion upon the Nicene-Constantinopolitan Creed.

Concerning the First Person: "I believe that this one God is the Father of all things, especially of angels and men; that he is in a peculiar manner the Father of those whom he regenerates by his Spirit, whom he adopts in his Son as coheirs with him and crowns with an eternal inheritance; but in a still higher sense, the Father of his only Son, whom he hath begotten from eternity."

Concerning the Son: Jesus of Nazareth, the Saviour of the world, anointed by the Holy Ghost for the messianic offices of prophet, priest, and king, is "the proper, natural Son of God, God of God, very God of very God," "Lord of all, having absolute, supreme universal dominion, but more peculiarly *our* Lord (who believe in him), both by conquest, purchase, and voluntary obligation"; he "was made man, joining the human nature with the divine in one person," was "conceived by the singular operation of the Holy Ghost and born of the Blessed Virgin Mary," "suffered death, even the death of the cross," "rose again from the dead," "ascended into heaven, where he remains in the midst of the throne of God in the highest power and glory as Mediator till the end of the world, as God to all eternity," and "in the end, he will come down from heaven to judge every man according to his works, both those who shall be then alive and all who have died before that day."

Concerning the Third Person: "I believe the infinite and eternal Spirit of God, equal with the Father and the Son, to be not only perfectly holy in himself, but the immediate cause of all holiness in us: enlightening our understandings, rectifying our wills and affections, renewing our natures, uniting our persons to Christ, assuring us of the adoption of sons, leading us in our actions, purifying and sanctifying our souls and bodies to a full and eternal enjoyment of God."

What Wesley says in expansion of the third article of the Creed is particularly important for our theme of "Trinitarian Theology and Wesleyan Holiness." Wesley's development of the third article bears a trinitarian watermark which becomes even clearer when it is read in the light of what he has already written in reference to the first and second articles. In the third article, the single most significant phrase for our purposes is the explicit confession that the Holy Spirit is "the immediate cause of all holiness in us." For we know from St Basil's accurate systematization of the scriptural record in his treatise, *On the Holy Spirit,* that all the works of God towards us start from the Father, proceed through the Son, and are completed in the Holy Spirit; and that our grateful response begins in the Spirit and ascends through the Son to the Father.[3]

Let us look, then, at the precise functions which Wesley in this text from the *Letter to a Roman Catholic* lists as the work of the Holy Spirit in us. These different aspects of the Spirit's work may be seen as occurring simultaneously and continuously in believers; but it is also possible to take them roughly in a temporal sequence that traces, according to what Wesley calls "The Scripture Way of Salvation" (1765), "the entire work of God from the first dawning of grace in the soul till it is consummated in glory"—provided that each successive stage integrates all that went before.[4]

Thus, first, the Holy Spirit "enlightens our understandings." In his sermon of 1785 "On Working Out Our Own Salvation," and in a way which refutes any possible accusation even of semi-pelagianism, Wesley attributes the very beginnings of salvation to the operation of divine grace, called here "preventing grace" in the sense of "prevenient":

> Salvation begins with what is usually termed (and very properly) "preventing grace"; including the first wish to please God, the first dawn of light concerning his will, and the first slight, transient conviction of having sinned against him. All these imply some tendency toward life, some degree of salvation, the beginning of a deliverance from a blind, unfeeling heart, quite insensible of God and the things of God.[5]

The recurrent image of the divine illumination of the human soul hitherto darkened by the ignorance of sin matches what Wesley has called the work of the Holy Spirit in "enlightening our understandings." Elsewhere, in his sermon of 1765 on "The Scripture Way of Salvation," Wesley may appropriate this prevenient work of God in the soul indifferently to any of the three Persons: "all the 'drawings' of 'the Father' [John 6:44], the desires after God, which, if we yield to them, increase more and more; all that 'light' wherewith the Son of God 'enlighteneth everyone that cometh into the world' [John 1:9], showing every man 'to do justly, to love mercy, and to walk humbly with his God' [Micah 6:8]; all the convictions [of sin] which his Spirit from time to time works in every child of man [John 16:8]."[6]

Next, according to Wesley's list in the *Letter to a Roman Catholic*, the Holy Spirit "rectifies our wills and affections." This is where the first stage merges into the second, for, after speaking in "On Working Out Our Own Salvation" of "preventing grace," Wesley immediately continues: "Salvation is carried on by 'convincing grace,' usually in Scripture termed 'repentance,' which brings a larger measure of self-knowledge, and a farther deliverance from 'the heart of stone' [Ezekiel 11:19]."[7] Repentance begins in the awakening of conscience, the human "faculty" to whose existence and exercise the "influence of the Spirit of God is absolutely needful" (as Wesley phrased it in his sermon of 1788 "On Conscience").[8] Wesley was so insistent on the need for repentance in the approach to faith, properly so called, and the gift of justification that he became suspected of "works-righteousness" on account of what he wrote in the Minutes of the 1770 Conference concerning "works meet for repentance": "Whoever desires to find favour with God, should 'cease from evil, and learn to do well' [Isaiah 1:16f.]."[9] According to a pattern wherein he often rang the terminological changes, Wesley considered repentance "the porch of religion," faith "the door," and holiness "religion itself."[10]

The next two items in Wesley's list—the work of the Holy Spirit in "renewing our natures" and "uniting our persons to Christ"—need to be taken together. Here we are dealing with a matter controversial between Protestants and Catholics, and even, in its nuances, among Protestants themselves, namely the relation between justification and sanctification. In saying that the two may not be separated even while they must be distinguished, Wesley both held to the temporal simultaneity between initial justification and the regeneration which was the beginning of holiness and yet also saw their grounding and result differently. Justification was what God did *for* us, pardoning us on account of the Son's redeeming work and thereby setting us in a new relation to himself; sanctification was what God did *in* us by the Holy Spirit, creating a real change in us through the renewal of our fallen nature.[11] Thus, in "uniting our persons to Christ," it is the business of the Holy Spirit to allow Christ to "reign in all believing hearts,"[12] so that believers may "have the mind of Christ" (a favorite expression of Wesley's) and "walk as Christ walked,"[13] and thus have "our natures renewed." Thus, in Lutheran terms, the *Christus extra nos* and the *Christus pro nobis* become also the *Christus in nobis*; or, in characteristically Catholic terms, we are "conformed" to Christ.

The next work of the Holy Spirit listed in Wesley's *Letter to a Roman Catholic* is his "assuring us of the adoption of sons." As in the Scriptures, regeneration may also be spoken of as adoption. A constant theme in Wesley's writings, and the subject of a cluster of sermons among the so-called Standard Sermons (numbers 9–12 in particular), is "The Witness of the Spirit." Wesley loved to cite Romans 8:15f.: "Ye have not received the spirit of bondage again unto fear; but ye have received the Spirit of adoption, whereby we cry, Abba, Father. The Spirit itself beareth witness with our spirit that we are children of God." The "inward witness" of the Spirit gave an assurance to believers of their filial relationship to God in Christ. Wesley calls such assurance "the common privilege of Christians." As the years went by after his own striking experience at the Aldersgate Society on 24 May 1738, Wesley came to the view that a believer might be justified even though not all doubts and fears were yet removed; but he never ceased to preach that the "child" of God, as distinct from the "servant," was characterized by the freedom of access to his heavenly Father. Moreover, the inward and direct witness of the Spirit is accompanied by an indirect witness, whereby our spirit concludes to our being children of God from the fruit of the Spirit in our lives—for "if the Spirit of God does really testify that we are the children of God, the immediate consequence will be the fruit of the Spirit, even 'love, joy, peace, long-suffering, gentleness, goodness, fidelity, meekness, temperance' [Galatians 5:22f.]."[14]

The passage just quoted from Galatians 5 goes on to say that "those who belong to Christ have crucified the flesh with its passions and desires. If we live by the Spirit, let us also walk by the Spirit." That brings us precisely to the next works of the Holy Spirit according to Wesley's enumeration in the *Letter to a Roman Catholic*: "leading us in our actions, purifying and sanctifying our souls and bodies." Notice first what Wesley said in a sermon of 1760, based on 1 Peter 1:6, entitled "Heaviness through Manifold Temptations":

> All inward holiness is the immediate fruit of the faith that worketh by love. By this the blessed Spirit purifies the heart from pride, self-will, passion; from love of the world, from foolish and hurtful desires, from vile and vain affections. Beside that, sanctified afflictions have (through the grace of God) an immediate and direct tendency to holiness. Through the operation of his Spirit they humble more and more, and abase the soul before God. They calm and meeken our turbulent spirit, tame the fierceness of our nature, soften our obstinacy and self-will, crucify us to the world, and bring us to expect all our strength from, and to seek all our happiness in, God.[15]

Like the apostle Paul, Wesley was well aware of the absurd reality that he addressed in a sermon of 1763 "On Sin in Believers."[16] In "The Scripture Way of Salvation," Wesley quotes from "Macarius the Egyptian" to the effect that "the unskillful (or unexperienced), when grace operates, presently imagine they have no more sin, whereas they that have discretion cannot deny that even we who have the grace of God may be molested again." He goes on to remark, in his own words, that sin certainly "remains" in the regenerate, even if it no longer "reigns": there is "our proneness to evil," a heart "bent to backsliding" [Hosea 11:7], the "still continuing tendency of the 'flesh' to 'lust against the Spirit' [Galatians 5: 17]"; and the sin which "remains" in our hearts also "cleaves" to all our words and actions.[17]

There is, therefore, plenty of work for the Spirit to do in "purifying and sanctifying our souls and bodies." But what, more positively put, is the Spirit's work in "leading us in our actions"? "Necessary to full sanctification," says Wesley in the same sermon, are both "works of piety" and "works of mercy." As works of piety he instances "public prayer, family prayer, and praying in our closet; receiving the Lord's Supper; searching the Scriptures by hearing, reading, meditating; and using such a measure of fasting or abstinence as our bodily health allows." The works of mercy, which may be directed to either the bodies or the souls of others, include "feeding the hungry, clothing the naked, entertaining the stranger, visiting those that are in prison, or sick, or variously afflicted" as well as "endeavouring to instruct the ignorant, to awaken the stupid sinner, to quicken the lukewarm, to confirm the wavering, to comfort the feebleminded, to succour the tempted, or to contribute in any manner to the saving of souls from death." This, Wesley concludes, "is the way wherein God hath appointed his children to wait for complete salvation."[18]

That last phrase brings us to a characteristic concern of Wesley's. Earlier in the sermon on "The Scripture Way of Salvation" he had said: "It is thus that we wait for entire sanctification, for a full salvation from all our sins, from pride, self-will, anger, unbelief, or, as the Apostle expresses it, 'Go on to perfection' [Hebrews 6:1; cf. Philippians 3]. But what is perfection? The word has various senses: here it means perfect love. It is love excluding sin; love filling the heart, taking up the whole capacity of the soul. It is love 'rejoicing evermore, praying without ceasing, in everything giving thanks' [1 Thessalonians 5:16–18]."[19]

Full salvation, entire sanctification, perfection, perfect love: these were controversial notions between Wesley and the Calvinists of his day, and they have remained controversial in Methodist relations with both Calvinists and Lutherans. Wesley knew, of course, that "God's love has been poured into our hearts through the Holy Spirit which has been given to us" (Romans 5:5), and he was reluctant to set limits to what God might accomplish in us even on this side of death: "What God hath promised"— towards the end of "The Scripture Way of Salvation" Wesley cites "the ancient promise" of Deuteronomy 30:6 that "I will circumcize thy heart, and the heart of thy seed, to love the Lord thy God with all thy heart and with all thy soul" and goes on—"He is *able* to perform," and God is indeed "both able and willing to sanctify us *now*" so as to "cleanse us from all sin" [1 John 1:7–9].[20] While this single devotion must certainly be prayed and striven for, it may perhaps be wondered whether the word "perfection" is worth fighting for, given the limits with which Wesley hedges it about: there is no problem in his saying that human perfection is not the absolute perfection of God or that it remains "improvable" with growth in grace, but it seems to accommodate too readily the errors that come from the ignorance and weakness consequent upon the Fall, and it appears to be rather too easily "amissable, capable of being lost."[21]

With all this we are approaching what Wesley names in the *Letter to a Roman Catholic* as the purpose and result of all the Spirit's sanctifying work, namely "a full and eternal enjoyment of God." In a brief sermon of 1773 "On Predestination," in which he expounds Romans 8:29f so as to stop short of Calvinism, Wesley speaks of God's final glorification of believers, where "having made them 'meet to be partakers of the inheritance of the saints in light' [Colossians 1:12], he gives them 'the kingdom which was prepared for them before the world began' [Matthew 25:34]":

Suppose then you stood with the "great multitude which no man can number, out of every nation, and tongue, and kindred, and people" [Revelation 7:9] who "give praise unto Him that sitteth upon the throne, and unto the Lamb for ever and ever" [Revelation 5:13], you would not find one among them all that were entered into glory, who was not a witness of that great truth, "Without holiness no man shall see the Lord" [Hebrews 12:14]; not one of all that innumerable company who was not sanctified before he was glorified. By holiness he was prepared for glory; according to the invariable will of the Lord, that the crown, purchased by the blood of his Son, should be given to none but those who are renewed by his Spirit.[22]

The Image of the Triune God

Thanks, then, to John Wesley's expansion upon the Creed in his *Letter to a Roman Catholic*, we have followed by a pneumatological thread the way of salvation from beginning to end, taking care to observe the trinitarian interweavings all along. Much more briefly, we may now display the theme of "Trinitarian Theology and Wesleyan Holiness" by another route. In his study *Der neue Mensch im theologischen Denken John Wesleys* (1970), Jürgen Weissbach showed better than most other scholars had done the prominence in Wesley's soteriology of the restoration of the image of God in humankind.[23]

In a sermon of 1760 on "The New Birth," Wesley set out a threefold understanding of the original creation of humankind in the divine image at Genesis 1:27f.:

> Not barely in his *natural image*, a picture of his own immortality, a spiritual being, endued with understanding, freedom of will, and various affections; nor merely in his *political image*, the governor of this lower world, having "dominion over the fishes of the sea, and over all the earth"; but chiefly in his *moral image*, which, according to the Apostle, is "righteousness and true holiness" [Ephesians 4:24]. In this image of God was man made. "God is love" [1 John 4:8, 16]: accordingly man at his creation was full of love, which was the sole principle of all his tempers, thoughts, words, and actions. God is full of justice, mercy, and truth: so was man as he came from the hands of his Creator.[24]

The passage from the sermon on "The New Birth" corresponds rather nicely to the three main strands in the traditional Christian understanding of the *imago Dei*: the human creature is ontologically capable of communion with God (our spiritual nature); is cosmologically located to "till the ground" (Genesis 2:5) or administer the earth on God's behalf; is constitutionally a society of neighbors with the opportunity for a life of mutual love. Fallen humankind needs redemption and renewal if it is to fulfill its divinely appointed ends.

For us in our ecologically sensitive times it is unfortunate that Wesley has rather little to say about the political aspect of the *imago Dei*, or the cosmic location of humankind. We shall concentrate rather on the other two aspects, doxology and social ethics. That is justified by Wesley's oft-repeated statement that true religion, in keeping with Jesus' summary of the Law in Matthew 22:37–40, basically consists in love of God and love of neighbor. In a sermon of 1789 on "The Unity of the Divine Being," for instance, Wesley said: "True religion is right tempers towards God and man. It is, in two words, gratitude and benevolence: gratitude to our Creator and supreme Benefactor, and benevolence to our fellow-creatures. In other words, it is the loving God with all our heart, and our neighbour as ourselves. It is in consequence of our knowing God loves us that we love him, and love our neighbour as ourselves."[25]

The dynamic link between love of God and love of neighbor is established by Wesley elsewhere in a phrase that he quotes from St. Augustine: *imitari quem colis*, "to imitate Him whom you worship."[26] In expounding from Matthew 6:24 what it means to "serve God," Wesley mentions, first, "the believing in God, as 'reconciling the world to himself through Christ Jesus' " [2 Corinthians 5:19], and second, "to love God," that is, "to desire God alone for his own sake," "to rejoice in God," "to delight in the Lord," "to enjoy God," "to rest in Him, as our God and our all"; and then Wesley continues (and the reference to "image" is to be noted):

> A third thing we are to understand by serving God is to resemble or imitate him.
>
> So the ancient Father: *Optimus Dei cultus, imitari quem colis:* "It is the best worship or service of God, to imitate him you worship."
>
> We here speak of imitating or resembling him in the spirit of our minds: For here the true Christian imitation of God begins. "God is a Spirit" [John 4:24, KJV]; and they that imitate or resemble him must do it "in spirit and in truth."
>
> Now God is love: Therefore, they who resemble him in the spirit of their minds are transformed into the same image. They are merciful even as he is merciful [Luke 6:36].
>
> Their soul is all love. They are kind, benevolent, compassionate, tender-hearted; and that not only to the good and gentle, but also to the froward. Yea, they are, like Him, loving unto every man, and their mercy extends to all his works.
>
> One thing more we are to understand by serving God, and that is, the obeying him; the glorifying him with our bodies, as well as with our spirits; the keeping his outward commandments; the zealously doing whatever he hath enjoined; the carefully avoiding whatever he hath forbidden; the performing all the ordinary actions of life with a single eye and a pure heart, offering them all in holy, fervent love, as sacrifices to God through Jesus Christ.[27]

The trinitarian shape of Wesley's doxology is clearly expressed in his sermon of 1780 on "Spiritual Worship": it consists in "the happy and holy communion which the faithful have with God the Father, Son, and Holy Ghost." The sermon is based on 1 John 5:20: "This is the true God, and eternal life," where the subject of the sentence is grammatically and exegetically established to be Jesus Christ. Accordingly, most of the sermon is devoted to establishing from a wide range of Scriptures that Jesus Christ is indeed "true God" and "eternal life." Wesley considers, however, that the entire First Epistle of John bears a trinitarian structure: it treats "first, severally, of communion with the Father (1:5–10), of communion with the Son (2 and 3), of communion with the Spirit (4); secondly, conjointly, of the testimony of the Father, Son, and Holy Ghost, on which faith in Christ, the being born of God, love to God and his children, the keeping his commandments, and victory over the world, are founded (5:1–12)." The "eternal life," which Jesus Christ "is," is expounded by Wesley in a trinitarian way, and it certainly includes that social love of others which has its source and model in the divine love, as John's Letter insists:

> This eternal life commences when it pleases the Father to reveal his Son in our hearts; when we first know Christ, being enabled to "call him Lord by the Holy Ghost"

[1 Corinthians 12:3]; when we can testify, our conscience bearing us witness in the Holy Ghost, "The life which I now live, I live by faith in the Son of God, who loved me, and gave himself for me" [Galatians 2:20]. And then it is that happiness begins; happiness real, solid and substantial. Then it is that heaven is opened in the soul, that the proper heavenly state commences, while the love of God, as God loving us, is shed abroad in the heart [Romans 5:5], instantly producing love to all mankind; general, pure benevolence, together with its fruits, lowliness, meekness, patience, contentedness in every state; an entire, clear, full acquiescence in the whole will of God; enabling us to "rejoice evermore, and in everything to give thanks" [1 Thessalonians 5:16–18].[28]

If such is the beginning of eternal life, Wesley describes its end, again in trinitarian terms, at the conclusion of his sermon of 1785 on "The New Creation":

And to crown all, there will be a deep, an intimate, an uninterrupted union with God; a constant communion with the Father and his Son Jesus Christ, through the Spirit; a continual enjoyment of the Three-One God, and of all the creatures in him![29]

Might that, I wonder, be viewed as Wesley's version of the final fulfillment of those "exceeding great and precious promises" that Wesley read in his Greek Testament at five o'clock in the morning of May 24th, 1738, that "by these ye might be partakers of the divine nature" [2 Peter 1:4]?[30]

Trinitarian Hymnology

From John Wesley (1703–1791), the principal founder of Methodism, we pass to his younger brother Charles Wesley (1707–1788), the hymnwriter, whose accomplishment was to stamp the evangelical faith on the hearts and minds of Methodists by way of their vocal chords. What John wrote in the calm prose of his printed sermons, Charles transmuted into an incandescent orthodoxy by the poetry of his hymns. Trinitarian doctrine runs as consistently through Charles's verse as it did through John's homiletics and dogmatics. That is natural, since both brothers were steeped in the Scriptures and in the classical literature of the Christian tradition. Since it is obviously impossible to work systematically through the 9,000 hymns and poems of Charles Wesley, the procedure here will be to introduce one particular collection that was devoted entirely to trinitarian themes, and then to lay out a few samples of some of his greatest trinitarian hymns from other collections that retained their places in the *lex orandi* of continuing Methodism.

In 1767 the Wesleys published from Charles's pen a collection of 188 pieces under the title *Hymns on the Trinity,* printed at Bristol by William Pine. The first 136 items were based on the treatise by the Reverend William Jones of Nayland (1726–1800), entitled *The Catholic Doctrine of a Trinity proved by above an hundred short and clear arguments, expressed in the terms of Holy Scripture, compared in a manner entirely new* (first published in 1756, with an enlarged third edition in 1767); the remaining 52

"Hymns and Prayers to the Trinity" were Charles Wesley's free composition. Charles had already in 1746 published a collection of twenty-four short versified doxologies under the title *Gloria Patri, &c., or Hymns to the Trinity*,[31] and scattered through his other collections one finds signs of his fierce concern, that was also William Jones's, about the various heresies that were threatening the trinitarian faith of the Church of England, as in the polemical prayer "for" (*sic*) "the Arians, Socinians, Deists, Pelagians, &c." included in Charles Wesley's *Hymns of Intercession for All Mankind* (Bristol, 1758).[32]

In the major part of the 1767 collection,[33] Charles Wesley followed the structure of Jones's treatise, with its four sections of "The Divinity of Christ" (1–57), "The Divinity of the Holy Ghost" (58–86), "The Plurality and Trinity of Persons" (87–109), and "The Trinity in Unity" (110–136). Under the rubric of the one or two scriptural texts on which Jones based each of his many theological arguments, Wesley would each time write a hymn, or very occasionally more. In these hymns Wesley would skillfully weave the phrases of Scripture, of conciliar creeds and dogma, of the Church's liturgy, and of Jones's theology into a cohesive pattern that owed much to Wesley's own lively faith and sought to commend the reality of the Trinity to the understanding and experience of singers or (in most cases, one suspects) readers.[34]

In a letter of April 17, 1776 to Mary Bishop, John Wesley wrote thus: "Mr. Jones's book on the Trinity is both more clear and more strong than any I ever saw on that subject. If anything is wanting, it is the application, lest it should appear to be a merely speculative doctrine, which has no influence on our hearts and lives; but this is abundantly supplied by my brother's *Hymns*."[35] A similar point is made, more flamboyantly, by George Osborn, the nineteenth-century editor of *The Poetical Works of John and Charles Wesley*:

> [The poet] has never lost sight of the experimental and practical bearings of [the catholic] doctrine [of the Trinity]. Mr. Jones has an excellent paragraph at the conclusion of his argument, warning his readers that a sound belief without a holy life will not profit them. But our poet, true to the mission of Methodism, makes experience the connecting link between knowledge and practice, and devotes an entire section of his work to "Hymns and Prayers to the Trinity," in which the doctrine is presented in most intimate connection with his own spiritual interests, and those of his readers. Such a mode of treating it is the best answer to those who represent it as a mere metaphysical speculation devoid of practical interest. The force of Scriptural argument, and the depth and tenderness of religious feeling, are here exhibited in inseparable combination, and the whole forms a manual, at once doctrinal and experimental, of great value. The "higher Christian life" is thus shown to be dependent upon the highest revealed mysteries, and these in their turn to minister illumination, help, and comfort to the humblest believer who receives the testimony of God concerning His Son.[36]

A first sample may be taken from the latter part of the collection, number 9 in the "Hymns and Prayers to the Trinity," where soteriology and doxology are characteristically fused. To each Person of the Trinity is recognized a particular role in the work of salvation, yet their cooperation is implied in the joint invocation of their blessing and presence, their plurality being integrated in their sameness of essence (grammatically reflected in the singular address "Thou" and the single name "Jehovah").[37] Thus:

> Fountain of Divine compassion,
>   Father of the ransomed race,
> Christ, our Saviour and salvation,
>   Spirit of consecrating grace:
> See us prostrated before Thee;
>   Co-essential Three in One,
> Glorious God, our souls adore Thee
>   High on Thine eternal throne.

> While we in Thy name assemble,
>   Overshadow'd from above,
> Let us at Thy presence tremble,
>   Holy, Triune God of love:
> Father, Son, and Spirit, bless us,
>   Who the true Jehovah art;
> Plenitude of God in Jesus,
>   Enter every contrite heart.

> Challenge now Thine humble dwelling,
>   O Thou high and lofty One,
> Thine own Deity revealing,
>   God in persons three come down:
> Thou, the Witnesses in heaven,
>   Dost on earth Thy record bear:
> Show us here our sins forgiven,
>   Show us all Thy glory there.

Again, in hymn 7 of the "Hymns and Prayers to the Trinity," the three Persons "meet" in the work of salvation and receive a common "admiration" or praise:

> All hail, mysterious Trinity!
> Every person of the three
>   In my salvation meets:
> The Father draws me to the Son,
> Accepts for Jesus' sake alone,
>   And all my sins forgets.

> The Son His cleansing blood applies,
> Breaks my heart, and bids me rise
>   A penitent forgiven.
> The Holy Ghost His witness bears,

> Numbers me with the royal heirs,
>   And gives a taste of heaven.
>
> The Father multiplies my peace,
> Jesus doth my faith increase,
>   And teaches me to pray;
> The Spirit purifies my heart,
> And makes me, Saviour, as Thou art,
>   And seals me to Thy day.
>
> Thus, only thus I surely know
> God was manifest below,
>   The pardoning God of grace,
> Whom saints in persons three admire,
> Whom I with all that heavenly choir
>   World without end shall praise.

Or, again from that latter part of the collection, hymn 30 takes up the theme of the restoration of the *imago Dei*:

> Come, Father, Son, and Holy Ghost,
> Restorer of Thine image lost. . . .

In the sixth and seventh stanzas, the renewal of the image is attributed to the work of the Holy Spirit ("He") before the concluding trinitarian summary ("Thou") and the striking last line with the linguistic coinage "imparadised":

> He sanctifies, without respect
> Of high or low, His own elect,
>   Regenerate from above,
> Into Thy glorious form converts,
> And stamps Thine image on our hearts
>   In purity and love.
>
> O wouldst Thou stamp it now on mine,
> The name and character Divine,
>   The holy One in Three!
> Come, Father, Son, and Spirit, give
> Thy love,—Thyself: and lo! I live
>   Imparadised in Thee.

And, finally from the independently composed section, hymn 48 makes a similar prayer for God's gifts of final justification and full sanctification to be given even now, on this side of death, as a prolepsis of the vision of God that will be granted in heaven ("*Gloria Dei vivens homo, vita autem hominis visio Dei,*" as St Irenaeus phrased it).[38]

This hymn varies "image" with the poetic alternative of "portraiture":

> Triune God, the New-Creator
>   Of our fallen souls appear,
> O communicate Thy nature,
>   Raise us to Thy image here,
> In true holiness renewed,
> Spotless portraitures of God.
>
> By a bless'd anticipation
>   Of Thy perfect righteousness,
> Qualify us for salvation,
>   Vessels of celestial grace,
> Meet by love and purity
> God without a veil to see.

And now a few examples from the earlier parts of the *Hymns on the Trinity*; first, hymn 87, where Charles Wesley follows William Jones on Genesis 1:26: "And GOD said, Let US make man in OUR image, after OUR likeness." The grammatically plural forms are taken, as frequently in traditional exegesis, for trinitarian; and, as in other places in the collection, one is doubtless meant to hear behind the compound singular-plus-plural name "Jehovah Elohim"—borrowed from Genesis 2:4b-3:24—the Holy Trinity:

> Hail, Father, Son, and Spirit, great
>   Before the birth of time,
> Enthroned in everlasting state
>   JEHOVAH ELOHIM!
> A mystical plurality
>   We in the Godhead own,
> Adoring One in persons three,
>   And Three in nature One.
>
> From Thee our being we receive,
>   The creatures of Thy grace,
> And raised out of the earth we live
>   To sing our Maker's praise:
> Thy powerful, wise, and loving mind
>   Did our creation plan,
> And all the glorious persons join'd
>   To form Thy favourite, man.
>
> Again Thou didst, in council met,
>   Thy ruin's work restore,
> Establish'd in our first estate
>   To forfeit it no more:

> And when we rise in love renew'd,
> Our souls resemble Thee,
> An image of the Triune God
> To all eternity.

Perhaps the three adjectives "powerful, wise, and loving" are to be especially associated with the three Persons respectively, Father, Son, and Spirit;[39] it might even be that the triune resemblance in the (renewed) human *soul* would follow the pattern of memory, understanding and will in the one mind, as in the *De Trinitate* of St. Augustine.[40]

In hymn 109, expounding the Thrice-Holy of Isaiah 6:3 and Revelation 4:8, Wesley follows Jones in the trinitarian interpretation familiar from the eucharistic liturgies of the Church, where the earthly choir adds its voices to the heavenly in anticipation of their ultimate junction, all united in praise of the God who alone is the proper recipient of worship:

> Hail holy, holy, holy Lord,
> Whom One in Three we know,
> By all Thy heavenly host adored,
> By all Thy Church below!
> One undivided Trinity
> With triumph we proclaim:
> Thy universe is full of Thee,
> And speaks Thy glorious name.
>
> Thee, holy Father, we confess,
> Thee, holy Son, adore,
> Thee, Spirit of true holiness,
> We worship evermore:
> Thine incommunicable right,
> Almighty God, receive,
> Which angel-choirs and saints in light
> And saints embodied give.
>
> Three persons equally Divine
> We magnify and love:
> And both the choirs ere long shall join
> To sing Thy praise above:
> Hail holy, holy, holy Lord,
> (Our heavenly song shall be,)
> Supreme, essential One adored
> In co-eternal Three.

And finally from the 1767 collection, two short hymns that are both of special interest for our theme of Christian holiness, and which each employ the exegetical technique of finding a particular saving function attributed in turn to all three Persons of the Godhead. In hymn 125, it is the "life-giving" function that is performed by the Father according to John 5:21 ("The Father RAISETH up the dead, and QUICKENETH them"), by the Son in the very same verse ("Even so the SON QUICKENETH whom He will"), and by the Spirit according to John 6:63 ("It is the SPIRIT that QUICKENETH"):

> Fountain of life Divine
> > The Three in One we know,
> The Father, Son, and Spirit join
> > To quicken all below;
> Each person of the three
> > The breath of lives inspires;
> And then we rise our God to see,
> > And do what He requires.

> Spiritual life to' impart
> > The Father's power we feel;
> The Son doth the same power exert
> > And quickens whom He will:
> The quickening Spirit stirs,
> > Infusing His own grace;
> And the whole Trinity concurs,
> > Me from the dead to raise.

In hymn 129, the theme is the divine "indwelling" of believers: "GOD hath said, I will DWELL in them" (2 Corinthians 6: 16), "That CHRIST may DWELL in your hearts" (Ephesians 3:17), "His SPIRIT that DWELLETH in you" (Romans 8:11):

> The Father, Son, and Spirit dwell
> > By faith in all His saints below,
> And then in love unspeakable
> > The glorious Trinity we know
> Created after God to shine,
> Fill'd with the plenitude Divine.

It would have been possible to develop the same theme from John 14:15–24, where Jesus promises that Father, Son, and Spirit will all make their home with his disciples. Perhaps this experience of the simultaneous and "collocative" presence of all three divine Persons in the believer constitutes, at the epistemological level of human cognition, the basis of what of course, at the ontological level of the divine reality, precedes it, namely, the eternal circumincession, circuminsession, or *perichoresis* of the three Persons, that is, their "mutual indwelling."

For a couple of examples of Wesleyan trinitarian hymns—not from the "Hymns on the Trinity" of 1767—that persisted long in the liturgical practice of Methodists, we may turn to the definitive *A Collection of Hymns for the Use of the People called*

Methodists of 1780, which constituted the backbone of subsequent hymnals in both the British and the American churches throughout the nineteenth century. The first example, which is doxological in emphasis, has continued without interruption in the hymnbooks of British Methodism until today:

> Father of everlasting grace,
> Thy goodness and Thy truth we praise,
>> Thy goodness and Thy truth we prove;
> Thou hast, in honour of Thy Son,
> The gift unspeakable sent down,
>> The Spirit of life, and power, and love.
>
> Send us the Spirit of Thy Son,
> To make the depths of Godhead known,
>> To make us share the life divine;
> Send Him the sprinkled blood t'apply,
> Send Him our souls to sanctify,
>> And show and seal us ever Thine.
>
> So shall we pray, and never cease,
> So shall we thankfully confess
>> Thy wisdom, truth, and power, and love;
> With joy unspeakable adore,
> And bless, and praise Thee evermore,
>> And serve Thee as Thy hosts above:
>
> Till, added to that heavenly choir,
> We raise our songs of triumph higher,
>> And praise Thee in a bolder strain,
> Outsoar the first-born seraph's flight,
> And sing, with all our friends in light,
>> Thy everlasting love to man.[41]

The second example, which is soteriological in emphasis, was scandalously dropped from the British hymnbook of 1983, *Hymns and Psalms:*

> Since the Son hath made me free,
> Let me taste my liberty;
> Thee behold with open face,
> Triumph in Thy saving grace,
> Thy great will delight to prove,
> Glory in Thy perfect love.
>
> Abba, Father! Hear Thy child,
> Late in Jesus reconciled;

> Hear, and all the graces shower,
> All the joy, and peace, and power,
> All my Saviour asks above,
> All the life and heaven of love.
>
> Heavenly Adam, Life divine,
> Change my nature into Thine!
> Move and spread throughout my soul,
> Actuate, and fill the whole!
> Be it I no longer now
> Living in the flesh but Thou.
>
> Holy Ghost, no more delay;
> Come, and in Thy temple stay;
> Now Thine inward witness bear,
> Strong, and permanent, and clear;
> Spring of life, Thyself impart,
> Rise eternal in my heart![42]

As a final curiosity, let me end this hymnological section with the versified para-phrase that John Wesley appends to his exposition of the Lord's Prayer. The text begins with three stanzas developing "Our Father, who art in heaven, hallowed be thy Name." The next two stanzas develop the next two petitions—"Thy kingdom come," "Thy will be done on earth as it is in heaven"—with a christological and a pneumatological address respectively. The sixth, seventh, and eighth stanzas take the remaining peti-tions of the Lord's Prayer according to a trinitarian sequence: the prayer for bread (addressed to the Father), the prayer for forgiveness (addressed to the "eternal, spot-less Lamb of God"), and the prayer for preservation from temptation and deliverance from evil (addressed to the "Giver and Lord of life"). The concluding doxological stanza is addressed to the Triune God. Doubtless adjudged too long for regular litur-gical use, the hymn was retained in abbreviated form—*with loss of the trinitarian structures*—as hymn 47 in the British *Methodist Hymn Book* of 1933. Occasional use of the original hymn in personal devotions would certainly enrich the spirituality of all who are prepared to learn from the Wesleys a pattern of trinitarian holiness:

> Father of all, whose powerful voice
> Called forth this universal frame,
> Whose mercies over all rejoice,
> Through endless ages still the same:
> Thou by Thy word upholdest all;
> Thy bounteous love to all is showed;
> Thou hear'st Thy every creature's call,
> And fillest every mouth with good.

In heaven Thou reign'st enthroned in light,
　　Nature's expanse beneath Thee spread;
Earth, air, and sea, before Thy sight,
　　And hell's deep gloom are open laid.
Wisdom, and might, and love are Thine;
　　Prostrate before Thy face we fall,
Confess Thine attributes divine,
　　And hail the sovereign Lord of all.

Thee, sovereign Lord, let all confess
　　That moves in earth, or air, or sky,
Revere Thy power, Thy goodness bless,
　　Tremble before Thy piercing eye;
All ye who owe to Him your birth,
　　In praise your every hour employ;
Jehovah reigns! Be glad, O earth,
　　And shout, ye morning stars, for joy.

Son of Thy Sire's eternal love,
　　Take to Thyself Thy mighty power;
Let all earth's sons Thy mercy prove,
　　Let all Thy bleeding grace adore.
The triumphs of Thy love display,
　　In every heart reign Thou alone,
Till all Thy foes confess Thy sway,
　　And glory ends what grace begun.

Spirit of grace, and health, and power,
　　Fountain of light and love below,
Abroad Thy healing influence shower,
　　O'er all the nations let it flow.
Inflame our hearts with perfect love,
　　In us the work of faith fulfil,
So not heaven's host shall swifter move
　　Than we on earth to do Thy will.

Father, 'tis Thine each day to yield
　　Thy children's wants a flesh supply;
Thou cloth'st the lilies of the field,
　　And hearest the young ravens cry.
On Thee we cast our care; we live
　　Through Thee, who know'st our every need;
O feed us with Thy grace, and give
　　Our souls this day the living bread.

Eternal, spotless Lamb of God,
    Before the world's foundation slain,
Sprinkle us ever with Thy blood;
    O cleanse, and keep us ever clean!
To every soul (all praise to Thee)
    Our bowels of compassion move,
And all mankind by this may see
    God is in us—for God is love.

Giver and Lord of life, whose power
    And guardian care for all are free,
To Thee, in fierce temptation's hour,
    From sin and Satan let us flee;
Thine, Lord, we are, and ours Thou art;
    In us be all Thy goodness showed,
Renew, enlarge, and fill our heart
    With peace, and joy, and heaven, and God.

Blessing, and honour, praise, and love,
    Co-equal, co-eternal Three,
In earth below, and heaven above,
    By all Thy works be paid to Thee.
Thrice holy, Thine the kingdom is,
    The power omnipotent is Thine;
And when created nature dies,
    Thy never-ceasing glories shine.[43]

Trinitarian Visions

As a closing pendant to the opening citation of John Wesley's sermon of 1775 "On the Trinity," the place of the Trinity in early Methodist soteriology and spirituality may be illustrated from a remarkable phenomenon occurring in the 1770s and 1780s. At a time when certain theological and ecclesiastical circles in England were declining into Unitarianism, and when the Wesleyan teaching on entire sanctification remained controversial, a number of Methodist men and women were vouchsafed visions of the Holy Trinity that both confirmed the orthodox doctrine of God and encouraged the hope of perfection, which of course depended on the divine status of the Son and his atoning work, and of the Spirit and his sanctifying work.[44] The visions are recorded of Charles Perronet, Betsy Ritchie, Hetty Roe, John Appleton, and Ann Cutler.

    In a letter of 8 August 1788 to Lady Maxwell, John Wesley wrote that "Mr. Charles Perronet was the first person I was acquainted with who was favored" with a vision of "the ever-blessed Trinity, Miss Ritchie was the second, Miss Roe (now Mrs. Rogers) the third. I have as yet found but a few instances; so that this is not, as I was at first apt to suppose, the common privilege of all that are 'perfect in love.' "[45]

Charles Perronet—son of Wesley's friend Vincent Perronet, vicar of Shoreham—described his experiences thus:

> Just after my uniting with the Methodists, the Father was revealed to me for the first time; soon after, the whole Trinity. I beheld the distinct Persons of the Godhead, and worshipped one undivided Jehovah, and each Person separately. After this, I often had equal intercourse with Christ and with the Father; afterward, with the Spirit also. But after four years, my usual communion was with Christ only: though at times, with the Father likewise; and not wholly without the Spirit. Of late I have found the same access to the Triune God. When I approach Jesus, the Father and the Spirit commune with me. . . . If it be asked, "In what manner I beheld the Triune God?" I answer, It is above all description: it differs so much from what is human. Who can describe Light, so as to make him understand that has never seen it? And he that hath thus seen God, can no more describe what he has seen, than he that hath not. In two of these Divine Interviews the Father spake, while I was in an agony of prayer for perfect Conformity to Himself; twice more, when I was in the depth of sorrow; and each time, in scripture words. . . . It may be asked, "Was the appearance glorious?" It was all divine: it was Glory, I had no conception of: it was God. The first time the Glory of Him I saw, reached even to me: I was overwhelmed with it, body and soul, penetrated through with the rays of Deity.[46]

John Appleton of Shropshire, in the account of his quest for perfection, related that "at a time of public prayer, I thought my mind was on a sudden enlightened to see three Persons, which it was revealed to me were the Holy Trinity. I saw them all joined together, and become as one. I saw one [the Holy Spirit] with a seal in his hand, which tongue can not express, which gave me to believe, that I was sealed by the Spirit to the day of redemption."[47]

Ann Cutler—a Lancashire woman affectionately known as "Praying Nanny"—used to "renew her covenant with God every day":

> Blessed Father, loving Jesus, Holy Spirit! I give my body and soul into Thy hands. . . .
>
> Father! I reverence Thy majesty, and sink before Thee: Thou art a holy God. I submit my all to Thee. I live under Thy inspection, and wonder at Thy glory every moment.
>
> Blessed Jesus! Thou art my constant friend and companion. Thou art always with me. We walk together in the nearerst union. I can talk with Thee as my Mediator. Thou showest me the Father, and I am lost in beholding His glory. Thou takest me out and bringest me in. Thou art with me wherever I go. Mine eyes are upon Thee as my pattern and continual help.
>
> Holy Spirit! Thou art my comforter. I feel for Thee a constant burning love. My heart is set on fire by Thy blessed influence. I pray by Thy power. It is through Thee I am brought to Jesus, through Jesus I am brought to the Father, and in the Father I am swallowed up in what I call glory: and I can say, Glory be to the Father, glory be to the Son, and glory be to the Holy Spirit!

I have union with the Trinity thus: I see the Son through the Spirit, I find the Father through the Son, and God is my all in all."[48]

When Ann Cutler had recounted her experience to John Wesley during a visit of his to Preston on 14 April 1790, the wise old pastor next day wrote to her thus:

My dear Sister: There is something in the dealings of God with your soul which is out of the common way. But I have known several whom He has been pleased to lead exactly in the same way, and particularly in manifesting to them distinctly the three Persons of the ever-blessed Trinity. You may tell all your experience to me at any time; but you will need to be cautious in speaking to others, for they would not understand what you say. Go in the name of God and the power of His might. Pray for the whole spirit of humility; and I beg you would write and speak without reserve to, dear Nanny, Yours affectionately, John Wesley.[49]

Endnotes

[1] *The Works of John Wesley* (*Bicentennial edition*) 2:373–386, here 385.

[2] *The Works of John Wesley* (*Jackson edition*) 10:80–86.

[3] St Basil the Great, *On the Holy Spirit*, e.g., 18(47), 26(63–64).

[4] *Works* (*Bicentennial edition*) 2:153–169, here 156.

[5] *Works* (*Bicentennial edition*) 3:199–209, here 203f.

[6] *Works* (*Bicentennial edition*) 2:156f.

[7] *Works* (*Bicentennial edition*) 3:204.

[8] *Works* (*Bicentennial edition*) 3:479–490, here 486; cf. *Works* (*Bicentennial edition*) 3:207.

[9] See Allan Coppedge, *John Wesley in Theological Debate* (Wilmore, KY: Wesley Heritage Press, 1987), 202f.

[10] "The Principles of a Methodist farther Explained" in *Works* (*Jackson edition*) 8:414–481, here 472f.

[11] See, for example, the sermon of 1746 on "Justification by Faith" in *Works* (*Bicentennial edition*) 1:181–199, here 187; the sermon of 1760 on "The New Birth" in *Works* 2:186–201, here 187.

[12] Sermon of 1750, "The Law Established through Faith, II" in *Works* (*Bicentennial edition*) 2:33–43, here 38; cf. *Charles* Wesley's sermon of 1742, "Awake, Thou That Sleepest" in *Works* (*Bicentennial edition*) 1:142–158, here 149.

[13] See, for example, sermon of 1786 "On Divine Providence" in *Works* (*Bicentennial edition*) 2:534–550, here 543.

[14] Sermon of 1767, "The Witness of the Spirit, II" in *Works* (*Bicentennial edition*) 1:285–298, here 297. On "the assurance of faith," see Geoffrey Wainwright, *Methodists in Dialogue* (Nashville: Abingdon/Kingswood, 1995), 57–71.

[15] *Works* (*Bicentennial edition*) 2:222–235, here 232f.

[16] *Works* (*Bicentennial edition*) 1:314–334.

[17] *Works* (*Bicentennial edition*) 2:159, 165.

[18] *Works* (*Bicentennial edition*) 2:166.

[19] *Works* (*Bicentennial edition*) 2:160.

[20] *Works* (*Bicentennial edition*) 2:167f.

[21] For a full statement of Wesley's teaching on the matter, see his "Plain Account of Christian Perfection" in *Works* (*Jackson edition*) 11:366–446; and for a critical discussion, Wainwright, *Methodists in Dialogue*, 143–158 ("Perfect Salvation in the Teaching of Wesley and Calvin").

[22] *Works* (*Bicentennial edition*) 2:413–421, here 418f.

[23] Jürgen Weissbach, *Der neue Mensch im theologischen Denken John Wesleys*, Beiträge zur Geschichte des Methodismus, Beiheft 2 (Stuttgart: Christliches Verlagshaus, 1970).

[24] *Works* (*Bicentennial edition*) 2:186–201, here 188. In his sermon of 1730 on "The Image of God" Wesley locates the "image of God wherein man was originally made" in his "unerring understanding, uncorrupt will, and perfect freedom," crowned by "happiness." In the renewal made possible through Christ, the understanding is corrected by humility ("a knowledge of ourselves, a just sense of our condition"), the will is reformed by charity (love towards God and neighbor), and, being thus set free by the Spirit of life from the law of sin and death, we are restored to virtue and happiness. The trinitarian hints in this early sermon are quite slight.

[25] *Works* (*Bicentennial edition*) 4:60–71, here 66f. The Johannine phrase "God is love" (I John 4:7–11, 16–21) can be unfolded in a trinitarian way after either an Augustinian manner (as in Eberhard Jüngel's *Gott als Geheimnis der Welt* [Tübingen: Mohr, 1977], 430–453) or a Cappadocian manner (as in John Zizioulas' *Being as Communion* [Crestwood, NY: St. Vladimir's Seminary Press, 1985], especially 46).

[26] See Augustine, *De civitate Dei* VIII.17.2 (Migne, *Patrologia Latina* 41:242).

[27] Sermon of 1748, "Upon Our Lord's Sermon on the Mount, IX" in *Works* (*Bicentennial edition*) 1:632–649, here 635f.

[28] *Works* (*Bicentennial edition*) 3:88–102, here 89f., 96.

[29] *Works* (*Bicentennial edition*) 2:500–510, here 510.

[30] For the significant events of May 24, 1738, see John Wesley's "Journal" in *Works* (*Bicentennial edition*) 18:249f.

[31] Printed in *The Poetical Works of John and Charles Wesley*, ed. George Osborn (London: Wesleyan-Methodist Conference Office, 1868–1872) 3:343–354.

[32] *Poet. Works*, 6:139f.

[33] The entire 1767 collection of "Hymns on the Trinity" is found in *Poet. Works* 7:201–348. A facsimile of the first edition of the 1767 book has been published by the Charles Wesley Society, ed. S T Kimbrough, Jr. (Madison NJ, 1998).

[34] In her Drew University dissertation "The Triune God in the Hymns of Charles Wesley" (Ann Arbor: University Microfilms International, 1989–90), Wilma J. Quantrille gives a few samples, in parallel columns, of Charles Wesley's text compared to William Jones's (22–24). In his preface (pages v–vi) to the facsimile edition (see note 33), S T Kimbrough, Jr lists the twelve texts from *Hymns on the Trinity* that were included, as the last items of the section "For Believers Rejoicing," in the 1780 *A Collection of Hymns for the Use of the People Called Methodists*. Kimbrough further points out that for the first twenty-four texts of the Jones-free "Hymns and Prayers to the Trinity" Charles Wesley deliberately specified tunes that had already been composed by John Lampe for other of his hymns.

[35] *The Letters of John Wesley*, John Telford, ed. (London: Epworth Press, 1931) 6:213.

[36] *Poet. Works* 7:204.

[37] While the Wesleys could use the word "office" to designate work appropriate to a particular named Person of the Trinity, they would not allow the Persons to be reduced to offices: "The quaint device of styling them three offices rather than persons gives up the whole doctrine" (John Wesley, Letter of 3 August 1771 to Jane Catherine March, in *Letters* 5:270). That clearly excludes such late twentieth-century substitutions for the Trinitarian Name as "Creator, Redeemer, Sustainer."

[38] Irenaeus, *Against the Heresies* IV.20.7.

[39] Against that, however, it must be said that many hymns emphasize that the divine attributes are common to the Persons. Thus, very clearly, hymn 19, where "The attributes Divine / Are all both His [the Father's] and Thine [the Son's]."

[40] For Augustine, see *De Trinitate* 10.17–19. A more likely (renewable!) *vestigium Trinitatis* for Charles Wesley is the tripartite anthropology found in 1 Thessalonians 5:23. Thus note in hymn 97 the constitution of the human being as summoned to proclaim and glorify the Creator: "Transcript of holiness Divine, / The Triune God proclaim, / And spirit, and soul, and flesh resign / To glorify His name"; cf. the fourth stanza of hymn 14 in "Hymns and Prayers to the Trinity": "O that we now in love renew'd / Might blameless in Thy sight appear, / Wake up in Thy similitude, / Stampt with the Tri-une character, / Flesh, spirit, soul to Thee resign, / And live, and die entirely Thine!"

[41] *Works* (*Bicentennial edition*) 7:535f. The hymn figures as number 300 in the British Methodist *Hymns and Psalms* of 1983. There is no need to take "the Spirit of Thy Son" in a filioquist sense; the reference is to the mission, not to the procession, of the Holy Spirit (cf. John 14:26; Romans 8:9; Galatians 4:6). This is not to suggest that the Wesleys showed any sign of actively abandoning the doctrine of the Spirit's double

procession inherited from the Anglican formularies of "the Nicene Creed" and the Quicunque Vult.

[42] *Works* (*Bicentennial edition*) 7:552. I have quoted the text in the version known to me from child-hood, in the British *Methodist Hymn Book* of 1933. David Tripp has documented—and deplored—the low proportion (especially in comparison with the 1780 *Collection*) of explicitly trinitarian hymns both in the British *Hymns and Psalms* (1983) and in *The United Methodist Hymnal* (1989); see his "Methodism's Trini-tarian Hymnody: A Sampling, 1780 and 1989, Some Questions," in *Quarterly Review*, Winter (1994–95): 359–85; cf. the same author's "Hymnody and Liturgical Theology: Hymns as an Index of the Trinitarian Character of Worship in some Western Christian Traditions," in *The Forgotten Trinity, 3. A Selection of Papers presented to the BCC Study Commission on Trinitarian Doctrine Today*, ed. Alasdair Heron (London: BCC/CCBI, 1991), 63–88.

[43] *Works* (*Bicentennial edition*) 1:589–591; 7:363–366.

[44] For the part played by these factors in the phenomenon, see Henry D. Rack, "Early Methodist Visions of the Trinity," in *Proceedings of the Wesley Historical Society* 46(1987–88): 38–44, 57–69.

[45] *Letters* 8:83. See also the letters of 11 February 1777 to Hester Ann Roe (*Letters* 6:252 f.) and of 16 June 1777 to Elizabeth Ritchie (*Letters* 6:266).

[46] From Charles Perronet's account in *The Arminian Magazine* 13 (1790): 203 f.; quoted by John Wes-ley, with minor variants, in *Letters* 6:253.

[47] From *The Arminian Magazine* 13 (1790): 638.

[48] See William Bramwell, *A Short Account of the Life and Death of Ann Cutler* (Sheffield: John Smith, 1796), 18 f.

[49] *Letters* 8:214 f.

4

The Practical Way of Holiness: Isaiah of Scetis and John Wesley

John Chryssavgis

Introduction

Eastern Christian mystics have normally been more reticent than their Western counterparts in terms of revealing their personal experiences in regard to the essence of God. Eastern theologians also generally have been more reserved about exhausting the inner life of God in their teachings. However, the representatives of the Eastern ascetic tradition have always sought to live out the depth of divine life in the rigor of daily life, and to reach out to the uncharted depth of divine truth through their personal discipline. Whether in early fifth-century Palestine where Abba Isaiah of Scetis lived in ascetic simplicity and spiritual struggle, or in eighteenth-century England where John Wesley (d. 1791) underwent a spiritual conversion to a more disciplined "method" or ascetic life-style, the practical way of holiness offered the possibility of and accessibility to the reality of the heavenly kingdom from this world and this age.

This paper will explore the *Ascetic Discourses* (AD) of Abba Isaiah in order to discover parallel insights in the writings of John Wesley. We shall expose certain points of correspondence and comparison between the asceticism of the early spiritual master of Egypt and Palestine and the "Methodism" of the more recent evangelistic leader of the Wesleyan movement. In brief, we shall consider the practical way of holiness as it emerges in the life and work of two very different representatives of two distinct traditions, the Eastern Orthodox communion of churches and the churches of Methodism.

During the last few decades, great strides have been taken to investigate and translate the hitherto unavailable early ascetic literature: the *Sayings* of the Desert Fathers, the *Correspondence* of Barsanuphius and John, the material contained in the *Philokalia*. One of the latest texts to be translated into modern European languages is the *Ascetic Discourses* of Abba Isaiah of Scetis. These writings would not immediately have appealed to John Wesley, or to his brother Charles, and in many ways to this day there exists a gap between the intellectual appreciation of the ascetic teaching of these early texts and its integration into everyday Christian rehearse.

People will sometimes feel that ascetic feats are too rigid or extreme. They are mistaken, for Abba Isaiah is an example of a monastic elder who holds the human body in the highest regard:

> Take care of your body; it is the temple of God. . . . [AD 15]. Taking care of the body in godly fear is a good thing. Adorning the body destroys the soul (AD 16).[1]

Other people often object to the austerity of ascetic discipline as being far removed from the gospel-reality of love. They are in denial, for Basil the Great defines the monastic way as none other than the communal "life according to the Gospel."[2] John Wesley, the founder of Methodism, one of Protestantism's most influential evangelistic renewal movements, also believed that ascetic spirituality applied to the whole of life which is intrinsically communal, not eremitic:

> Christianity is essentially a social religion, and to turn it into a solitary religion is indeed to destroy it.[3]

In the spiritual life there is no sharp distinction between monastics and non-monastics; the external circumstances may vary but the path is essentially one.

Still others may feel uncertain about the connection or indeed the relevance of early ascetic customs to our contemporary society and culture. They are perhaps a source of embarrassment, yet Abba Isaiah regards monasticism as a social event, not a selfish practice:

> Perform your handiwork, so that you may feed the poor (AD 16).

The "charitable" dimension of Abba Isaiah's ascetic spirituality would be appealing to the "societary" aspect of Wesleyan pietistic thought, according to which there is "no holiness but social holiness,"[4] precisely perhaps because of its scriptural foundation. Like the Wesleys, Abba Isaiah was inspired by the exhortation of St Paul:

> Share in suffering for the gospel in the power of God, who saved us and called us with a holy calling, not in virtue of our works but in virtue of His own purpose and the grace which He gave us in Christ Jesus ages ago, and now has manifested through the appearing of our Savior Christ Jesus, who abolished death and brought life and immortality to light through the gospel. For this gospel I was appointed a preacher and apostle and teacher (2 Tim 1:8–11).

In similar fashion, Wesleyan Methodism heeded the "holy calling" to perfection through public proclamation, itinerant instruction, and scriptural interpretation. Isaian spirituality, on the other hand, preferred the way of practical asceticism, spiritual direction, and personal application. Where John Wesley was a preacher, Abba Isaiah was a practitioner. Where John Wesley proclaimed the power of the Word, Abba Isaiah underlined "the power of the cell" (AD 4). Isaiah is described by his biographer as a *praktikos,* and this term appropriately defines the character of this hermit and of his *Ascetic Discourses.* They constitute a practical guide for the monk on the life of *ascesis,* the way of perfection, the discipline of work, the fulfillment of the commandments, and the attainment of accordance with the nature of Jesus.

The *Ascetic Discourses* are not a systematic exposition of monastic thought or Christian spirituality. The work does indeed have a sense of unity in its basic structure and theme, but—in contrast to the more methodical system of religious observance articulated by the Wesleys—the writing of Abba Isaiah does not contain any explicitly methodical articulation of practice or doctrinal elaboration of principles. Naturally, John Wesley too did not provide an exhaustive systematic exposition of the Christian articles of faith. Again, similarly to the trend of Pietism in more recent centuries, at times Isaiah's writing is expressly hostile towards any intellectualism (see AD 6), though perhaps far more so than Wesleyan Methodism ever is. In the tradition of the *Sayings of the Desert Fathers*—whose teachings Abba Isaiah espouses and extends into fifth-century Palestine, as well as a legacy to which Abba Isaiah contributed and with which he is sometimes even confounded—the chapter headings of the *Ascetic Discourses* reveal the text as a loose collection of counsels and commands, of didactic propositions in the form of a spiritual "constitution" for monks choosing to follow the way of perfection under the supervision and guidance of Abba Isaiah (cf. AD 3). These rules and regulations indicate the subtle yet profound perception that the mystery of divine grace speaks a language that may be absorbed primarily through "being" rather than by doing, thinking, or teaching.

The Kingdom of God: the End, the Way, and the Struggle

The end as criterion

For Abba Isaiah, the way of perfection and holiness is properly and clearly approached only from an eschatological perspective. Each moment is an expectation of that Last Day. The 1780 Methodist hymnbook, *A Collection of Hymns for the Use of the People called Methodists,* prayed:

> Jesus, my strength, my hope,
> On thee I cast my care
> . . .
> Give me on thee to wait.[5]

Every virtue that we acquire, just as every vice that we avoid, prepares us for that moment "when He [Christ] comes to meet us on the day of judgment," a phrase repeated several times in Discourse 16 alone. The light of the heavenly kingdom illumines every detail of our earthly life as we "press on toward our goal" (Philippians 3:14). In the way of the Psalmist (cf. Psalm 16:8) then, "we are to hold God before our eyes in everything that we do" (AD 5).

The kingdom of God is not simply "inherited through obedience" (AD 4) or even merely "acquired through virtue" (AD 4). It is in fact "expected in hope" (AD 17; see also 8) and "desired with passion" (AD 16):

> Love the faithful, so that you may find mercy in them. Desire the saints, so that their zeal may consume you. Remember the heavenly kingdom, so that its passion may very gradually attract you (AD 16).

Further, this heavenly kingdom is more than "a new reality of the future age" (AD 13);

it is "the spiritual pledge of the present life" (AD 19; see also 16):

> Truly you have become the bridge [of Christ], and the Holy Spirit has made you its
> heir, even while you are still in the body (AD 19).

The grace of the Paraclete at once refreshes (lit., "gives rest": see AD 4) and revitalizes (lit., "gives breath": AD 7). Although in this age the fullness of "divine glory is not yet revealed" (AD 7), nevertheless "the flame of divine grace is already alight" (ibid.). On that final day:

> ... each of us will be shown up by the very torch that is in our hand (AD 16).

Therefore, the ascetic is called to "struggle with violence" until the last breath, to the moment of death (AD 5, 8, and 16), for:

> ... alas, our body, which is susceptible of the eternal light, is likewise vulnerable to
> the eternal darkness (AD 29).

For John Wesley too, we are to "gladly urge our way to heaven."[6] And Charles Wesley writes of "the kingdom of an inward heaven."[7] Yet the attainment of perfection, even if limited in this life, is an ongoing process of growth and movement toward the end of all things and of all times. The "last times" imply not so much an escapist attitude to the world, as they do in fact teach about the "last-ness" and the "lasting-ness" of all things. Eschatology is not the teaching about the end, the last—perhaps unnecessary, sometimes unintelligible—chapter in a manual of Christian doctrine; rather, it is the vision about the relationship of everyone and everything to the end of all. Christian perfection is possible through Christ's Incarnation, writes Charles Wesley:

> For God is manifest below.[8]

Eschatology signifies the appreciation of the earth below in relation to the heavens above. It is the Omega that gives meaning to the Alpha, the heavenly sacrament of the Eucharist, which is the only true perception of the present. For John and Charles Wesley, we are already sharers of that final banquet:

> By Faith and Hope already there
> Ev'n now the Marriage-Feast we share,
>   Ev'n now we by the Lamb are fed,
> Our Lord's celestial Joy we prove,
>   While ...
>   [He] lulls us in his Arms to rest!
> ...
> This the Pledge the Earnest This
> ...
> Here He gives our Souls a Taste,

> Heaven into our Hearts He pours;
> . . .
> Walking in all thy Ways we find
> Our Heaven on Earth begun.[9]

The way as movement

Abba Isaiah likens the spiritual way to traveling on a journey:

> There are [he writes] two roads, one leading to life and the other to death. Someone traveling on one road cannot also follow the other. Indeed, the person who walks both ways is reckoned as walking neither—whether that leading to the kingdom, or that leading to hell (AD 21; see also 25).[10]

If there are two characteristics of the practical way of perfection, they are ongoing struggle and never-ending progress:

> On the way of virtues are . . . change, variation . . . measure . . . heartache . . . progress and violence. For it is a journey, and you must travel this route until you attain rest (*anapausis*) (AD 24).

In his *Brief Thoughts on Christian Perfection*, John Wesley also relates perfection to the attainment of "the promised rest" which he identifies with "the Canaan of [God's] perfect love."[11] And the desire for perfection is equally intense in both of the Wesley brothers:

> Eager for thee I ask and pant,
>   So strong the principle divine,
> Carries me out with sweet constraint,
>   Till all my hallow'd soul be thine;
> Plunged in my Godhead's deepest sea,
> And lost in thine immensity.[12]

Abba Isaiah addresses the subject of spiritual perfection in two of his twenty-nine *Discourses* (13 and 23), claiming that the way of perfection is discerned and discovered amid two spiritual poles: the recognition of one's human limitations (AD 23) and the imitation of Christ's divine measure (AD 13). The stages along the way of holiness begin from *ascesis* against the passions and lead to *ascent* upon the Cross:

> For the Cross of Jesus is abstinence from every passion, until it is cut off (AD 16).

Below we shall develop the stages of the way of the cross, but here it is important to emphasize the way itself, which always remains an orientation toward the age which is to come, a constant expectation of the last things. Perfection is therefore perpetual progress. The soul constantly moves forward, opening up to "grace upon grace" (John 1:16), "forgetting those things which are behind, and stretching forward to those things which are ahead" (Philippians 3:13). The process of growth is infinite, quite simply because God is limitless; this is the classical teaching developed by Gregory of Nyssa on mystical "*epectasis.*"[13] And in his Sermon 40, *On Christian Perfection*, John Wesley observes:

> Christian perfection, therefore, does not imply (as some men seem to have imagined) an exemption either from ignorance, or mistake, or infirmities, or temptations. Indeed, it is only another term for holiness. They are two names for the same thing. Thus, every one that is holy is, in the Scripture sense, perfect. Yet we may, lastly, observe, that neither in this respect is there any absolute perfection on earth. There is no 'perfection of degrees,' as it is termed; none which does not admit of a continual increase.[14]

To this Abba Isaiah might add that the levels of intensity in the spiritual way are ever deepening, precisely because there is no comfortable way of sitting on the cross.

The struggle with nature

When Abba Isaiah speaks of this discomfort, he recalls the forcefulness required to enter the kingdom (cf. Matthew 11:12). And if he speaks of violence in the struggle toward perfection, it is to describe the forceful attraction of the heavenly kingdom. However, whenever he speaks of sin as the barrier along this way, he prefers to adopt medical rather than juridical imagery:

> We are all as if in surgery. One feels pain in the eye, another in the head, yet another in the veins, or whatever other diseases may exist. . . . Some wounds are already healed, but then one eats something harmful, and they return once more . . . (AD 8).

> Truly blessed then is the person who deals with one's own sins (AD 10).

"Sin results from denial of one's proper limits" (AD 17), and virtue from knowing oneself (see AD 19 and 23). Dispassion, or the overcoming of sin, is identified with love (AD 21), and passion with an "eclipse of the heart's proper desire" (AD 22). The wise Palestinian elder will present his monks with the traditional view of sin as being *unnatural or destructive forces to be eradicated* (AD 4 and 8); he even offers a list of the numerous branches of evil (AD 28 and 29).[15] Nevertheless, he also understands passions as natural or misguided forces to be redirected (see esp. AD 2). It is a matter of spiritual preference, a question of "where our treasure lies" (Luke 12:34):

> When we love the desires of our heart more than we love God, then we do not have as much love for God as we do for the passions (AD 5).

Virtue or vice depend on the direction of our heart (AD 16). And the natural commitment, the innate priority of our love is toward God:

> . . . everything that is contrary to nature is called faithlessness or prostitution (AD 25).

> In the beginning, when God created Adam, God placed him in paradise with healthy, natural senses. Later, when Adam listened to the one who deceived him, all the senses were twisted toward that which is contrary to nature . . . (AD 2; see also 16).

Abba Isaiah adopts the terms "twisting" or "turning" (ultimately, it is a matter of "perversion" or "madness" [AD 29]) and "transformation" or "conversion" (even of "saneness" [AD 25]). The ascetic must be turned, indeed surrendered, to God totally and passionately, never partially (AD 25):

> For sin is not particular, but it is the entire human person, the 'old person', that is called sin (AD 21).

Yet our nature has been hardened, and it is not easily changed unless one is unconditionally submitted to the will of God. This is the teaching and example of Jesus Christ at the Incarnation. Thus great emphasis is placed in ascetic literature on the power of human will:

> Every person either binds oneself for hell, or else becomes free for heaven. For there is nothing harder than the human will, whether it is directed towards death or towards life (AD 18).

Certainly this concept of the "hardening" of human nature comes closer to the manner in which John Wesley perceives the doctrine about the origin of sin. In his work published in 1757 and entitled *The Doctrine of Original Sin, According to Scripture, Reason, and Experience*, Wesley writes:

> Adam, by his sin, became not only guilty but corrupt; and so transmits guilt and corruption to his posterity. By this sin he stripped himself of his original righteousness and corrupted himself (p. 458).

> . . . our nature is deeply corrupted, inclined to evil, and disinclined to all that is spiritually good; so that, without supernatural grace, we can neither will nor do what is pleasing to God (p. 273).[16]

For the Wesleys, this understanding of human nature was not merely theological information learned from their reading of Calvinist manuals of doctrine. It was their own very formation learned from their mother, who remained John Wesley's counselor until her death in 1742. In a letter to her son John, written on 24 July 1732, Susanna Wesley described the way in which she maintained order in her family within an unstable world. Her thesis would today receive much attention in terms of child development, inasmuch as it focused on pure obedience, but it constituted the structure within which John Wesley understood the notion of free will:

> I insist upon conquering the will of children . . . because this is the only strong and rational foundation of a religious education, without which both precept and example will be ineffectual. But when this is thoroughly done, then a child is capable of being governed by the reason and piety of its parents, till its own understanding comes to maturity and the principles of religion have taken root in the mind.[17]

Certainly one may encounter in early monastic texts similar teachings about the human will in relation to the struggle against evil. In the way of perfection, demons are normally cited far more frequently than angels. This is true of the ascetic literature of the desert as it is of the pietistic tradition of the Methodists. Struggling against the deceitful wiles and unruly ways of the demons is the source of spiritual understanding and authority. Yet Abba Isaiah appears also to be aware of the subtle truth that the ladder of divine ascent, where we are called to struggle against the evil spiritual forces, may easily be transformed into the ladder of Jacob, where we realize that we are wrestling with God himself. There is a sense in which our demons may also reveal our very angels. Our life is filled with moments that either attract us toward God or else estrange us from God. There is no vice that is unrelated to virtue, no darkness that is bereft of light, and no brokenness that cannot lead to wholeness. Charles Wesley prays in one of his hymns:

> Shine on thy work, disperse the gloom;
> Light in thy light I then shall see.[18]

Every aspect of human nature is, by divine intention and by natural inclination, filled with a heavenly spark. This is a reality that Abba Isaiah would have learned from his experience in the desert of Egypt, where Anthony the Great taught:

> "Whoever has not experienced temptation cannot enter into the Kingdom of Heaven."

He even added, "Without temptations, no-one can be saved."[19]

The Way of the Cross: the Inner Kingdom and the Imitation of Christ

The grace of the sacraments

Like the Wesleyan revival, the spirituality of Abba Isaiah is not only radically evangelical but also surprisingly sacramental. However, while Abba Isaiah respects the sacraments of the Church—he writes, for instance, on baptism (AD 8, 13, 16, 22, and esp. 25), the Eucharist (AD 3, 4, 8, 26, 29, and esp. 4), marriage (AD 25), and ordination (AD 5)—he strives to develop an inspirational model based on the sacramental life. Isaiah wants his monks to be more than merely "Christians by name" (AD 21 and 22). John Wesley too speaks of those who, "though they are called Christians, the name does not imply the thing: They are as far from this as hell from heaven."[20] Therefore, Abba Isaiah invites his readers to a rebirth through repentance, which alone will allow entrance to the kingdom of God. In Discourse 25, for example, he explores the Lord's saying in Matthew 18:3, "Unless you repent and become like little children, you will not enter into the kingdom of heaven."

Together with faith and holiness, John Wesley placed much practical emphasis on repentance; these three comprised the "main doctrines" of Methodism.[21] So the aim of the way of holiness is, paradoxically perhaps, not spiritual maturity but in fact sacred infancy, not education but "regeneration," not formation at all but actually recreation. In the words of Abba Isaiah:

> . . . arriving at the measure of a child . . . and attaining to the measure of sacred infancy (AD 25).

The Wesleyan revival preached of this "new birth" through the Holy Spirit (cf. Romans 8:15), which was the beginning of Christian transformation and personal sanctification, a moral restoration to the image of God revealed in Jesus Christ. Spiritual regeneration was the assurance of divine favor and pious fervor (cf. 2 Peter 1:4) alike. John Wesley wrote that:

> . . . justification implies only a relative, the new birth a real, change. God in justifying us does something for us; in begetting us again, He does the work in us. . . . The one restores us to the favor, the other to the image, of God.[22]

For Abba Isaiah, this assurance is achieved by means of Holy Communion, the sacrament of thanksgiving that colors every detail of this new life as a gift from God:

> The gift of thanksgiving comes from God. For it is God who gives us the grace to render thanks to Him in all things (AD 22).

Finally, Abba Isaiah underlines the royal priesthood of all believers:

> Rather, become in purity an altar of God, having the inner priest always offering sacrifices, both in the morning and in the evening, so that the altar is never left without sacrifice (AD 5).

> Therefore, examine yourself . . . for you have been baptized into Christ and into His death (AD 22).

This manner of thinking would no doubt have appealed to John and Charles Wesley, who also prayed:

> Erect thy Tabernacle here,
> The New Jerusalem send down.[23]

Although deliberately distancing himself from specific Roman Catholic doctrines on Holy Communion, the sacramentalism of John and Charles Wesley was firmly centered on the Eucharist:[24]

> Affix the Sacramental Seal,
>   And stamp us for thine own.
> Return, and with thy servants sit,
>   Lord of the Sacramental Feast
> And satiate us with the heavenly Meat,
>   And make the World thy happy Guest.[25]

What is there in common between Abba Isaiah, Thomas à Kempis, and John Wesley?

One aspect of Abba Isaiah's thought, that is perhaps indicative also of his Monophysite inheritance, is his emphasis on the imitation of Jesus Christ and on the intimacy of the monk's relationship with the Lord Jesus. Although not entirely absent from Eastern Byzantine thought and spirituality, such an emphasis is certainly afforded a centrality by Isaiah not frequently found in spiritual and mystical writers of the East. Perhaps it is further evidence of the open-mindedness of Isaiah's work, that in reading, for example, *Ascetic Discourse* 16 one can almost imagine that one is reading the *Imitation of Christ* by Thomas à Kempis. However, this is more likely to be a reflection of the practical nature of the Isaian *corpus*. References to the "tenderness" and "sweetness" of Jesus (AD also 25 and 13) are typical of a simple piety and practical spirituality. Yet, much more than this, it is also a sign of Isaiah's own very delicate nature and of his sensitivity to details in the interpersonal relations among the members of his monastic community (cf. AD 4). Isaiah believes that we ought to "follow in the steps" of Jesus (AD 25 and 22), and quite plainly, in Pauline terms (cf. Galatians 3:27), to be "dressed with Jesus" (AD 21 and 2) through the power of the sacraments. It should be noted briefly here that, like the author of the *Macarian Homilies,* Isaiah is also one of the few early ascetic authors to stress the importance of the Holy Spirit (see especially AD 19).

We know that John Wesley came across Thomas à Kempis' *Imitation of Christ* for the first time as early as 1725 in a seventeenth-century translation by George Stanhope. After reading this mid fifteenth-century Augustinian treatise on the progress of the soul to perfection and union at the tender age of twenty-one, initially Wesley was "very angry with Kempis for being too strict." Yet he decided to:

> watch against all sin, whether in word or deed. [He] began to aim at, and pray for, inward holiness.[26]

For Abba Isaiah, in the sacraments, the Christian enjoys communion with the Son of God, with the Lord Jesus Christ (AD 8 and 22). Jesus Christ "reveals to us the will of the Father" (AD 23). Although the comparison with Christ appears awesome, yet the parallel is critical:

He is sinless, and offered us an example [*typos*] in everything. . . . He endured abuse, whereas we do not in the least. He did not return evil for evil, whereas we cannot do likewise. He was not angered in suffering, while you are angry whenever in pain. . . . He gave Himself for the life of those who sinned against Him, until He redeemed them, while you cannot do similarly even for those who love you. . . . Know Him through His deeds; and know yourself through your own deeds (AD 22).

In his Discourse 27, Abba Isaiah twice draws attention to the power of Christ's redeeming blood:

Attend diligently, knowing that the Lord, though rich, became poor for our sake and died. In dying for us, He bought us with His own blood, in order that you also may consider living no longer for yourself but for the Lord, being His perfect slave in everything, living always before God like a very gentle animal who does not answer back but is submissive to his master . . . and not having a will or desire of his own but aspiring only to do the work of God.

Attend diligently, believing firmly that our Lord Jesus Christ, who is God, who possesses glory and ineffable majesty, has made Himself a model [*typos*] for us in order to follow His footsteps.

"The invitation is to all . . . Let every soul be Jesu's guest," writes Charles Wesley, for whom "Christ and heaven are one."[27] And in *A Plain Account of Christian Perfection*, John Wesley notes that "Thy [Christ's] presence is the perfect day."[28] For Abba Isaiah, to "follow in His footsteps" is to "look for His traces" (AD 25; Charles Wesley writes in one hymn: "Jesu, we follow thee / In all thy footsteps tread"),[29] which in turn means— through the sacraments of baptism and repentance—to "reach the measure of Christ" (cf. Ephesians 4:13). In the final analysis, in the words of Abba Isaiah, this implies turning toward and fixing our gaze upon the crucified Christ:

. . . try hard to fix your eyes on the bronze serpent which Moses made according to God's command. He placed this on the wood at the top of the mountain in order that anyone bitten by a serpent may gaze upon it and immediately recover. Our Lord Jesus on the cross resembled the bronze serpent. . . . Our Lord Jesus assumed this model [*typos*] in order to extinguish the venom that Adam had eaten from the serpent's mouth and in order to bring back nature—which had become contrary to nature— to conform once again to nature (AD 25).

On the cross, everything that Christ endured—the gall, the spitting, the crown of thorns, the beating, the nakedness, the suffering, the isolation, the entombment (*this is the order in which these are presented by Abba Isaiah*)—was in order to offer us a model; "it is an example for us," as Abba Isaiah observes sixteen times in just a single paragraph of Discourse 13.

The stages of the Cross

Abba Isaiah's indebtedness to St. Paul is particularly evident in Discourse 13, where he develops his favorite notion of "ascending the cross of Jesus." It is a passionate devotion to and contemplation of the cross (see also AD 21, 25, and 27). The cross therefore becomes the key to the way of perfection:

> The cross is the abolition of all sins, and engenders love. For without love there is no cross (AD 21).

Similarly, Wesley's prayer to Christ is none other than to "lead [him] to [His] holy hill" of the cross, which is tantamount to the ascent to heaven.[30] Charles Wesley states this reality clearly in his hymns:

> We in thy birth are born,
> Sustain thy grief and loss,
> Share in thy want, and shame, and scorn,
> And die upon thy cross.
>
> Made like him, like him we rise,
> Ours the cross, the grave, the skies.[31]

However, while adhering to the Pauline model of holiness as being crucified with Christ (cf. Gal. 2:20), Abba Isaiah introduces a new distinction in the way of the cross. Beyond the distinction between Martha and Mary, who symbolize "practical endurance" and "the state of mourning"; and even beyond Lazarus bound and the risen Lazarus, who symbolizes "the intellect fettered" and "the intellect carefree" (cf. AD 21); there is a further perceptive distinction between "*beholding* the cross" (which we have already considered; cf. AD 25), "*bearing* the cross" (AD 21), and simply "*being on* the cross". The latter implies a higher stage of silence, while the former signifies the preparatory stage of struggle (cf. also AD 8). The follower of Christ is called to "accompany the Lord to the cross" (AD 16) and to "ascend the cross" (AD 17): "we are to *climb on the cross* and to *stay on the cross*" (AD 13) [italics, author's emphasis]. Indeed these two stages are distinct, and "to wish to stay on the cross prematurely is to attract the wrath of God" (AD 8 and 13).

Nonetheless, the natural home, the *topos* of the soul, is the cross. In similar fashion Charles Wesley speaks of the crucified Christ in heaven as preparing our natural place of rest:

> Near himself prepares our place
> harbinger of human race.[32]

We are therefore called, writes Abba Isaiah, to render thanks to the Lord for enabling us to endure the cross (AD 17), and to renounce those who wish us to descend from the cross (AD 26).

Blessed therefore is the person who is crucified, dead, buried, and risen in newness, when he sees himself in the natural condition of Jesus, following His holy footsteps which were made when He was incarnated for the sake of His holy saints. Thus it is to Him that belong [the virtues of] humility, baseness, poverty, detachment, forgiveness, peace, enduring reproach, not caring for the body, not fearing the conspiracies of evil people, and – the greatest of these – knowing everything before it occurs, and treating people with kindness. So one who has reached these and eliminated the condition that is contrary to nature, shows that he is truly from Christ, and is the Son of God and brother of Jesus (AD 18).

The Life of the Community: Prayer, Love, Doctrine

The power of prayer

The way of the cross is realized and remembered through prayer, "much prayer" (AD 13 and 9): "continual prayer. . . . Overlooking prayer even slightly gives rise to forgetfulness of this truth" (AD 16). The way of the cross is the way into the heart (cf. AD 2), which is illumined through prayer (cf. AD 4 and 16). Abba Isaiah understands prayer as communion with God, or as compassion deriving from God, rather than as some communication for the sake of petition:

> Do not ask for this or that in prayer, but simply say, ". . . Have compassion on your creature. . . . I have no other refuge but you, Lord" (AD 4; see also 26).

Otherwise prayer is neither cathartic nor authentic:

> [Such a person is] not praying genuinely with the intellect, but ignorantly with the lips. . . . One is deceived, because no one listens to such prayer. For it is not the intellect that is in prayer, but only the habit of regular discipline (AD 18; see also 25).

And John Wesley underlines the importance of prayer for the Christian in the way of perfection:

> For indeed he *prays without ceasing*; at all times the language of his heart is this: *Unto you is my mouth, though without a voice; and my silence speaks unto you.* His heart is lifted up to God at all times, and in all places. In this he is never hindered, much less interrupted, by any person or thing. In retirement or company, in leisure, business, or conversation, his heart is ever with the Lord. Whether he lie down or rise up, *God is in all his thoughts*; He *walks with God* continually; having the loving eye of his soul fixed on him, and everywhere *seeing him that is invisible.*[33]

The grace of love

Not only are we to "*love praying* ceaselessly," but Abba Isaiah notes that "we are to *love to love*" (AD 16). Love is the purpose (*telos*: cf. AD 16), the climax (*oros*) of all virtue, while "the end of all passion is self-justification" (AD 7). Nothing is more detestable and dangerous in the spiritual life, for Isaiah, than insensitivity towards others and towards God (AD 5, 16, 26, and 18). When we are not sensitive to others, when we do not love, "when we bear hatred towards even a single person, then our prayer is unacceptable" (AD 16). Love is identified with life (cf. AD 21; see also I John 3: 13–14); it is the other side of the same coin known as "dispassion" (AD 21 and 26), and characterized as "blessed" (AD 29). Love is "the seal of the soul" (AD 7), "the image of Christ within us" (AD 25). In his hymn "Hark the Herald Angels Sing," Charles Wesley adopts the same image:

> Adam's likeness now efface,
> Stamp thine image in its place:
> Second Adam from above,
> Reinstate us in thy love.[34]

Paradoxically, love is the highest expression of passion, as John Wesley notes in *A Plain Account of Christian Perfection*:

> Thy soul break out in strong desire
> The perfect bliss to prove!
> Thy longing heart be all on fire
> To be dissolv'd in love![35]

Often we reduce the concept of love to outward actions. Yet love may also involve the more "visible" dimensions of charity or counseling, as well as the "invisible" aspects of support and silence. Conversely, being silent when we are supposed to speak "can be the cause of our spiritual death"; at the same time, a word out of place "can also be the death of our soul" (AD 5). The context within which Abba Isaiah perceives the virtue of love is the Pauline image of the body, wherein the least significant members deserve the greatest attention, and the most vulnerable are invaluable, indeed indispensable (1 Corinthians 12:12):

> Again he said: if it comes to you, while you are sitting in your cell, to judge your neighbor, consider how more numerous your own sins are than your neighbor's. If you believe that you are doing righteous things, do not think that these will please God. Every one of the body's stronger limbs takes care of the weaker members in order to attend and care for them. But the cruel person who busies himself, asking: "What have I to do with the weak?" does not belong to the body of Christ, because the strong sympathize with the weak until the latter are healed; and they say: "I am the weak one" (AD 26).

The path to perfection in Wesleyan spirituality is also connected to the fulfillment of the two great commandments: love of God and love of neighbor. And wholeness of heart is identified with oneness of soul by John Wesley in his letters. In 1738, he wrote:

> Their faith hath made them whole. And these are of one heart and of one soul. They all love one another, and are knit together in one body and one spirit, as in one faith and one hope of their calling.[36]

This is the way of love that we have learned directly from the Incarnate Son of God. John Wesley states this succinctly:

> Where there is no love of God, there is no holiness, and there is no love of God but from a sense of his loving us.[37]

And, in his hymn *Wrestling Jacob,* Charles Wesley repeats seven times:

> Thy nature, and thy name, is LOVE.[38]

For God has nurtured us, and then gradually weaned us, through the vulnerability of childhood to the maturity of sainthood. The image of the providential love of God is colorfully depicted by Abba Isaiah in his 25th Discourse:

> While the young infant is still in its mother's bosom, she guards it at all times from every evil. When it cries, she offers it her breast. Gradually, she gives it breath with all her strength, helping it to learn fear . . . in order that its heart is not filled with bold-ness. But when it cries, she is moved to pity, for it is born of her entrails. She consoles, embraces, and comforts it again, by giving it her breast. If it is greedy for gold, silver, or precious stones, nevertheless it overlooks these while being in the mother's bosom. It scorns everything in order to take the breast. Meanwhile, the father does not scold it for not working, or for not warring against the enemy, since it is yet small and weak. It may have healthy feet, but it cannot stand up. It may have hands, but it cannot hold weapons. The mother treats it with condescension until gradually it grows. When it has grown a little and wishes to fight someone who is stronger, its father is not angry, knowing that it is only a child. When it has finally matured, its zeal is apparent. . . . It confides in its father because it always remains his son.

Love is the very milk on which we are raised, the "great mystery" that reveals us to be "members of Christ's body, of His flesh and of His bones" (says Abba Isaiah, par-aphrasing Paul in Ephesians 5:30), and "members one of another." Instead of the image of the mother and child, John Wesley prefers to speak of our constant dependence on Christ's grace:

> In every state we need Christ in the following respects. (1) Whatever grace we receive, it is a free gift from him. (2) We receive it as his purchase, merely in consideration of the price he paid. (3) We have this grace, not only from Christ, but in him. For our

perfection is not like that of a tree, which flourisheth by the sap derived from its own root, but . . . like that of a branch which, united to the vine, bears fruit; but, severed from it, is dried up and withered. (4) All our blessings, temporal, spiritual, and eternal, depend on his intercession for us, which is one branch of his priestly office, whereof therefore we have always equal need. (5) The best of men still need Christ in his priestly office, to atone for their omissions, their short-comings, (as some not improperly speak), their mistakes in judgment and practice, and their defects of various kinds.[39]

In a short essay of eight paragraphs entitled "A Thought on the Manner of Educating Children," which is essentially a broad statement of his own educational philosophy, John Wesley proposes an education:

. . . in holy tempers; in the love of God and our neighbour; in humility, gentleness, patience, long-suffering, contentedness in every condition . . . in the image of God, in the mind that was in Christ.

His definition of religious education—or, we might say, of spiritual formation—is simple:

to turn the bias from self-will, pride, anger, revenge, and the love of the world, to resignation, lowliness, meekness, and the love of God.[40]

In his Sermon 76, *On Perfection*, John Wesley states:

What is then the perfection of which man is capable while he dwells in a corruptible body? It is the complying with that kind command, 'My son, give me thy heart.' It is the 'loving the Lord his God with all his heart, and with all his soul, and with all his mind.' This is the sum of Christian perfection: It is all comprised in that one word, Love. The first branch of it is the love of God: And as he that loves God loves his brother also, it is inseparably connected with the second: 'Thou shalt love thy neighbour as thyself': Thou shalt love every man as thy own soul, as Christ loved us. 'On these two commandments hang all the Law and the Prophets': These contain the whole of Christian perfection.[41]

The ecumenical imperative

It is this sensitive nature and evangelical conviction that guide Abba Isaiah in his relations with others, both personal and confessional, as a monk and as a Christian alike. His outlook is always balanced, never extreme. Abba Isaiah appreciates how an untold number of variables interact upon and influence the dance that we call life. More than we perhaps often realize, our lives hinge on little things: on a word, a gesture, a nod, a smile, a glance. And so his gentle approach extends to "the slight and trivial" (AD 15) details of daily routine: from how one greets another to how one holds a vessel given by another; from how one stands in prayer to how one behaves in the privacy of the cell; from how one notices a person of the opposite sex to how one walks with a friend of the same sex; from how one carries out the shopping to how one converses in public; from discussions about the Scriptures to disputes about theology (cf. AD 3–5). These details are personal, yet so general; they are particular, yet so universal. Our words and deeds have profound impact on our neighbor and the world. Even minor actions have significant spiritual consequences. And so John Wesley will define Christian perfection as being no more and no less than:

> the humble, gentle, patient love of God, and our neighbour, [and the] ruling our tempers, words, and actions.[42]

Whether considering scriptural interpretations or doctrinal aberrations, Isaiah always recommends humility, discernment, and compassion (cf. AD 4–5). The purpose is not "the desire to prove your faith right" (AD 4) or "the enjoyment of futile diatribe" (AD 6), but the "personal education from God" (AD 8) and "the spiritual encouragement of the heart" (AD 25).

An anecdote from the life of Abba Isaiah reveals an openness and kindness, as well as a gentle ecumenical conviction toward Christians of different persuasion. When two monks once approached the renowned Monophysite elder to ask whether they should remain firm in their adherence to the Chalcedonian definition as formulated in the Great Council of 451, Abba Isaiah's closest disciple Peter conveyed to them the words of the wise spiritual elder:

> The Old Man says: "There is no harm in the Church, you are well as you are, you believe well."[43]

Although Peter clearly did not share the opinion of his spiritual father—he hastened after all to add his own commentary: "But I tell you that the Old Man lives in heaven, and does not know the ills that were done in that council"—it is Isaiah's sensitivity that gained the respect of Chalcedonians, Monophysites, and Nestorians alike in the centuries that followed. Wesley maintained the similar ecumenical principle of "we think and let think" in "opinions that do not strike at the root of Christianity."[44] In his plea for mutual respect and tolerance, Wesley did not recognize matters of ecclesiastical governance to be church-dividing.[45]

Conclusion

Like most of us today, Methodists and Orthodox alike, the Wesleys were more familiar with Isaiah the prophet[46] than with Isaiah the hermit;[47] they were clearly more comfortable with the message of the Scriptures than with the monasticism of Scetis. Had the work of Abba Isaiah been readily available to John Wesley, the latter may well have recognized similar qualities in the fifth-century Egyptian and Palestinian ascetic literature of the desert to those writers which he admired in the contemporaneous

Syrian tradition, whether in the person of Ephrem or in the Homilies of Macarius. The spirituality of the Wesleys was expressed in both inward and outward forms, a way of perfection and a holiness of practice alike.

The practical way of holiness as developed by these two writers, from so diverse theological and cultural backgrounds, and in so different periods and circumstances of church history, allows their readers to sense a commonality of purpose. In 1756, John Wesley expressly stated that his aim was:

> to provide, so far as I am able, vital, practical religion; and by the grace of God to beget, preserve, and increase the life of God in the souls of men.[48]

This is precisely the ascetic intent of Abba Isaiah.

At the same time, the sensitivity of these two spiritual leaders, in their understanding of the "method" of Christian living, reveals in their writings a sense of openness in personal relations and of breadth in confessional tolerance. Is it any wonder that the heirs of their spiritual legacy—Orthodox Christians of the East and Methodist adherents of the West—have strongly participated in the multilateral ecumenism of the World Council of Churches, as well as in bilateral dialogues among the Christian communions? Is it also any wonder that the Ecumenical Patriarchate and the World Methodist Council have already taken significant steps toward official theological discussions?

Endnotes

[1]For the French translation, see Abbé Isaïe, *Recueil ascétique—Introduction et traduction françaises par les moines de Solesmes*, Collection Spiritualité Orientale, no. 7, Abbaye de Bellefontaine 49 (Bégrolles, 1970). In this chapter the *Ascetic Discourses* are cited in parenthesis throughout the main body of the text as (AD) followed by the number of the Discourse in the volume cited.

[2]See *Epistle 207*, 2 *Patrologia Graeca* 32: 761.

[3]See Thomas Jackson, *The Works of John Wesley* (London: Wesleyan Conference Office, 1829–1831), vol. 5, *Sermon on the Mount IV*, 296. Cited in Frank Whaling, ed., *John and Charles Wesley: Selected Prayers, Hymns, Journal Notes, Sermons, Letters, and Treatises*, Classics in American Spirituality (New York: Paulist Press, 1981), 58.

[4]See eds. C. Jones, G. Wainwright, and E. Yarnold, *The Study of Spirituality* (London: SPCK, 1986), 450–459 and 603–605.

[5]See Whaling, *John and Charles Wesley,* 51. See also the hymn by Charles Wesley on Christ's Kingdom in Whaling, 287 and 289: "On thee we humbly wait. / . . . We long to see thy kingdom now. / Hasten that kingdom of thy grace."

[6]See *Hymns on the Lord's Supper by John and Charles Wesley* (London: Strahan, 1745; facsimile reprint, Madison, NJ: Charles Wesley Society, 1995), Hymn 46, p. 34. In his *Plain Account of Christian Perfection*, John Wesley writes: "Bring thy heavenly kingdom in," see Whaling, *John and Charles Wesley,* 325.

[7]See Whaling, *John and Charles Wesley,* 190.

[8]See Whaling, *John and Charles Wesley,* 49.

[9]See *Hymns on the Lord's Supper,* Hymns 93 (p. 82), 103 (p. 89), and 96 (p. 83). See also Whaling, *John and Charles Wesley,* 264–265: "A drop of heaven o'erflows our hearts / . . . Sure pledge of ecstasies unknown."

[10]See also the *Didache*, or the *Teaching of the Apostles*, ch. 1, J.B. Lightfoot, ed., *The Apostolic Fathers* (Grand Rapids: Baker Book House, 1956), 123.

[11]See *Works* (Jackson) 11:385–386.

[12]From a hymn by Charles Wesley, quoted by John Wesley in *A Plain Account of Christian Perfection*;

cited in Samuel J. Rogal, *John and Charles Wesley* (Boston: Twayne Publications, 1983), 91.

[13]*Homily on Perfection, Patrologia Graeca* 26:285.

[14]Cited in Rueben Job, *A Wesleyan Spiritual Reader* (Nashville: Abingdon Press, 1997), 210. See also John Wesley's *A Plain Account of Christian Perfection* found in Whaling, *John and Charles Wesley,* 329.

[15]In Discourse 4, for instance, Abba Isaiah refers to the "seven passions"; and in Discourse 17, he connects these to the "seven demons" (cf. Also Luke 8:2).

[16]See S. Rogal, *John and Charles Wesley,* 88–89.

[17]This educational philosophy would be harshly criticized today, and it is surely not unrelated to Wesley's own difficult relationship with his wife, whom he reprimanded in a letter of 1760, echoing his maternal upbringing: "Every act of disobedience is an act of rebellion against God and the King, as well as against your affectionate Husband." See his *Letters,* vol. 4; quote in S. Rogal, *John and Charles Wesley,* 44.

[18]See Whaling, *John and Charles Wesley,* 191.

[19]*Apophthegmata,* saying no. 5. See B. Ward, ed., *The Sayings of the Desert Fathers* (Kalamazoo: Cistercian Publications, 1975), 2.

[20]*Sermon* 61: "The Mystery of Iniquity," cited in R. Job, *A Wesleyan Spiritual Reader,* 41.

[21]Cf. *Works* (Jackson) 1984, 8:472.

[22]Sermon 19 on "The Great Privilege of those that are Born of God," in *Works,* vol. 5, cited in Whaling, *John and Charles Wesley,* 48. See also John Wesley's *A Plain Account of Christian Perfection,* in Whaling, 312: ". . . He is a child of God, and if he abide in him, an heir of all the promises."

[23]See *Hymns on the Lord's Supper,* Hymn 146, p. 141.

[24]See G. Wainwright, introduction to *Hymns on the Lord's Supper,* v–xiv.

[25]Ibid., see Hymns 30 (p. 23) and 46 (p. 141).

[26]See N. Curnock, ed., *The Journal of the Rev. John Wesley* (London: Charles Kelly, 1909), 1:466–467.

[27]Cf. Whaling, *John and Charles Wesley,* 179 and 182. See also 183: " 'Tis heaven to see our Jesu's face."

[28]See Whaling, *John and Charles Wesley,* 324.

[29]See Whaling, *John and Charles Wesley,* 32.

[30]See Whaling, *John and Charles Wesley,* 17 and 33.

[31]See Whaling, *John and Charles Wesley,* 267–268 and 285.

[32]See Whaling, *John and Charles Wesley,* 286.

[33]See Whaling, *John and Charles Wesley,* 304.

[34]See Whaling, *John and Charles Wesley,* 49. Cf. also ibid., 216: "We bear the character divine / The stamp of perfect love."

[35]See Whaling, *John and Charles Wesley,* 336.

[36]Dedication of the book by Samuel J. Rogal, *John and Charles Wesley.* Cf. Also J. Telford, ed., *The Letters of the Rev. John Wesley,* 8 vols. (London: Epworth Press, 1931).

[37]Sermon 5: *On Justification by Faith,* cited in R. Job, *A Wesleyan Spiritual Reader,* 205.

[38]See Whaling, *John and Charles Wesley,* 192–194.

[39]See *Works* (Jackson) 11:395–396.

[40]*Arminian Magazine,* 1783.

[41]Cited in R. Job, *A Wesleyan Spiritual Reader,* 209–210.

[42]See *Works* (Jackson) 11:446.

[43]See *Patrologia Orientalis,* 8:164.

[44]Cf. *Works* (Jackson) 1984, 8:340.

[45]A. McGrath, *The Blackwell Encyclopedia of Modern Christian Thought* (Blackwell: Oxford, 1993), 373–376.

[46]See especially Charles Wesley, for instance his hymn entitled "Adoration and Return to God" in Whaling, 177–178. Charles Wesley wrote 225 poetic paraphrases of the Old Testament prophet Isaiah, capturing the latter's personality and prophesy in the form of eighteenth-century congregational song, and emphasizing particularly the special relationship between Israel and its God (cf. Isa. 1:3), as well as the "new heaven and new earth" (cf. Isa. 65:17 and 66:22).

[47]Hitherto unavailable in an English translation, the twenty-nine *Ascetic Discourses* of Abba Isaiah of Scetis will soon appear in Cistercian Publications (Kalamazoo, MI), with introduction and notes by John Chryssavgis and Robert Penkett.

[48]From his *Works,* vol. 13, cited in Whaling, *John and Charles Wesley,* 44.

5

Holiness in the Perspective of Eucharistic Theology

Petros Vassiliadis

In the Biblical tradition, both the Old and the New Testament, holiness is by no means a moral concept; it rather connotes a characteristic feature of deity.[1] In terms, therefore, of modern theological language one could easily argue that it has dogmatic and not ethical dimensions. As a matter of fact, as an attribute associated with God, by extension it can also be associated with his holy people, which in the New Testament is identified with the church. In other words, it is not an exaggeration to state that it constitutes an "ecclesial" rather than a "personal" process, a "collective" and not merely an "individual" character. Even in later Christian tradition, when—as the result of the encounter with Greek philosophy (Stoic, etc.)—a more personal understanding of holiness has gradually developed, it was always within this ecclesial framework that the concept of "holiness" of any individual believer (monastic, or nonmonastic) has been understood. It is this ecclesial dimension of holiness that I propose to deal with in my presentation. More precisely, I will try to approach the Christian understanding of holiness from the perspective of a "eucharistic theology."

Because, however, in almost all handbooks of Christian spirituality[2] the eucharistic spirituality is normally juxtaposed, or at least addressed with the monastic one,[3] I will critically refer to these two essential expressions of Christian spirituality, analyzing as far as possible their relationship, differences, and mutual interaction, having as a basic point of reference the radical biblical eschatology of the early church. By underlining the tension between these two basic components of Christianity, one can better grasp, I believe, the subject we set out to examine.[4]

A few preliminary observations, nevertheless, seem absolutely necessary. First of all, I adhere to the view that "the fundamental principles of Christian spirituality are the same in the East and in the West";[5] after all, a great deal of Wesleyan spirituality and of the Methodist movement is exceptionally based on a rediscovery of the Eastern Christian heritage.[6] Secondly, despite my firm conviction that a trinitarian (i.e. pneumatological) approach is more veracious to my Orthodox tradition, I will follow instead a christological one. In the framework of a meaningful encounter between the Orthodox and Wesleyan traditions, I decided to have as an overall starting point Christ and his basic kerygma. Thirdly, what follows is not a historical, namely confessional (i.e. Orthodox), approach, based on my church's spiritual heritage, but as far as possible an ecumenical contemporary theological reflection, based on the biblical foundation.

The Christological Background of the Understanding of Holiness

Christian spirituality in general, and the understanding of holiness in particular, is based and determined by the teaching, life and work of Christ. His teaching, however, and especially his life and work, cannot be properly understood without reference to the eschatological expectations of Judaism. Without entering into the complexities of Jewish eschatology, we can very briefly say that this eschatology was interwoven with the idea of the coming of a Messiah, who in the "last days" of history (the *eschaton*) would establish his kingdom by calling the dispersed and afflicted people of God into one place to become one body united around him. As it was expressed in the prophetic tradition of the Judaism (Joel 3:1; Isaiah 2:2, 59:21; Ezekiel 36:24, among others), the start of the eschatological period will be sounded by the gathering of all the nations and the descent of God's Spirit to the sons and the daughters of God.[7] The statement in the Gospel of John about the Messiah's role is extremely important. There the writer interprets the words of the Jewish High priest by affirming that "he prophesied that Jesus should die . . . not for the nation only but to *gather into one* the children of God who are scattered abroad" (11:51–52).[8]

Throughout the Gospels Christ identifies himself with this Messiah. We see this in the various Messianic titles he chose for himself, or at least as witnessed by the most primitive Christian tradition ("Son of man," "Son of God,"), most of which had a collective meaning, whence the Christology of "corporate personality"). We see it as well in the parables of the kingdom, which summarize his teaching, proclaiming that his coming initiates the new world of the kingdom of God, in the Lord's Prayer, but also in his conscious acts (e.g. the selection of the Twelve). In short, Christ identified himself with the Messiah of the *eschaton* who would be the center of the gathering of the dispersed people of God.

It was on this radical eschatological teaching of the historical Jesus about the kingdom of God (which, as modern biblical research has shown, moves dialectically between the "already" and the "not yet"; in other words, begins already in the present but will be completed in its final authentic form in the *eschaton*) that the early church has developed its ecclesiology, on which their missionary activities, as well as their struggle for perfection and holiness, were based.

In the first two decades after Pentecost the Christian community understood its existence as the perfect and genuine expression of the people of God.[9] With a series of terms taken from the Old Testament the early Christian community believed that it was the "Israel of God" (Galatians 6:16), the "saints" (Acts 9:32, 41; 26:10; Romans 1:7; 8:27; 12:13; 15:25), "the elect" (Romans 8:33; Colossians 3:12, etc.), "the chosen race," "the royal priesthood" (1 Peter 2:9), namely, the holy people of God (*laos tou theou*), for whom all the promises of the Bible were to be fulfilled at the *eschata*. During this constructive period the concept in which the early church understood herself was that of a *people* and not of an organization. An examination of both the Old and the New Testament terminology makes this quite clear. The chosen people of God were an '*am* ("people" in Hebrew, especially in the prophets) or a *laos* ("people" in Greek), whereas the people of the outside world were designated by the words *goim* in Hebrew and the *ethne* in Greek (cf. Acts 15:14).

This consciousness that when God created a new community, he created a people, distinguished the church from those guilds, clubs or religious societies so typical of the Graeco-Roman period. It is quite significant that the first Christian community used the term *ecclesia* in the Old Testament meaning; it is not accidental that this term (*ecclesia*) in the Septuagint, corresponds to the Hebrew *qâhâl,* a term denoting the congregation of God's people. The Septuagint never translates *ecclesia* by the Hebrew *'edhah,* the usual translation of which is *synagogue.* In this primitive period, therefore, the members of the Christian community do not just *belong to* the church, i.e. they are not simply members of an organization; *they are* the church.

The second generation after Pentecost is certainly characterized by the great theological contribution of St Paul. The apostle takes over the above charismatic notion of the church, but, in addition, he gives it a universal and ecumenical character. To the church belong all human beings, Jews, and Gentiles, for the latter have been joined to the same tree of the people of God (Romans 11:13–25). The church, as the new Israel, is thus no longer constituted on grounds of external criteria (circumcision), but of its faith to Jesus Christ (cf. Romans 9:6). The term, however, with which St Paul reminds the reader of the charismatic understanding of the church is *body of Christ.* With this metaphorical expression St Paul was able to express the charismatic nature of the church by means of the Semitic concept of corporate personality. He emphasized that in the church there exists a variety of gifts, exercised by the individual members of the community, and necessary for the building up and the nutrition of this body, Christ alone being its only head and authority.

The Johannine figure of the vine (John 15:1–8) is equally impressive. As with the Pauline term *soma,* the double scheme vine-branches indicates the special relationship existing between people and Christ, which reveals the inner basis of ecclesial life. The other New Testament terms for the church, "household of faith" (*oikos*) (Ephesians 2:11–22), "fellowship" (1 Corinthians 1:9), "bride of Christ" (Ephesians 5:31–33; Revelation 21:9), "little flock" (Luke 12:32), "family of Christ" (Luke 8:21), all point to the same direction: namely, that the new community is a *people,* bound together by love and the Spirit provided by God in Christ, and not by external structure.

St Paul in particular was absolutely convinced that all who have believed in Christ have been incorporated into his body through baptism, completing with the Eucharist their incorporation into the one people of God. However, even during the period of oral tradition there were clear indications of similar concepts as witnessed, for example, by the account of the multiplication of loaves and the words of institution[10] of the Eucharist. The Gospel of John develops this radical eschatological teaching even further in regard to the unity of the people of God around Christ and their incorporation into Christ's body through the Eucharist above all. The main contribution of the early church, as it is recorded in the New Testament, emphasized and underlined most sharply by St Luke, was that with Christ's resurrection and especially with Pentecost the *eschaton* had already entered history. The messianic eschatological community becomes a reality each time the church, the new Israel, the holy people of God, gathers *epi to auto* (in one place), especially when they celebrate the Holy Eucharist. This development is undoubtedly the starting point of Christian mission, the springboard of the church's witnessing *exodus* to the world, which in fact interpreted the imminent expectation of the *parousia* in a dynamic and radical way.

The understanding of holiness stems exactly from this awareness of the church. The people of God as being an eschatological, dynamic, radical, and corporate reality, struggled to become "holy," not in terms of individualistic perfection, but in order to authentically witness the kingdom of God "on earth as it is in heaven" (Matthew 6:10).[11] The apostles were commissioned to proclaim not a set of given religious convictions, doctrines, or moral commands, but the coming kingdom, the gospel, the good news of a new eschatological reality, which had as its center the crucified and resurrected Christ, the incarnate Logos of God and his permanent dwelling among us human beings, through the continuous presence of the Holy Spirit.

Therefore, all faithful are called to holiness not as individuals, but as a corporate ecclesial entity. That is why they are called "holy"; because they belonged to that chosen race of the people of God. That is why they were considered "royal priesthood"; because all of them, without exception (not just some special cast, such as the priests or levites) have priestly and spiritual authority to practice in the diaspora the work of the priestly class, reminded at the same time to be worthy of their election though their exemplary life and works.[12] That is why they were called to walk towards unity ("so that they may become perfectly one," John 17:23), to abandon all deeds of darkness and to perfect themselves. They are to become holy, because the One, who called them out of darkness into light, "from non existence into being," who took them as non-members of the people of God and made them into genuine members of the new eschatological community ("Once you were no people, now you are God's people," 1 Peter 2:10) is holy ("You shall be holy, for I am holy" 1 Peter 1:16, cf. Leviticus 11:44, 19:2, 20:7) and perfect ("I sanctify myself that they also may be sanctified in truth," John 17:19). Matthew 5:48 in particularly states, "You, therefore, must be perfect, as your heavenly Father is perfect."

One can summarize by saying the ideal of holiness is based on the firm conviction that the church sanctifies and saves the world not by what she does, or by what she says, but *by what she is*. In other words, the primary status of holiness is inextricably related to a life of communion, experienced in the "eucharistic," in the wider sense, life itself.

The Eucharistic Dimension of Holiness

Vladimir Lossky in his monumental work, *The Mystical Theology of the Eastern Church*, has for almost half a century determined the characteristic feature of Orthodox theology, and by extension also the Orthodox understanding of holiness.[13] His mystical approach was coupled with his "pneumatological," or "trinitarian" one. Trinitarian theology points to the fact that God is in God's own self a life of communion and that God's involvement in history aims at drawing humanity and the whole of creation into this communion, into God's very life. The implications of this assertion for a profound understanding of holiness are extremely important: holiness does not primarily aim at individual perfection, but at sharing of the life of communion that exists in God.[14]

This trinitarian approach seems to be the prevailing one among almost all Orthodox in recent time. One of the most serious contributions of modern Orthodox theology was the reintroduction into current theological thinking of the trinitarian doctrine of the undivided church.[15] Nevertheless, despite the fact that the trinitarian approach is widely recognized, and more and more applied even by non-Orthodox[16] in dealing with current theological issues, I will approach, as I said, our theme from the *eucharistic* perspective. I came to this decision not so much in order to avoid a strictly contextual (i.e. Orthodox) approach, but purely for *methodological* reasons. It is time, I think, to distance ourselves as much as possible from the dominant modern scholarship syndrome of the priority of the texts over the experience, and of theology over ecclesiology. There are many scholars who still cling to the dogma, imposed by the post-Enlightenment and post-Reformation hegemony over all scholarly theological outlook (and not only in the field of biblical scholarship or of Protestant theology), which can be summarized as follows: the core of our Christian faith can be extracted only from expressed theological views, from a certain *depositum fidei,* (hence the final authority of the Bible according to the evangelicals, or of the Fathers, the canons and certain decisions of the Council, according to the Orthodox). Very rarely is there any serious reference to the eucharistic communion that has been responsible for and produced these views.[17]

It is almost an assured result of modern scholarship, reinforced recently by the insights of cultural anthropology, that ritual in general and the liturgy in particular constitute an element of primal importance for a proper understanding of the religious experience. Christian scholarship in particular (biblical and liturgical alike) has come to the conclusion that the Eucharist in the early church was "lived" not as a mystery cult, but as a foretaste of the coming kingdom of God. It was a proleptic manifestation within the tragic realities of history of an authentic life of communion, unity, justice, and equality, with no practical differentiation (soteriological and beyond) between Jews and gentiles, slaves and freemen, women and men (cf. Galatians 3:28). This was, after all, the real meaning of the Johannine term "eternal life," and St Ignatius' expression "medicine of immortality."

According to some historians, the church was able a few generations later, with the important contribution of the Greek Fathers of the golden age, to develop the doctrine of Trinity, and much later to further develop the important distinction between substance and energies, only because of the eschatological experience of *koinonia* in the Eucharist (both vertically with its head, and horizontally among the people of God, and by extension with the entire humanity through the church's mission) of the early Christian community, an experience which ever since continues to constitute the only expression of the church's self-consciousness, its Mystery *par excellence.*

No one, of course, can deny that early on in the Christian community, even from the time of St Paul, the paradigm shifted from a self-consciousness understanding the Eucharist as a *koinonia* of the *eschata* and as a proleptic manifestation of the coming kingdom of God. For whatever missionary reasons, the eucharistic experience gave way to the Christian message, eschatology to Christology (and further and consequently to soteriology), and the event (the kingdom of God) to the bearer and center of this event—Christ, and more precisely his sacrifice on the Cross. However, the

Eucharist (the *theia koinonia*) has always remained (with the exception perhaps of some marginal cases in later church history) the sole expression of the church's identity. To their merit, modern theologians from all Christian traditions, and most recently of Metropolitan of Pergamon John Zizioulas,[18] reaffirmed the paramount importance of the *koinonia* dimension of the Eucharist. They stressed that not only the identity of the church, but all its expressions (structure, authority, mission and so on) are in fact *relational*.[19] In summary, if one wants to approach, and reflect on, any specific issue, like holiness, it is the *eucharistic theology* in its broad sense that should guide this effort.[20]

Towards a Proper Understanding of Eucharist

In a mutual and meaningful encounter between Orthodox and Methodists one has at least to affirm a proper understanding of Eucharist, the Sacrament *par excellence* so revered and honored by the Orthodox. Wesleyan spirituality, of course, has laid a great deal of emphasis on the Eucharist,[21] and this makes our task easier.

Nevertheless, one should never forget that a proper understanding of Eucharist has always been a stumbling block in Christian theology and life. This is so, not only when the infant church struggled against a multitude of mystery cults, but also much later when scholastic theology (mostly in the West) systematized a latent "sacramentalistic" view of *the* Mystery *par excellence* of the One, undivided, Holy, Catholic, and Apostolic Church. In vain, distinguished theologians of the East (most notably in the case of Nicholas Cabasilas in the fourteenth century) attempted to redefine the Christian sacramental theology on the basis of the trinitarian theology, that is, pneumatology. From a modern theological perspective, this was a desperate attempt to reject certain tendencies that overemphasized the importance of Christology at the expense—and to the detriment—of the importance of the role of the Holy Spirit.

The controversy between East and West on the issues of the *filioque*, the *epiclesis*, and so on, are well known, though their consequences to the sacramental theology of the church have yet to be fully and systematically examined. The tragic consequences of those tendencies were in fact felt a few generations after the final schism between East and West with the further division of Western Christianity. One of the main focuses during the Reformation, and rightly so, was the "sacramentalistic" understanding of the Eucharist in Western Christianity which resulted, among other things, in divergent views between evangelical and Orthodox theology. The dialectic between "sacramentalism" on the one hand, and "the complete rejection of sacraments" on the other, resulted in the tragic secularization of our society and the transformation of the *church* into a *religion*. The traditional churches (some Orthodox included) became cultic religions, evangelical Christianity became exclusively evangelistic.

The first serious reflection upon the profound meaning of the Eucharist is in the Bible itself, and in particular in the Gospel of John.[22] There we have the beginnings of what has become later axiomatic in Christian theology: to have eternal life—in other words to live in a true and authentic way and not just live a conventional life—one has to be in *koinonia* (communion) with Christ. Communion with Christ, however, means participation in the perfect communion that exists between the Father and the Son: "Just as the living Father sent me, and I live through the Father, he who eats me will live through me," (6:57). As the Fathers of the Church later stated, it is participation in the perfect communion that exists within the Holy Trinity.

What we have in John, is in fact a parallel expression to the classic statement of 2 Peter 1:4 ("partakers of the divine nature"), which has become in later patristic literature the biblical foundation of the doctrine of divinization (*theosis*). In the Gospel of John, however, this idea is expressed in a more descriptive and less abstract way. Taking this argument a little further, we can say that Johannine theology develops the earlier interpretation of the Eucharist as the continuously repeated act of sealing the "new covenant" of God with his new people. This interpretation is evident in both the synoptic and the Pauline traditions. In the latter, though, the covenantal interpretation of Jesus' death in the phrase "this is my blood of the covenant," in Mark 14:24 and 2 Corinthians 11:25, is somewhat hidden by the soteriological formula "which is shed for you."

What comes out of this biblical understanding of Eucharist (with its more direct emphasis on the covenant and of *koinonia*) is the transformation of Jeremiah's vision, which was at the same time also a promise, from a marginal to a central feature. Just as in the book of Jeremiah, so also in early Christianity, at least in John, it is the ideas of *a new covenant*, of *communion*, and of the church as *a people*, that are most strongly emphasized. Listen to what the prophet was saying: "and I will make a *covenant . . . a new covenant*," Jeremiah 31:31; and "I will give them a heart to know that I am the Lord. . . . and they shall be unto me *a people*" (Jeremiah 24:7).

During this normative period, the Eucharist was understood in its "ecclesial" dimension, as a communion event, and not as an act of personal devotion, or even a merely cultic act. It was an expression of the church as the people of God and as the body of Christ mystically united with its Head, not as a sacramentalist quasi-magical rite.[23] The eucharistic theology of the early church was by no means related to any "sacramental" practices of the ancient mystery cults.

In sum, the Eucharist, as the unique and primary Mystery of the church, is the authentic and dynamic expression of the communion of the people of God, and a proleptic manifestation of the kingdom to come. As such, *mutatis mutandis*, is a reflection of the communion that exists between the persons of the Holy Trinity.

The Tension between Eucharistic and Therapeutic Spirituality

There is no doubt that quite early in the history of Christianity the original eucharistic-horizontal-eschatological spirituality (stemming from a biblical/Semitic background) was mingled with a more personal-vertical-soteriological one (influenced by Greek philosophy). Nevertheless, it is more than clear that the horizontal-eschatological view was the predominant one in New Testament and in other early Christian writings. The vertical-soteriological view was always understood within the context of the horizontal-eschatological perspective as supplemental and complementary. This is why the liturgical experience of the early church is incomprehensible without its social dimension (see Acts 2:42; 1 Corinthians 11:17–22, Hebrews 13:10–16; Justin, *1 Apology* 67; Irenaeus, *Adver. Her.* 18:1, as examples).

This understanding of spirituality in the early church is also clearly reflected within its liturgical order. From the time of St Ignatius of Antioch onwards, the church considers the eschatological people of God, gathered in one place around Christ, as reflected in the offices of the church: the bishop is the image of Christ, while the presbyters around him "re-present" the apostles. Above all it is the eucharistic gathering which authentically expresses the Mystery of the church. This *eucharistic/liturgical* understanding identified the Christian community as an icon of the *eschaton* and defined holiness as an imperative duty to be a witness, an authentic expression in a particular time and place of the eschatological glory of the Kingdom of God—with all that this could imply for social life. A conviction began to grow among church writers, beginning with the author of Hebrews (10:1) and more fully developed in the writings of St Maximus the Confessor, that the events of the Old Testament were a "shadow" of future riches, and that the present church is only an "image" (*eikon*) of a "truth" to be revealed only in the *eschaton*.

This fundamental biblical and early Christian understanding of spirituality, based on the eucharistic/liturgical and eschatological understanding of the church, began gradually to fall out of favor. By the third century, under the intense ideological pressure of Christian Gnosticism and especially Platonism, it began, at best, to coexist with concepts promulgated by the Catechetical School of Alexandria. The main representatives of this school, Clement of Alexandria and Origen, gave Christian ecclesiology (and by extension its missiology and its struggle for perfection and holiness) a new direction which, as Metropolitan John Zizioulas emphatically put, was "not merely a change (trope), but a complete reversal (anatrope)."[24] Gradually the church ceased to be an icon of the *eschaton*; it became instead an icon of the origin of beings, of creation. The Alexandrines, under the influence of the ancient Greek philosophy, particularly Platonism, believed that the original condition of beings represents perfection and that all subsequent history is a decline. The mystery of the Incarnation contributes almost nothing to this system of thought,[25] Christ being primarily considered as the source of the union of humankind with God, and as the recapitulation, in some sense, of the human fallen nature. But if earlier in the church's life "recapitulation" was understood in the biblical sense,[26] with the Alexandrines the concept is torn completely from its biblical roots in eschatology. The *eschaton* is no longer the focal point and apex of the Divine Economy. The direction of interest has been reversed, and now the focus is on creation. Thus we have a cosmological approach to the church and to its mission, and not a historical one, as in the Holy Scriptures. The church is now understood, completely apart from the historical community, as a perfect and eternal Idea.

Naturally, therefore, interest in the collective character of spirituality and the ecclesial dimension of holiness has diminished, and along with that any concern for the historical process, and even for the institutional reality of the church. The latter's purpose is now characterized, at best, as "sanatorium of souls." The church's spirituality is now directed not in bringing about *synergically* and *proleptically* the kingdom of God, but toward the salvation of the souls of every individual Christian. Historically this new development of spirituality is connected with the origins of monasticism. In the Eastern, but also the Western, monasteries the works of Origen were studied with great reverence, even after his synodical condemnation.

A decisive turning point in the development of Christian spirituality came when the *corpus Areopagiticus* affected the Christian liturgy. Pseudo-Dionysius the Areopagite was the catalyst in departing from eucharistic ecclesiology and spirituality. His theological analyses made a tremendous impact on the shaping of subsequent theology,[27] affecting the very heart of Christian eschatology as expressed in the eucharistic Liturgy.[28] Using the anagogic method[29] of approach, Pseudo-Dionysius interpreted the liturgical rites of the church by attempting to raise them from the letter to the spirit, from the visible acts of the sacraments to the mystery of the Unseen.[30] The bishop's very movements within the church are seen now as a divine return to the origin of beings. With this method, however, the eschatological view of the Eucharist finally disappears. The sole function of worship is now to mystically lead the soul (*mystagogia*) to the spiritual realities of the unseen world.[31]

It has been rightly maintained that "in the dionysian system there is little room for biblical typology. Allegorical anagogy predominates: the liturgy is an allegory of the soul's progress from the divisiveness of sin to the divine communion, through the process of purification, illumination, perfection imaged forth in the rites (*Eccl. Hier.*, I PG 3 cols. 369–77). There is very little reference to the earthly economy of Christ, and none whatever to his divine-human mediatorship, to his saving death and resurrection (*Eccl. Hier.*, III 1, 3.3 PG 3 cols. 424 ff.)."[32] It was inevitable, therefore, that in the dionysian system a mediating "hierarchy" was absolutely necessary.[33] But this was something which according to the fundamental teaching of Hebrews had been abolished "once and for all" (*ephapax*) by Christ's sacrifice on the cross. According to the late Fr John Meyendorff, "those who followed Dionysian symbolism approached the Eucharist in the context of a Hellenistic hierarchical cosmos, and understood it as the center of salvific action through mystical contemplation."[34] That is why there is no mention here at all of Christ's self-sacrifice, nor of his mediatory and high-priestly role;[35] mediation is the work of the earthly hierarchy and the rites that it (and not the community as a whole) performs.

However, where the dionysian system reaches its most extreme is in overturning the eschatological and historical dimensions of the Eucharist. There is not a single reference to the fundamental Pauline interpretation of the Eucharist, according to which at every eucharistic gathering "we proclaim the Lord's death until he comes," (1 Corinthians 11:26). Even communion, the most important act of the Eucharist, is no more than a symbol of human union and absorption with the divine hypostasis.[36] In other words, there is a clear shift from a communion *of* the body of Christ (the incarnate Logos) and *in* the body of Christ (the church), to a communion *with* the pre-existing Logos.

Under this peculiar mysticism, holiness is no longer connected with the coming kingdom, i.e. with the anticipation of a new eschatological community with a more authentic structure. It is rather identified with the soul's union with the Logos, and therefore, with the *catharsis*, the purification from all that prohibits union with the primal Logos, including all that is material, tangible, historical. Continuous prayer and the struggle against the demons and the flesh replace the *maranatha* of the Pauline communities and the "come Lord" of the seer/prophet of the Apocalypse.

In contrast, therefore, to the eucharistic spirituality and ecclesial holiness, this *therapeutic/cathartic* one has put the emphasis on the effort toward *catharsis* (purification) of the soul from passions, and toward *therapy* (healing) of the fallen nature of the human beings (men/women). In other words, the reference point is not the eschatological glory of the kingdom of God, but the state of blessedness in Paradise before the Fall.

In the life of the church these two basic expressions of spirituality have always remained parallel to each other, sometimes meeting together and forming a creative unity, and some other times moving apart creating dilemmas and conflicts. Where should one search to find personal wholeness and salvation, and what is the authentic mode of holiness? Is it in the eucharistic gathering around the bishop, where one could overcome creatively all schizophrenic dichotomies (spirit/matter, transcendence/immanence, coming together/going forth) and social polarities? Or in the desert, the hermitage, the monastery, where naturally the effort for catharsis and for the healing of passions through ascetic discipline of the individual is more effective? This was, and remains, a critical dilemma in the life of the church, especially in the East.

No doubt, the center of the church's spiritual life, with few exceptions, has always remained the Eucharist, the sole place where the church becomes what really is: the people of God, the body of Christ, the community of the Holy Spirit, a glimpse and foretaste of the kingdom of God. And it was this eschatological dimension of the Christian ecclesiology that determines the authentic expression of holiness.[37] In other words, *holiness is inextricably linked with the eucharistic understanding of the church as a communion of the eschaton.*

The Rediscovery of the Eucharistic Awareness and Vision

It was exactly this understanding of the church and of holiness, that made Orthodox theologians in recent times speak of the "eucharistic ecclesiology," a term coined for the first time in 1957 by Nicholas Afanassieff,[38] in his intervention to the deliberation of the II Vatican Council of the Roman Catholic Church. Afanassieff had successfully argued for the existence from the very old times of the church's life of two clearly distinguished views about the church: the widespread—even today—"universal ecclesiology," and the "eucharistic ecclesiology." More importantly, he has convincingly proved the priority and the authenticity of the latter. According to Afanassieff the effect of the universal ecclesiology was so strong, that for centuries it seemed the only possible option, almost an ecclesiological axiom, without which every single thought about the church seemed impossible. However, Afanassieff went on, the universal ecclesiology was *not* the only one. And what is even most important, it was not the primitive ecclesiology; it took the place of a different ecclesiology, (which Afanassieff for the first time) called "eucharistic,"[39] thus creating a new era in the ecumenical and ecclesiological discussions.[40]

We do not propose to enter into more details of this radical ecclesiological view. We only want to underline that, by using the eucharistic ecclesiology as a tool, the Eucharist remains the basic criterion of holiness, the only expression of unity of the church, and the point of reference of all the other mysteries (and of course of the priesthood and of the office of the bishop). That is why the catholicity of the church is manifested completely in every local church. "Wherever there is a eucharistic meeting there lives Christ too, there is also the Church of God in Christ."[41] On the other hand, the "universal ecclesiology" (the beginnings of which are to be found in Cyprian of Carthage[42]) having as point of departure the fact that the whole is made up by parts,[43] understands the church as having a strictly hierarchical structure (hence the theological importance of "primacy"[44]). But in this case first in importance and extremely determinative is the role of the bishop, whose office constitutes the preeminent expression of the unity of the church, and in consequence the Eucharist one of his functions.[45]

The focal point of the eucharistic ecclesiology (and by extension also the eucharistic theology) in all her expressions and variations, is the concept of the *communion* (hence the importance of pneumatology). In contrast, universal ecclesiology, is characterized by the priority that it gives to the *external structure* (hence the importance of Christology, and by extension of the role of the bishop, and consequently of primacy). In addition, eucharistic theology underlines the eschatological dimension of the church. That is why it understands all the offices of the church, and especially those of the ordained priesthood, not as authorities or offices in the conventional sense, but as *images* of the authentic eschatological kingdom of God. In opposition to this, the universal ecclesiology, having as its point of departure the *historical* expression of the church, understands the unity and catholicity of the church, as well as the apostolic succession, in a *linear way*.[46] That is why the bishop, even when he is interpreted as type and image of Christ, has priority over the eucharistic community. Thus, the sacrament of priesthood theoretically surpasses the sacrament of the Holy Eucharist.

This eucharistic vision, thanks to the contribution of the Orthodox, has also been the guiding principle of the ecumenical movement, ever since the VI assembly of the WCC (Vancouver 1983). As it has officially stated there: "Christ—the life of the world—unites heaven and earth, God and world, spiritual and secular. His body and blood, given to us in the elements of bread and wine, integrate liturgy and diaconate . . . Our eucharistic vision thus encompasses the whole reality of Christian worship, life and witness."[47]

Concluding Remarks on the Eucharistic Spirituality and Holiness

The ultimate goal of holiness cannot be dissociated from the problem of the evil. According to the eucharistic approach of holiness, the problem of overcoming the evil in the world is not at all a moral issue; it is basically, primarily and even exclusively an *ecclesial* one. The moral and social responsibility of the church (both as an institution and also on the part of its individual members), as the primary results of holiness, are the logical consequence of their ecclesial/eucharistic self-consciousness. Only in this do they bear witness to the fundamental characteristics of the church, those of *unity* and *catholicity*. Only in this way will "exclusiveness" give its place to the priority of the "communion" with the "others." And only thus can all kinds of nationalistic and phyletistic behavior be definitely overcome, promoting not only church unity, but also actively contributing to the struggle for the unity of humankind.

In terms of tangible effects, a eucharistic understanding of holiness always points towards a *common* evangelistic witness. According to the biblical references (cf. Matthew 25:31–46) what really matters is not so much accepting and believing in the abundant love of our Triune God (confessional, religious exclusiveness), but exemplifying it to the world through witness (ecclesial inclusiveness). Additionally, the eucharistic understanding of holiness goes far beyond denominational boundaries, beyond Christian limitations, even beyond the religious sphere in the conventional sense; its aim is the manifestation of the kingdom of God, the restoration of God's "household" (*oikos*) of God, in its majestic eschatological splendor.

It was such a eucharistic understanding of holiness that has in many cases helped the church to overcome the corrupted hierarchical order (which is a reflection of the fallen earthly order, and not of the kenotic divine one) both in society and in the priestly ecclesiastical order. An authentic understanding of holiness has traditionally insisted on the "iconic" perception of all priestly ministries. It has also contributed to a "conciliar" status in all sectors of the ecclesiastical life (i.e. participation of the entire *laos* to the priestly, royal, and prophetic ministry of the church), and to a genuine community of men and women. Finally, a eucharistic understanding of holiness has prevented the church from all kinds of "Christocentric universalism," always directing her towards a "trinitarian" understanding of the divine reality and pointing to a mission that embraces the entire *oikoumene* as the one household of life.

We live in a world different from our Fathers' who developed unique expressions of holiness and spirituality; from a world that experienced the existence of saints, of martyrs, of confessors, of defenders of the apostolic faith, of monks and nuns who day and night were saying the *monologistos* prayer; from a world in which existed *puritan* expressions of the Christian life. The secular world we live in today, as well as broken and divided humanity, need new forms of holiness. For Christians across denominational boundaries the future of humanity depends on a spiritual life that pays more attention to the perspectives of unity and communion.

As during Jesus' time, when the Son and Word of God came down to earth, that we "may have life, and have it more abundantly" (John 10:10), today once again the survival of humanity is based on unity: "I in them and You in me, that they may be *perfectly one*," John 17:23. Without excluding any (traditional or otherwise) expression of holiness, as well as the various forms of spirituality, which act as "therapy,"[48] it is essential to return to forms of "proleptic" spirituality and holiness. This is what *eucharistic spirituality and holiness* is all about: an act, behavior, and struggle directed towards the unity of the universe (humankind and the whole of creation). It is the affirmation of the created world (history and everything in material creation), and the referring of it all (*anaphora*) back to the Father Creator, while always keeping alive the vision of the *eschaton*.[49]

Endnotes

[1]More in O. L. Procksch, "hagios etc.," *Theological Dictionary of the New Testament*, ed. G. Kittel, et al, trans. by D. E. Green (Grand Rapids, 1995) 1:88–97, 100–115. Cf. Also Frederic Raurell, *"Doxa" en la teologia I antropologia dels*, LXX (Barcelona, 1996).

[2]Cf. The three-volume book *Christian Spirituality*, ed. by Jill Raitt-Bernard, Bernard McGinn, John Meyendorff (New York: Crossroad, 1985), which is part of a twenty-five-volume encyclopedia of world spirituality under the general title, *World Spirituality. An Encyclopedic History of the Religious Quest*; also the three-volume work by Louis Bouyer, J. Leclercq, F. Vandenbroucke, *A History of Christian Spirituality* (New York, 1982), translated from the French *Histoire de la Spiritualité de l'Orient Chrétien* (Paris, 1978 and 1988); and also John Meyendorff, *St Gregory Palamas and Orthodox Spirituality* (Crestwood, NY: St Vladimir's Seminary Press, 1974).

[3]Two were, after all, the tendencies which from the very beginning were developed within Christian ecclesiology: the therapeutic or cathartic one and eucharistic or liturgical one, which for one reason or another have been connected with the above expressions of Christian spirituality. Cf. the introductory to the above trilogy article by John Zizioulas, "The Early Christian Community," B. McGinn and John Meyendorff, eds., *Christian Spirituality I. Origins to the Twelfth Century* (New York, 1985), 23–43; and *Issues of Ecclesiology* (Thessaloniki, 1991), 25 ff., in Greek.

[4]It is exactly for that purpose that I have pointed out on another occasion that authentic Christian spirituality—despite the fact that it is generally identified with "the inner dimension of the *human* person, which in different traditions is called *pneuma*. . . . where it is open to the transcendent dimension, and lives the ultimate reality" (from the working definition of *World Spirituality* [*Christian Spirituality I.*, xiii])—is in fact related to the *Holy Spirit*, without of course denying the human person (cf. my "La pneumatologia ortodossa e la contemplazione," *Vedere Dio* [Bologna, 1994], 86).

[5]*Orthodox Spirituality*, x.

[6]*John and Charles Wesley. Selected Writings and Hymns*, F. Whaling, ed. (New York: Paulist Press, 1981), 12. What makes Wesleyan Christianity very close to Eastern Orthodoxy is its founder's claim that "Christianity was not primarily a set of beliefs, it was an experimental way, a process, an inwardness based on orthodox doctrines and resulting in outward practice," ibid., 8; (cf. this with Florovsky's famous statement: "The Church is first of all a worshipping community. Worship comes first, doctrine and discipline second. The *lex orandi* has a privileged priority in the life of the Christian Church. The *lex credendi* depends on the devotional experience and vision of the Church," Georges Florovsky, "The Elements of Liturgy," in G. Patelos, ed., *The Orthodox Church in the Ecumenical Movement* [Geneva, 1978], 172–182; also Petros Vassiliadis, "Orthodoxy and Ecumenism," *Eucharist and Witness. Orthodox Perspectives on the Unity and Mission of the Church* [Geneva: WCC and Boston: Holy Cross, 1998], 7–28, 9).

[7]In Luke's writings (Acts 2:1–4), and also in the later liturgical tradition of the church, the descent of the Holy Spirit was understood as the eschatological event *par excellence*, and an act of the unity of church. In other words eschatology and pneumatology run parallel to each other. Thus, the church's perception of holiness has in addition a reference to pneumatology.

[8]The idea of "gathering into one place the scattered people of God" is also to be found in Isaiah 66:18; Matthew 25:32; Romans 12:16; *Didache* 9:4b; *Martyrium Polycarpi* 22:3b; Clement of Rome, 1 Corinthians 12:6.

[9]Most of what follows is taken from the ecclesiological studies of my book *Biblical Hermeneutical Studies* in *Bibliotheca Biblica* 6 (Thessaloniki, 1988), 364 ff., in Greek.

[10]More on this in my "The Biblical Foundation of the Eucharistic Ecclesiology," *Lex Orandi. Studies of Liturgical Theology*, in *Ecclesia-Koinonia-Oikoumene* 9 (Thessaloniki, 1994), 29 ff., in Greek.

[11]Cf. St John Chrysostom's comment on the relevant petition of the Lord's Prayer: "(Christ) did not say 'Your will be done' in me, or in us, but everywhere on earth, so that error may be destroyed, and truth implanted, and all wickedness cast out, and virtue return, and no difference in this respect be henceforth between heaven and earth." (*Patrologia Graeca*, 57 col. 280).

[12]J. H. Elliott, *The Elect and the Holy*, (1966), has redetermined on the part of the Protestant biblical theology the real meaning of the term "royal priesthood," which has been so vigorously discussed since the time of Luther. Cf. R. Brown, *Priest and Bishop: Biblical Reflections* (New York, 1971).

[13]Vladimir Lossky, *The Mystical Theology of the Eastern Church* (London, 1957).

[14]I. Bria, ed., *Go forth in Peace* (Geneva: WCC, 1986), 3.

[15]Cf. e.g. the application of the trinitarian theology to the *structure* of the church. By nature the church cannot reflect the worldly image of secular organizations, which is based on power and domination, but the kenotic image of the Holy Trinity, which is based on love and communion. If one takes a little further this trinitarian approach and takes into consideration the distinction of the hypostases (persons) within the Holy Trinity, one can come to the conclusion that the church is a church of "God" (the Father) before it becomes a church of "Christ" and of a certain place. In eucharistic liturgy all the proper eucharistic prayers are addressed to God. This has revealing implications also on a number of issues ranging from the profound meaning of episcopacy (bishop = image of "Christ"?) to the dialectics between Christ-church, divine-human, unity of man and woman, and so on.

[16]K. Raiser's *Ecumenism in Transition* is a perfect example of a well documented argumentation for the necessity, and to our view also for the right use, of the trinitarian theology to address current burning issues in modern theology. Cf. also sister Elizabeth A. Johnson's *She Who Is: The Mystery of God in Feminist Theological Discourse* (New York, 1992), especially ch. 10 under the title "Triune God: Mystery of Revelation," 191 ff.

[17]I have come to the conclusion that out of the three main characteristics, that generally constitute the Orthodox theology, namely its "eucharistic," "trinitarian," and "hesychastic" dimension, only the first one can bear a universal and ecumenical significance. If the last dimension and important feature marks a decisive development in Eastern Christian theology and spirituality after the eventual schism between East and West, a development that has determined, together with other factors, the mission of the Orthodox Church in recent history; and, if the trinitarian dimension constitutes the supreme expression of Christian theology, ever produced by human thought in its attempt to grasp the mystery of God, after Christianity's dynamic encounter with the Greek culture; it was, nevertheless, only because of the eucharistic experience, the matrix of all theology and spirituality of our church, that all theological and spiritual climaxes in our Church have been actually achieved.

[18]Cf. his address to the Fifth World Conference of Faith and Order "The Church as Communion," T. F. Best and G. Gassmann, eds., *On the Way to Fuller Koinonia* (Geneva: WCC, 1994), 103–111.

[19]Ibid., 105 ff.

[20]One should, of course, avoid the temptation to project later theological interpretations into this primary eschatological experience; but on the other hand, it would be a methodological fallacy to ignore the wider "social space" (to put it in socio-[cultural-] anthropological terms), i.e. the primary eucharistic ecclesial and eschatological experience, the matrix of all theology that produced all theological interpretations.

[21]Cf. the famous 1745 *Hymns on the Lord's Supper*, by John Wesley and Charles Wesley, facsimile ed. with an introduction by Geoffrey Wainwright (Madison, NJ: Charles Wesley Society, 1995).

[22]Most of what follows is taken from my article "The Understanding of Eucharist in St John's Gospel," L. Padovese, ed., *Atti del VI Simposio di Efeso su S. Giovanni Apostolo* (Rome, 1996), 39–52.

[23]Cf. also John Zizioulas' affirmation that "when it is understood in its correct and primitive sense— and not how it has come to be regarded even in Orthodoxy under the influence Western scholasticism— the Eucharist is first of all an assembly (*synaxis*), a community a network of relations . . ." (*Being as Communion: Studies in Personhood and the Church* [Crestwood, NY, 1985], 60). Cf. also his interesting remark: "the Fourth Gospel identifies eternal life, i.e. life without death, with truth and knowledge, (which) can be accomplished only if the individualization of nature becomes transformed into communion—that is if communion becomes identical with being. Truth, once again, must be communion if it is to be life," (105).

[24]John Zizioulas, *Issues of Ecclesiology*, 28.

[25]On Origen's soteriology and its minimal salvific significance of the Christ's human nature see A. Grillmeier, *Christ in Christian Tradition* (Atlanta, 1975); also R. Taft, "The Liturgy of the Great Church: An Initial Synthesis of Structure and Interpretation on the Eve of Iconoclasm," *Dumbarten Oaks Papers* 34–35 (1980–81): 45–75, and 62, n. 79.

[26]Cf. St Irenaeus' use of "anakephalaiosis" (recapitulation) (*Adversus Haereses* 3) based on the Pauline theology. One can also cf. how finally St Athanasius the Great articulated this concept more definitively in his classic statement that "He [God] became man so that we could become God." (*On the Incarnation*, 54).

[27]Vladimir Lossky insists that the orthodoxy of the writings of the Areopagite cannot be questioned;

The Vision of God (Crestwood, NY, 1963/1983), 99; cf. also his influential work *The Mystical Theology of the Eastern Church* (Crestwood, NY, 1976). On the other hand, all Orthodox theologians who are in favor of a liturgical renewal are critical of the theology of Pseudo-Dionysius (cf. John Meyendorff, *Byzantine Theology. Historical Trends and Doctrinal Themes* [New York, 1974, 1987], 28, 202 ff.; Georges Florovsky, "Pseudo-Dionysios' Works," *Religious and Ethical Encyclopedia*, vol. XII, col. 473–480, in Greek; Alexander Schmemann, *An Introduction to Liturgical Theology* [New York, 1986] 150 ff.; 232 ff.; Paul Meyendorff, *Saint Germanus of Constantinople On the Divine Liturgy*, 1984/1999).

²⁸The alleged neoplatonic influence of the Areopagite literature (on this cf. L. Siasos, *The Lovers of Truth. Searching the Beginnings and Building-up of the Theological Gnosiology according to Proclos and Dionysios Areopagite* [Thessaloniki, 1984], in Greek) is in fact of less importance compared with their catalytic redirection of what we call eucharistic ecclesiology and spirituality. Hieromonk Auxentios and James Thornton ("Three Byzantine Commentaries on the Divine Liturgy: A Comparative Treatment," *Greek Orthodox Theological Review* 32 [1987]: 285–308) fail to discern this dimension, for although they rightly recognize that the Byzantine liturgical commentaries touch the heart of Orthodox spirituality, they try to refute the negative position of Alexander Schmemann about the value of this philological sort, siding as they say with other Orthodox scholars such as . . . Florovsky, Fountoulis, Popovic and so forth (288). If in Origen we find the beginnings of the spiritualization of the understanding of the Holy Eucharist, in the treatises of the works of Pseudo-Dionysios we find their final theological polishing. Cf. L. Lies, *Wort und Eucharistie bei Origenes. Zur Spiritualisierungstendenz des Eucharistie-verständnisses* (Innsbruck, 1978).

²⁹According to R. Taft "mystagogy is to liturgy what exegesis is to scripture. . . . the commentators on the liturgy used a method inherited from the older tradition of biblical exegesis" ("The Liturgy of the Great Church," 59).

³⁰Cf. E. Boulard, "L'eucharistie d'après le Pseudo-Denys l'Aréopagite," *Bulletin de littérature ecclésiatique* 58 (1957): 193–217 and 59 (1958): 129–69.

³¹*Ecclesiatical Hierarchy* II 3,2, *Patrologia Graeca*, 3:379. A wonderful analysis of it in R. Bornet's classical work, *Les Commentaires byzantins de la Divine Liturgie du VIIe au XVe siècle* (Paris, 1966).

³²R. Taft, "The Liturgy of the Great Church," 61–62. Cf. also his *The Great Entrance. A History of the Transfer of Gifts and Other Pre-anaphoral Rites of the Liturgy of St John Chrysostom* (1975), 1978; "How Liturgies Grow: The Evolution of the Byzantine Divine Liturgy," *Orientalia Christiana Periodica* 43 (1977): 357 ff.; *The Liturgy of the Hours in the Christian East* (Kerala, 1988). For a thorough critical consideration of the eucharistology of the areopagites see R. Roques, *L'univers dionysien. Structure hiérarchique du monde selon le Pseudo-Denys* (Paris, 1954).

³³H. Wybrew, *The Orthodox Liturgy. The Development of the Eucharistic Liturgy in the Byzantine Rite* (London, 1989), and the St Vladimir's Seminary Press 1990-edition with a preface by Bishop Kallistos Ware, 115. This reminds us, *mutatis mutandis*, of Paul's opponents in Colossians, and also marks the latent return of a mediatory priesthood.

³⁴John Meyendorff, *Byzantine Theology*, 207.

³⁵R. Taft, "The Liturgy of the Great Church," 62.

³⁶*Ecclesiastical Hierarchy* III 3,13.

³⁷It was in the heart of an ancient Liturgy, in one of St James' post-anaphoral prayers, that we find the dominical admonition to holiness (*"you shall be holy, for I am holy"*).

³⁸"The Church Which Presides in Love," J. Meyendorff, ed. *The Primacy of Peter. Essays in Ecclesiology and the Early Church* (Crestwood, New York, 1992), 91–143, whence all references hereafter (1963), 57–110. Afanassieff's views had appeared earlier in a shorter form in French ("La doctrine de la primauté à la lumière de l'écclesiologie," *Istina* 4 [1957]: 401–420).

³⁹"The Church Which Presides in Love," 106 f.

⁴⁰Cf. e.g. M. Edmund Hussey, "Nicholas Afanassiev's Eucharistic Ecclesiology: A Roman Catholic Viewpoint." *Journal of Ecumenical Studies* 12 (1975): 235–252; P. McPartlan, "Eucharistic Ecclesiology," *One in Christ* 22 (1986): 314–331; K. Raiser, *Ecumenism in Transition* (Geneva: WCC, 1991), 97 ff. Also John Zizioulas, *The Unity of the Church in the Eucharist and the Bishop in the First Three Centuries* (Athens, 1966, 1990, in Greek); cf. nevertheless the traditionalist reaction by P. Trembelas, "Unacceptable Theories on the Unum Sanctum," *Theologia* 41 (1964): 167 ff. (in Greek); etc. also my "The Biblical Background of the Eucharistic Ecclesiology."

⁴¹N. Afanassieff, "Una Sancta," *Irenikon* 36 (1963): 436–475, 459.

[42]Cyprian of Carthage provided for the first time the theological foundation of the universal ecclesiology. . . . while the connection between the Roman empire and the Roman pontiff on the one hand, and the religious life from the time of Constantine the Great onwards on the other, facilitated its wide acceptance. N. Afanassieff, "The Church which Presides in Love," 141.

[43]"Deus unus est et Christus unus, et una ecclesia," (*Epistula* XLIII, 5, 2) and "ecclesia per totum mundum in multa membra divisa," (*Epistula* LV, 14, 2).

[44]N. Afanassieff, referring to the theological discussion between East and West on the issue of the primacy of the Bishop of Rome, has rightly suggested that the starting point for any solution must be sought in ecclesiology: i.e. whether any idea of primacy is necessary for the identity of the Church ("The Church which Presides in Love," 91).

[45]This was the view finally adopted in Vatican II.

[46]More on this in John Zizioulas, "Apostolic Community and Orthodox Theology: Towards a Synthesis of Two Perspectives," *Saint Vladimir's Theological Quarterly* 19 (1975): 75–108.

[47]In my recent book, *Eucharist and Witness*, I argue for a "costly eucharistic vision."

[48]Orthodox monasticism is undoubtedly more than a means of spiritual therapy; its authentic expression has definitely to do with overcoming all divisions in human life (cf. *Mount Athos and the Paideia of our Genos* [Karyes, 1984], in Greek; Arch. Vassilios Gontikakis [Now Abbot of Iviron Monastery], *The Entrance Hymn* [Athens, 1974], English translation [Crestwood, NY: Saint Vladimir's Seminary Press, 1987]).

[49]It is quite a promising development that modern Orthodox monastic communities, where traditionally all important spiritual journeys were initiated, are nowadays concerned with new forms of authentic spirituality and liturgical expression. This is the case with the monastic communities of the New Skete near Cambridge, New York, with their pioneer liturgical editions (cf. R. Taft, "The Byzantine Office in the Prayerbook of New Skete: Evaluation of a Proposed Reform," *Orientalia Christiana Periodica* 48 [1982]: 336–370). Cf. also the concern in liturgical matters of the Simonopetra Monastery of Mount Athos, as it is shown by their critical editions of the Divine Liturgy (*Ieratikon*). Also the concern, unusual in traditional monastic spirituality, in social or ecological issues, as it is the case with the convent of The Annunciation of the Theotokos in Ormylia, Chalkidiki, Greece (cf. *Ormylia the Holy Cenobion of the Annunciation of the Theotokos* [Athens, 1992], in Greek). All are indirect evidence that there is not just one form of spirituality in Orthodoxy.

6

The Way of Holiness

Dimitar Popmarinov Kirov

The idea of "the holy" is basic to every religion. In the central worship of the Ortho-dox Church, in the liturgy, one of the most utilized words is "holy." The sacraments are holy; the Divine Liturgy, the worship, and the church are holy. Everything, accord-ing to the Orthodox tradition, which springs out from the life of the church, is holy, because God in the person of Jesus Christ dwells in the church.

The etymology of "holiness" is rooted in the word "holy." It shows the presence of the Divine and distinguishes the sacred from the profane. In this sense "holiness" is the expression to the essential nature of the "sacred." It is therefore to be understood, not as one attribute among other attributes, but as the innermost reality to which all others are related. The term itself cannot express the fullness of the idea that it con-tains. It is only a symbol, a sign, about a reality that goes beyond the possibility of every human word and expression.

Therefore, behind the holy there is always mystery. Holiness and mystery are interrelated. In the pagan world a mystery is accepted as something which is hidden, which is not to be shown, lest it be profaned. Only special people keep the mystery. The greatest mystery is the Divine Being. Therefore mystery is a secret which has great religious meaning. The most sacred place for a religious person is the temple, the altar, the place where there is the presence of the Divine, which is mystery itself. Therefore, if the temple is the place wherein the Divine dwells, it is also the place from whence the holy radiates.

Holiness and the Bible

In the Bible holiness and mystery are connected. God is mystery, and everything around God is mystery, so God is simultaneously holy and mystery. Behind God's holiness and mystery is hidden the divine ontological essence, a totally transcenden-tal reality. Thus mystery and holiness are vehicles of God's revelation. God reveals the divine mystery announcing that he is holy (1 Samuel 2:2).

The idea of the holy derives from the common Semitic root *qds* (Hebrew *qadosh*). The provenance of the term's derivation is believed to be Canaan. Theoretically, the origin of the term contains the idea that the holy is distinct from the commonplace, from the profane. The difference is, in a sense, that it is separated from the other. It can be a person or object. There can be holy ground (Exodus 3:5), or a holy nation (Exodus 19:6). This separation from the other has no moral significance. Rather, the separated object is devoted to God. Israel is holy not because she is better than others but because she is God's choice. So, this nation has no priority over the other nations because of character, but rather priority in time with the mission of preserving the faith in the true God, as a witness to surrounding nations. The holy separates itself from the rest. After choosing the people of Israel, God gave them the law and their moral code. So everything is holy when it is chosen by God and follows the given law. The manifestation of the holy is in the realm of God's will; God decides what is holy.

Thus begins the process of relation—relation between God and the devoted things, God and the devoted people. Therefore, God sanctifies the chosen people with whom he is in relationship. The way of the Israelites to the Holy Land is symbolical of the way of holiness. In order to attain holiness the Israelites are obliged to keep God's commandments and to obey God's will. This is an example of the positive dimension of devotion to God.

But there is also a negative dimension. Everything alien to God is alien to God's holiness. Whatever is not devoted to God has to be eliminated. "And the city shall be accursed, even it, and all that are therein, to the Lord," (Joshua 6:17). God does not allow his people to touch and take unclean things that may tempt them. Otherwise they will become like the pagans, and their sanctity will go away: "As for you, keep away from the things devoted to destruction," (Joshua 6:18).

God is holy (1 Samuel 2:2), so God's people should also be holy. When they do not obey God, they lose their holiness and provoke divine anger (Joshua 7:10). Then the holiness of God is removed and people are without protection. In order to restore their holiness, they must repent. This means that the chosen people must return to God (Hosea 6:1), and in this relationship share in God's holiness (Hebrews 12:10).

God is holy. God creates all things with the opportunity to have real life, to be close to God and to be holy. God wants people to accept divine holiness; he loves them and transmits holiness to them through this love. In this sense all Israel should endeavor to become holy, so that through Israel the whole world, everything, may become holy. God declares: "I am the Lord, and there is no other." God is One and radiates life. As an act of holy love God created the people and everything that supports their life, "formed the earth and made it, . . . formed it to be inhabited" Isaiah 45:18. In this sense the whole world becomes holy. The holiness of God is related to God's creation of life and therefore is dynamic, not static. Through his divine energies, God goes beyond divine transcendence and makes possible relations with created beings.

God is holy because God is love (1 John 4:8, 16). This New Testament revelation makes understandable God's jealousy towards humanity. In the Old Testament God reveals this love for all human beings through Israel. In the New Testament God's love is realized in the person of Jesus Christ. God's love towards people is the same, but its saving power is manifested in different ways. In the Old Testament God is faithful to Israel despite her apostasy. When God's people act wrongly, he exposes their sin. God promises in holiness (Amos 4:2) to remain faithful to the covenant by punishing Israel. Fulfilling the law means life; fulfilling the law means remaining faithful to God. Remaining faithful to God means seeking God permanently, which grants life (Amos 5:6).

In Slavonic holy is *svjat*, and in Sanskrit it means "pure," "shine," and "bright." Everything holy is bright, it shines; that is to say, it is visible, transparent, not hidden.

Its meaning is close to the Akkadian word *qadasu* (to be bright, to shine). The same word in Bulgarian is used also to denote "world," everything that is visible, that can be recognized by the senses and the mind, everything which is intelligible. Therefore holiness is the opposite of darkness. From the same root, the word for priest is also derived. In Slavonic holiness also corresponds to the creative activity of God. One of the very first things which God creates is the light (Genesis 1:3). Light is equivalent to life, so God creates life that exists in its absolute state in the person of Jesus Christ, who is light (John 1:4). Light penetrates everything and makes it transparent. Therefore holiness, understood as light, enlightens everything. People who have holy life, who are enlightened, cannot remain unnoticed (Matthew 5:14–16). Holiness enlightens the people, through spreading Christ's light.

Further, holiness obviously has much in common with truth, life, and knowledge, and in the Old and New Testaments God is revealed as the Giver of Life. The prophet Isaiah speaks about the One, who "created the heavens," who "formed the earth and made it," who "established it," who "formed it to be inhabited!"(Isaiah 45:18). God in the New Testament, as Giver of Life, is fully revealed in the face of the incarnate *Logos*, Jesus Christ, as expressed in the Gospel of John: "I came that they may have life, and have it abundantly" (John 10:10).

The same idea of holiness is behind the term "light." Jesus Christ is life and light simultaneously. He created life which is light. "In him was life and the life was light of all people" (John 1:4). He is the light that shines in the world. This same light shines in the Old Testament as confirmed by God: "I did not speak in secret, in a land of darkness" (Isaiah 45:19). The New Testament reveals it according to new conditions: "The light shines in the darkness, and the darkness did not overcome it" (John 1:5). Therefore, holiness that radiates from God is the same in the Old Testament and New Testament but is revealed in different ways, depending on God's plan for saving the world.

God reveals the Divine Self in order to be known by the chosen people. God's holiness is uniquely God's and is not attainable by the people, but God reveals the Divine Self to them in accordance with divine choice. God's self revelation in the Old Testament is awesome; people are filled with fear and dread (Deuteronomy 11:25). No one can see God. Even those who hear God may die (Exodus 20:19). But God's holiness can be attained only if God so desires, in accordance with the possibility of people's perception. There are different means through which God is revealed; one is through the way of the Old Testament people. The history of revelation is the history of the way of the holiness with God and the people.

God desires that his people, the chosen people, be holy. Therefore, the whole of Israel should become holy. The presence of God among the people makes them holy, but at the same time, only God is absolutely holy. The holiness of the people is dependent on God's holiness, because the primary source of life is God. God is the author of life itself. In this sense the whole meaning of creation is life—perfect life meant to become holy is the purpose of the creation. The holiness of God derives, radiates from, God's life, from the Divine Being. The purpose of the person is to take part in God's given life, to strive to become holy. The one who attains holiness becomes perfect. This is what Jesus Christ wishes from his followers: "Be perfect, therefore, as your heavenly Father is perfect" (Matthew 5:48).

The Christian Mind and the Ethical Approach to Holiness

Ethics is a human concept embodying a sense of utilitarianism: we behave in accordance with our own best interests; we prefer certain behaviors, such as seeking good relations with the others. Such an approach is more or less the approach of a secularized Christianity: "I do good things because it is satisfying me." Such behavior is far from the Christian deep understanding of sacrifice. Love separated from Christianity becomes egoistic, self-centered—*cosmophilia.*

However, the Orthodox ascetics did not abide by this ethic. Their path was intended to attain holiness, to be on the way toward God, toward perfection. In drawing nearer to God, through grace God sanctified them and the world around them. A sign of this perfecting process is peace of heart, which means that God already dwells within. Having peace in one's heart is already the path of salvation, a sign of holiness. Peace is attained not by ethical prescriptions, but by following Christ and the grace of the Holy Spirit. This is the advice of the saints towards those who are looking for salvation. St Seraphim of Sarov stated, "Acquire inward peace, and thousands around you will find their salvation." On this path there are no ethical guideposts. Everything issues from the heart and moves outward, not vice versa.

In ethical relationships there are no sacrifices, because ethical prescriptions usually are aimed at social benefits. Although often presented broadly as Christian values in order to be accepted, ethical values have utilitarian aims. Their goal is good, a perfect society, and a frame of reference that will grant a good life for the individual. A proper societal framework affords the individual "the good life." In such an understanding ethics becomes the internal fabric of the society. The individual obeys secular laws and principals for the common good. The freedom of the person in such a way is limited.

This is one of the ways in which the secular and Orthodox understanding of the way to perfection differ. Secular behavior strives ultimately to build a perfect society. Christian behavior purposes to build a perfect person. The methodologies are different. Socialism is a secular Western idea, therefore it can succeed only in the West, not in the East. In the East this idea was transformed and taken as religion (*Berdyaev*)[1] and failed. Western societies are attempting to build this social dream more precisely than the East. This is the easier way, the secular way.

In the Orthodox understanding, the way to perfection is different; it concentrates not on society, but on the person. Collective salvation is not promised in the gospel. The promise of the gospel is for personal salvation through relations with others. Jesus Christ, as a true man and true God, embodies the fullness of God, as a person. Perfect personhood can be attained only through life in Christ in the church. "Apart from him we can do nothing" (Jn 15:5), because he is "the Way, and the Truth, and the Life" (Jn 14:6). Following this Way everyone who is seeking perfection becomes holy. Being holy, he or she radiates in such a way that the surrounding society becomes holy. As people are enlightened, the society of holy people is increased. But this kind of society can only be the church. The church is the true focal point of the reality and in the church are the realization of spiritual perfection and the attainment of holiness.

Nowadays, some ethical visions and patterns are closer to the Old Testament understanding of salvation—salvation for the society (Israel) as a whole. Here is the cornerstone of the Old Testament interpretation of salvation, the one is not more important than the many. In the New Testament, however, there is a strong emphasis on the value of the individual (Mt 6:26, Mk 8:36), yet not solely at the expense of the whole world.

In modern ethical systems, the individual has freedom, but at the same time cannot contradict the ethical, social paradigm. In this sense there is no place for holiness. Ethical rules that are more or less anthropocentric and autonomous govern the individual. From a Christian and biblical perspective, holiness eclipses such ethical paradigms because the essence of its relationship and strivings issue from the personhood of God.

God as Trinity, as Three Persons in One, has relationships within the Godhead itself. The Three Persons in One are in relationship with one another, in perfect agreement, and this relationship is based on perfect love (1 Jn 4:8 ff.). Love exists only when it has an object towards which it is oriented. Therefore, God's love is relational. It is relational among the Persons of the Trinity in the Godhead, between God and the created world, between God and his people. So, the church, established by the Triune God, as catholic and universal, in its essence is relational. In this sense, John Zizioulas writes: "The Church is catholic not as community which aims at a certain ethical achievement (being open, serving the world, and so forth, but as a community which experiences and reveals the unity of all creation insofar as this unity constitutes a reality in the person of Christ."[2]

Viewed from this perspective, Orthodox spirituality whispers not a word about ethics. It is easier to speak about the Way—the way of perfection. Examples in the Orthodox tradition are not abstract values and ideas, but virtues fulfilled in an enlightened, holy people. Holiness is acquired not through the secular society but through the church. The society is sanctified by the holy people—members of the church. Secular society itself is not greater than the sum of its members. It does not have a real relationship with God. Only the person relates to God. The more people that have a real relation with God, the more people that have a holy life, and the more the society becomes holy and bears the fruits of God's grace.

The ethical approach to holiness is not the church's approach, nor is it even biblical. Ethics has largely to do with solving sociological problems. As John D. Zizioulas writes: "Sociological views of catholicity must be only derived views and not vice versa"[3] Ethics provide more or less rules, and is on a level that is not necessarily that of Scripture. In the Bible and in the church there are moral problems, which are spiritual in essence and depth, but they may not be ethical in nature. Confusion can result when people mix ethical and spiritual problems. Indeed, ethical problems may issue from spiritual ones, but one may not assume that every ethical problem has a corresponding and obligatory spiritual problem. Therefore, it is precarious to attempt to solve spiritual problems found in the Old Testament on the basis of ethical systems, as some theologians are trying to do today.

A person under the Old Covenant did not merely maintain a certain ethic but wanted to live according to God's will. The person strove to follow God's will in accordance with the historical situation, the social environment, and his or her own perception. Ethical problems, which modern scholars "discover" in the Old Testament texts, did not exist as such in the mind of the Old Testament person. The goal was not a certain ethic but the Person of God. If a person attained a relationship with God, he or she at the same time solved ethical problems! Conversely, if ethics becomes the priority, or is used as a means to attain to God, to follow God's ways, ethics become an obstacle. Ethics affirm persons in their way toward God, providing them with a framework of human understanding and practice of what God desires of them.

The purpose of the Old Testament was not primarily to give information about morality, but to provide standards which, when pondered and absorbed into the mind, suggested the pattern or shape of a life lived in the presence of God.

The people of God were those who keep the covenant with God, who followed the divine commandments. They were holy because they obeyed God's will. The consciousness of the people about God's holiness is kept in the law, the Holy Scripture, in the tradition. This fence kept the chosen people from the temptations of the gods of the neighboring peoples. If the chosen people worshiped God in the correct way, it meant that they knew God and participated in divine holiness, God's gift to them. Their "spirituality" was a matter of lifestyle, not just particular rulings on "moral issues." "Torah" is a system by which to live one's whole of life in the presence of God, rather than a set of detailed regulations to cover every individual situation in which a moral ruling might be required. The main desire and drive of a person in a covenantal relationship with God was to present one's life into the hands of God, under God's will, control, and ruling.

In this same sense one cannot speak about ethics in the New Testament. In Christ's teaching there is no ethical system. Instead, he brings God closer to people. "For in him the whole fullness of deity dwells bodily" (Colossians 2:9). When we speak about Christianity today and about its moral values but do not live them, when we do not live in Christ, we make of his teaching an ideology. In making it an ideology we secularize it. Christianity thus becomes an ethical system useful in producing "good results." In the Christian world an ethic is the secondary product. But nowadays, after secularization, ethics is a prime principle of social relations. Today, with the globalization of the world, a global ethic is needed. Sooner or later such an ethic may be established, but it surely will not satisfy everyone in the global village.

In the New Testament the holiness of God is revealed in three ways: God is holy (John 17:11), is totally transcendental and all-powerful, and is the eschatological Judge (Revelation 4:8, 6:10). God's holiness as revealed to people is relational. It is uncovered or revealed when one pronounces the divine name (Luke 1:49); when there is concern about God's law (Romans 7:12); about the spirituality of the law (14); when the holiness of the Old Testament is reaffirmed; and when the covenant in the New Testament is established (Luke 1:72). Following this perception of holiness, everything which relates to God is holy – the prophets, the writers of the Scriptures (Luke 1:70; Mark 6:20; Romans 1:2), God's temple, the heavenly Jerusalem (1 Corinthians 3:17; Revelation 21:2) and the chosen of God as followers of Christ (1 Pet 1:15).

The holiness of God is hypostasized. Through Jesus Christ human beings become potential objects of the holiness. Jesus was conceived by the Holy Spirit. Therefore the holiness of Jesus Christ is relational to the person of God and to the people who accept

God as Lord. This act of opening the door of holiness starts with baptism and chrismation and is permanently actualized through receiving Holy Communion. In the New Testament holiness is perfect and absolute in the person of Christ. He is holy in all his nature. From one perspective he is the true Son of God (Matthew 3:17), from another he is the true Son of Man (Matthew 11:27; Luke 10:22). Having in his nature the fullness of God and at the same time the fullness of humankind, he becomes the bridge through which the way of holiness is opened. Holiness issues from God to the people through Jesus Christ. Through him people acquire holiness and come closer to God.

Holiness and the Church

According to the Nicene Creed, the church is holy. This holiness issues from the reality that its founder is holy. Jesus Christ as Head of the church sanctifies her. His sanctifying act, however, is not only as God but also as a human being. In this sense the holiness of the church is determined not only from the total presence of God but also from the total presence of humanness, of the human essence in the person of Jesus Christ. So the holiness of the church issues from the Triune God, One essence in Three Persons. At the same time, existence of the church is possible only because of the Incarnation and the union of the Logos with human nature. This union between God and humanity in the person of Jesus Christ is a full act of resurrected human nature. Following the true life of Christ in the church, every Christian becomes a partaker in God's holiness. Such participation in this holiness, however, depends on the spiritual growth of every Christian. All members of the church are invited to become holy, they are called to be holy. As members of the church, they become holy to a certain degree, but they have not attained perfect holiness. They are on the way to becoming holy and perfect.

God's holiness is transmitted through the mysteries of the church. All those who participate in the mysteries and the things that surround God become sanctified. The deeper one participates in the mysteries of the church, the deeper one's spiritual life grows. Then comes the moment of *theosis*, attaining grace that transforms one into a holy person. Such a person by his/her relationship with God through prayer and the spiritual life, becomes a saint, holy. This is the way toward holiness in the church. Outside the church there is no holiness. Therefore the church was established to give everybody the chance to be saved, to partake of the divine. Everyone in the church is called to transformation, to become a new person (Ephesians 2:15). Becoming a new person entails growing in the likeness of God, the transfiguration of oneself, and the world around.

Holiness in itself is also action, effort. Only through the efforts of the whole person can holiness be attained. Even so, it is God's gift. The result of all spiritual effort, attainable by everyone willing, is to love—to love God, the neighbor, and the church. In the act of love resides real holiness. In this sense Christ himself is the example, who: "loved the church and gave himself up for her, in order to make her holy by cleansing her with the washing of water by the word, so as to present the church to himself in splendor, without a spot or wrinkle or anything of the kind—yes, so that she may be holy and without blemish" (Ephesians 5:25–27).

Holiness, therefore, penetrates everything. Those who attain holiness become saints. Their inner life is transformed. Everything in them, every thought is oriented to the Lord. Their lives are defined by the prayer. They pray constantly so they are in permanent relationship with the Lord. Life itself becomes a prayer. Being in such a relationship with God, they spread holiness to others and also to the entire world, the cosmos. Being closer to God, they attain possibilities that are far beyond usual life. They influence the people and even physical environment around them, because they are already reconciled with the surrounding world, with nature. Abba Isaac witnesses: "the humble man approaches the destructive animals and as soon as they see him, their wildness is calmed, and they approach him as their master and they wag their heads and lick his hands and feet, because they sense that he has upon himself that fragrance which Adam gave off before the Fall. And that which was taken away from us at that time, Jesus Christ gave back to us anew through his presence on earth, granting a sweet-smelling fragrance to mankind."[4]

As regards holiness and the saints of the church, we turn to the Homilies of St Macarius: "The bodies of the saints, being members of the Christ, must needs be what Christ is, and nothing else."[5] So that these are the fruits of the holiness—attaining the fullness of life, life eternal, becoming members of God's kingdom here on earth, where it is among us (Luke 17:21).

Hence, the way of the holiness is channeled only through the church, because our Lord Jesus Christ is the Head of the church (Ephesians 4:15; Colossians 1:18), and through the presence of the Holy Spirit in the church. Things that are unthinkable in the Old Testament in the church become reality. In the Old Testament the word "holy" is used only for the chosen people, for particular places, and in an eschatological sense. In the New Testament church, the Christians are holy. Therefore, it is possible for everyone to become holy. Through Christ's divine and human nature, the possibility is given to everyone, who participates in the sacraments of the church, to become holy. Of course, this holiness is not absolute. It is received through the life in the church. Thus holiness always is relational—between God and the people (1 John 4:20).

Life in Christ and the way of holiness are the way of sacrifice. To begin the path toward holiness one should sacrifice love of the world, of sin. Christians are a "chosen race, a royal priesthood, a holy nation," a people who are called "out of darkness" into the light of God (1 Peter 2:9). To attain holiness means to pass through suffering. The apostles viewed the way of the holiness as the true life of a Christian. St Peter demanded: "If any of you suffer as a Christian, do not consider it a disgrace, but glorify God because you bear this name" (1 Peter 4:16).

Holiness and the Contemporary World

Modern humankind is "secular-minded." The role of Christianity in the world is decreasing. Therefore, we speak today about the post-Christian world. People concentrate mostly on material things. With globalization, the minds of the people are enslaved very easily, in part due to the great influence of technology, communications, and electronic networks. Every part of human life becomes dependent on these influences. Human beings voluntarily involved in this process finally become obedient to them. Every day and every hour the freedom of persons is diminished. All people of the world become more and more interdependent. At the same time people have to sustain this snowballing development. Objects of the world attract the whole imagination of people with less and less room for prayer and for God. The human mind is engaged with the external world and with solving problems that are external in nature, thus increasing the gap between the human heart and God.

We see these trends everywhere, which are quite the opposite of holiness. Today's world seems to create its own secular "holiness." This trend unfortunately seems irreversible. It is described in a document of Orthodox theologians: "the secular news of the mass media has taken the place of prayer and substituted the need to listen to the voice of God. We can observe how men and women of the twentieth century desperately look to the arts, eroticism, drugs, technology, or different forms of revolution— as substitutes for God. For many the idea of God has become meaningless, the only reality and value being the world and the search for material progress. In the face of this situation our words have become empty."[6] This new secular "holiness" has its own attractiveness, its own philosophy, and its own "spirituality." It can be found in the new literature, arts, music, fashion, and so forth. In this kind of fallen "holiness" one can find incarnated ideas of the evil. Evil creates its own cult with its "clergy" and worshippers. Evil attracts, and many voluntarily become its followers.

What can be done in this seemingly helpless situation? Can such a world accommodate Christian holiness? Many people are facing these questions, and the answers are not easy. We have to go back to the principles of Christianity. The Christian faith is personal. Salvation is personal. Holiness is personal. All three are personal yet communal. When we are personally in a right relation with God, when we have been saved, we will then help our neighbors to find their salvation. This is one way the community of the church grows and becomes holy, living the faith in Christ. This kind of a Christian community becomes "holy" in the primary sense of the word, separated from the secular world in order to live in Christ. The community of faith is "in" the world but not "of" the world. This community is distinguished from the secular world through its faith, behavior, and mind. At the same time it lives in this world and witnesses to the faith, lighting the way. It opens the way of true holiness in the alien world and offers the opportunity of faith to those "of" the world. In this sense today we emulate the life of Christians during the first centuries of the church. Christians conquered the world not by structures, not by external force, but through the power of the Spirit through which the holiness of the church was spread.

Conclusion

Essentially Christianity is concerned not with quantity, but with quality (Matthew 18:20). God's holiness radiates from heaven, through the Holy Spirit and the sacraments of the church, through the saints of the church, through the life in Christ of every Christian. Therefore, it is relational. Despite the visible advances of evil, faith is firm and "the gates of hell cannot prevail against it" (Matthew 16:18). The power of Christianity is in its weakness (in the eyes of the secular world). Holiness is not visible for those who close their spiritual eyes.

The situation in countries that were previously communist is encouraging. Viewed from the vantage point of institutions, from that of the structure, it is difficult to say that the church is alive. This is the case in Bulgaria today. But being in the midst of the people, one can find how the grace of God works in their hearts. God can reveal holiness which one never expects. Here is the highest point of the mystery of faith— the opening of hearts and the receiving of salvation. This way of the holiness is not visible, but it can be revealed. It emerges in the hearts of the faithful, following the principle of the Orthodox Church—to propose, not to impose. Orthodox spirituality is the cornerstone of the Orthodox faith. It is the eternal in the temporal, the unchangeable in the changing.

With the growth of the secularization and the strength of the external powers of the world, the grace and power of God are growing among the faithful at the same time. This is because God in the person of Jesus Christ promised: "Take courage; I have conquered the world" (John 16:33) and "I am with you always, to the end of the age" (Matthew 28:20).

Endnotes

[1] Nikolai Aleksandrovich Berdyaev (1874–1948) was one of the greatest religious philosophers of the twentieth century. Though his origin was from a family of nobility, as a young person he became a Marxist and was imprisoned in 1898. At the beginning of the twentieth century, together with many young intellectuals, he converted from Marxist ideology to religion. After the Bolshevik revolution in 1917, he and many other Russian intellectuals were expelled by Lenin from Russia. Berdyaev went to Paris and became famous with his severe criticism of Marxism. It may be that he is the best critic of Marxist ideology. He considered Marxism as a quasi-religious system and created a brilliant analysis of the social and religious roots of the communism in Russia and of its totalitarian character. One of the best books on this topic is *Istoki I Smisl Russkogo Komunizma* (*The Origin of Russian Communism*), in Russian. In 1947, he was awarded the title Doctor *Honoris Causa* from Cambridge University, England. During the communist regime in the previous Soviet Union his books were forbidden and, if someone was found to have them, he/she could be imprisoned. See Nikolai Aleksandrovich Berdyaev, *Tsarstvo Duha I Tsarstvo Kessarya* (*Kingdom of the Spirit and Kingdom of the Caesar*), in Russian (Paris, 1951), chapter 3, p. 48 ff.; *Smisl Istorii* (The Meaning of History), in Russian, Paris, 1969, p. 116, ff.

[2] John D. Zizioulas, *Being As Communion* (Crestwood, NY, 1985), 159; cf. 214 ff.

[3] Ibid., 158, note 68.

[4] Antonios Alevisopoulos, *The Orthodox Church, Its Faith, Worship and Life* (Athens, 1994), 107–108.

[5] Quoted from Bishop Kallistos Ware, *The Orthodox Way* (Crestwood, New York, 1998), 127.

[6] "Preaching and Teaching the Christian Faith Today," *Orthodox Thought, Reports of Orthodox Consultations* (Geneva: World Council of Churches, 1983), 65.

Other Eastern Sources and John Wesley

7

A Testimony to Christianity as Transfiguration: The Macarian Homilies and Orthodox Spirituality

Hieromonk Alexander Golitzin

It is an honor and pleasure for me to be part of a discussion which features the names of so many scholars who are either acquaintances of some years' standing, or else whose works I have long admired without the benefit of personal encounter. I must also confess a certain sense of inadequacy. I am not at all familiar with one half of our theme, that of Wesleyan spirituality, and am consequently obliged to take refuge in the hope that the nature of my subject will at least serve to provide some material for further thought and discussion. Kallistos Ware, for instance, begins his "Preface" to the recent, Paulist Press edition of *The Fifty Spiritual Homilies* with a quotation from John Wesley, "I have read Macarius and my heart sang," while Ernst Benz and Herman Doerries wrote some years ago on Macarian influences in, respectively, Anglo-Saxon Protestant thought and continental Pietism.[1] So it is at least clear that others have felt that my author does supply a number of points of contact between the Christian East and the later, post-Reformation West.

Given my limitations, I am obliged to focus on "Macarius" himself, with an eye perhaps toward pointing on occasion to his relationship with and influence on certain central themes, or, to borrow an expression from Jaroslav Pelikan, "melodies" within the harmonies and, once in a while, disharmonies of the theological and ascetic-mystical tradition in the Orthodox East[2]—thus, for example, the "transfiguration" of this paper's title. I could as easily have said "transformation" or "deification," or else, particularly given the two traditions meeting here this week, "holiness" or "sanctification," since I take the transfiguration of my title as inclusive for "Macarius" of all of these.

To touch briefly on some of the points to follow, he understands Christianity as the renewal of the human being. God in Christ has entered into our world and, in baptism, into the Christian's body and soul. The latter is thus, in potential, the royal throne of Christ (a note I shall come back to in detail below), and to work toward the conscious fulfillment of that potential, that is, to a loving awareness and even perhaps vision of the indwelling glory of Christ in the Spirit, is the whole aim of Christian life on this side of the *eschaton*. Hope and longing for that encounter engage one in a total effort of moral and psychological reform, an effort which, once committed to, reveals in its turn the limitations of any purely human effort, and so the necessity of grace to overcome the force of sin rooted in the soul. Humility, thus, and constant prayer provide the necessary ground for that stress on the visitation of grace for which the *Macariana* are primarily known: the light-filled experience (*peira*) of the divine presence "perceptibly and with complete assurance" (*en pasei aisthesei kai plerophoriai*).[3] This program was not without controversy, but by way of arriving at that discussion perhaps we should have a look first at "Macarius" himself, at least as much as can be known about him, together with a few more details of his thought.

The *Macarian Homilies* were written in Greek at the end of the fourth century, but we do not have any exemplars in that language earlier than four medieval Byzantine collections, of which three (including the best known *Fifty Spiritual Homilies*) exist in critical editions.[4] We do not know, moreover, who the author of the Macarian Homilies was. He was certainly not Macarius the Great of Egypt, though it was under the latter's name that his writings were eventually to find a safe haven.[5] In this respect, our anonymous author has much in common with another late-fourth-century monastic writer, Evagrius of Pontus (†399), several of whose works were also handed down under the protection of someone else's name.[6] In each case the pseudonymity was a posthumous device, and likely a necessary one, since both writers were controversial and even judged (if not always accurately or fairly, particularly in our writer's case) to have been heretical. In spite of those condemnations, Evagrius and Macarius—to give our author the name he has gone by for centuries—can fairly be called the most influential of the fourth century monastic writers. So influential, in fact, that it is no exaggeration to say that together they gave to the spirituality of the Christian East the shape which it has held to the present day. "Evagrius," in the words of a contemporary scholar who reflects the modern academic consensus, "established the categories; Macarius . . . provided the affective content."

While I am myself not entirely happy with casting Evagrius as the mystic of the head and Macarius as the avatar of mystical *Gefühl*, I will admit that there is considerable justice to seeing the works of the two men as "mutually corrective and complementary."[7] Evagrius is the theoretician, often (though not always) cool and even remote in tone, whose preferred diction features the brief, dense, and highly allusive sentences which he adapted from the style of biblical wisdom literature and contemporary, Cynic discourse, and which he intended his disciples and other readers to ponder slowly in the solitude of their desert hermitages.[8] Macarius, though he is also clearly a monastic *geron* or *staretz*, a charismatic and inspired elder charged with the guidance of souls, is much more the preacher intent on encouraging, exhorting, warning, and persuading.[9] His language in consequence is open and immediately accessible, flooded with imagery borrowed from the Scriptures, contemporary society, and the natural world. He is also, unlike Evagrius in the latter's retreat in Egypt's empty wastes, fully immersed in the life of his own and related communities in the heavily populated regions of upper Mesopotamia (or southern Asia Minor), laying down a rule for his spiritual children, engaging in question and answer sessions with his own and other monks, sometimes fighting with the local hierarchy, defending himself and his followers, arguing for his understanding of the faith, and correcting other ascetics whose thinking and behavior he believes has strayed from the ways of Christian life and into demonic delusions.[10] Macarius is, in addition, clearly a man in whom several different Christian (and even pre-Christian) currents of tradition converge. He shares with Evagrius in his debts to the Christian Platonism of Alexandria through Clement and especially Origen, and—as appears increasingly clear—in personal ties with the Cappadocian Fathers, but he combines with these connections the different, Syrian Christian currents represented by Aphrahat and Ephrem, by the likewise anonymous and ascetic work called the *Book of Steps* or *Liber Graduum*, and by the encratism of the Thomas tradition and of the wandering Manichaean ascetics, together with elements from Jewish and Jewish-Christian apocalyptic and related literature.[11] Yet Evagrius may himself also, less the specifically Syrian element, have been aware of and responding to lines of biblical exegesis related to apocalyptic and rabbinical thought.[12] All in all, the differences in style, personality, and background are real enough, but do not point necessarily to the head versus heart distinction so favored by modern scholarship ever since Irenée Hausherr's famous article sixty years ago delineating the purported "schools" of Eastern Christian spirituality, according to which schema Evagrius represented the "school of intellect" and Macarius that of "feeling"; a taxonomy which is not a little—and, to my mind, suspiciously—reminiscent of the "intellective" and "affective" labels long applied to such Western Medieval writers as, say, Eckhardt and other Dominican Rhinelanders, on the one hand, and Bernard, together perhaps with the Franciscans, on the other.[13]

One area where we can speak of a certain real difference in the doctrines that the two men teach concerns the ultimate role and eschatological destiny of the body. Put simply, for Evagrius the body has no role in the world to come while for Macarius it does. Both men teach an assimilation to the presence and activity of the living God, and both teach the vision of God as light, but Evagrius has no place for the transformation or transfiguration of the body.[14] The latter, together with the lower faculties of the soul, are for him providential and necessary, but, rather like booster rockets in a space-shuttle launch, are to be jettisoned once their purpose has been performed. They propel the initial phase of the ascent—or return—to God.[15] Macarius, though certainly also a Platonist and devoted to the allegorizing exegesis of Christian Alexandria, remains too firmly rooted in biblical realism to dispense with the body's share in the kingdom of heaven. Rather than an ultimately disembodied spirit (or *nous*), as in Evagrius, he sees the transfigured human being at the *eschaton* as one in whom the illumined and glorified soul shares its splendor and light with the risen body. The Gospel account of Christ's Transfiguration on Mount Tabor serves as the image and promise both of the *visio dei* accorded the soul in this life, and of the eschatological transformation of soul and body: "Just as when the Lord had ascended the mountain He 'was transfigured' into His divine glory, so are there souls which even in the present time are illumined and glorified with Him, while on the last day their bodies as well will be glorified and flashing with light" (I.18.7.3). What is visible to the eyes of the illumined soul now and within, that is, the abiding and glory of Christ and the Spirit in the "inner man," will then become visible outside, in the very limbs of the transformed body.[16]

Macarius' thought turns constantly around this duality or tension of "inner" and "outer," and it is always the former to which he accords priority. He uses a number of different words for it: heart, soul, *nous* or intellect, and, after the usage of St Paul (and of Origen!), "inner man." Very occasionally he distinguishes among them, as for example when he speaks of the *nous* as the "eye" of the heart or soul, but more often he appears to employ them interchangeably as rough equivalents. The characterization of his thought as a mysticism of "the heart," at least insofar as heart is understood as denoting a primarily emotive or affective emphasis, strikes me therefore as misleading, or at least as one sided.[17] What he is concerned with first and foremost is the inner life where emotions, appetites, thought, and will all have their place, and perhaps most especially the will, the *autexousion* or capacity for self-determination.[18] It is the inner life of the human being, after all, which for him is first and most radically affected by the original Fall. It is there, within the soul, that Satan and his angels have set up their dwellings and palaces amid the cloud or, to use Macarius' own favored phrase, the "veil" of disordered drives and appetites which he covers with the term, "passions." The veil of the passions brought about by Adam's Fall and the devil's inhabitation prevent communion and conversation with God.[19] They block the vision of and share in divine glory that was Adam's original inheritance, his royal "robe" and "crown."

The robe and crown of divine glory are ancient themes in Jewish and Syrian Christian literature.[20] So is the language of the warfare between God and devil, light and dark, and of the "two ways" which Macarius also draws on in order to describe the post-lapsarian, human condition.[21] Stripped of participation in divine glory and life, naked in its own inadequacy, humanity is in a state of constant conflict in a disordered and perishing world. Though the power of self-determination, the capacity to choose the right and refuse the evil, never departs us (Macarius is the heir of such as Ephrem Syrus as much as of Origen in his refusal to accept fatalism of any kind), the cure for our condition is beyond our powers. We can of our own volition neither remove the veil that the evil one has wrapped around us, nor heal what Macarius calls the "incurable passions" (*ta aniata pathe*), nor dry up the "bubbling spring" of evil impulses which lies in the deeps of the heart or soul.[22] More powerfully and realistically, I think, than Evagrius, our Syrian Christian ascetic is aware of the power of evil. He is, though, marginally more optimistic than an Augustine. He believes that the human being can refuse to *do* what is sin*ful*. The acts of the body are largely within our control. What we cannot do, in his view, is rid ourselves of sin within the soul, of the condition that renders us opaque to the vision and indwelling of God. In regard to the healing of the inner life, all that the human being can do is cry out for divine help.[23]

So it is for God to act on our behalf in order to cure and to restore. Macarius' Christology is entirely orthodox and traditionally Eastern—if I may speak so broadly —in its emphasis on the ontological effects of the Word of God's incarnation, death, and resurrection. *Theosis,* deification, is quite as much the point of Christ's saving action for Macarius as it is for Athanasius, for Basil the Great, or for Ephrem Syrus.[24] Perhaps, though, we find somewhat more emphasis in his writings on Christ as precisely healer or physician, *iatros,* of the soul than we do in other Greek writers. The Lord as *osyo,* healer, is a very ancient and popular Syrian Christian theme, though certainly not absent in other early Christian writers.[25] In any case, it is only in and through Christ dwelling within the soul in the power of the Holy Spirit that the wellsprings of evil can be dried up, the veil removed, that we may be transfigured "from glory to glory" through looking on the "light of the face of Christ within the heart."

The allusion just now to St Paul, specifically to 2 Corinthians 3:7–4:6, is deliberate. I might even venture to suggest that the whole Macarian corpus comprises a kind of extended meditation on this scriptural passage. Macarius seems to understand it as encapsulating virtually all the essentials of what he has to say to his monks.[26] It includes the contrasts between the Old and New Covenants, between veiled and unveiled, between outward and inward, between body and soul, and between Moses as type of the salvation to come and Christ and the Spirit as its fulfillment. Even more, it speaks of the change, alteration, or transfiguration—*metabole, alloiosis, metamorphosis*—which occurs in the Christian soul through the indwelling Spirit, and of the glory (*doxa*) of God in which the soul and ultimately the body are called to share. Finally, there is the overlap, I might say, between Christ and the Holy Spirit, which is also a feature of the *Homilies*. All of these notes occur repeatedly. The obedience enjoined by the Law was an outward thing whereas, Macarius observes, in Christianity "everything is within (*endon*)."[27] The whole of Israel's sacred history, of God's relations with his chosen people, becomes thus for the Christian the story of the soul's relation with Christ.[28]

The echo of Alexandrian spiritual exegesis from Philo through Origen, mediated in Macarius' case perhaps especially through Gregory of Nyssa, is surely unmistakable. I should like, though, to underline what I take to be the *Homilies'* particular emphasis on the Old Testament motifs of the promised land and holy city, Jerusalem, and of the tabernacle and temple as the place of God's abiding. Christ is the reality of these images. He is the heavenly fatherland and the celestial city, the place of God's presence and—to borrow an expression from the Targumim, since I think the traditions the latter represent are close to Macarius' own heart—the "glory of the *Shekinah*" which dwells there and fills all with light.[29] This presence or abiding, the literal sense of *Shekinah,* which comes to the Christian through baptism and the gift of the Holy Spirit, renders the soul in its turn the city and temple of God, at least in potential.[30] Here we arrive at once at the place of the ascetical life for Macarius, and at the question of the church's sacraments and their relation to his thought. I will begin with the first: *ascesis* as the action of the body and soul, cooperating with divine grace, in order to ascend the inner Sinai and arrive at the conscious perception, and even the vision, of the Presence Who, even now, awaits the believer within the latter's heart of hearts, in its innermost recesses, at the sanctuary and altar of the soul.

Cooperation, *synergia*, is certainly a key term for Macarius, as it is for the Eastern Christian tradition generally.[31] If true healing and ultimate transformation come about only through the power of God, the human will is still required to contribute its part. Testing and trials are of the essence of being a Christian. We are called patiently to endure sufferings, and thereby to imitate the passion and death of Christ. Macarius returns again and again to this theme in his answers and sermons to his monks. Never, he insists, is the Christian—a term which he uses, in the fashion of Basil the Great, as more or less synonymous with, and even preferable to, "monk" or "solitary" (*monazon*)—going to be without trials in this life.[32] There is no security here below. All is struggle, though by God's mercy the glory and splendor of heaven may occasionally be glimpsed. Furthermore, as one of his homilies puts it:

> The warfare is . . . double for Christians . . . For after someone [i.e., a monk] has with-
> drawn from parents, spouse, possessions, comfort, fatherland, and customs. . . . then,
> when he has gathered himself together and is concentrating on the Lord, and after he
> has so to speak pried open the inside of his soul, he faces another war, a great battle
> against opposing powers, against invisible enemies and the activities of darkness,
> against which he is obliged to take up heavenly armor in order to be able to emerge
> victorious.[33]

This battle, he continues, is "inside, in the soul, in the thoughts."[34] The inner and
deeper warfare requires divine assistance, precisely the "heavenly armor" mentioned
above and borrowed from Ephesians 6:14–17. Heavenly aid begins and ends with love,
the yearning desire for Christ which is at once the expression of the soul's own deepest longings and, simultaneously, the Lord's gift and presence. Like Origen and Gregory of Nyssa, Macarius uses *eros* and *agape* effectively as synonyms.[35] They express
at bottom the dynamism of both the Creator-Redeemer, and of the created human
being in process of redemption and, for Gregory and Macarius together in conscious
opposition to Origen, in the everlasting growth of beatitude.[36] If love is the alpha and
omega of the virtues, in between come the others: faith, repentance, hope, endurance,
patience, long-suffering, meekness, humility, dispassion (*apatheia*), and, beginning as
willed activity and ending as divine gift, perseverance in prayer.[37]

The emphasis on prayer will surely remind us of Evagrius, as must Macarius'
insistence on the mutually supporting chain of the virtues, his emphasis on the battle
with the "thoughts," *logismoi,* and the value he accords dispassion. There are, just as
clearly, important differences. First, there is next to none of Evagrius' careful effort to
systematize these elements, most of them held in common virtually throughout the
more learned monastic literature of the day, and arrange them into a precisely articulated pedagogy of the soul.[38] Again, we find here the contrast between the theoretician and the preacher.

Second, certain of Macarius' emphases are typical of the specifically Syrian asceticism of his day and long afterwards. At this point we arrive at the matter of his alleged
"heresy": the monastic movement or, perhaps better, bundle of ascetical beliefs and
tendencies which the church hierarchy of Syria and Asia Minor condemned in a series
of councils at the end of the fourth and beginning of the fifth centuries under the label
of "Messalianism." The word comes from the Syriac "to pray" (*tslo,* hence the partici-
ple, *metsalyane,* the "praying ones"), and it was the bishops' contention that these
monks' emphasis on prayer and dispassion had led them into error. For our purposes
here, we may single out the accusations that the monks claimed that human beings
are entirely subjected to the devil, that the latter's presence within the soul could not
be eradicated by baptism, but only by prayer and by the subsequent indwelling of the
Spirit which, once given, assured a permanent state of dispassion and freedom from
sin. Together with these charges, we also find the assertion that these ascetics claimed
a vision of the Holy Spirit, indeed, even of the Trinity, with their bodily eyes.[39] Now,
it is beyond doubt that certain of these propositions were culled from the *Macarian
Homilies,* in particular the co-indwelling of sin and grace even after baptism, insistence on the importance of prayer, and—though only in a falsified way where the texts

were clearly taken out of context—in the possibility and experience of divine light.[40]

While there may doubtless have been individuals and even groups who espoused the extremes these condemnations describe, it is also the case that Macarius himself was, on the one hand, struggling against certain of these ideas—at least in their cruder form—among his monks, and, on the other hand, that both he and they were heirs of long-standing elements in Syrian, particularly Syriac-speaking Christianity. Here I have especially in mind the twin emphases on asceticism and pneumatology, together with a frankly visionary element, so prominent in, for example, the *Acts of Thomas.* These are as well to the fore in such later and more "orthodox" fourth-century writers as Aphraates and (a little more controversially) the *Liber Graduum,* and which at the same time draw on ancient currents dating from Second Temple Judaism, notably the literature of apocalyptic.[41] As one recent scholar remarked, with perhaps a little exaggeration: "Messalianism is originally no more and no less than an obvious irruption of Syrian Christianity, and it could have been taken as heterodox only from the narrow perspective of an imperial orthodoxy."[42] Somewhat less fiercely, Columba Stewart has convincingly demonstrated that much of the Messalian controversy derived from what amounted to a kind of culture clash: Greek-speaking bishops confronted with, and reacting without either much sympathy or comprehension to a phenomenon and vocabulary whose origins lay in the Semitic earth of Syria-Palestine.[43] Macarius, we might say, was caught in the middle and branded quite indiscriminately with the same stigma that was attached with a trifle more justice to some of his more extreme countrymen. We have to thank those early generations of monks, wiser in at least this regard than their bishops, who sheltered the *Homilies* under the protective cover of a famous and uncontroversial name for the fact that these invaluable texts survived at all—and, indeed, more than survived, since they have continued to nourish and influence both Eastern and, later on, Western Christians to the present day.

To speak of Macarius as a man in the middle is apt in a couple of ways. He is, as I have noted, someone who stands at the confluence of several different currents of Christian thought and tradition, though to what degree he is doing so consciously I will leave for others to determine. He is also, however, on occasion and very consciously facing in two directions at once: toward his monks, whom he is trying to guide and whose enthusiasms he is often seeking to temper and direct; and toward the bishops and other church authorities whose concerns for the sacramental and doctrinal integrity of the church he is seeking to satisfy, while at the same time defending as vigorously as he can, and often rather sharply, those elements of faith and practice which the heresiologists have fingered as doctrinal error, most notably the certainty which he shares with his monks that it is possible to experience and even—if only momentarily—to see God while still in this present life.[44] Regarding, for example, the debate around the Trinity which so preoccupied the fourth century, he is careful to include a confession of faith at the beginning of his *Great Letter,* otherwise devoted to setting out a community rule for his monks, which both precisely reflects the trinitarian settlement following the Council of Constantinople in AD 381 and insists on his faith in the "one baptism" of the church.[45] Elsewhere in his works we can pick out strains of anti-Eunomian polemic that recall the controversial works of Basil the Great and Gregory of Nyssa.[46] In the space remaining to me, however I would like to focus on what Macarius has to say both about the *visio dei,* and about the relation which the church's sacraments and, more generally, the liturgical assembly have with the life of the "inner man." What he wrote with respect to both would have great influence in subsequent Eastern Christian tradition. Let me begin with the first, the matter of vision.

There is no question that visions of heavenly things were much on the mind of Macarius' monks. Consider, for example, the following exchange:

> *Question:* What should one do who is led astray by Satan through, for example, an appearance of blessedness, or else by what seems to be a revelation of grace in light? *Answer:* One needs a great deal of discernment for this in order to recognize and understand the exact difference between good and evil . . . So, too, should you receive even heavenly beings with careful testing, knowledge, and discernment . . .[47]

Even angels are to be asked for their credentials and not accepted until after a careful perusal. On the other hand, it is evident that both Macarius and his interlocutor took for granted the possibility of such visitations. The chief criterion for distinguishing the true from the false light is the effect it has on the recipient. The reply thus continues:

> . . . even if, wishing to deceive the soul, he [Satan] were to create fantasies by transforming himself into brilliant visions . . . he is unable to effect love in you for either God or for the brethren without immediately causing conceit and arrogance. Nor can he bring humility, nor joy, nor peace, nor quieting of the thoughts, nor hatred of the world, nor rest in God, nor desire for the good things of heaven . . . All these things are the results of grace . . . It is therefore from its activity within you that you are to know whether the intelligible light that has shone in your soul is of God or of Satan.[48]

Moreover, he concludes, the experienced soul should be able to differentiate between "the gifts of the Spirit and the phantasms of Satan" by virtue of its "spiritual perception" (*aisthesis*), just as "the throat knows the difference" between wine and vinegar. They look alike, but their taste distinguishes them immediately.[49]

I should like to underline three things about this passage. There is, first, the insistence that the virtues, in particular love of God and neighbor, necessarily accompany any true visitation, and, as a kind of corollary, the implication that these virtues are not necessarily accompanied by vision. They stand, therefore, as in a sense primary, which is to say that the Christian experience of grace is not necessarily visionary, a matter of extraordinary experiences.[50] Second, the "spiritual perception" of which Macarius speaks recalls the "spiritual senses" of Origen and, again, it is this perception, broader than simply vision and itself the fruit of the experience of grace, together with its accompanying discernment, which he appears to hold out to his interlocutor as of more lasting importance for the spiritual life than vision per se.[51] Third, however, he is convinced that an experience of God in the form of a vision of light within the soul is not only possible, but—and here I add to the passage cited above—a foretaste of the eschatological transformation to come. This conviction doubtless derives in great part from his own experience. In the best known of the several Macarian collections, Collection II or the *Fifty Spiritual Homilies,* the eighth homily lists in the third person a series of visions, including a "cross of light" plunging itself "deep into the inner man," a "splendid robe . . . not made by human hands" like the clothes of Christ on the mount of the Transfiguration, and finally, citing from George Maloney's recent translation:

> Sometimes indeed the very light itself, shining in the heart, opened up interiorly and in a profound way a hidden light, so that the whole person was completely drowned with that sweet contemplation . . .[52]

Later on in the same homily, in an exceptionally rare instance of the autobiographical in Greek patristic literature, he makes it clear that he was himself the subject of these experiences: "After I received the sign of the cross . . . grace quiets all my parts and my heart."[53] Elsewhere he is emphatic that this light of grace is not a human or created thing.[54] In the following citation from Collection I, for example, he takes issue with what appear to be critics of visionary experience. Against their claim that any experience of light is to be understood as metaphorical, or perhaps as intellectual, that is, as the kind of mental illumination or flash of insight that may come from studying the Scriptures, Macarius opposes scriptural accounts of a *visio luminae,* including Paul's conversion on the Damascus Road, the vision of Stephen at the latter's martyrdom, and his favorite text, 1 Corinthians 3:18, in order to conclude:

> We ourselves acknowledge that revelation does take place by the Spirit through interpretation as well, but let them admit in their turn that it may also be a divine light, shining essentially and substantially [*en ousiai kai hypostasei*] in the hearts of the faithful . . . [the] divine and essential [*ousiodes*] light which is that which appears and shines in souls more than the light of the sun.[55]

The relevance of this citation, and like passages in the Homilies, to the fourteenth century Hesychast debate over the "light of Tabor," and particularly to Gregory Palamas, must be clear, further evidence of what one scholar refers to as "an astonishing continuity in Church history."[56]

In still another homily from the same Collection he presents a longer catena of proof texts, moving from 2 Corinthians 3:18 to 4:6 (the "glory" of Christ within the heart), Psalms 118:18 and 42:3 (on light), Acts 9 and 22 (the light at St Paul's conversion), 1 Corinthians 15:49 ("the image of the heavenly man"), Philippians 3:21 (the "body of Christ's glory"), 1 Corinthians 2:9–10 ("What eye has not seen . . ."), and Romans 8:11 (the indwelling Spirit).[57] In yet other places, he will appeal to Moses' shining face in Exodus 34:29–35, to Ezekiel's vision of the chariot throne of God's Glory, to the Synoptic Transfiguration narratives, as well as to the Johannine passages, particularly John 14:21–23 and 17:22–24, which promise an indwelling manifestation and participation in divine glory, and to Revelation 22 on the celestial city and the glory which shines within it.[58] Glory, *doxa,* is a key term for Macarius. There are some scholars, most recently Hans Veit Beyer, who see in this preoccupation with the vision of glory and light a fundamental surrender to Neoplatonism.[59] I beg to differ. Macarius certainly owes much to the Platonic tradition, though not specifically to the Neoplatonist writers (I do not find any echoes of Plotinus or the later Platonists in him—perhaps through Gregory of Nyssa?), and I must also add that I cannot think of any single, important patristic writer who does not owe a fair bit to Plato. Given the background of Graeco-Roman culture, the Platonism of the *Homilies* is an inevitable feature of their general emphasis on interiority. What is surely more significant about Macarius' use of *doxa* is that term's long-standing use in Greek-speaking Jewish and Christian traditions as the translation of the Hebrew *kabod* YHWH, such as, for example, in such texts of the Septuagint as Exodus 24 and 33–34, Numbers 12:8 (where *doxa* translates the divine form, *temunah*, in the context of the *visio dei*), I Kings 8:1–11, Isaiah 6 and 40 (the eschatological manifestation, "all flesh shall see . . ."), Ezekiel 1, 8–11, and 43, and—not mentioned specifically, but implied—in the shining of the righteous in Daniel 12.[60] The texts cited at the head of this paragraph give some idea of the term's importance for the New Testament, a feature of earliest Christian thought which is only very lately beginning to come into the prominence it deserves. *Kabod* and its Greek equivalent are, put simply, the biblical terms of choice for theophany.

What is at work in Macarius' use of *doxa* is therefore a persistent and conscious interiorization of the biblical glory tradition, of theophany. He is scarcely alone in this among monastic writers of the late fourth century. Evagrius, too, is engaged in exactly the same enterprise, and he is not the only such parallel.[61] I myself think that this common endeavor owes not a little to the sea-change[62] in Christian thought entailed by the Nicene *homoousion*, whose confirmation at Constantinople we have already seen Macarius endorsing. The spirituality required by the doctrine of divine consubstantiality did not allow for the sort of crudely materialistic or frankly anthropomorphite cast to the *visio dei* suggested by the episcopal heresiologists' accusation, noted above, that the Messalians taught a vision of the Trinity accessible to the physical eye. We can find similar concerns and debate operative in the anthropomorphite controversy among Egyptian monks at the close of the fourth century, in Augustine's *Confessions* (recall his delight at discovering the Platonists!), as well as in his *De Trinitate* and Epistles 147–148, or in Cyril of Alexandria's correspondence with Palestinian monks in the 430's.[63] To sum up an argument I have made at length elsewhere, there was widespread controversy in the late fourth and early fifth centuries about the nature of the vision of God, and, further, this *controversy* was particularly associated with the monks.[64] Ancient traditions among Christian ascetics were in process of being re-shaped, and monastic leaders like Macarius and Evagrius were at the forefront of this reconfiguration.

The nature and provenance of these ancient traditions, together with an instructive glimpse into Macarius' program, are perhaps most stunningly displayed in the first homily of the better known Collection II. The latter begins by summarizing Ezekiel's vision on the banks of the Chebar (Ezekiel 1:1 ff.), and then goes on to add the following interpretation:

> The prophet truly and assuredly saw what he saw, but [his vision] also suggested something else. It depicted beforehand something secret and divine, a mystery truly

hidden from eternity and, after generations, made manifest in the last days with the appearance [lit. epiphany] of Christ. For Ezekiel beheld the mystery of the soul that is going to receive its Lord and become His throne [*thronos*] of glory, since the soul which has been made worthy of fellowship with the Spirit of His [Christ's] light, and which has been illumined by the beauty of His ineffable glory after having prepared itself for Him as a throne [*kathedra*] and dwelling place [*katoiketerion*], becomes all light and all face and all eye.[65]

There are a number of things worth pointing out in this passage. First, there is the emphatic statement that Ezekiel's was a true vision. He really did see the glory of God. One might contrast this with Augustine's systematic reduction of the Old Testament theophanies to angelophanies, or to mere symbols. I do not think, though, that Macarius is primarily concerned here with countering such an interpretation, but that he wants rather to make it clear that he is in agreement with the interest of his monastic audience in, first of all, according this text its full, literal value. Second, I would suggest that they were so interested because they hoped to enjoy the sort of vision for which Ezekiel's was the likely prototype, by which I mean the sight of the enthroned glory of God in the heavenly sanctuary that we find so often to the fore in apocalyptic literature and, later on and perhaps simultaneously with writers like Macarius and Evagrius, in the *merkabah* (chariot) lore of the talmudic-era *hekhalot* texts.[66] This is not to say that Macarius' monks were reading rabbinic literature. They did not need to, since they—or, certainly, other Christian ascetics—were busy at the time and thereafter translating and copying the earlier apocalyptic and other pseudepigraphical materials for themselves.[67] Recall, for example, Athanasius' *39th Festal Epistle* of 367, where the modern scriptural canon of the Christian churches (less the deuterocanonical books) appears for the first time, and note that the great archbishop provides a list of authoritative books exactly in order to exclude apocalyptic texts like the Enochic books and the *Ascension of Isaiah*, about which he tells us certain overly enthusiastic ascetics, "the wretched Meletians" in this case, "have been boasting."[68] We might also bear in mind the fact that Athanasius was markedly unsuccessful. Old Testament pseudepigrapha and related literature did not disappear immediately even in Egypt, let alone in other regions, such as, in our case, Syria-Mesopotamia. Jacob of Serug's long homily, *On the Chariot that Ezekiel the Prophet Saw*, provides significant testimony that, a century after Macarius, some Syrian monks were still interested—unhealthily so, in Jacob's view—in what I take to be an apocalyptic or *hekhalot* type of mystical ascent to see the human form, Christ, of the glory enthroned. I might add that I think similar concerns were at work in Jacob's anonymous (though more famous) contemporary, the unknown Syrian Christian who wrote under the name of Dionysius Areopagites, though no one else seems to have picked up on this element in "Dionysius."[69]

Macarius in any case does not oppose this tradition head-on. Instead, he affirms Ezekiel's vision, and only then adds his qualifying "but": "but [this] also suggests something else." The "something else" in question is my third point: Macarius engages in nothing less than a recasting of the ancient literature of ascent and vision to which his monks were so attached. As Gershom Scholem put it, in an offhand remark at the close of the chapter on "Merkabah Mysticism" in his epochal study, *Major Trends in Jewish Mysticism*, Macarius is engaged in "a mystical reinterpretation" of the *Merkabah* tradition.[70] There is no need to go "up" to heaven to see God on his glorious throne, since, "with Christ, everything is within," and therefore the chariot-throne of divinity, the place of divine abiding and heavenly palace or temple (*hekhal, naos*), has, through Christ and the gift of the Holy Spirit, become the Christian soul itself. Just as Evagrius, in the words of Nicholas Sed, provides us with "the first interiorization" of Moses' ascent at Sinai "of which we have a written attestation," such that the true mount of revelation is relocated to the intellect, so does Macarius rework the motifs of tabernacle, temple, and of the ascent to heaven for initiation into its mysteries.[71] The "all face and all eye" in the passage cited just above, for example, deliberately recalls the four faces and many eyes of the angelic bearers of Ezekiel's chariot throne, the "living creatures" or *hayyot* which feature so prominently in both apocalyptic throne visions and in the angelological speculations of the later *hekhalot* texts.[72] Macarius thus continues:

> The four living creatures which carry the chariot were also carrying a type of the four governing faculties [lit., "thoughts," *logismoi*] of the soul . . . I mean the will, the conscience, the intellect [*nous*], and the power to love [*agapetike dynamis*], for through them the chariot of the soul is steered, and upon them God takes up His rest [*epanapauetai*].[73]

The One who rides and directs these steeds, the charioteer, Macarius stresses a few lines later, is the Same who rode upon Ezekiel's cherubim, "Who holds the reigns and guides with His Spirit." While this passage obviously owes a great deal to Plato's *Phaedrus*, it is surely also Platonism with a difference. For the pagan philosopher, it is the rational faculty, the *logistikon*, which holds the reigns and directs the soul, but, for our Christian ascetic, the intellect has been bumped out of the driver's seat and buckled into harness together with the other faculties in order to make room for the true Charioteer, Christ God, Who guides the soul with the Holy Spirit.[74] Visionary traditions and enthusiasms are not denied in this reworking, for theophany is still held out as possible and desirable, but they are tempered, redirected into channels more conducive to ascetical sobriety, toward, in fact, that inner warfare we noted earlier and the divine help needed to wage it. Attaining to vision within must and will only come as the result and gift of the soul's entire restoration and transfiguration, and then again, as Macarius frequently puts it elsewhere, only—and fleetingly—as an anticipation of the Day of Resurrection when the divine fire now hidden within the soul will, as it were, emerge and shine forth openly from a transformed and risen body.[75]

My fourth observation about the chariot passage provides us with our entry into the second area of concern I promised to discuss, the matter of Macarius' relation to the sacraments and liturgical assembly which, as we have seen, was at issue in the Messalian controversy. In the passage on the chariot we find two Greek words used for "throne," *thronos* and *kathedra*. The second term has an obviously ecclesiastical ring to it, recalling the place of the bishop's teaching and presidency at the church's liturgy. I think that this association is quite deliberate on Macarius' part. While he does not pursue the echo of church liturgy and even architecture in this particular homily, he certainly does so elsewhere, frequently, and, on one occasion at least, at some length. Throughout, perhaps his key scriptural texts are 1 Corinthians 3:16 and 6:19–20, especially the latter's equation of the individual Christian's body and the temple of the Spirit.[76] This is clearly the basis for the following passage, which joins the imagery of sanctuary and, very popular among Syrian Christians, of nuptial union:

> The body of the human being is a temple of God . . . and the human heart is an altar of the Holy Spirit . . . With the temple of the Lord let us also sanctify the altar, that He may light our lamps and that we may enter into His bridal chamber.[77]

The Jerusalem Temple was, of course, the place *par excellence* of divine abiding in Israel, the object of the Psalmist's frequent desire to look upon God's glory. Thus, just as with Ezekiel's *Merkabah* (itself written in part as a response to the imminent loss of the Solomon's temple), Macarius also picks up and makes interior this motif: the holy of holies, the *debir* of the *Shekinah's* abiding, is now the Christian soul. Likewise, the priesthood of the sons of Aaron celebrating within the holy place, and the ministry of the angels in the heavenly sanctuary, a frequent theme in intertestamental literature, is now also fulfilled and active within the soul once the latter has acquired—and been given—freedom from the passions: "For it is in such a heart that God and all the Church of heaven take their rest";[78] and also, with the related imagery of the heavenly Jerusalem, the following: "[Christ] Himself ministers [*diakonei*] to her [the soul] in the city of her body, and she in turn ministers to Him in the heavenly city."[79]

The body as temple is the sphere thus of Christ's unique priesthood: "The true priest of the future good things . . . has entered into the tabernacle of their [the believer's] bodies, and he ministers to and heals the passions."[80] That which He effects within is, earlier in the same homily, specifically likened to the sacramental change, *metabole*, of the eucharistic elements, and in such a way as also to recall the Eastern (and especially Syrian) Christian tradition of the consecratory invocation of the Holy Spirit, the *epiklesis*:

> For our Lord came for this reason, that He might change [*allaxai*] and transform [*metabalein*] and renew and recreate the soul which had been overturned by the passions . . . mingling with it His own Spirit of divinity . . . to make new men, anointing them with His own light of knowledge, that He might put in them the new wine which is His Spirit.[81]

Another term Macarius uses with this same kind of echo is the word, *synaxis*. It means gathering or assembling, or a gathering or assembly, and is of course familiar to liturgists as an ancient expression for the liturgical assembly of the church.[82] In several passages, Macarius employs it simply, or with at least apparent simplicity, for the soul's "gathering" of its scattered thoughts, *logismoi,* in order, as he puts it in one such passage, that Christ may "gather her unto Himself and make her thoughts divine, and teach her true prayer."[83] I say apparent simplicity because it becomes evident elsewhere that he does mean it to carry a specifically ecclesiastical and liturgical resonance, as in the following:

> "Church" is therefore said with regard both to the many and to the single soul. For that soul which gathers [*synagei*] all its thoughts is also the Church of God . . . and this term [thus] applies in the case both of many [Christians] and of one.[84]

This citation is an obvious and open appeal to the principle of microcosm and macrocosm, the soul as a microcosm of the church's macrocosm. Put another way, and borrowing an expression from Macarius' equally anonymous contemporary, the author of the *Liber Graduum,* the Christian, and particularly the Christian heart or soul, is a "little church."[85] Mention of the *Liber* leads me to point out that, in all that we have touched on so far regarding Macarius' use of the language of temple and church, he is drawing on a manner of speaking which has many precedents, some of them very old indeed. The notion of the Christian as ecclesiastical microcosm —and, indeed, microcosm as well of the Paradise Mountain and of the Sinai of theophany— is at the least adumbrated in Ephrem Syrus' *Paradise Hymns,* while the body as "temple" goes back, as noted, to St Paul.[86] We might also look to the *Acts of Thomas* in the earlier Syrian milieu where the bodies of the ascetics are hailed as temples, places of Christ's indwelling, and where the "holy ones" are in consequence even accorded sacerdotal powers, "empowered to forgive sins."[87] Aphraates speaks similarly of the Christian's priestly office of prayer.[88] The Alexandrian writers from Philo to Origen draw conscious comparisons between the worship of the community and liturgy of the soul,[89] while Macarius' placing of the ascetic's body and soul in parallel with the eucharistic elements may also draw on Ignatius of Antioch's and Polycarp of Smyrna's second-century characterization of the martyr's body as locus of theophany and sacramentally transformed, as well as their obvious deployment of eucharistic language in order to depict that transformation, and we should note that they in their turn were the heirs of still older, Jewish traditions of the martyr as a holy and reconciling sacrifice.[90] It is, by the way, a truism that the fourth century monastic movement drew on the imagery of martyrdom. What is perhaps less appreciated is the real possibility that the same imagery, and for likely just as long, had been applied to the ascetics. Christianity in Persian Mesopotamia seems to bear this out. There it was martyrdom that was the more recent, fourth century experience. When it thus came time to write the martyrologies, the language the authors used was that which previously their communities had employed for their ascetics—precisely the reverse of the sequence in the Roman world.[91]

Traditional, yes, and even ancient, but it is equally evident that many bishops at the end of the fourth century felt that this language threatened proper regard for the sacraments and, to be sure, that thereby their own authority was placed in question. With respect to the second concern, I would say that they were probably in part justified, though I would add that the real authority of the charismatic saint, almost inevitably an ascetic or monastic, has been a constant thorn in the Eastern hierarchy's side from the Messalian controversy and before to the present day, and that there is no sign that it will ever be removed short of the *eschaton*—for which God be praised.[92]

Regarding the bishops' concern over proper evaluation of the sacraments, however, there was surely misunderstanding, at least so far as Macarius was concerned. The latter not only wrote of baptism and the Eucharist in such a way as to make it clear he accepted and indeed embraced the church's doctrine, but in one of his homilies he also sought to reply both to the bishops and, on the other side of his typically two-way dialogue, surely as well to some of his monks who were raising questions, by elaborating on the notion of the ecclesiastical microcosm in such a way as to exercise profound influence on subsequent Eastern Christian thought, practice, piety, and even, I think, church architecture. I shall touch first and briefly on his affirmations of the traditional teaching before turning to his contribution.

Baptism and the Eucharist are realities for Macarius. Dom Vincent Desprez in an article published ten years ago most usefully discussed his understanding of the former.[93] While acknowledging that Macarius shared with his Syrian Christian background in a certain neglect respecting the Pauline theme of baptism as a sharing in Christ's death, Dom Vincent points out his equally Syrian emphasis on the sacrament as the "earnest," *arrabon,* of the gift of the Holy Spirit.[94] This eschatological emphasis is at the fore, of course, throughout all of his writings. In the case of baptism, the use of the imagery of the "earnest" and "talent" given the believer in the sacrament looks ever toward eschatological fulfillment, and opens thus onto the dynamic of growth into a conscious and perfected Christian life. Macarius is always interested in process. He thus criticizes in one homily what he takes to be his critics' static and in effect magical view of sacramental efficacy, insisting instead that, though participation in the Spirit through baptism is real indeed, that participation is an invitation to progress, to an increase in love and virtue and awareness "according to the measure" of each believer's faith, *kat'analogian tes pisteos.*[95] On the other hand, if baptismal grace is left uncultivated, the "earth of the heart" can indeed revert to weeds and thorns, that is, suffer again the inhabitation of evil. To be sure, later ascetic writers such as Mark the Monk and Diadochus of Photiki in the following century would, in view of the episcopal condemnations, develop and refine the Macarian teaching, laying more stress on baptism's ties with the cross, stressing the plenitude of the gifts received, and moderating his language concerning the post-baptismal indwelling of evil, but in substance their modifications have much more in common with Macarius than they differ from him.[96]

As for the Eucharist, Macarius admittedly speaks relatively little of it, at least when he is not in a polemical mode replying to his critics. Yet this is scarcely untypical of monastic writers, and, when he does write of it, his language is fully traditional, as in the following citation with its typical emphasis on the Spirit:

> Those who have truly partaken of the bread of the eucharist are made worthy of becoming partakers of the Holy Spirit, and thus holy souls are enabled to live everlastingly. Just as he who drinks wine possesses the latter mingled with all his members . . . so, too, with him who drinks the blood of Christ, for the Spirit of divinity which is drunk is mingled with the perfect soul and the latter is mingled with the Spirit and, thus sanctified, becomes worthy of the Lord.[97]

Then there is also the passage where, interpreting 1 Corinthians 2:9, "what eye hath seen," he holds out the sacraments as that which the prophets did not see, though they foretold Messiah's coming:

> . . . neither did it come to their understanding that there would be a baptism of fire and the Holy Spirit, and that bread and wine would be offered in the Church as an antitype of the Lord's body and blood, and that those who partake of the visible bread spiritually eat His flesh, and that the Apostles and Christians would receive the Comforter and be clothed with power from on high and filled with divinity, and that souls would be mingled with the Holy Spirit. None of this did the prophets know.[98]

I would also add the texts that I cited above in connection with the believer as microcosm. Macarius would surely not be using a word like *metabole,* with its echo of eucharistic consecration, for the inner transformation of the soul unless both he and his audience understood and accepted the term's original reference to the mysterious change of the sacramental elements. The allusion and implied analogy would otherwise lose their intended force, that is, as the elements are truly changed through the action of the Spirit at the church's altar, so must it be with the "inner man" at the altar of the heart.

In sum, throughout the Macarian corpus the Eucharist is understood as at once the real anticipation and the illustration of the Christian's eschatological transformation. The latter element, the illustrative character, or perhaps we might better say, the iconic aspect of the eucharistic assembly is what draws Macarius' particular attention in Homily 52 of Collection I, where I would see him as, typically, addressing both his episcopal critics and certain among his own monks, or monastic correspondents, who had raised questions about the importance of the liturgy.[99] Here, too, is where he makes another signal contribution to the thought of Greek-speaking Christianity: the visible church as the divinely given icon here below of the transfigured inner man called to participate in the heavenly liturgy. This is the note on which he begins his homily:

> The whole visible arrangement of the Church of God came to pass for the sake of the living and intelligent substance [*noera ousia*] of the rational soul which was made according to the image of God, and which is the living and true Church of God . . . For the Church of Christ and temple of God and true altar and living sacrifice is the man of God.[100]

He criticizes his critics for their superficiality: "They have complete confidence in the temporary arrangement and only trust in statutes of the flesh." Neglecting "the seeking according to the inner man and the renewal of the soul . . . they slander us out of ignorance." This does not mean that Macarius denies the reality of the present dispensation of altar and sacraments: "God gave His Holy Spirit to the holy and catholic Church, and arranged that He be present at the holy altar and in the water of holy baptism," so that, through this presence and divine action, "faithful hearts . . . might be renewed and refashioned by the power of grace."[101] The Spirit was present in the Ark of Covenant of the Old Dispensation, so how much more then is this not the case for the Christian altar? But visible realities, as we have seen, are for Macarius always subordinate to the invisible, to the unseen and secret work within, thus:

> Because visible things are the type and shadow of the hidden ones, and the visible temple [a type] of the temple of the heart, and the priest [a type] of the grace of Christ, and all the rest of the sequence of the visible arrangement [a type] of the rational and hidden matters according to the inner man, we receive the manifest arrangement and administration of the Church as an illustration [*hypodeigma*] of what is at work in the soul by grace.[102]

In the concluding section of the homily he develops this statement by taking up the sequence, *akolouthia,* of the Eucharistic Liturgy and the physical arrangement, *oikonomia,* of the assembled believers, by which he means, respectively, the two halves of the service, the Liturgies of the Word (*synaxis*) and of the Eucharist proper (*anaphora*), and the progression from the catechumens in the church porch to the baptized believers in the nave to the presbyters on either side of the bishop's throne in the sanctuary apse. The first he presents as an image of the relationship of ascetic efforts to the grace of the Spirit. Just as the consecration of the gifts and Holy Communion crown and complete the reading and meditation on the Scriptures in the service's first part, so does the "mystical activity of the Spirit" crown and complete the efforts of "vigil, prayer, ascesis, and every virtue." Neither one is sufficient without the other; both are required. The *anaphora* must have the *synaxis* to precede it, while the latter is obviously incomplete without the consecration and Communion. Similarly, there is no point to ascetic labors without the visitation of the Spirit, but He will not rest upon us unless we labor in our turn. The physical ordering of the assembly likewise mirrors the ascent of the believer to God and participation in the heavenly liturgy. Just as "those who do not sin and make progress . . . come eventually to the priesthood, and are transferred from some outer place [presumably referring to the church porch] up to the altar so that they may become God's ministers and assistants [*leitourgoi kai paredroi*]"—the sequence of promotion in the church's hierarchy, with the last phrase likely referring to the deacons and presbyters at the bishop's throne— so the soul,

> If . . . it does not embitter grace . . . but rather pleasingly follows the dominical statutes . . . and with all its faculty of choice cleaves at all times to the Lord and welcomes grace, then indeed . . . progresses and is made worthy . . . of promotion and spiritual rank, and . . . will be inscribed in the Kingdom among the perfect workers and with the blameless ministers and assistants [*leitourgoi kai paredroi*] of Christ.[103]

In its temporal sequence and spatial ordering, the order (*kosmos*) of the church's liturgy therefore reflects both the order of the Spirit's activity within and cooperation with the soul, and the latter's rise to share in the ministry of the angels in the heavenly temple, that is, with those who serve (*leitourgoi*) and who stand beside (*paredroi*) the throne of Christ.

The notion of the church's prayer as a participation in and reflection of the liturgy of heaven is very old, indeed, arguably with roots in the New Testament and, even before, in Second Temple Judaism,[104] while the idea of the human soul as microcosm of the church is, as I noted above, likewise very old. What Macarius brings to these themes is a more precise development and coordination. He argues systematically in this homily that what we see when we participate in the liturgy is a divinely established image or—in the fully sacramental sense that the term would later acquire—icon both of heaven, and of ourselves and our calling as Christians. Now, some might feel—and have felt—that this is an unfortunate allegorization of the liturgy and thereby a surrender, again, to Platonism.[105] We certainly do have a kind of allegorization here, and, equally, it owes not a little to Plato, but I do not agree that it is so regrettable. Let us first recall that Macarius is writing to his monks, and that, secondly, he does so at least as much to persuade them of the importance of the visible church's worship as to engage his critics among the bishops. It is in this effort to reconcile his ascetics to the liturgy by demonstrating its relevance and application to their own intense focus on the inner life that we discover the lasting importance of what he has to say. He insists that the communal and objective character of public worship is both true, being grounded in divine revelation, and that it at once aids and reflects the Christian's own subjective appropriation of the unique sacrament, *mysterion*, of Christ. I would insist that the key here is the "both, and," and the reconciliation or harmony that it seeks to effect between the sacramental and the mystical, objective and subjective, public and private, institutional and charismatic, or—in Macarius' own terms—altar and heart. As the revealed icon of heaven and of the heart, the church's altar becomes the necessary, middle term between the two, at once communicating heaven to us and leading us to its manifestation within us. Its role is a temporary one, since "the whole arrangement and ministry of the heavenly mysteries of the church will pass away at the conclusion of the age," then, when heaven and glorified humanity will merge and become one, but, for now, in the present time of attendance and anticipation, it mediates the *eschaton* to us in image and in truth.

I cannot then regard Macarius' efforts here as in any sense a surrender or betrayal, for it seems to me that what he accomplished served in a very fundamental way to preserve the unity of the church of the bishops, sacramentally based and necessarily structured, with the enthusiasm, charismaticism and generally inward thrust of the monastic movement. He helped establish the two in a union which, while it has had its tensions, has never since been broken. He was not alone in this endeavor. To be sure, Athanasius and Basil had also contributed significantly to this project, though not with respect to the specific matter of the "inner church."[106] I have, however, already mentioned Ephrem Syrus' adumbrations of this reconciliation in his *Paradise Hymns,* and can point as well to the exact same ideas as Macarius, and probably for the exact same reasons, in the twelfth *mimro* of the *Liber Graduum.*[107] But both of the latter two works were written in Syriac, and neither one to my knowledge was ever translated into Greek, certainly not the *Liber.* So it is chiefly at Macarius' door that I would place the later works of Dionysius Areopagites, especially on the hierarchies, and Maximus Confessor's *Mystagogy,* together with pervasive strains in, for example, the writings of Symeon New Theologian, Gregory of Sinai, and Nicholas Cabasilas.[108] These writers reflect more than a thousand years of Greek-speaking Christianity. They also represent much of the best that the Eastern Christian world has to offer.

Macarius fully deserved the efforts his immediate successors must have expended to preserve his writings from the oblivion that befell too many others who ran afoul of hasty condemnations. He wrote about what he knew, both from Scripture and tradition, and from his own experience, and he did so in such a way as to weave together into a single compelling tapestry threads from many, not always harmonious earlier Christian and pre-Christian groups and traditions. His was a genuine ministry of synthesis and reconciliation whose power to speak to subsequent generations sprang from the quality of its living and lived witness to the transfiguration promised by the gospels and apostles, to that change, effected by the Spirit of the risen Christ, which is at work in Christians even now, provided only they pledge their trust and longing.

Some years ago, after having been invited to sit in on a session of the Orthodox-Lutheran dialogue, I remember asking a prominent Lutheran theologian of my acquaintance how he pictured a Lutheran saint. He was at a loss for words for a moment, and then graciously admitted that he had never really given the matter any thought. For me, on the other hand, it still seems a very important question, even fundamental. What is the ideal we have of the Christian life in this world? Can it be lived? Whom may we look to for examples in our own and recent times, and throughout the history of the church? Some of this perspective strikes me as having been shared by the Wesleys. Thus when, at the sessions of their Holy Club, John and Charles Wesley picked up and read Macarius, and loved him in spite of the gulf of time and space, and equally of the centuries-old divisions of culture and in the church which separated fourth century Mesopotamia from eighteenth century England, I would like to think that they were responding to the same Spirit who inspired him.[109] If, moreover, that Spirit is the one and unique river of life which flows from the throne of God and of the Lamb, then might we not find in the welcoming response of two saintly Englishmen to this Syrian holy man, who so deeply impressed the thought and practice of Eastern Christianity, a kind of proof that those ages of difference and division can in fact be transcended and—who knows?—perhaps even the hope that they can be reconciled? Surely, if we look first to our saints for the truth of Christ's promises, for the presence in this age of the age to come, for the signs of the Spirit in short, will we not find a more certain, or at least a more promising ground for ecumenical encounter than merely the mutual exchange of confessional statements? We Orthodox are fond of saying that Orthodoxy is most fundamentally neither a system of doctrine nor an institution, important as both those are, but first and last a way of life, as in Bishop Kallistos Ware's little book, *The Orthodox Way*. We do not very often live up to that claim, but we can and do point to those whom we believe have done so, to our saints, as the proof of things unseen and embodying the substance of things hoped for. I have the impression that that is part of the purpose of the discussions in this volume. If so, it is a worthy project, and I hope that this paper has made some small contribution to it.

Endnotes

[1]K. T. Ware, "Preface," in *Pseudo-Macarius: The Fifty Spiritual Homilies and the Great Letter*, tr. G. Maloney (New York: 1992,) xi. See also E. Benz, *Die protestantische Thebais. Zur Nachwirkung Makarios des Ägypters im Protestantismus des 17. und 18. Jahrhunderts im Europa und Amerika* (Göttingen, 1963), and H. Doerries, *Die Theologie des Makarios-Symeons* (Göttingen, 1978), 16 ff. I am indebted for the reference to Benz' book to R. Staats, "Messalianerforschung und Ostkirchenkunde," in *Makarios-Symposium über das Böse*, ed. Werner Strothmann (Göttingen: 1983), 60, n.39.

[2]I take the phrase from J. Pelikan's *The Spirit of Eastern Christendom (600–700)*, (Chicago/London, 1974).

[3]The expression, "perceptibly and with complete assurance," is one of the signature phrases of the Macarian Homilies. For an analysis of the phrase, together with the related term, *peira* (experience), see esp. C. Stewart, *"Working the Earth of the Heart": The Messalian Controversy in History, Texts, and Language to A.D. 431* (Oxford/New York, 1991), 96–168. For *peira* alone, see P. Miquel, *Le vocabulaire de l'expérience spirituelle dans la tradition grecque du IVe au XIVe siècle* (Beauchesne, 1991).

[4]Collection I appears in *Makarios/Symeon. Reden und Briefen: Die Sammlung I des Vaticanus Graecus 694 (B)*, ed. H. Berthold (Berlin, 1973); Collection II in *Die 50 geistlichen Homilien des Makarios*, ed. H. Dörries, E. Klostermann, and M. Kröger (Berlin, 1964); and Collection III in *Neue Homilien des Makarios/Symeon. Aus Typus III*, ed. E. Klostermann and H. Berthold (Berlin, 1961). The last has also been more recently edited and supplied with a French translation by V. Desprez, OSB: *Pseudo-Macaire, Oeuvres spirituelles*, vol. 1: *Homelies propres à la Collection III*, in *Sources chrétiennes 275* (Paris, 1980). When referring to or quoting from Macarius below, I shall be using my own translations unless otherwise stated, and referring to the original language texts above. Citations in the notes below will begin with uppercase Roman numerals for the Collections, followed by arabic numerals for the specific homily and its subsections.

The first item in the MSS of Collection I, Macarius' *Great Letter*, is not included in Berthold's edition as it was edited previously by W. Jaeger, *Two Rediscovered Works of Ancient Christian Literature: Gregory of Nyssa and Macarius* (Leiden, 1965). It was Jaeger's thesis that Macarius had based this treatise on Gregory's shorter work, *On Christian Perfection* (also included in *Rediscovered Works*). A second edition of the *Letter*, however, together with the close analysis of its editor, R. Staats, in the latter's *Makarios-Symeon: Epistola Magna* (Göttingen, 1980), demonstrated convincingly that the relationship was in fact the reverse, i.e., that Gregory edited Macarius. In that Macarius elsewhere appears often to have availed himself of ideas characteristic of Gregory (as well of as Basil the Great, see below, n. 11), the evidence has been building for "an environment of mutual exchange" between the author of the *Homilies* and the great Cappadocian, to quote from S. Burns' paper, "'Sober Intoxication' as a metaphor for divine ecstasy in Gregory of Nyssa and Ps-Macarius," given at the North American Patristics Society Conference at Loyola, Chicago, in June 1998. I look forward to the eventual publication of Burns' thesis on this subject as it promises to be the most thorough study on Macarius' Syrian and Greek background available in English.

[5]The name, Symeon of Mesopotamia, is often attached (particularly by German scholars) to "Macarius," owing to the appearance of that name, a leader in the Messalian movement, in a few of the ancient MSS. H. Dörries was the first to raise the possibility of Symeon in *Symeon von Mesopotamien. Die Überlieferung des messalianischen Makarios-Schriften* (Leipzig, 1941), and was followed by many thereafter. For a brief consideration of the question of Macarius' identity, see V. Desprez, "Macaire," in *Dictionnaire de spiritualité* X:27, and at greater length in his "Introduction" to the sc edition of Collection III, 32–37.

[6]Evagrius was preserved, partially, in Greek under the name of Nilus of Sinai, but the *Kephalaia Gnostica*, his main doctrinal work, survives only in two Syriac translations, tr. and ed. by A. Guillaumont, *Patrologia Orientalis* XXVIII. His Origenism was the source of his later condemnation in 553, and the best study of his thought in that regard is still Guillaumont's *Les "Kephalaia Gnostica" d'Évagre le pontique* (Paris, 1962). More recent studies by, especially, G. Bunge have served to place Evagrius more securely in the setting of Egyptian eremeticism, and somewhat to ameliorate the charge of heresy. Thus, in chronological order, see the latter's "Évagre le Pontique et les deux Macaires," *Irénikon* 56 (1983): 215–227 and 323–360; "On the Trinitarian Mysticism of Evagrius of Pontus," *Studia Monastica* 17 (1986): 191–208; "Origenismus-Gnostizismus: zum geistesgeschichtlichen Standort des Evagrios Pontikos," *Vigiliae Christianae* 40 (1986): 24–54; *Geistliche Vaterschaft: Christliche Gnosis bei Evagrios Pontikos* (Regensburg, 1988); and perhaps especially "Hénade ou

Monade? Au sujet des deux notions centrales de la terminologie évagrienne," *Le Muséon* 102 (1989): 69–91.

[7]Desprez, "Macaire," *Dictionnaire de spiritualité*, 39.

[8]For the background in Wisdom literature and Cynic diatribe to the literary form Evagrius largely invents for Eastern monastic literature, the "chapters" or short sayings, see W. R. Schoedel, "Jewish Wisdom and the Formation of the Christian Ascetic," in R. Wilken, ed., *Aspects of Wisdom in Judaism and Early Christianity* (Notre Dame, 1975), 169–199; and also, specifically in Evagrius, J. Driscoll, OSB, *The "Ad Monachos" of Evagrius Ponticus: Its Structure and a Select Commentary* (Roma: 1991), 307–384. On meditation in the Egyptian hermitages, see D. Burton-Christie, *The Word in the Desert: Scripture and the Quest for Holiness in Early Christian Monasticism* (Oxford/New York, 1993), 76–177.

[9]For Macarius as himself the recipient of revelations, see II.8, cited below, esp. II.8.6. On the necessity of an inspired guide, see I.4.12; II.14.4; 15.20 (saints as *theodidaktoi*); 18.5–6; III.7.3–4 (vs. false guides); 14.1; and 16.3; but against false claims to perfection, impossible in this life, see II.8.5; 15.36 (we are always free to fall); 17.5–6; 38.4–5; I.31.6; 39 and 64 (the need for meekness vs. conceit); III.22.1–2 (vs. pretenders to knowledge through intellectual effort alone); and for comment, Dörries, *Theologie*, 336–366. On the phenomenon of the enlightened elders in the fourth century (and afterwards) and their claims to authority, often in tension with the official hierarchy, see, e.g., P. Rousseau, *Ascetics, Authority, and the Church* (Oxford, 1978) 18–67; P. Brown, *Society and the Holy in Late Antiquity* (Berkeley, 1982), 103–195; and A. Golitzin, *St Symeon the New Theologian on the Mystical Life*, vol. 3, *Life, Times, Theology* (New York, 1997), 19–21 and 38–53.

[10]On the social and ecclesiastical setting of monasticism in Asia Minor and upper Mesopotamia, see J. Gribomont, "Le monachisme au sein de l'église en Syrie et en Cappadoce," *Studia Monastica* 7 (1965): 7–24; I. Pena et. alii, *Les réclus syriens: récherches sur les anciennes formes de vie solitaire en Syrie* (Milano, 1980), especially 93–162 on the life and continual contacts of Syrian hermits with larger groups; and S. H. Griffith, "Asceticism in the Church of Syria: The Hermeneutics of Early Syrian Monasticism," in ed. V. L. Wimbush and R. Valentasis, *Asceticism* (Oxford/New York, 1995), 220–245. On Macarius' *Great Letter* as a "rule" for his community ascetics, see Staats, "Messalianerforschungen," 56–57, and in detail, *Epistola Magna*, 63–72.

[11]Dörries' annotations in his edition of *Die 50 geistliche Homilien* are especially good on noting links to apocryphal materials, as well as other echoes of earlier Christian writers. See also G. Quispel, *Makarius, das Thomasevangelium, and das Leid von der Perle* (Leiden, 1967) on the echoes of the earlier Syriac literature of the Thomas tradition; together with A. Baker, "Syriac and the Scriptural Quotations of Pseudo-Macarius," *Journal of Theological Studies* 20 (1969): 133–149; and Stewart, *"Working the Earth,"* 84–95, 188–203, and 211–233 for parallels in later, fourth century Syriac literature. I know of no studies devoted to the influence of Clement and Origen, but see Desprez, "Introduction," SC, 275, 55–56; and for the Cappadocians, esp. R. Staats, *Epistola Magna*, and, ibid., *Gregor von Nyssa und die Messalianer* (Berlin, 1968), as well as the forthcoming work by S. Burns, n. 4 above. I shall touch on some possible parallels with Jewish thought on specific issues below.

[12]See above, n. 6, and especially N. Sed, "La shekina et ses amis araméens," in *Cahiers d'Orientalisme* XX (1988): 233–242 for Evagrius' links with Jewish exegesis on the *visio dei*.

[13]I. Hausherr, "Les grands courants de la spiritualité orientale," *Orientalia Christiana Periodica* 1 (1935): 114–138, esp. 121–124 and 126–128. See my remarks on this influential article in "Temple and Throne of God: Pseudo-Macarius and Purity of Heart," in *Purity of Heart in Early Ascetic and Monastic Literature*, ed. H. Luckman and L. Kunzler, (Collegeville, MN, 1999), 107–112.

[14]On the vision of light in Evagrius, see again Sed, op.cit., together with A. Guillaumont, "Un philosophe au désert: Évagre le Pontique," *Revue de l'histoire des religions* 181 (1972): 29- 56; ibid., "La vision de le l'intellect par lui-même dans la mystique évagrienne," *Mélanges de l'Université Saint Joseph* 50 (Beirut, 1984): 255–262, and, critical of both Evagrius and Macarius (together with the later Byzantine Hesychasts) as in thrall to the light mysticism of Neoplatonism, H.V. Beyer, "Die Lichtlehre der Mönche des vierzehnten und des vierten Jahrhunderts," in *XVI Internationaler Byzantinistenkongress*, Akten I:2, *Jahrbuch des österreichischen Byzantinistik* 31,1 (1981): 473–512.

[15]See my discussion of Evagrius in *Et introibo ad altare dei: The Mystagogy of Dionysius Areopagita* (Thessalonica, 1994), 322–340; and, in greater detail, M. O'Laughlin, *Origenism in the Desert: An Origenist Christolog* (Washington, DC, 1970), 89–111, may also be consulted with profit.

[16]The citation is from I.18.7.3. For other references to the Transfiguration, see I.10.3.1; II.4.13; 8.3; 15.38. For more examples of the contrast between the "now" (*nyn*) of the light within, and the "then" (*tote*) of the body's visible glorification, see I.18.6; 24; 28.1; 58.3; II.2.5; 5.7–12; 11.1; 15.38; 34.2; and III.2.1. On the place of

the Transfiguration in particularly Eastern Christian thought, see J. A. McGuckin, *The Transfiguration of Christ in Scripture and Tradition* (Lewiston/Queensland, 1986), 99–128, esp. 117–128 on the Gospel episode taken as an illustration of the deification of the flesh, and as an epiphany of the age to come.

[17]Macarius certainly makes use of "heart" as equivalent to "inner man," thus see I.3.2; 4.30; 27.2; 39; 54.2–3; II.4.4; 5.4; 8.3; 10.1; 11.9–13; 13.1; 15.8,20,28,33–34; 19.7; 24.2; 26.21–22; 32.3; 43.3 and 7; III.3.2; 20.2; 28.4; *Great Letter* 6, 22, 34, 40, and 42. Elsewhere, however, he will freely use "inner man" soul, or even intellect (*nous*) instead of "heart," as in, for example, virtually all his references to the inner temple (*naos*), church (*ekklesia*), house (*oikos*) or dwelling-place (*oiketerion*) or palace (*palation*) or throne (*thronos*) or city (*polis*) or altar (*thysiasterion*) or tabernacle (*skene*) of God: I.3.3; 4.7 (soul); 5.3 (intellect); 7.18 (soul and inner man); 25.1 (soul); 29.2 (soul); 40.1 (soul); II.1.2 (soul); 6.5 (intellect); 12.15 (soul); 27.19 (soul and intellect); 28.1 (soul); 32.5–6 (soul); 33.2 (soul); 37.8–9 (soul); 45.5 (soul); 47.14 (soul); III.6.2 (soul); 19.2 (soul); 21.3 (soul); 25.4 (soul); and 27.6 (soul). Relatedly on the importance of the soul or "inner man," see I.5.2; 18.7 ("inner man" as the image of God); 23.2; 24 (soul as key to the spiritual reading of the Scriptures); 25.1 (soul as locus of interior warfare); 40.1; 54.2–3; 62 (intellect called to rule over passions); 64; II.28.1; 30; 37.1; 43.7 (the intellect as the "eye of the heart," and cf. II.6.8 for the intellect as "eye of the soul"); 47.2–14; III.18.2; 26.4 and 7 (soul as the image); and 28.2.

[18]On the *autexousion* and its rooting in the image of God, see; e.g., I.41; 42; II.15.23 and 36; 19.1ff.; III.25.2 and 5; and 26.3; and, for comment, Dörries, *Theologie*, 96–100.

[19]For the "veil of the passions," II.2.2–3; together with I.2.2–3; 35 (Adam's loss of glory); 50.1 (the "mingling" of the soul with the passions); II.15.25; and III.26.5, together again with Dörries, *Theologie*, 41–58, on this and related imagery.

[20]See especially S. P. Brock, "Clothing Metaphors as a Means of Theological Expression in Syriac Tradition," in M. Schmidt and C. F. Geyer, editors, *Typus, Symbol, Allegorie bei den östlichen Vätern und ihren Parallein in Mittelalter* (Regensburg, 1982), 11–38. For the donning of the luminous robes of the angelic priesthood as an image of transformation in apocalyptic literature, see M. Himmelfarb, *Ascent to Heaven in Jewish and Christian Apocalypses* (Oxford/New York, 1993), 3–4 and 9–46, and C. R. A. Morray-Jones, "Transformational Mysticism in the Apocalyptic-Merkabah Tradition," *Journal of Jewish Studies* 43 (1992): 1–31, esp. 16–21.

[21]For "two ways," "two spirits," "two kingdoms," and similar language in Macarius, see I.18.4; 27.2; 33.3; 34; III.4; and 31.1 and 3. For military language, see I.20.2; 60.2; II.5.5; 11.14; 15.28 and 33; 21; 27.20–23; III.9.4; 23.5 ("holy war"); and esp. I.50.4, with its appeal to Deuteronomy 20's call to "holy war," together with R. Murray, "An Exhortation to Candidates for Ascetical Vows at Baptism in the Ancient Syrian Church," *New Testament Studies* 21 (1974): 59–80 on the antiquity of this appeal, going back to the texts of Qumran.

[22]For the "bubbling spring" and related imagery, see I.6.3 (the spring); 25.1 (invisible wounds of soul); 36 (serpent within); 50.1 (mingling of passions with soul); II.2.2–3 (inhabitation of evil); 15.48 (inner spring of evil); 20.4; III.25.11; 26.5 (veiling of soul); and for comment, Dörries, *Theologie*, 63–75.

[23]III.26.3; and see M. Canevet, "Macaire," *Dictionnaire de spiritualité*, X:32–33.

[24]See, for example, Macarius on the traditional scriptural locus for deification, 2 Peter 1:4 ("partakers of the divine nature"), in I.1.8; 14.23; 54.5.6; II.25.5; 34.2; 39; 49.9; III.8.2; 18.1; and Dörries, *Theologie*, 316–348. For deification in Ephrem and a comparison with the Alexandrians and Cappadocians, see S.P. Brock, *The Luminous Eye: The Spiritual World Vision of Ephrem the Syrian* (rev. ed., Kalamazoo, 1992), 145–154.

[25]For Christ the healer of the soul's wounds and the "hidden passions," see I.2.10; 25.1; 63.3; and II.20.4 and 6. On the importance of Christ as physician in Syrian Christian thought, see R. Murray, *Symbols of Church and Kingdom* (Cambridge, 1975), 199–203.

[26]For a by no means exhaustive sampling of 2 Corinthians 3:7–4:6 in Macarius, see I.10.3; 28.2; 48.2; II.5.5; 25.3; III.3.2 and 28.2.

[27]III.8.1.

[28]See I.2.3 (on Genesis 3 as at once historical and psychological); 24 (Israel's history as that of the soul); II.25.7 (the Christian and the Exodus narrative); 28.1 (the soul as Jerusalem despoiled); 42.15 (Passover and Exodus as "mysteries of the soul"); 47.2–13 (again, the soul and Israel's history); III.20.1 (the soul and resurrection); and 24 (soul as tabernacle of David).

[29]See especially II.34.1–2 for Christ as house and tabernacle and city. On the development of the post-biblical term, *Shekinah*, in the Targumim and early rabbis, see A.M. Goldberg, *Untersuchungen über die Vorstellung von der Shekhinah in der frühen rabbinischen Literatur* (Berlin, 1969), especially 439–530; and,

particularly for the antiquity of the expression, "glory of the *Shekhinah*," D. Munoz-Leon, *Gloria de la Shekina en los Targumim del Penteteuco* (Madrid, 1977), especially his conclusions, 487–494. The term, *shekinto*, turns up in Christian writers in Syriac, for example in Ephrem's *Paradise Hymns* 2.12; 3.1, 6, and 12–13; and 10.12 (identified with the Presence enthroned at the Tree of Life and visible atop Sinai, respectively), and, over a century later, in Jacob of Serug's "On the Chariot that Ezekiel the Prophet Saw," in *Mar Jacobi Sarugensis: Homiliae Selectae*, ed. P. Bedjan (Paris, 1908), vol. IV, 569:19–29; 570:13; and 602:20; and for the related term, *yikoro* (glory), see 559:13; 571:17; 576:2; 592:5; and 593:13. In each case, Ephrem and Jacob, the terms in question seem primarily identified with Christ. Macarius, I think, stands within this tradition, thus see my remarks on light and glory below.

[30]See n.17 above, and my discussion of baptism in Macarius below.

[31]A glance at Lampe, *A Patristic Greek Lexicon*, 1323–1324, should suffice for the widespread use of this term and its relatives in Greek Christian authors.

[32]On the need for trials and struggles, see for example I.2.3.7–9; 20.1–2; 62; II.3.4; 5.5; 15.28; 19.1ff (need of "violence"); III.1; 4.3; 5; and 9.1.

[33]I.50.4.4.

[34]Ibid., 4.6.

[35]For Macarius on the equivalence of *eros* and *agape*, see II.5.5; 10.4; 15.37; and *Great Letter* 23; in Gregory Nyssa, e.g., *Vita Moysii* II.231–232 (SC 1:106–107), and for comment, J. Danielou, *Platonisme et théologie mystique* (Paris, 1944), 201 ff., and Origen's "Prologue" to his commentary on *The Song of Songs* (tr. Lawson, *Ancient Christian Writers* 26, pp. 30–38).

[36]See thus Macarius on the insatiable (*akorestos*) yearning (*eros*), love (*agape*), or longing (*pothos*) in I.21; and II.10.1–2, together with the endless appropriation of grace in II.8.6 and continual "stretching" (*epekteinesthai*) in *Great Letter* 14. It is difficult not to see in this a reaction to the notion of "satiation" with divinity traditionally ascribed to Origen, and an echo of Gregory of Nyssa's notion of *epektasis*. For the latter, see P. Deseille, "Epectase," *Dictionnaire de Spiritualité* IV:1785–788.

[37]For lists or chains of vices and virtues, see I.2.1; 39; II.40.1; and *Great Letter* 10 and 21.

[38]On the Evagrian pedagogy, see Driscoll, *The "Ad Monachos,"* 25–44 and 361–384, and on the sources of the vocabulary through fourth century usage in monastic circles, J. Raasch, "The Monastic Concept of Purity of Heart and its Sources," *Studia Monastica* 8.1–2 (1966): 7–33 and 183–213, 10.1 (1968): 7–55, 11.2 (1969): 269–314, and 12.1 (1970): 7–41.

[39]For the "Messalian" dossier, see M. Kmosko, *Liber Graduum*, in *Patrologia Syriaca* III (Paris, 1926) clxxii–ccxciii; and for discussion of the lists of errors and evolution of the controversy, Stewart, *"Working the Earth,"* 12–69.

[40]The modern literature on Macarius as "Messalian" begins with L. Villecourt, "La date et l'origine des 'Homelies spirituelles' attribuées à Macaire," *Comptes rendus du l'Académie des Inscriptions et Belles-Lettres* (Paris, 1920), 250–258, and reaches perhaps its most virulent expression in I. Hausherr's "L'erreur fondamentale et la logique du Messalianisme," *Orientalia Christiana Periodica* 1 (1935): 328–360, where Macarius emerges as a virtual compendium of heresies. For a more recent and balanced discussion, see V. Desprez, "Introduction," *Sources chrétiennes* 275, 38–56.

[41]On Jewish asceticism in the Second Temple era, see S. P. Fraade, "Ascetical Aspects of Ancient Judaism," in *Jewish Spirituality*, vol. 1: *From the Bible to the Middle Ages*, ed. A. Green (New York, 1988), 253–288; and for the visionary element in temple worship and apocalyptic, see for example J. Levenson, "The Jerusalem Temple in Devotional and Visionary Experience," ibid., 32–64, and C. R. Rowland, *The Open Heaven: A Study of Apocalyptic in Judaism and Early Christianity* (New York, 1982), especially 9–22 and 214–247. On motivations for earliest Christian asceticism, see G. Kretschmar, "Ein Beitrag zur Frage nach dem Ursprung frühchristlicher Askese," *Zeitschrift für Theologie und Kirche* 64 (1961): 27–67, and P. Nagel, *Die Motivierung der Askese in der alten Kirche und der Ursprung des Mönchtums* (Berlin, 1966), especially 20–74 on eschatological anticipation and the ascetic as pneumatophor. On the Thomas tradition, see A. F. J. Klijn, "Das Thomasevangelium und das altsyrische Christentum," *Vigiliae christianae* 15 (1961): 146–159; G. Quispel, "The Study of Encratism: A Historical Survey," in *La Tradizione dell'Enkrateia*, ed. U. Bianchi (Rome, 1985), 35–81; A. De Conick, *Seek to See Him: Ascent and Vision Mysticism in the Gospel of Thomas* (Leiden, 1996); and H. Drijvers' "Introduction" to the *Acts of Thomas*, in *New Testament Apocrypha*, ed. W. Schneemelcher, tr. R. McL. Wilson (rev. ed., Louisville: 1992), 2:322–338, especially 327–337. On the *Liber*, see A. Guillaumont, "Situation et signification du 'Liber Graduum' dans la spiritualité syriaque," *Orientalia*

Christiana Analecta 192 (Rome: 1974): 311–325. For Aphraates, see again Murray, "Exhortation," and for early Syrian Christian literature generally and the Holy Spirit, S. P. Brock, *Holy Spirit in the Syrian Baptismal Tradition* (Poona, India, 1979), 37–69, and ibid., *Spirituality in the Syrian Tradition* (Kottayam, India, 1989), 60–83.

[42]Staats, "Messalianerforschungen," 53.

[43]Stewart, *"Working,"* 69 and 234–240.

[44]For some echoes of this controversy in Macarius, see the citations below from I.17.3 and 52.1–2, together with my discussion. Macarius also clearly takes issue against the exaggerated claims of perfection and dispassion singled out by the bishops' complaints. See his insistence that no one in this life is either perfect or secure in I.39 (conceit is the enemy); 64; II.8.5; 15.8 and 20; 17.5–6; 38.4–5; and III.7–3-4 (vs. pretended spiritual guides). See also his occasional reminders that grace can work hiddenly, i.e., without conscious perception, in the soul, as in, e.g., I.34 and III.14.2l.

[45]*Great Letter,* 1–3, and see Staats, *Epistola Magna,* 23–26 and 63–66.

[46]See especially III.22.1–2.

[47]I.1.10.1–2.

[48]I.1.10.4–5.

[49]I.1.10.5.

[50]I offer this particularly in response to I. Hausherr's assertions, in "L'erreur fondamentale," 337–338, that Macarius simply identifies grace with the conscious—and necessarily spectacular—perception of grace. This not true, as also in n. 44 above.

[51]For the spiritual senses in Origen, see especially his *Dialogue with Heracleides,* in *Sources chrétiennes* 67, 78–102, together with K. Rahner, "Le début d'une doctrine des cinq sens spirituels chez Origène," *Revue d'ascétique et de mystique* 13 (1934): 113–145, and, for a wider survey of the theme in Greek Christian literature, B. Julien-Fraigneau, *Les sens spirituels et la vision de Dieu chez saint Symeon le nouveau théologien* (Paris, 1985). On the use of *aisthesis* in Macarius, see Stewart, *"Working,"* 116–138.

[52]II.8.3, in *Pseudo-Macarius: The Fifty Spiritual Homilies,* 82.

[53]II.8.6, ibid., 84.

[54]See, for example, his insistence that the visitation is foreign, *xenon,* to our nature and, by implication and occasionally specifically, not a created thing in I.18.6.2 ("foreign" and "eternal light"); 50.1 (the "uncreated [*aktiston*] Spirit"]; 58.2 (not a product of the intellect, a *noema,* but *phos hypostatikon*); II.4.7–8; 6.5–7 ("uncreated crowns"); 24.5–6 ("foreign to our nature"), 26.19 (the same); III.2.1 (same); 22.2 ("divine power and fire"); 25.3 ("light of the Holy Spirit"); and the *Great Letter,* 25–27 (the activity of the Holy Spirit is "supernatural," *hyper physin*).

[55]I.17.1.3.

[56]For example, the following from the *Tomos of the Holy Mountain,* the hesychast manifesto written by Palamas around 1339, "If anyone maintains that the light which shone about the disciples on Mount Tabor was an apparition and a symbol of the kind that now is and now is not, but has no real being . . . [he] contends against the doctrine of the saints . . . [who] call this light ineffable, uncreated, eternal, timeless . . . archetypal and unchanging beauty, the glory of God, the glory of Christ, the glory of the Spirit . . . ," from the translation by K. T. Ware, et alii, *The Philokalia* (London, 1995) 4:422. Macarius is, in fact, one of the saints Gregory invokes by name earlier on (ibid., 421) I shall come back to the importance of the term, "glory," in my discussion and n. 59 below.

[57]I.58.1–2; cf. the shorter catenae in I.17.1; 21; and 29.2

[58]For appeals to Moses' encounter with the divine glory on Sinai in Exodus 34 as a type of the Christian, see I.2.3.14; II.12.14; and 47.1; for Ezekiel's chariot, see I.29.1; II.1 ff. (discussed below); and 33.2; and, for a sampling of Macarius' use of the Johannine texts, I.4.7; 18.4; 22.2; 29.1; 35; II.15.38; III.16.4 and 28.2.

[59]Beyer, "Lichtlehre," 498ff.; and cf. Hausherr, "Les grands courants," 121–124. "Neoplatonist" is one of those words, beloved of some scholars, which is too often used without a great deal of precision and simply attached to phenomena which the writer does not like very much. With regard to most fourth-century Christian writers, it really serves more as an epithet than as a useful designation. For "glory" in Macarius, see I.2.1; 10.3; 35; 58.1; II.4.13 (identified with the "unapproachable light" of I Timothy 6:16); 12.8–9 (Adam and Moses clothed with it); 15:38 (citing John 17:22–24); 20.2 ("vesture of glory"); 25.3 (to be "participants of divine glory"); 47.1; III.2.1; 3.3; 16.8 ("vesture of glory"); 28.4 (to become "pure temples" with "glory in heart").

[60]For *kabod* in the Hebrew scriptures, see M. Weinfeld, *"Kavod"* in *The Theological Dictionary of the Old Testament*, ed. G. J. Botterwick et alii, tr. D. E. Green (Grand Rapids, 1995), vol. 7:23–38; and, at greater length, T. D. N. Mettinger, *The Dethronement of Sabaoth: Studies in the Shem and Kabod Traditions* (Lund, 1982) 80–123. For *doxa*, G. Kittel, *"Doxa," Theological Dictionary of the New Testament*, ed. G. Kittel, tr. G.W. Bromily (Grand Rapids, 1968), 3:233–253; and for carrying on the trajectory into later Christian literature, P. Deseille, "Gloire de Dieu," *Dictionnaire de spiritualité*, VI:421–463. For the visionary importance of this term and these texts in Jewish and Christian thought, see the articles by Levenson and Morray-Jones cited above, n. 20, as well as the articles and books by A. Segal, notably *Two Powers in Heaven: Early Rabbinic Reports about Christianity and Gnosticism* (Leiden, 1977), 159–237, *Paul the Convert: The Apostolate and Apostasy of Saul the Pharisee* (New Haven, 1990) especially 9–11 and 58–64; C.C. Newman, *Paul's Glory Christology* (Leiden, 1992); and J. Fossum, "Jewish-Christian Christology and Jewish Mysticism," *Vigilae christianae* 37 (1983): 260–287. This is merely to scrape the surface of a large and growing bibliography.

[61]See N. Sed, "La Shekinta" (above, n.12) for Evagrius with regard to the glory theophany on Sinai in Exodus 24:10, and cf. the "Letter 13" of Ammonas, *Patrologia Orientalis* XI:612–613 for reference to Ezekiel, and "Letter 10," XI:594, citing the *Ascension of Isaiah*.

[62]The expression "sea-change" comes from William Shakespeare's *The Tempest* and refers here to the generally acknowledged revolution in the Christian thought that Nicea brought in its train:

> Full fathom five thy father lies,
> Of his bones are coral made,
> Those are pearls that were his eyes;
> Nothing of him that doth fade
> But doth suffer a sea-change
> Into something rich and strange.

William Shakespeare, *The Tempest*, Act 1, scene 2, lines 396–401.

[63]See John Cassian, *Collationes* X, in *Corpus Scriptorum de ecclesiasticorum latinovum*, 13:288–308, for the Anthropomorphite debate in Egypt, together with G. Florovsky, "Theophilus of Alexandria and Apa Aphou of Pemdje," *The Collected Works of Father Georges Florovsky* (Belmont, MA, 1975), 4:97–129; Augustine, *De Trinitate*, Books II-III (Latin in *Oevres de S. Augustin* 15 [Paris, 1955], 183–321, and *Epistles*, 147–148 (*Obras de San Augustin*, 11 [Madrid, 1972], 41–113); and, for Cyril, *Cyril of Alexandria: Select Letters*, ed. L. R. Wickham (Oxford, 1983), especially 140–149, 156–157, and 168–171.

[64]A. Golitzin, "The Form of God and Vision of the Glory," extant at present only in Rumanian translation, as "Forma lui Dumnezeu si Vederea Slavei: Reflectii asupra Controversei Anthropomorfite din Anul 399 d. Hr.," in Hieromonk Alexander Golitzin, *Mistagogia: Experienta lui Dumnezeu in Orthodoxie*, tr. I. Ica (Sibiu, 1998), 184–267, especially 232–236.

[65]II.1.2 (my translation).

[66]On the rabbinical literature of ascent to the divine "palaces" (*hekhalot*), and its dating to the era of the Talmud, the pioneer of modern studies was Gershom Scholem. See especially his *Major Trends in Jewish Mysticism* (3rd rev. ed., Jerusalem, 1973), 1–79, and *Jewish Gnosticism, Merkabah Mysticism, and Talmudic Tradition* (2nd. ed., New York, 1965). I. Gruenwald traces the continuity from apocalyptic literature in *Apocalyptic and Merkavah Mysticism* (Leiden, 1980) and, although his and Scholem's views on continuity were subsequently challenged by P. Schaefer, "New Testament and Hekhalot Literature: The Journey into Heaven in Paul and Merkavah Mysticism," *Journal of Jewish Studies* 35 (1984): 19–35, and ibid., *The Hidden and Manifest God: Some Major Themes in Early Jewish Mysticism* (New York, 1992), which rejects "mysticism" altogether, xi-10, in which he is joined by D. Halperin's resolutely skeptical and literary approach in *Faces of the Chariot: Early Jewish Responses to Ezekiel's Vision* (Tübingen, 1988), especially 1–114, Morray-Jones has recently published an impressive response, "Paradise Revisited (2 Corinthians 12:1–12): The Jewish Mystical Background of Paul's Apostolate," in *Harvard Theological Review* 86 (1993): 177–217 and 265–292, seconded with some reservations by A. Goshen-Gottstein, "Four Entered Paradise Revisited," *Harvard Theological Review* 88 (1995): 69–133. P. J. Alexander's "Comparing Merkavah Mysticism and Gnosticism," *Journal of Jewish Studies* 35 (1984): 1–18, provided useful models for pursuing the trajectory of apocalyptic ascent to heaven from the Second Temple era through Gnosticism, on the one hand, and simultaneous rabbinical developments leading to the *hekhalot* texts, on the other. For the texts themselves and critical comment, see Schaefer, *Synopse zur Hekhalot Literatur* (Tübingen: 1981). On their precedents in the literature of Qumran, see C. Newson, *Songs of the Sabbath Sacrifice: A Critical Edition* (Atlanta, 1985), espe-

cially 39–72, and more recently the articles by J. Baumgarten, "The Qumran *Sabbath Shirot* and the Rabbinic Merkabah Tradition," *Revue de Qumran* 13 (1988): 199–213, and D. Diamant and J. Strugnell, "The Merkabah Vision in *Second Ezekiel* (4Q 385 4)," *Revue de Qumran* 14 (1990): 331–348, especially 344–48 suggesting a wider interest in the "Chariot" than simply among the Qumran sectaries. Thus see also the studies by Rowland et alii cited above, nn. 40 and 60. For striking echoes in Macarius of the imagery of the heavenly realm found often in apocalyptic and the *hekhalot* texts, see esp. I.33.3; II.14.4–5 (the "bright land" of divinity and "creatures of fire"); and III.13.2 where the "palaces" and "camps" of the angels in the heavens are held out as present possibilities within the soul.

[67]We would have none of the Old Testament Pseudepigrapha today were it not for Greek, Coptic, Syrian, Ethiopian, Armenian, and even Latin monks. On the continued interest in these materials, see most recently R. A. Kraft, "The Pseudepigrapha in Christianity," in *Tracing the Threads: Studies in the Vitality of Jewish Pseudepigrapha*, ed. J. C. Reeves, (Atlanta, 1994), 55–86. Reeves has himself written a valuable study on the impact of the visionary aspect of this literature on Mani and early Manichaeanism, *Heralds of that Good Realm: Syro-Mesopotamian Gnosis and Jewish Traditions* (Leiden, 1996), especially 5–30, a movement which we note was certainly active in the regions where Macarius lived and wrote.

[68]From D. Brakke's translation of the Coptic version of the letter, in Brakke's *Athanasius and the Politics of Asceticism* (Oxford, 1995), 330–332.

[69]See *On the Chariot* in Bedjan, *Homiliae* IV, especially Jacob's emphatic warning that it is not for his listeners to ascend the chariot on high, "else you sin in your seeking!" in 605:16–606:6, and his insistence a little earlier that "there is no chariot either to ascend to or to seek out" (601:1), since, as he argues earlier, the *merkabah* is not God's secret home, but a condescension to the needs of the angels (569:16–572:8). For Christians, however, the church's altar offers the same presence and a greater: they are to "hold Him fast in the hollows of their hands" whom the cherubim carry on their backs with trembling (609:13–14). On Dionysius' focus on the altar and liturgy, see A. Golitzin, "Hierarchy vs. Anarchy? Dionysius Areopagita, Symeon New Theologian, Nicetas Stethatos and their Common Roots in Ascetical Tradition," *St Vladimir's Theological Quarterly* 38 (1994): 131–179, especially 142–152; and ibid., *Et Introibo*, 222–230.

[70]Scholem, *Major Trends*, 79.

[71]Sed, "La Shekinta," 240–242, and for Macarius see above, n. 17 and n. 65.

[72]See, for example, P .S. Alexander's translation of *3 Enoch* 19–26, a later *hekhalot* text, in J. Charlesworth, *The Old Testament Pseudepigrapha* (New York, 1985), 2:275–281 for the *hayyot* and their "princes."

[73]II.1.2.

[74]For a like combination of Ezekiel and the *Phaedrus*, see II.2.3 and 9; and 33.2. For the *Phaedrus* taken straight, as it were, with the *nous* as charioteer, II.40.5. St Symeon New Theologian will take up precisely this combination of Ezekiel and Plato, together with the related imagery of the Byzantine offertory hymn, the *cherubikon*, at the conclusion of his third Ethical Discourse. See *St Symeon the New Theologian, On the Mystical Life: The Ethical Discourses*, tr. A. Golitzin (New York, 1995), 1:137–138 and 138, n.5.

[75]See again II.8.6, and the now/then distinctions in n.16 above.

[76]On the believer as "temple of God," see again n. 17 above.

[77]I.7.18.3. For the importance of the "bridechamber" and bridal imagery in early Syrian Christianity, see Murray, *Symbols*, 131–142.

[78]II.15.45.

[79]II.44.3.

[80]II.44.4.

[81]II.44.1 and also 2. For a like use of *metaballo/metabole*, see I.21.11; 26; 52.1; 63; III.18.2; 22.2; and 25.5. On the term's association with the eucharistic change from the time of Justin Martyr, see Lampe, *Patristic Greek Lexicon*, 848 and 850.

[82]See again Lampe, 1302–1303.

[83]I.4.7.1, and see also II.24.2; 31.1–2; and 33.1–2.

[84]II.21.5; and cf. 37.8.9 and III.27.6.

[85]Kmosko, *Patriologia Orientalis* III:285–304, English trans. in S. P. Brock, *The Syriac Fathers on Prayer and the Spiritual Life* (Kalamazoo, 1987), 45–53, and 294 (English trans.: 49) for the "three churches" of heaven, the visible assembly, and the heart. On this coordination of liturgy, heaven, and heart in Syrian Christian writers, see Murray, *Symbols,* 262–276, on its presence in Macarius and the *Liber*; Stewart, "Work-

ing," 218–221; Golitzin, *Et Introibo,* 371–384; and on Macarius, Doerries, *Theologie,* 367- 434. Relatedly, see also S. P. Brock, "Fire from Heaven: From Abel's Sacrifice to the Eucharist. A Theme in Syrian Christianity," *Studia Patristica* XXV, 229–243 (especially 239 ff.); ibid., "Prayer of the Heart in the Syriac Tradition," *Sobornost* 4:2 (1982): 131–142; and ibid. "The Priesthood of the Baptized: Some Syriac Perspectives," *Sobornost/ Eastern Churches Review* 9 (1987): 14–22. See also V. Desprez, "Le Baptême chez le Pseudo-Macaire," *Ecclesia Orans V* (1988): 121–155, esp. 125–130.

[86]On Ephrem's *Paradise Hymns,* see Brock's "Introduction" to his translation, *Hymns on Paradise* (New York, 1990), 7–75, esp. 39–74, and the chart of parallels on p. 53; and Golitzin, *Et Introibo,* 368–371.

[87]*Acts of Thomas* 92, English trans. in Schneemelcher, *New Testament Apocrypha* II:375.

[88]For references in *Aphraates,* see Brock, "Fire from Heaven" and "Prayer of the Heart."

[89]See Philo, *de somnis* II:215, on the two temples of the universe and the inner man typified by the worship of the Jerusalem Temple; Clement, *Stromateis* VII.13.82.2–5, citing 1 Corinthians 6:19 on the "Christian gnostic" as temple paralleling the Church; and for Origen, *Comm. in Mt, Patriologia Graeca* 16:161BC, and *Fragments on I Cor.,* cited by P. Brown, *The Body and Society* (Oxford/New York: 1988), 175, respectively on the "true bishop" as the spiritual man and the virgin as "priest" within the temple of her heart.

[90]See Ignatius, *Romans* 4 and 7; on Polycarp's martyrdom, the *Letter of the Smyrneans,* 14–15, and for discussion, A. Golitzin, *Et introibo,* 245–247. On the Jewish origins of the theology of martyrdom, W. H. C. Frend, *Martyrdom and Persecution in the Early Church* (Garden City, NJ, 1967), 22–57.

[91]See S.A. Harvey, "The Edessan Martyrs and Ascetic Tradition," *V Symposium Syriacum,* ed. R. Lavenant (Roma, 1990), 195–206, esp. 196–201. Relatedly to this theme and n. 89, the transfigured body, see also Harvey's remarkable article on Symeon Stylites, "The Sense of a Stylite: Perspectives on Symeon the Elder," *Vigilae christianae* 42 (1988): 376–394, esp. 381–386.

[92]See K. Holl, *Enthusiasmus und Bussgewalt beim griechischen Mönchtum: Eine Studie zum Symeon dem neuen Theologen* (Leipzig, 1898), which is largely devoted to this theme, together with the references in n. 9 above.

[93]Desprez, "Baptême," especially 131–154.

[94]Ibid., 140–145; relatedly, see A. Guillaumont, "Les 'Arrhès de l'Esprit' dans le Livre des Degrés," *In Memorian Msgr. Gabriel Khouri-Sarkis* (Louvain, 1969), 107–113.

[95]Ibid., 135–7 and 145, citing Macarius, I.43, and noting parallel expressions in Gregory of Nyssa, Basil the Great, and others.

[96]Ibid., 153–154, and see also esp. K.T. Ware, "The Sacrament of Baptism and the Ascetic Life in the Teaching of Mark the Monk," *Studia Patristica* 10 (1970): 441–452.

[97]I.22.1.7–8.

[98]II.27.17.

[99]See n. 84 above for the scholarly discussion of this homily.

[100]I.52.1.1.

[101]I.52.1.3.

[102]I.52.2.1.

[103]I.52.2.2–8.

[104]See, for example, Revelation 4–5 and Hebrews 12, and recall the Qumran *Songs of the Sabbath Sacrifice* cited above, n. 65. This is not, to be sure, an issue without debate. On the one hand, see P. Prigent, *Apocalypse et liturgie* (Neuchatel, 1964), 14–68, and E. Petersen, *The Angels and the Liturgy,* tr. Walls (1964), and, on the other, E. Schüessler-Fiorenza, "Cultic Language in Qumran and in the New Testament," *Catholic Biblical Quarterly* 38 (1976): 159–177.

[105]See the criticisms of Macarius in this regard summarized by Desprez, "Baptême," 123–124, and, more generally and with application to Eastern Orthodox critics of "platonizing" the liturgy, the argument and the many references cited in P. Vassiliades, *Greek Orthodox Theological Review* 42 (1997): 1–23.

[106]On Athanasius, see again Brakke, *Athanasius and the Politics of Asceticism,* and for Basil, Gribomont, "Monachisme au sein de l'Eglise," together with, more recently, P. Rousseau, *Basil of Caesarea* (Berkeley, 1994), esp. 190–232.

[107]See the references in n. 84 above.

[108]For a sketch of this trajectory, see Golitzin, *Et introibo,* 402–413, and 219–230 for Dionysius in particular. On Maximus in this regard, see A. Louth, *The Wisdom of the Byzantine Church: Evagrius of Pontus and Maximus the Confessor,* ed. J. Raitt (University of Missouri, 1998), esp. 34–43; and R. Bornert, *Les com-*

mentaires byzantins de la divine liturgie du VIIe au XVe siècle (Paris, 1966), 83–104. For Symeon, see A. Golitzin, *On the Mystical Life*, 3:156–173; and for Gregory of Sinai, M. Van Parys, "La liturgie du coeur chez S. Gregoire le Sinaïte," *Irénikon* 51 (1978): 312–337 (though without reference to either Dionysius or Symeon).

[109]See A. C. Outler, "Preface," and F. Whaling, "Introduction," to the Paulist Press edition, *John and Charles Wesley: Selected Writings* (New York, 1981), xiv-xvi and 12–13, respectively.

8

Inner Struggle:
Some Parallels between the Spirituality of
John Wesley and the Greek Fathers

Frances Young

The principal focus of this paper will be on the relationship between Wesley's spirituality and that of the Macarian Homilies. However, in order to set the scene and bring
out key characteristics in the Macarian material that Wesley then takes over in a very
different historical and social context, I shall begin by focussing on the notion of
struggle and its significance in the world of early Christianity.

The "Agon"

Heroism was very important in the culture of the ancient world. The importance of
the great Homeric epics to Greek education was one factor in the glorification of the
hero who carried off the victor's crown in combat, literally on the battlefield. But such
was not in practice a heroic possibility once the *pax romana* had turned the army into
professionals and for the most part distanced war to remote frontiers. Another form
of combat was the struggle in athletics. Through competition the same struggle for
glory could be peacefully enacted. Education in the Greek tradition took place in the
gymnasium and embraced intense physical training as well as reading the classics,
acquiring oratorical skills and, for some, sitting at the feet of philosophers. The crown
of olive brought glory, *doxa*, to the victor in the games. It is no wonder early Christian texts evidence images drawn from this scene, as pervasive as it was then as sport is
today.

The most well known New Testament example is doubtless that phrase in
Hebrews 12:1 about running the race (*agon*) set before us with perseverance, as a great
crowd of onlookers cheers us on. For St Paul, the Christian life involves an *agon*: there
is the struggle he and his converts have with opponents (Phil 1:27–30); and speaking
the gospel involves struggle (1 Thess 2:2). The most graphic description occurs in 1
Corinthians 9:24–27 (NRSV):

> Do you not know that in a race the runners all compete, but only one receives the
> prize? Run in such a way that you may win it. Athletes exercise self-control in all
> things; they do it to receive a perishable wreath, but we an imperishable one. So I do
> not run aimlessly, nor do I box as though beating the air; but I punish my body and

enslave it, so that proclaiming to others I myself should not be disqualified.

The English translation obscures one or two significant words for the history we are to trace: the word "athlete" represents Greek which means the one who "agonizes," in other words, engages in an *agon*; the "self-control" is *encrateia*, soon to be associated in Christianity with asceticism; the winner's crown or "wreath" will reappear in much literature about martyrs attaining the victory; and the subjection of the body, here an image drawn from sports training, will become a more literal theme in the struggle of martyr and monk.

Such comments immediately open up the key themes for us. It has been argued[1] that the withdrawal of monks into the deserts that happened so dramatically in the fourth century was a kind of replacement of martyrdom, by now a thing of the past because of the peace of the church under Constantine. And the representation of both as front-line troops in a battle, as athletes striving for the crown, rising above the natural needs and fears of the body, is not the least of those features that encourage this association. Many early Christian writers depict suffering as a school of discipline, but more specific is the way the *agon* of the martyr was characterized in the early *Acts* as a spectacle, entertainment in the amphitheater:[2] Tertullian addressed prospective martyrs, saying, "You are going to submit to a good *agon* in which God is the *agono-thetes* (the person who gives the spectacle), the *xystarches* (president of the wrestling match) is the Holy Spirit and the *epistates* (the steward of the games) is Christ." The heroism displayed in this stylized battle represented the real struggle with the powers of evil. The notion of *Christus Victor* [3] overcoming the devil through the Cross and breaking the power of death through the Resurrection, inspired the troops he led to engage with hope in the struggle. Through suffering and death lay the victor's crown.

The *agon* of the martyr was replayed in that of the desert monk. Theodoret's picture of the Syrian ascetics is of heroes

> who have undertaken a campaign against evil and paganism, a combat with the devil who is overcome by their exorcisms and cures, a race in which they will win an imperishable crown; for they are imitators of God's prophets, indeed the imitators of Christ himself.[4]

In taking the offensive against the powers of evil the monks, like the martyrs before them, were engaged in what Gustaf Aulen called a "mopping-up operation," for Christ had already won the essential victory.[5]

Athanasius in the long recension of his work *On the Incarnation* suggests that Christ suffered the specific death by crucifixion so as to confront the devil in his own element, by hanging in the air, and in the *Life of Antony*, following Christ involves invading the devil's own territory, the tombs and the desert. The victorious Christ works through Antony to overcome the powers of evil. The weapons are prayer and the sign of the Cross. The tales of the monks collected by Palladius and others demonstrate the way in which this struggle was interiorized. It was to do with the overcoming of temptations, of passions, anger, and pride. Ministering angels assisted in the battle against interior demons, which particularly attacked the soul through the body, through needs and desires for sleep, for food, for sex. Physical mortification became the vehicle through which the spiritual struggle was played out.

Some collections of the *Apophthegmata Patrum* make this the more apparent by arranging their material by topic, so highlighting the twenty or so monastic virtues: of quiet; of patience; that a monk might not possess anything; that nothing ought to be done for show; of humility; and so on. The sense of struggle with demonic temptations remains:

> Who sits in solitude and is quiet has escaped three wars: hearing, speaking, seeing; yet against one thing shall he continually battle: that is, his own heart.[6]

And the difficulties of focussing on the right struggle is captured in the saying:

> We have not been taught to kill our bodies, but to kill our passions.[7]

That the battle with demons was a way of representing internal conflict was recognized:

> Our own wills become demons.[8]

> They attack us from outside, and they also stir us up from within.[9]

One of the desert fathers recalled the words of James 1:14: Each person is tempted when he is lured and enticed by his own desire.[10]

Indeed, the struggle against temptation drew much from the Scriptures.[11] The forty days Jesus spent in the wilderness were literally played out in periods of solitude. Demons were often chased away by words from Scripture. Biblical heroes, Job and others, provided examples of endurance. Perseverance in time of trial was assisted by scriptural words:

> Rejoice that God visits you and keep this blessed saying on your lips, "The Lord has chastened me sorely but he has not given me over unto death." (Ps 118:18) . . . Have you been given a thorn in the flesh? (2 Cor 12:7) Exult, and see who else was treated like that; it is an honour to have the same sufferings as Paul. Are you being tried by fever? Are you being taught by cold? Indeed scripture says, "We went through fire and water; yet thou hast brought us forth to a spacious place." (Ps 66:12) . . . By this share of wretchedness you will be made perfect. For he said: "The Lord hears when I call him." (Ps 4:3) So open your mouth wider to be taught by these exercises of the soul, seeing that we are under the eyes of our enemy.[12]

They were sure that temptations could not destroy hope in God.[13]

So far then we have seen how central was the notion of struggle in the world of early Christianity, and how early Christian construction of the spiritual life drew upon this range of imagery, sometimes almost literally, more often in parabolic ways. We have also traced a movement towards interiorizing the struggle with evil, and focusing upon the war within one's own heart. It is this legacy as it appears in the Macarian Homilies to which we now turn.

The Macarian Homilies

I shall not digress into any discussion of the provenance of or critical problems raised by the Macarian Homilies, but simply assume that they are the product of the monastic tradition and note that their influence upon both Eastern Orthodox spirituality and upon John Wesley is incontestable.

If there is any significance in the order in which the Homilies appear in the best known collection of fifty, it is noticeable that the opening homily on Ezekiel's vision of the chariot-throne, interpreted as an image of the soul with Christ as the charioteer, is immediately followed by a series of homilies which set out the need for liberation from the powers of darkness. These describe the struggle in which the soul has to engage as a "war" in one's "inner thoughts" against "arrogance, presumption, unbelief, hatred, envy, deceit, hypocrisy," and use images of journeying and running races victoriously. The kind of material we have been observing has certainly shaped the language and imagery here: conflict whether in war or the arena is how the Christian life is envisaged. By Homily 21 it is explicit that whoever wishes to please God has to

> wage battle on a double front. One battle takes place in the material affairs of this life by turning completely away from the earthly preoccupations and the attraction of worldly bonds and from sinful passions. The other battle takes place in the interior against the evil spirits themselves of whom the Apostle spoke: "For it is not against human enemies that we have to struggle but against the Sovereignties and the Powers, against the rulers of the darkness of this world, against spiritual armies of evil in the heavens" (Eph 6:12).[14]

This latter, interior struggle only becomes apparent when the first is won, and can only be brought to a conclusion through the grace and power of God. It is the person who has really rejected the world, has persevered wholeheartedly, who "discovers the opposition, the hidden passions, the invisible bonds, the unseen warfare, the battle and interior struggle"; and then

> he receives the heavenly armour of the Spirit, which the blessed Apostle described as "the breastplate of justice, the helmet of salvation, the shield of faith and the sword of the Spirit" (Eph 6:14). Armed with these weapons, he is able to stand against the hidden deceits of the devil . . .[15]

The battle is with one's own nature, with its old habits and the customs with which one grew up;

> for a certain hidden and subtle power of darkness is revealed that has been entrenched in the heart. And the Lord . . . puts in you secret, heavenly thoughts and

he begins interiorly to give you rest. But he allows you to be disciplined, and grace directs you in these very afflictions.[16]

The following image of a child being chastised encourages gratitude to the tutor who inflicts punishment. So grace in God's providence disciplines until arrival at full maturity.

The individual has to struggle with great patience; the spiritual power of God's grace also works with great patience. Perseverance in the face of temptation is vital. Homily 9 illustrates this with one biblical example after another: Joseph, David, Moses, Abraham, Noah—these examples are offered

> to show that the power of divine grace is in man and the gift of the Holy Spirit which is given to the faithful soul comes with much contention, with much endurance, patience, trials and testings.[17]

Someone who really strives, battling, longing, diligently seeking, should be able to escape from the darkness of the evil demons, and attain to holiness and perfection, because they receive the love of Christ and the Holy Spirit. Yet even when a person is deep and rich in grace, there still remains inside a remnant of evil.[18] Someone overwhelmed by temptations, however, ought not to lose hope. For evil diminishes and dries up in persons who constantly put their hope in God. Those abounding in grace can overcome the reality that evil lives in the human heart and operates by suggesting wicked and obscene thoughts, for it has entered into our souls and touched all our bones and members. Sin and grace are at war within us.

The points just made come from Homily 16, which is one from which John Wesley abstracted certain paragraphs to form Homily VIII in the first volume of his *Christian Library*. Anticipating comparison with Wesley, I shall continue by drawing attention to passages which are to be found among the selections that Wesley published in translation. Here there can be no dispute about influence—indeed, we find Macarian material in the dress of Wesleyan English, and this brings out the deep similarities in their spirituality. Both identify struggle as an essential element in attaining to perfection, though perfection comes entirely through God's grace and the gift of the Spirit.

The person who has not yet come "to the perfect love of Christ, and to the fullness of the Godhead"

> still inwardly retains the war. He is one hour refreshed in prayer, and another in a state of affliction: for so is the will of the Lord; because he is as yet but an infant, he trains him up to the battle: and there spring up in him both light and darkness, and rest and affliction: and that, whatever gifts he hath, for many of the brethren have had gifts of healing, and revelation, and prophecy; however, not having attained to perfect charity, the war came upon them, and they fell.[19]

In the Homily which follows in Wesley's selection, we find that although Christians are "possessed of so much joy and comfort, they are yet *in fear and trembling.*" Now and again Macarian material takes the form of question and answer, so the question arises here: What fear and trembling? The answer is:

> A jealous fear, that they make no false step in any one instance; but harmonize with grace. For a man does not immediately arrive at perfection. First he enters the lists and fights with satan, and after a long course and fight he carries off the trophies of victory, and becomes a Christian.[20]

The following discussion makes it clear that struggle and trouble is unavoidable; the way into the kingdom is "*strait and narrow*," and "we must go through this rugged way, and hold out with patience, and be afflicted, and so enter life."

In these Homilies is a tension in the reasons given for the struggle in which the Christian is engaged. The context of the first passage we noted suggests that, whereas war is the condition of those not yet perfect, the (true) Christian is clothed in the Spirit, at rest, fortified against external attack by the inner power of the Lord, no longer worried about satan. In fact, an analogy is drawn with Christ in the wilderness, and the suggestion is made that because God was within, there was no harm in Satan approaching. "Christians, though outwardly they are tempted; yet inwardly are they filled with the Divine nature and so nothing injured." Elsewhere,[21] however, the varied states of believers are attributed to God's wisdom and providential dispensation, some receiving the gifts of the Spirit "without toil and sweat, and fatigue," and others subject to all kinds of trials despite having withdrawn from the world and persevering in prayer and fasting and diligence. Not having received the consolation of grace, they are the more keen to advance, and should certainly not be subject to criticism:

> Let not therefore any of the brethren be lifted up against his brother, so as to say, I have the spiritual gift, and thou hast not. For you know not what the morrow may bring forth; or what end his will be, and what your own.

Indeed, there are real dangers for those who think they are secure. A beautiful garden can still be destroyed by flood, and

> Even thus is the heart of man; it has good thoughts and desires, but there are rivers of corruption ever approaching. And if the mind give but a little way to unclean thoughts; lo, the spirits of error have entered in, and overturned all the beauties that were there, and laid the soul waste.[22]

In fact, without the power of God, dealing with the powers of darkness is impossible. Christ is needed as pilot to navigate the "waves of wickedness and the strong winds of sin."[23] The soul has to be brought out of Egypt protected by the pillar of fire and the pillar of the cloud; the spiritual Pharaoh pursues the soul hard with afflictions and temptations—in fact, this is the way God has appointed,

> to be in affliction, and in straits, and temptations; that thence the soul may afterwards make her way to the true land of the glory of the sons of God. When therefore the

soul has no hope in herself, through the overbearing affliction, and the death before her eyes; in that very juncture doth she, with a strong hand, and an high arm, through shining of the Holy Spirit, break through the power of darkness . . .[24]

It would be an over-simplification to say that Wesley's Macarian material holds out a picture of struggle in this life and rewards in the life to come. Rather, there is a contrast between Christians and others, a sharp distinction between

the children of this world . . . tossed to and fro by unsettled reasonings, by earthly desires, and a variety of gross imaginations, whereby Satan is continually sifting the whole sinful race of men

and true Christians who

have their heart and mind constantly taken up with thoughts of heaven; . . . and being arrived, through many conflicts and labours to a settled and fixed state, to an exemption from trouble, to perfect rest, are never sifted more by unsettled and vain thoughts.[25]

In other words, heaven is anticipated among those who are born of God. But this is "purchased only with labour, and pains, and trials, and many conflicts;" and as we have seen, always vulnerable. Ultimately it is entirely dependent upon God's grace. Yet we are exhorted to "strive," so that "the inward man may be made partaker of that glory in this present life."[26] And to become "the pure habitation of the Holy Spirit" is to attain

heights which the soul does not reach all at once; but through many labours and conflicts, with variety of trials and temptations, it receives spiritual growth and improvement, till at last it comes to an entire exemption from its old afflictions . . .[27]

In fact the striving is described as taking care to work out our salvation with fear and trembling; and in another question and answer session, it is stated that if a person grows careless, he certainly falls from grace; because his enemies are never idle or backward in the war.[28] The soul should not be "surprised as at a strange or unusual thing," when it "falls into divers temptations"; nor should it "despond, because it knows that they come by permission, that it may be tried and disciplined by the evil that befalls it."[29] There is assurance that "they in whom the Divine law is ingrafted in the heart" are "able to get clear of the stumbling-blocks of the wicked one"; but not if they imagine they have done it in their own strength. Only those who constantly seek help from God will be "made partaker of the Divine glory." Prayer is enjoined for "the Divine fire" that enlightens souls, that tries them "as pure gold in the furnace," that consumes "sin as thorns and stubble," "burns up the beam in the inward eye, and restores the mind to its purity"; for "this burning of the Spirit" is what "kindles up new life in the heart."[30]

Thus we see that for Macarius, as read by Wesley, perfection is perfect love, and in the true Christian this is anticipated on earth; but it is never secure, and the discipline of temptation always possible. This struggle towards perfection is at the heart of prayer and spirituality.

John Wesley

That John Wesley was influenced by the Macarian Homilies is a fact not simply dependent upon their presence in the *Christian Library*. His diary entry for July 30, 1736, indicates that travelling by boat during his mission in Georgia, with the wind set fair, and later in the rain, he read Macarius and sang. Even when "not a little affrighted by the falling of the mast . . . , he again read Macarius and sang." Though a man of "one book," the Bible, Wesley early determined that a sure rule for its interpretation was the consensus of the ancients, and describes in his *Journal* how he daily checked his reading of Scripture against the early authors as he crossed the Atlantic. This before his so-called conversion; but the continuing significance of the Fathers in general and Macarius in particular is evident in the *Plain Account of Genuine Christianity* (1753) where he expresses his reverence for the primitive Fathers, naming Clement of Rome, Ignatius, Polycarp, Justin Martyr, and others, adding to the list, Macarius and Ephraim Syrus.[31]

Wesley believed that the Macarian Homilies were written by the "great Macarius of Egypt," and in his preface offers an exemplary sketch of his life, suggesting that

> what he continually labours to cultivate in himself and others is, the real life of God in heart and soul, that kingdom of God, which consists in righteousness, and peace, and joy in the Holy Ghost.

Commending the homilies, he deduces that "Macarius" was educated in the Holy Scriptures, and his knowledge of them was "not merely literal or speculative," but "true and practical," "able to save his soul." Using phrases that indicate his perception of congruence between his own thought and that of "Macarius," he writes:

> He is ever quickening and stirring up his audience, endeavouring to kindle in them a steady zeal, an earnest desire, and inflamed ambition, to recover that Divine image we were made in; to be made conformable to Christ our Head; to be daily sensible more and more of our living union with him as such; and discovering it, as occasion requires, in all the genuine fruits of an holy life and conversation, in such a victorious faith as overcomes the world, and working by love, is ever fulfilling the whole law of God.

Wesley and "Macarius" have a common practical theology, a common drive towards perfection as the goal of the Christian life, a common emphasis on the Incarnation and the Holy Spirit as the generators of perfection, a common stress on the love of God.

In the Macarian Homilies, then, Wesley found the doctrine of Christian perfection, but it was perfection earthed in the reality of struggle. To what extent is struggle characteristic of Wesley's own account of Christian living? It would seem to have a more significant place than might appear at first sight, given that for him genuine Christianity was a matter of love, joy, and peace.

Faced with misunderstanding by opponents and over-enthusiasm among supporters, he had to spell out what was and was not meant by Christian perfection, and like Macarius before him, stressed that security was never possible in this life. The contentious nature of his doctrine of Christian perfection and the need to explain exactly what he meant is clear in *A Plain Account of Christian Perfection*.[32] Here he insists that his teaching on the subject has been consistent from 1725 to 1765; indeed, the work, written in haste, abstracts from earlier writings to prove exactly that. Time and again we see how the doctrine is built up out of the promises of Scripture. Those who cannot accept it do not trust God to fulfill the divine promises. Perfection is defined as "perfect love" and as something dynamic—not a state attained, nor something absolute, but something always improvable: indeed, "one perfected in love may grow in grace far swifter than he did before."[33] In other words, it is not something of which anyone can boast, nor does it eliminate the possibility of struggle or future fall.

This is apparent in the sermon on "Christian Perfection" which is among the works retrospectively surveyed. Here Wesley tried to spell out in what sense Christians are not perfect, and in what sense they are. They are not perfect in knowledge—they can make mistakes, they are not infallible; they are not free from infirmities—they may be slow of understanding, lack quickness of imagination, may be unrefined in language and, to put it in our terms, have a local working-class accent. This is one way in which Wesley acknowledges that everyone remains limited by the flesh, by being a creature. Wesley also affirms that none are ever wholly free from temptation—the servant is not greater than the master, he says, maybe picking up a comment we have already noted in Macarius.[34] Elsewhere he suggests that if the Spirit has purified the heart, evil thoughts cannot spring up any more, and that in a sense those saved are free from temptation:

> for tho' numberless temptations fly about them, yet they trouble them not. At all times their soul is even and calm, their heart is steadfast and unmovable.[35]

Yet such immunity still presupposes that temptation is the environment in which the perfected one must exist. In the very next paragraph Wesley gives comfort to those tempted to give up their confidence in God because "tried by fire," with a soul "in heaviness through manifold temptations." The peace that comes with knowing God's salvation may last for days, weeks, months, and the belief arise that war will be known no more; and then

> some of their old enemies, their bosom sins, or the sin which did most easily beset them (perhaps anger or desire), assault them again, and thrust sore at them that they may fall.[36]

Doubt about the forgiveness of sins will then arise, along with fears that they will not endure to the end. But Wesley is sure that God will soon answer.

In fact Wesley's account of his own so-called conversion experience shows how he was dogged by such doubts and temptations.[37] Once he had testified to what had happened, it was not long before the enemy suggested, "This cannot be faith, for where is thy joy?" After all he had only had his heart "warmed"; it wasn't set on fire! Later after he had returned home, he says he was "much buffeted with temptations"; and though they fled when he cried out, they returned again and again. The difference was, however, that whereas before he was often conquered by temptation, now he was always conqueror, as long as he asked for divine help. The next day the enemy continued to suggest doubts and fears; but a Pauline text came to his rescue, "Without were fightings, within were fears" (2 Cor 7:5). Wesley felt he had to go on and tread them under his feet. The following day he claims that his soul continued in peace, but yet in heaviness because of manifold temptations. And the day after still he was assaulted by many temptations, though through these experiences he discovered that trust in the wounds of Christ and rejoicing in God his Saviour was enough to enlarge his spirit and make him more than conqueror. Thus Wesley presents himself as a type of the soul being converted, discovering that God provides the weapons that are most effective in battle.

Wesley did not believe that sanctification came immediately. In a sermon on the fullness of faith, he describes the process. It began at the moment of justification, but soon "temptations return and sin revives; showing it was but stunned before, not dead."[38] The experience of converts is that two principles are at war within them, the flesh lusting against the Spirit, nature opposing grace. Such persons may still have the power to believe in Christ and to love God, yet feel in themselves something of pride or self-will, sometimes anger or unbelief. They find these things frequently stirring in their hearts but not conquering; he admits they may fall, but the Lord is their help. At this point he explicitly turns to Macarius, and quotes words expressing the view that while the inexperienced may imagine they have no more sin, the more mature recognize that even those who have the grace of God may be molested again.

> So it is necessary to mortify the deeds of the body, of 'our evil nature'. As we are more and more dead to sin, we are more and more alive to God. We go on from grace to grace.[39]

Thus we wait for entire sanctification, for full salvation from all our sins, from pride, self-will, anger, unbelief, for Christian perfection. Even then temptation and struggle are not incompatible with Christian perfection, though attainment of perfect love implies victory through the power of the Spirit. To facilitate the process of sanctification, every meeting of "the bands" had an agenda of questions: What known sins have you committed since our last meeting? What temptations have you met with? How were you delivered?[40] Wesley regards as blessed the person who endures temptation; for once tried and proved, he shall receive the crown of life (Jas 1:12). Thus he picks up the biblical language of the *agon*. But he warns against attributing such temptation to God, despite the words of the Lord's Prayer: "Lead us not into temptation," which refers to any kind of trial, and the prayer is that we be not enticed into it through our own lust or by the "evil one" from whom we pray to be delivered (*Forty-four Sermons,* no. XXI = no. VI on the "Sermon on the Mount"). Here Wesley alludes to James 1:14 exactly as one of the Desert Fathers had before him (see above).

In his published sermons Wesley does not ignore the problems of "Satan's devices" (*Forty-four Sermons*, no. XXXVII), or "heaviness through manifold temptations" (*Forty-four Sermons*, no. XLI); indeed, given the extent to which the struggle is internalized, it is not surprising that he also needs to address the issue of "wandering thoughts" (*Forty-four Sermons*, no. XXXVI). In these sermons it is clear that Wesley has a lively sense of all those distractions offered by the world, the flesh, and the devil. Bodily weakness or pain may distract and the person be innocent; but if the distraction allows room for sinful tempers to increase, such as pride, anger, love of the world, that innocence is gone. Heaviness through manifold temptations does not threaten the basic characteristics of those born again, those in whom the love of God is shed abroad in their hearts, those whose peace passes understanding, those filled with joy in the Holy Ghost. They may be sorrowful, grieved, under a fiery trial, yet that is God's way of refining faith. Trials increase faith, hope, love, and advance holiness of heart. The important thing is to endure to the end, through watching and praying. As long as we are in the world we cannot escape the subtleties of Satan. We have the first-fruits of God's Spirit; but the harvest is not yet. And Christians are open to attack precisely where their strength lies: by concentrating on their guilt and sinfulness rather than the hope of the gospel; by letting their confidence in God's salvation wane. This is perhaps Wesley's version of the sin of *akedia*.

John Wesley's life was marked with conflict, so it is not surprising that conflict motifs appear in his writings. He recognized that the more God's kingdom prevailed, the more the prince of this world would cause "a flood of opposition."[41] He was not dead or asleep. He stirred up the people, magistrates, and even the King to "take a course to stop these run-about preachers." Wesley recognizes that in all ages and nations, all they that will live godly in Christ Jesus shall suffer persecution (2 Tim 3:12). Yet predominantly it is the inner struggle that fills the pages of his published work.

Wesley's preaching is full of the need to strive, to run the race and win the prize (e.g., *Forty-four Sermons*, no. XXVI = no. XI on the "Sermon on the Mount"). But this "striving as in an agony" to enter in at the strait gate (Wesley quotes the Greek: *agonizesthe eiselthein*) means turning from the broad way which is "void of poverty of spirit, and all that inward religion, which the many, the rich, the wise, account madness" and seeking that "holiness without which no man can see the Lord." There is a profound consonance between the interiority of the struggle as it is found in Wesley and Macarius. Wesley democratizes the spirituality he found in those he regarded as the early interpreters of Scripture, namely the Fathers of the fourth and earlier centuries. That much of it emerged from the monastic movement does not deter him from presenting it as the true Christianity every believer should aspire to.

Conclusion

In this he was anticipated by St John Chrysostom. We know from John Wesley's lists of the early authors he valued and read that Chrysostom was among them, and indeed that he learned the importance of good works from Chrysostom, to whom he attributes the statement:

> So soon as a man hath faith, he shall flourish in good works. For faith is full of good works and nothing is good without faith.[42]

Wesley came nearer to the Eastern doctrine of synergism than most Western theologians, largely through his reading of Chrysostom. The very first paper I ever wrote (produced for a graduate seminar and never published) showed that the two Johns, Chrysostom and Wesley, have much in common, and we can certainly assume familiarity with St John's attempt to live the monastic virtues in the world and to preach repentance and transformation of life to everybody. While we cannot suggest actual familiarity with the more recently rediscovered texts of Chrysostom's *Catechetical Homilies*, these texts confirm this consonance of thought, and precisely because they are addressed to all who seek baptism and graphically bring together the themes we have traced, they provide a fitting climax to the study, and exemplify common themes in Orthodox and Wesleyan spirituality.

> Chrysostom urges each of those to be baptised to approach his daily task with fear and anguish, and spend his working-hours in the knowledge that at evening he should . . . render account to the Master for the whole day.[43]

Like Wesley he sees prayer and thanksgiving as the way to secure the gifts of salvation, as the remedy for the soul, the cure for passions which surge up within. Prayer is the cleansing of our souls, ransom for our sins, the foundation and source of countless blessings, but also a fortress of the faithful, an invincible weapon.[44]

The military imagery runs right through, for the neophytes are enlisted in Christ's army[45] and must show themselves good fighters from the very outset, doing battle with the desires and passions of the flesh, their whole decorum providing evidence that they are enrolled as citizens of another state, the heavenly Jerusalem.[46]

> Like valiant and vigilant soldiers of the Spirit, shine up your spiritual weapons each day, so that your enemy may see the glitter of your arms, retreat far off, and never even consider making a stand from close at hand.[47]

The enemy is, of course, the devil, and in describing the combat in which every Christian is engaged, the *agon* in the arena provides variant imagery:[48]

> When the day of the games arrives, when the stadium is open, when the spectators are seated above the arena, and the judge of the contest is on hand, then must those who are slothful fall and leave the arena in deep disgrace, or be energetic and win the crowns and prizes.[49]

The thirty days of preparation are like training for wrestling. The catechumens up to now have been in a school for training and exercise; there falls were forgiven. But from today on, the arena stands open, the contest is at hand, the spectators have taken their seats.[50]

Using words of St Paul, Chrysostom notes that "we have been made a spectacle to the world and to angels and to men," suggesting that while the angels are spectators, the Lord of angels presides over the contest as judge. But this judge is not impartial, like judges at the Olympic games. Christ is entirely on our side:

He anointed us as we went into the combat, but He fettered the devil; He anointed us with the oil of gladness, but He bound the devil with fetters that cannot be broken to keep him shackled hand and foot for the combat.[51]

The contrast is developed: "If I win, I shall receive a crown; if he wins, he is chastised." So

let us . . . take courage and strip ourselves for the contests. Christ has put on us armor that is more glittering than gold, stronger than steel . . . God has made my breastplate not from metal but justice; he has prepared for me a shield which is made not of bronze but of faith. I have, too, a sharp sword, the word of the Spirit.[52]

The martyrs provide examples of this kind of courageous engagement, and are powerful to assist and heal their followers.[53] However, it is the Cross which provides the most powerful type of the struggle. Chrysostom quotes St Paul, "They who belong to Christ have crucified their flesh with its passions and desires (Gal 5:24)," and continues:

When a man is fastened to a cross and has been pierced with those nails, he is broken by the pain and tormented, so to speak, in every fiber of his being. In this state he never could be troubled by desires of the flesh, but every passion and wicked desire is put to rout by the pain which leaves no room for those passions. In the same way, those who have dedicated themselves to Christ have nailed themselves to Him by this dedication and have jeered at the concupiscence of the body, just as if they had crucified themselves together with their passions and desires.[54]

For Chrysostom the struggle is personal, but empowered by Christ with the promise of glory, as it would be centuries later for John Wesley.

My final challenge is: how do we reclaim this perspective for the twenty-first century? In different ways secular psychology and the charismatic movement have made it problematic to appropriate it uncritically for the twentieth century. But I suspect that a spirituality of peace, love, and joy needs the mettle of contest and struggle, if it is not to become merely sentimental.

Selected Bibliography

To assist the general reader, this author has made use of readily available collections, editions and English translations, and referred to the following volumes by page number:

For the Apophthegmata Patrum

Waddell, Helen, *The Desert Fathers* (Collins: Fontana Library, 1962 [1st published 1936]).
Ward, Benedicta, *The Sayings of the Desert Fathers* (London: Mowbrays, 1975).

For the Macarian Homilies

Wesley, John, M.A., *A Christian Library:* consisting of extracts from and abridgements of the choicest pieces of Practical Divinity which have been published in the English tongue, vol. I of the 1819 edition.
Pseudo-Macarius, The Fifty Spiritual Homilies and the Great Letter, translated, edited and with an introduction by George A. Maloney, S.J., The Classics of Western Spirituality series (New York: Paulist Press, 1992).

For John Wesley

Wesley, John, *Sermons on Several Occasions:* first series consisting of forty-four discourses (London: The Epworth Press, 1944 [with subsequent reprints]).
John Wesley, ed. Albert C. Outler (New York: Oxford University Press, 1964).
John and Charles Wesley. Selected Writings and Hymns, ed. Frank Whaling, The Classics of Western Spirituality series (New York: Paulist Press, 1981).

For John Chrysostom

St John Chrysostom, Baptismal Instructions, translated and annotated by Paul W. Harkins, Ancient Christian Writers series, no. 31 (New York: Newman Press, 1963).

Endnotes

[1] For example see E. E. Malone, *The Monk and the Martyr* (Washington, D.C.: Catholic University Press, 1950).
[2] As, drawing on earlier work, G. W. Bowersock noted, *Martyrdom and Rome* (Cambridge: Cambridge University Press, 1995), 50 ff.
[3] The title of the classic study by Gustaf Aulen, trans. (abridged) by A. G. Herbert (London: SPCK, 1931).
[4] From my work *From Nicaea to Chalcedon* (London: SCM and Philadelphia: Fortress Press, 1982), 55.
[5] Aulen, *Christus Victor*.
[6] *Verba Seniorum* ii.2, in Helen Waddell, *The Desert Fathers* (London: Collins, Fontana Library, 1962, first published London: Constable, 1936), 81.
[7] *Alphabeticon*, Poemen, 184, in Benedicta Ward, *The Sayings of the Desert Fathers* (London: Mowbrays, 1975), 162.

[8] *Alphabeticon*, Poemen, 67, in Ward, *The Sayings of the Desert Fathers*, 148.

[9] *Alphabeticon*, Syncletica, 24, in Ward, *The Sayings of the Desert Fathers*, 196.

[10] *Alphabeticon*, Sisoes, 44, in Ward, *The Sayings of the Desert Fathers*, 185.

[11] Cf. Douglas Burton-Christie, *The Word in the Desert. Scripture and the Quest for Holiness in Early Christian Monasticism* (New York and Oxford: Oxford University Press, 1993).

[12] *Alphabeticon*, Syncletica 7, in Ward, *The Sayings of the Desert Fathers*, 194.

[13] *Alphabeticon*, Poemen 102, in Ward, *The Sayings of the Desert Fathers*, 152.

[14] *Pseudo-Macarius, The Fifty Spiritual Homilies and the Great Letter*, translated, edited, and with an introduction by George A. Maloney, S.J., The Classics of Western Spirituality series (New York: Paulist Press, 1992), 153; henceforth cited as Maloney, *Pseudo-Macarius*.

[15] Maloney, *Pseudo-Macarius*, 155.

[16] Hom. 32, in Maloney, *Pseudo-Macarius*, 200–201.

[17] Maloney, *Pseudo-Macarius*, 85.

[18] Hom. 16, in Maloney, *Pseudo-Macarius*, 130.

[19] *Christian Library* (Hom. XIV.5) in John Wesley, M.A., *A Christian Library: Consisting of Extracts from, and Abridgements of the Choicest Pieces of Practical Divinity in the English Tongue*, 50 vols. (Bristol: F. Farley, 1749–1755; reprinted in 30 vols., London: T. Cordeux, 1819–1827), vol. 1 of the 1819–1827 edition, 111; henceforth cited as *Chr. Library* with document cited within parenthesis followed by page number(s).

[20] *Chr. Library* (Hom. XV.5), 114.

[21] *Chr. Library* (Hom. XVII), 116 ff.

[22] *Chr. Library* (Hom. XVIII.8), 120.

[23] *Chr. Library* (Homily XIX. 5–6), 123.

[24] *Chr. Library* (Hom. XXI.8), 128–129.

[25] *Chr. Library* (Hom. IV.1,4), 84–85.

[26] *Chr. Library* (Hom. IV.9), 87.

[27] *Chr. Library* (Hom. VI.4), 92.

[28] *Chr. Library* (Hom. VII.2.3), 93.

[29] *Chr. Library* (Hom. VIII.1), 94.

[30] *Chr. Library* (Hom. XIII), 108–109.

[31] Albert Outler, ed., *John Wesley* (New York: Oxford University Press, 1964), 195.

[32] This work is reproduced in Frank Whaling, ed., *John and Charles Wesley, Selected Writings and Hymns*, The Classics of Western Spirituality series, (New York: Paulist Press, 1981); henceforth cited as Whaling, *John and Charles Wesley* and page number(s).

[33] Whaling, *John and Charles Wesley*, 374.

[34] Whaling, *John and Charles Wesley*, 307.

[35] Whaling, *John and Charles Wesley*, 311.

[36] Whaling, *John and Charles Wesley*, 312.

[37] Outler, *John Wesley*, 66 ff.

[38] Outler, *John Wesley*, 274.

[39] Outler, *John Wesley*, 275.

[40] Outler, *John Wesley*, 181.

[41] Outler, *John Wesley*, 113.

[42] Outler, *John Wesley*, 132.

[43] *St John Chrysostom, Baptismal Instructions*, translated and annotated by Paul W. Harkins, Ancient Christian Writers series, no. 31, (New York: Newman Press, 1963), 127; henceforth cited as Harkins, *St John Chrysostom* with page number(s).

[44] Harkins, *St John Chrysostom*, 114–115.

[45] E.g., Harkins, *St John Chrysostom*, 182, 191.

[46] Harkins, *St John Chrysostom*, 74–77.

[47] Harkins, *St John Chrysostom*, 91.

[48] Harkins, *St John Chrysostom*, 182–183.

[49] Harkins, *St John Chrysostom*, 140.

[50] Harkins, *St John Chrysostom*, 58.

[51] Ibid.

[52]Harkins, *St John Chrysostom,* 59.
[53]Harkins, *St John Chrysostom,* 106.
[54]Harkins, *St John Chrysostom,* 77.

9

From Glory to Glory:
The Renewal of All Things in Christ:
Maximus the Confessor and John Wesley

Kenneth Carveley

Within this paper I want to explore themes which came to mind through a parallel reading of texts of Wesley's sermons and Maximus the Confessor—striking, recurrent, coincidental themes. Although it is unknown as to whether Wesley read Maximus, both had a common interest in Macarius and other church fathers.

Maximus was born in A.D. 580 in Constantinople. It is said he became head of the Imperial Chancellery, a position he left to become a monk at Chrysopolis, and later at St George, Cyzicus. The monks later fled south, and we find Maximus in Carthage ca. A.D. 630. In the Christological controversy of the seventh century he rejected monothelitism. Such resistance brought about his exile in Thrace, and later tortures, which resulted in the loss of his right hand and tongue. His teaching of a divine and human will in Christ was later vindicated by the Sixth Ecumenical Council at Constantinople A.D. 680.

John Wesley was born in 1704 and raised in the family rectory at Epworth, Lincolnshire. After schooldays at Charterhouse during his student days and a fellowship at Lincoln College, Oxford, he was the focal figure in the group called "Methodists" because of their methodical practices of fellowship and spiritual life. Having come under Pietist influence via the Moravians, he underwent an evangelical conversion experience on May 24, 1738 which sparked the Methodist revival within the Church of England.

Maximus from his ascetic context, and Wesley from his Anglican/Pietist one, both seek the religion of the heart. There may be a line of research which leads us from Maximus via Bernard of Clairvaux[1] to Pietism and hence to Wesley, though it may be less taxing to think that both simply drank from the same source. I want to hold a dialogue between Maximus and Wesley on these themes, a conversation as it were, minuted in the hymns of Charles Wesley.

If for Maximus God alone knows his own being and essence, a secret which even angels do not understand, such ultimate self-knowledge in terms of heart religion may be echoed in Charles Wesley's hymn,

> God only knows the love of God;
> O that it now were shed abroad
> In this poor stony heart![2]

Incarnation and Deification

It is interesting to find in Maximus the continual use of 2 Peter 1:4: "He has given us through these things his precious and very great promises . . . so that through them you may . . . become participants of the divine nature"; a favorite Pietist and Wesley text, with its emphasis on becoming sharers in the life of God. This accords with Maximus' emphasis on deification.

> "The future deification of those who have now been made children of God" was the way Maximus described the stages of salvation. Having been transformed into 'children of God' in this life, believers could anticipate yet a further transformation in the life to come, into participation in the very nature of God.[3]

> "The blessed promise . . . this grace of deification laid up in hope for those who love the Lord, which already exists figuratively and can be received in advance."[4]

John Wesley speaks of:

> ". . . the great end of religion," which is "to renew our hearts in the image of God, to repair that total loss of righteousness and true holiness which we sustained by the sin of our first parent.
>
> "Ye know that all religion that does not answer this end, all that stops short of this, the renewal of our soul in the image of God, after the likeness of him that created it, is no other than a poor farce, and a mere mockery of God, to the destruction of our own soul."[5]

In Maximus this renewal in God's image retains the distinction between God's image and likeness in humankind, the image being regarded as ineradicable, but both needing restoration because of our fallen nature. For Maximus the Incarnation restores and recapitulates humanity and its place in creation.

For this reason (humankind) is said to be made "to the image and likeness of God," to the image of his being by our being, to the image of his eternal being by our eternal being, . . . to the likeness of his goodness by our goodness, to the image of his wisdom by our wisdom. The first is by nature, the second by grace. Every rational nature indeed is made to the image of God, but only those who are good and wise are made to his likeness.[6]

Deification, with its anticipation below of the joys of heaven, is recurrently found in Wesleyan spirituality, and grounded, as with Maximus, in the Incarnation as the basis of our sharing and renewal in the life of God:

> He deigns in flesh to appear,
> Widest extremes to join;
> To bring our vileness near,
> And make us all divine:
> And we the life of God shall know,
> For God is manifest below.[7]

Or as Maximus puts it:

> He deigned in his kindness that we be one and the same with him . . . by joining and
> knitting us closely together with himself in spirit and leading us to the measure of the
> spiritual maturity which springs from his own fullness.[8]

If we ask Maximus and Wesley what brings about this change in the status of
humankind through the Incarnation, it is clear:

> Love is therefore a great good and of goods the first and most excellent good, since
> through it God and humankind are drawn together in a single embrace, and the cre-
> ator of humankind appears as human, through the undeviating likeness of the dei-
> fied God in the good so far as is possible to humankind.[9]

To Love as God Loves

It is this pure universal love of God toward humankind, which for Wesley is the
ground, and truth of the gospel. The human response to such love in both writers is
love for all humankind. The test of true religion for Wesley, the acid test of purity for
Maximus, is whether within the believer there develops not only love for God but also
an all-embracing love for others.

Maximus says:

> . . . there is nothing that can make the human being who loves God ascend any higher,
> for all other ways of true religion are subordinate to it. This we know as love and so
> we call it, not divisively assigning one form of love to God and another to human
> beings, for it is one and the same and universal: owed to God and attaching human
> beings to one another. For the activity and proof of perfect love towards God is gen-
> uine disposition of goodwill towards one's neighbour (1 Jn 4:20).[10]

> The one who loves God cannot help but love also everyone as himself even though
> he is displeased by the passions of those who are not yet purified. Thus when he sees
> their conversion and amendment he rejoices with unbounded and unspeakable joy.
>   The one who loves God surely loves his neighbour as well. Such a person can-
> not hold on to money but rather gives it out in God's fashion to each one who has
> need. [Here Methodists may well recall Wesley's sermon on the "Use of Money."]
>   The work of love is the deliberate doing of good to one's neighbour as well as
> long suffering and patience and the use of all things in the proper way.[11]

Wesley says:

> Dost thou now believe? Then the love of God is now shed abroad in thy heart. Thou
> lovest him because he first loved us. And because thou lovest God thou lovest thy
> brother also. And being filled with "love, peace, joy," thou art also filled with "long-

suffering, gentleness, fidelity, goodness, meekness, temperance" and other fruits of the Spirit, in a word, whatever dispositions are holy, are heavenly or divine. For while thou "beholdest with open uncovered face (the veil now being taken away) the glory of the Lord," his glorious love, and the glorious image wherein thou wast created, thou art changed into the same image from glory to glory by the Spirit of the Lord.[12]

So for Wesley the love of God shed abroad in the heart leads to the mount of Transfiguration and the renewal of the image of God in us.

As enjoined by the Lord, such love extends to enemies and is made perfect in the witness of loving those who may not return it. This is so both for Maximus and Wesley.

Maximus:

But I say to you, says the Lord, love your enemies, do good to those who hate you and pray for those who mistreat you. Why did he command this? To free you from hatred, grief, anger and resentment, and to make you worthy of the supreme gift of perfect love. And you cannot attain such love, if you do not imitate God and love all men equally.[13]

Wesley:

"Love your enemies" see that you bear a tender good will to those who are most bitter of spirit against you: who wish you all manner of evil . . . "Bless them that curse you" . . . "Do good to them that hate you": let your actions show that you are as real in love, as they in hatred . . .

In patience, in longsuffering, in mercy, in beneficence of every kind, to all, even to our bitterest persecutors: "be ye" Christians "perfect", in kind, though not in degree, "even as your Father which is in heaven is perfect" (Mt 5:48).[14]

For him and for Maximus training in love means to learn to love as God loves. As Charles Wesley puts it:

> Pure, universal Love thou art;
> To me, to all, Thy mercies move:
> Thy nature and Thy name is Love.[15]

Kenosis

In Christ this pure universal love of God moves towards humankind, as Methodists sing:

> He left His Father's throne above—
> So free, so infinite his grace—
> Emptied himself of all but love,
> And bled for Adam's helpless race.[16]

Or as Maximus more expansively describes this *kenosis*:

> God, who made nature and wisely healed it when it was sick through wickedness, through his love toward us, emptied himself taking the form of a slave, and without change united himself to this (nature) hypostatically, for our sake, and from us and through us he became wholly man to such a degree that unbelievers thought that he was not God, while existing as God to such a degree that to believers was granted the ineffable and true meaning of reverent religion.[17]

Such *kenosis* requires also a corresponding *kenosis* in all who are God's children by adoption and grace. For Maximus this means ascetic striving, in Wesley, incessant watchfulness.

God became incarnate says Maximus

> that he might make men gods and sons of God . . . we shall be there where Christ himself now is as head of the whole Body, who has also become Forerunner to the Father for us with his human body.[18]

Charles Wesley echoes this:

> And soon my spirit, in his hands,
> Shall stand where my Forerunner stands.[19]

Louth points out that whereas in Origen we move away from the Incarnation to some eternal reality, in Maximus *the wisdom in a mystery* becomes an ever-increasing engagement with the incarnate Word. It is such for Charles Wesley who in the suffering Christ sees God as:

> Wisdom in a mystery
> Of bleeding love unfold.[20]

The Circumcision of the Heart

In Maximus, the one who is in Christ has gone beyond the righteousness of the law and of nature, and therefore in Christ there is neither circumcision nor uncircumcision. He develops this theme, as does Wesley, in his writing on the circumcision of the heart:

Maximus:

> the circumcision of the heart in spirit is the complete stripping away of the natural actions of sense and mind with respect to sensible and intelligible things by the presence of the Spirit, who directly transfigures the entire body and soul together into something more divine.[21]

For Wesley it is:

a right state of soul, a mind and spirit renewed after the image of him that created it, being sanctified throughout in spirit, soul and body. A constant and continued course of self-denial.[22]

The circumcision of the heart from all filthiness, all inward as well as outward pollution. It is a renewal of the heart in the whole image of God, the full likeness of him that created it.[23]

In Hope of Perfect Love

> And bid our inmost souls rejoice
> In hope of perfect love![24]

Maximus:

perfect love does not split up the one nature of men on the basis of their various dispositions, but ever looking steadfastly at it, it loves all men equally, those who are zealous as friends those who are negligent as enemies. It is good to them and forbearing and puts up with what they do.

It does not think evil at all but rather suffers for them, if occasion requires, in order that it may even make them friends if possible. If not, it does not fall away from its own intentions as it ever manifests the fruits of love equally for all men.

In this way Our Lord Jesus Christ manifesting his love for us, suffered for all mankind and granted to all equally the hope of resurrection, though each one renders himself worthy of either glory or punishment.[25]

Perfect love casts out the first fear from the soul which by possessing it no longer fears punishment.[26]

The one who is perfect in love and has reached the summit of detachment knows no distinction between one's own and another's, between faithful and unfaithful., between slave and freeman, or indeed between male and female, but having risen above the tyranny of the passions and looking to the one nature of men he regards all equally, and is equally disposed to all.[27]

The one who has been able to acquire perfect love and who has let it control his whole life can say 'Lord Jesus' in the Holy Spirit.[28]

Nothing is more truly God-like than divine love, nothing more mysterious, nothing more apt to raise up human beings to deification.[29]

Wesley:

A Methodist is one who loves the Lord his God with all his heart, with all his soul, with all his mind and with all his strength. God is the joy of his heart and the desire of his soul ... He is therefore happy in God and having in him a well of water springing up into everlasting life and overflowing his soul with peace and joy. Perfect love having cast out fear, he rejoices evermore.[30]

> Made perfect first in love,
>   And sanctified by grace,
> We shall from earth remove,
>   And see his glorious face:
> Then shall His love be fully showed,
> And man shall then be lost in God.[31]

As we might expect, this theme is more fully expounded in John Wesley's *A Plain Account of Christian Perfection*.

Salvation as a Universal and Cosmic Process

For Maximus the Incarnation is the central turning point in the history of the cosmos. He quotes Gregory of Nazianzus: "the natures are instituted afresh and God becomes man."

His anticipation of the healing of the divisions found in everything that is, is, according to Louth, part of his cosmic theology. In this the cosmos is analogous to a human creature endowed with a body and a soul. It is part of Christ's saving work to restore the whole cosmos.[32]

Christ divinely recapitulates the universe in himself showing that the creation exists as one, like another human being, completed by the gathering together of its parts one with another in itself and inclined towards itself by the whole of its existence in accordance with the one, simple, undifferentiated and indifferent idea of production from nothing, in accordance with which the whole of creation admits of one and the same undiscriminated logos as having not been before it is.[33]

Here the human being is a microcosm and bond of creation mediating between its divisions.

Maximus' singularity and unity in creation as a single human being has a curious parallel in Wesley, though from a more anthropological angle in which he contrasts God, eternity, and our limitedness:

But God is not a man. A day and million of ages are the same with him. Therefore there is the same disproportion between him and any finite being as between him and the creature of a day. Therefore whenever that thought recurs, whenever you are tempted to fear lest you should be forgotten before the immense, the eternal God, remember that nothing is little or great, that no duration is long or short before him. Remember that God "*ita praesidet singulis sicut universis et universis sicut singulis*" That "he presides over every individual as over the universe and the universe as over each individual."

So that you may boldly say:

> Father how wide thy glories shine
> Lord of the universe—and mine!
> Thy goodness watches o'er the whole
> As all the world were but one soul;
> Yet counts my every sacred hair,
> As I remained thy single care.[34]

For Maximus the renewal of all things in heaven and earth is focussed in the person and work of Christ.

For the wisdom and sagacity of God the Father is the Lord Jesus Christ who holds together the universals of beings by the power of wisdom and embraces their complimentary arts by the sagacity of understanding, since by nature he is the fashioner and provider of all and through himself draws into one what is divided and abolishes war between beings and binds everything into peaceful friendship and undivided harmony, both what is in heaven and what is on earth, as the divine Apostle says.[35]

Again "the natures are instituted afresh", the divine through its measureless goodness and love for humankind and by its will, in a way beyond nature, voluntarily accepted our fleshly birth and paradoxically without seed tilled our flesh endowed with a rational soul.[36]

The human person unites the created nature with the uncreated through love . . . showing them to be one and the same through the possession of grace, the whole creation interpenetrated by God and become completely whatever God is, save at the level of being and receiving to itself the whole of God himself and acquiring us as a kind of prize for its ascent to God, the most unique God himself as the end of the movement of everything that moves towards it and the firm and unmoved rest of everything that is carried towards it, being the undetermined and infinite limit and definition of every definition and law and ordinance, of reason mind and nature.[37]

In becoming incarnate, God unites the fragments of universal nature, showing how they all take their origin in the Logos, and in this union Christ fulfills God's purpose by uniting and recapitulating in himself everything that has been created both on earth and in heaven.[38]

Christ unites earth and heaven with his earthly body consubstantial with us, bearing the whole of our nature, body, and soul. He united the sensible and intelligible and showed the convergence of all creation in the One divine Logos, and bears our humanity to the Father showing himself to God for us.[39]

In this continuing dialogue we might ask where in the corpus of the Wesleys' writing we might we find any expression of this cosmic vision of Christ and his saving work.

I want to indicate that not for once does John Wesley let go of the nature of saving faith, of the necessity of this for every believing Christian, and its corollary of pressing on towards perfect holiness. Yet this is held within a universal call in the gospel, and a universal hope for all humankind. When pressed to the question if all humankind are made alive in Christ he answers:

> That all mankind are not "made alive in Christ" as they are, is not God's fault, but their own.[40]

We might, however, want to pursue the qualifier "as they are." Wesley is clear:

> Without holiness no man shall see the Lord. By faith we are saved from sin and made holy. The God of love is willing to save all the souls he has made. This he has proclaimed to them in his word, together with the terms of salvation, revealed by the Son of his love, who gave his own life that they that believe in him might have everlasting life. And for these he has prepared a kingdom, from the foundation of the world. But he will not force them to accept of it, he leaves them in the hands of their own counsel, he saith: "Behold I set before you life and death, blessing and cursing; choose life that ye may live." Choose holiness by grace, which is the way, the only way, to everlasting life. He cries aloud: "be holy and be happy, happy in this world and happy in the world to come. Holiness becometh his house for ever". This is the wedding garment of all that are called to "the marriage of the lamb".
>
> But as to all those who appear in the last day without the wedding garment, the judge will say, "Cast them into outer darkness; there shall be weeping an gnashing of teeth."[41]
>
> If you ask "Why then are not all men saved? the whole law and the testimony answer, Not because of any decree of God; not because it is his pleasure they should die," for "as I live," saith the Lord God, "I have no pleasure in the death of him that dieth" (Ezek 18:32). Whatever be the cause of their perishing, it cannot be his will, if the oracles of God are true, for they declare "he is not willing that any should perish but that all should come to repentance" (2 Pet 3:9) "he willeth that all men should be saved". And they, secondly declare what is the cause why all men are not saved, namely that they will not be saved. So our Lord expressly: "ye will not come to me that ye might have life" (Jn 5:40); "the power of the Lord is present to heal them" but they will not be healed. They reject the counsel, the merciful counsel "of God against themselves," as did their stiff necked forefathers. And therefore are they without excuse because God would save them, but they will not be saved. This is the condemnation ; "How often would I have gathered you together and ye would not" (Mt 23:37).[42]

> Let the whole stream of thy thoughts, word and actions flow from the deepest con-
> viction that thou standest on the edge of the great gulf, thou and all the children of
> men, just ready to drop in, either into everlasting glory or everlasting burnings.[43]

I have, of course, like a good Methodist preacher, dangled you over the pit. In this you may see nothing at all that corresponds with Maximus the Confessor, apart per-haps from ascetic stringency, and certainly between them both he and Wesley empha-size watchfulness over one's own soul. Maximus says:

> God provides equally to all the power that leads to salvation so that each one who
> wishes can be transformed by divine grace.[44]

We may find a resonance and likeness in Wesleyan thinking that relates to the cos-mic vision of Maximus in what we might describe as the universal call and hope of the gospel grounded in the mercy and love of God in the Incarnation and the Atone-ment.

In the light of contemporary inter-faith dialogue, we might note that Wesley says that he has no authority from the Word of God to judge those who are outside the Christian dispensation.

> Not do I conceive that any man living has a right to sentence all the heathen and
> Mahometan world to damnation. It is far better to leave them to him that made them
> and who is "the Father of the spirits of all flesh" who is the God of the heathens as
> well as the Christians, and who hateth nothing that he hath made. All those under the
> law, the Christian law, shall undoubtedly be judged thereby.[45]

He concludes this sermon with

> I believe the merciful God regards the lives and tempers of men more than their ideas.
> I believe he respects the goodness of the heart rather than the clearness of the head;
> and that if the heart of man be filled (by the grace of God, and the power of his Spirit)
> with the humble, gentle, patient love of God and man, God will not cast him into
> everlasting fire, prepared for the devil and his angels, because his ideas are not clear
> or because his conceptions are confused. "Without holiness, I own, no man shall see
> the Lord", but I dare not add "or clear ideas".[46]

I suggest that there is in Methodism this universal strain, which echoes Maximus' understanding of all things recapitulated in Christ. It calls all creation to rejoice in what God has done in Christ, invites all humankind to recognize and receive Christ as Lord and Saviour.

> Methodism, so called, is the old religion, the religion of the Bible, the religion of the
> primitive Church, the religion of the Church of England. This old religion . . . is no
> other than love, the love of God and of all mankind; the loving God with all our heart,
> and soul and strength, as having first loved us, as the foundation of all good we have
> received, and of all we ever hope to enjoy; and the loving every soul which God hath
> made, every man on earth as our own soul.[47]

If indeed God had decreed before the foundation of the world that millions of men should dwell in everlasting burnings because Adam sinned hundreds or thousands of years before they had a being, I know not who could thank him for this, unless the devil and his angels; seeing on this supposition all those millions of unhappy spirits would be plunged into hell by Adam's sin without any possible advantage from it. But, blessed be God, this is not the case. Such a decree never existed. On the contrary, every one born of woman may be an unspeakable gainer thereby; and none ever was or can be a loser but by his own choice.[48]

Maximus too speaks of God's providence and judgment

through which the universe is led in an orderly manner to that end which is known beforehand by God alone. Of this no one knows its nature, or how it will be, and then only to those who have purified their souls through the virtues and have inclined the whole of their mind wholly toward the divine. To them is granted, as has been said, an apprehension of the providence and judgement of the whole nature of visible things.[49]

In his future hope Wesley sees the transformation of all creation, for all creatures:

all the deformity of their aspect will vanish away, and be exchanged for their primeval beauty. And with their beauty their happiness will return; to which there can be no obstruction. As there will be nothing within, so there will be nothing without to give them any uneasiness—no heat or cold, nor storm or tempest, but one perennial spring. In the new earth, as well as in the new heavens, there will be nothing to give pain, but everything that the wisdom and goodness of God can create to give happiness. As a recompense for what they once suffered while under "the bondage of corruption" when God has "renewed the face of the earth" and their corruptible body has put on incorruption, they shall enjoy happiness suited to their state, without alloy, without interruption and without end.[50]

The whole creation shall then be delivered from moral and natural corruption. Sin and its consequence, pain, shall be no more. Holiness and happiness shall cover the earth. Then shall all the ends of the world see the salvation of our God. And the whole race of mankind shall know and love and serve God and reign with him for ever and ever.[51]

In the end humankind will enjoy a greater state of happiness than Adam enjoyed in paradise. The vision of Revelation of the absence of pain and sorrow and sighing will become a reality and this will be accompanied by a deep communion in the life of the Divine Trinity.

To crown all, there will be a deep, an intimate, an uninterrupted union with God; a constant communion with the Father and his Son Jesus Christ through the Spirit; a continual enjoyment of the Three-One-God, and of all the creatures in him.[52]

This glorious liberty of the children of God is eternally doxological, but anticipated in hymns below.

A form of cosmic Christology is clear in a line which John Wesley translates from
Johann Andreas Rothe's hymn which echoes a line of Faustus:

> While Jesu's blood through earth and skies,
> Mercy, free, boundless mercy! cries.[53]

This aspect of salvation is represented in the recent Orthodox comment on the
program "Justice Peace and the Integrity of Creation":

> Thanks to Christ's sacrifice on the cross, every human being and the whole of cre-
> ation receive the gift of victory over sin, evil and corruption (Col 1:14–17). Death did
> not triumph on Calvary. Christ is Risen. Christ's resurrection is a solid and funda-
> mental hope for every believing human being in the struggle against evil in all of its
> manifestations. It is already a guarantee of the ultimate triumph of life and therefore
> hope for the salvation of every person and of the entire creation.[54]

This universal strain in Christology is continued in Charles Wesley:

> Universal Saviour, thou
>   Wilt all thy creatures bless;
> Every knee to thee shall bow,
>   And every tongue confess:
> None shall in thy mount destroy,
>   War shall then be learnt no more:
> Saints shall their great King enjoy,
>   And all mankind adore.
>
> Then according to thy word,
>   Salvation is reveal'd;
> With thy glorious knowledge, Lord,
>   The new-made earth is fill'd:
> Then we sound the mystery,
>   The depths and heights of Godhead prove,
> Swallow'd up in mercy's sea,
>   Forever lost in love.[55]

It is this overwhelming image of being "swallowed up" in God's mercy and love,
like some unsuspecting surfer overcome by the greatest tunnel wave ever, that persists
throughout Wesley's imagery:

> This the universal bliss,
>   Bliss for every soul design'd
> God's original promise this,
>   God's great gift to all mankind;
> Blest in Christ this moment be!
> Blest to all eternity![56]

So shall the world believe
  Our record, Lord, and thine;
And all with thankful hearts receive
  The Messenger divine,
Sent from his throne above,
  To Adam's offspring given,
To join and perfect us in love,
  And take us up to heaven.[57]

Believing against hope,
  We hang upon thy grace,
Through every lowering cloud look up
  And wait for happy days;
The days when all shall know
  Their sins in Christ forgiven,
And walk awhile with God below,
  And then fly up to heaven.[58]

Till all the earth, renew'd
  In righteousness divine,
With all the hosts of God
  In one great chorus join,
Join all on earth, rejoice and sing;
Glory ascribe to glory's King.[59]

One cannot eradicate this universal desire from the Wesleyan message. It comes rooted in the work of God in the Incarnation and saving work of Christ for all humankind. It sounds the note of joyful hope for all the earth, for all nations and peoples, for all creation. It comes intimately linked to the call to conversion of life, to faith and holiness, to growing into perfect love, the stature of the fullness of Christ.

Dominic Unger summarizes Maximus' teaching as giving two reasons for the Incarnation: the deification of human nature and the redemption from sin. This, I believe, accords with the Wesleyan view. Unger describes Maximus' Christological perspective as "Christ, the Final Scope of All Creation."[60] And we sing with Charles Wesley:

Finish then Thy new creation,
  Pure and spotless let us be;
Let us see Thy great salvation,
  Perfectly restored in Thee;
Changed from glory into glory,
  'Til in heaven we take our place,
'Til we cast our crowns before Thee,
  Lost in wonder, love and praise.[61]

In expounding Wesley's theology, Colin Williams regards him as being firmly convinced that the time will come "when Christianity will prevail over all and cover the earth." In our more pluralistic context we may consider this to be a real optimism of grace. To this he appends the comment of Gordon Rupp that the depths of human tragedy and the world's fallenness must be attached to the heights of grace, the solidarity of mankind in the Second Adam, Jesus Christ of whom Charles Wesley sings "Head of all mankind art thou." Total depravity, says Rupp, is set within the context of total grace, of the great salvation.[62]

Such optimism of grace is found too in the work of Brian Frost in which he sought to relate the concept of "fullness" in the Wesley's writings to Orthodox theology. He understands fullness there as the restoration of all things to their true state,[63] though whether this ever reaches the *apocatastasis* some find in Maximus may be doubtful. True, Charles Wesley can speak of the fullness of God's grace:

> Its streams the whole creation reach,
> So plenteous is the store.[64]

Maximus says that in Christ there dwells in bodily form the completeness of the Deity by essence, in us the fullness of the Deity dwells by grace, whenever we have formed in ourselves every virtue and wisdom, lacking in no way which is possible to man in the faithful reproduction of the archetype.[65]

This is close to the Wesleyan concept which appears with echoes of Transfiguration in Charles Wesley's eucharistic hymn:

> Till all Thy life we gain,
>   And all thy fullness prove,
> And, strengthened by Thy perfect grace
> Behold without a veil Thy face.[66]

It is perhaps, for Methodists, unremarkable that throughout this dialogue I have referred constantly to Charles Wesley's hymns. These we are told are Methodism's liturgical heartbeat, our sung dogmatics, our true liturgy. For Maximus too, the liturgy focuses mystically on the themes he explores.

Maximus says:

Thus, we will be found giving worship in every way in imitation of the angels in heaven, and we shall exhibit on earth the same manner of life as the angels.[67]

Charles Wesley says we shall

> Live the life of heaven above,
> All the life of glorious love.[68]

Perhaps where dogma stammers those things into which angels may desire to look but not sound their depths, we like them are drawn to love and praise.

God grant us this grace, where earth and heaven meet in Christ, to join with Maximus, the Wesleys, and all the saints in this praise for ever.

Selected Bibliography

Maximus the Confessor: Selected Writings, trans. and notes by George C. Berthold (London: SPCK and Paulist Press: London, 1985).
Maximus the Confessor, A. Louth, Routledge (London and New York, 1996).
The Works of John Wesley, 14 vols., ed. by Thomas Jackson (London: Wesleyan Conference Office, 1872).

Endnotes

[1]Cf. D. J. Geanakoplos, "Some Aspects of the Influence of the Byzantine Maximos the Confessor on the Theology of East and West," *Church History* 38 (1969): 152.
[2]Charles Wesley, *Methodist Hymn-Book* (London: Methodist Conference Office, 1933) Hymn 434, v3. This volume will be cited henceforth as MH1933 followed by hymn and stanza number preceded by "v."
[3]Jaroslav Pelikan, "Introduction" in *Maximus Confessor: Selected Writing,* trans. G. C. Berthold (New York/Oxford: Paulist Press/SPCK, 1985), 10. This volume will be cited henceforth as: Berthold, *Maximus* followed by the page number and the document reference.
[4]A. Louth, *Maximus the Confessor,* (London and New York: Routledge, 1996), 150: Difficulty, 10.45A 1200A. This volume will be cited henceforth as: Louth, *Maximus the Confessor* followed by the page number and the document reference.
[5]John Wesley, Sermon 44, "The New Birth," *Works* (Jackson), 6:64, 65.
[6]Berthold, *Maximus,* 64: Century 3:25.
[7]Charles Wesley, MH1933, Hymn 142, v4.
[8]Maximus: Ambiguorum Liber, *Patrologia Graeca,* 91. 1097.
[9]Louth, *Maximus the Confessor,* 90: Letter 2 To John the Cubicularius. 401C.
[10]Louth, *Maximus the Confessor,* 90: 404A.
[11]Berthold, *Maximus,* 37, 39: Century I: 13, 23, 40.
[12]John Wesley, Sermon 7, "On the Way to the Kingdom," 2:13, *Works* (Jackson), 5:86.
[13]Berthold, *Maximus,* 41 and Louth, *Maximus the Confessor,* 39, 40: Four Hundred Chapters on Love. Century 1.61.
[14]John Wesley, Sermon 23, "Sermon on the Mount," III:13, *Works* (Jackson), 5:292, 293.
[15]Charles Wesley, MH1933, Hymn 339, v7.
[16]Charles Wesley, MH1933, Hymn 371, v3.
[17]Louth, *Maximus the Confessor,* 87: Letter 2. 397B.
[18]*Capitum theologica et oeconomica centuria,* in *Patrologia Graeca,* 90. 1136BC.
[19]Charles Wesley, MH1933, Hymn 232, v3.
[20]Charles Wesley, MH1933, Hymn 465, v3.
[21]Berthold, *Maximus,* 1.36: On Knowledge, 1:46.
[22]John Wesley, Sermon 17, "The Circumcision of the Heart," 3, *Works* (Jackson), 5:203.
[23]John Wesley, *A Plain Account of Christian Perfection,* Q,38.27, *Works* (Jackson), 9:444.
[24]Charles Wesley, MH1933, Hymn 718, v5.
[25]Berthold, *Maximus,* 42, 43: Four Hundred Chapters on Love. Century 1:71.
[26]Berthold, *Maximus,* 44: Century I:82.
[27]Berthold, *Maximus,* 51: Century. 2:30.
[28]Berthold, *Maximus,* 79: Century 4:39.
[29]Louth, *Maximus the Confessor,* 85: Letter 2: On Love. To John the Cubicularius. 393B.

[30]John Wesley, "The Character of a Methodist" in *A Plain Account of Christian Perfection*. 10. *Works* (Jackson), 11:371.

[31]Charles Wesley, MH1933, Hymn 142, v5.

[32]Charles Wesley, MH1933, Hymn 142, v5.

[33]Louth, *Maximus the Confessor*, 160: Difficulty 41. 1312A.

[34]John Wesley, Sermon 54, "On Eternity," *Works* (Jackson), 6:198.

[35]Louth, *Maximus the Confessor*, 161, 162: Difficulty 41. 1313B.

[36]Louth, *Maximus the Confessor*, 162: Difficulty 41. 1313CD.

[37]Louth, *Maximus the Confessor*, 158: Difficulty 41. 1308B.

[38]Louth, *Maximus the Confessor*, 159: Difficulty 41. 1308D.

[39]Louth, *Maximus the Confessor*, 159, 160: Difficulty 41. 1309C.

[40]John Wesley, "The Doctrine of Original Sin," Part II:7, *Works* (Jackson), 11:246.

[41]John Wesley, Sermon 120, "The Wedding Garment," 18, 19, *Works* (Jackson), 7:316, 317.

[42]John Wesley, Sermon 127, "On Free Grace," 22, *Works* (Jackson), 7:381.

[43]John Wesley, Sermon 32, "Upon Our Lord's Sermon on the Mount," Discourse XIII.12, *Works* (Jackson), 5:433.

[44]Louth, *Maximus the Confessor*, 118: Difficulty 10:20b. 1144.

[45]John Wesley, Sermon 125, "On Living without God," 14, *Works* (Jackson), 7:353.

[46]Ibid., 15, 7:354.

[47]John Wesley, Sermon 132, "At the Foundation of City Road Chapel," II:1, *Works* (Jackson), 7:423, 424.

[48]John Wesley, Sermon 58, "God's Love to Fallen Man," II: 10–20, *Works*, Bicentennial edition, 2. Sermons II: 34–70. (Nashville: Abingdon Press, 1983), 434.

[49]Louth, Maximus the Confessor, 134: Difficulty 10:31h. 1169A.

[50]John Wesley, Sermon 60. "The General Deliverance," *Works*, Bicentennial edition, vol. 2, Sermons II.34–70: III 4: 446, I.34–447, I.12.

[51]John Wesley, Sermon 61, "The Mystery of Iniquity," *Works*, Bicentennial Edition, vol. 2, Sermons II: Sermons 34–70. 470, I.5–15.

[52]John Wesley, Sermon 64, "The New Creation," *Works*, Bicentennial edition, vol. 2: Sermons II 34–70/ 510, 1.17–21.

[53]John Wesley, MH1933, Hymn 375, v3.

[54]G. Limouris, ed., "Orthodox Perspectives on Creation: III The Transfigured Creation: 26," *Justice, Peace and the Integrity of Creation: Insights from Orthodoxy* (Geneva: WCC, 1990), 9.

[55]Charles Wesley, *A Collection of Hymns for the Use of the People Called Methodists* (London, 1780), Hymn 703, vv3,4.

[56]Ibid., Hymn 20, v4.

[57]Ibid., Hymn 460, v3.

[58]Ibid., Hymn 453, v5.

[59]Ibid., Hymn 635, v6.

[60]Dominic J. Unger, OFM, "Christ Jesus, Center and Final Scope of All Creation According to St Maximus Confessor," *Franciscan Studies* 9 (1949), 61.

[61]Charles Wesley, MH1933, Hymn 431, v3.

[62]Gordon Rupp, *Principalities and Powers* (London, 1952), 81. C. Williams, *John Wesley's Theology Today* (London, 1960), 190.

[63]Brian Frost, "The Idea of Fullness in Methodist Hymns," chapter 5 in *Living in Tension Between East and West* (London: New World Publications, 1984), 40, 41.

[64]Charles Wesley, MH1933, Hymn 49, v4.

[65]Berthold, *Maximus*, 152: Chapters on Knowledge, 2:21.

[66]Charles Wesley, MH1933, Hymn 764, v2.

[67]Berthold, *Maximus*, 113: Commentary on The Our Father, 4. Thy will be done on earth as it is in heaven.

[68]Charles Wesley, MH1933, Hymn 319, v3.

10

All Creation in United Thanksgiving: Gregory of Nyssa and the Wesleys on Salvation

Peter C. Bouteneff

for Canon A. M. Allchin

When those now lying in sin have been restored to their original state, all creation will join in united thanksgiving, both those whose purification involved pain and those who never needed purification at all.[1]

This short passage summarizes several key aspects of St Gregory of Nyssa's teaching on salvation. From it we may glean that salvation consists in restoration to an original, pure state; that it concerns the removal of evil from an essentially good creation; and also that it applies to all creation. This last point, on the *universality* of salvation, involved something of a risk for Gregory of Nyssa, particularly as his doctrine came at times to be seen as intertwined in some way with that of Origen.

Fourteen centuries later, the Wesleys would likewise distinguish themselves from their immediate context, which often insisted on a strict Calvinist doctrine of predestination. Against that backdrop, they presented salvation as something that was available to everyone. Despite writing under vastly different circumstances, the Wesleys put forward many ideas concerning human salvation which find parallels with ideas being set out in the late fourth century by the Cappadocians, especially Gregory of Nyssa. There are also of course differences, and these, together with the similarities, are of interest to investigate.

Comparison between the Wesleys and the Greek Fathers is a highly attractive pursuit for both Wesleyan and Patristic scholars, for Methodists and Orthodox, particularly for those with an interest in the modern ecumenical implications of the frequent overlaps which one finds. Yet it would be a mistake to treat the Wesleys and the Fathers simply side by side. The Wesleys are not, nor do they pretend to be, systematic theologians. And while they were surely influenced by the Fathers, it is no longer possible to press the idea of direct influence too far. The ideas of Albert Outler, one of the premier Wesleyan scholars of this century, that John Wesley relied upon the Fathers for much of what he said, have been tempered in recent years by scholars who have found that the Wesleys read and cited patristic literature much less than originally thought, and moreover, often not accurately.[2] And while Outler and others liked to cite Wesley's "exceeding reverence" for the Fathers, as stated in *A Plain Account of Genuine Christianity,* they tend to omit the context of that passage, where Wesley says that despite the genuineness of their Christianity, these Fathers were generally short on learning, and their writings contained "many mistakes, weak suppositions and ill-drawn conclusions."[3] Still, while such qualifications of the notion of Wesleyan fidelity to the Fathers might affect the *methodology* of any comparative effort, it does not make the comparison any less interesting, or indeed any less worth attempting: the Wesleys can also be said to have been "patristic" owing as much to the spirit of Anglican renewal in the seventeenth and eighteenth centuries, a renewal that was, among other things, patristic in character.[4]

For the purposes of this paper, I would like to draw out the Wesleys on what they say concerning human salvation. But I will do so with the eyes of a Cappadocian scholar, in particular hearing the questions posed by the teaching of St Gregory of Nyssa, who had the most of the three Cappadocians to say on that subject. Of what Gregory of Nyssa says, together with some of the other early Christian writers, about salvation, its universality, and its relationship to "perfection" or "holiness" (Gregory's *teleiotetos* or perhaps *arete*), what is picked up by the Wesleys, and what form does it take in their context? The exploration of this question could provide a key to the relationship between "apostolic traditions and holiness" which was to be one of the themes of this conference. I will give Gregory of Nyssa the first word, setting out the salient features of his soteriology as it is set out in his treatise *De anima et resurrectione* (On the Soul and the Resurrection).[5] In order to frame this summary, I will begin with some reflections on the notion of universal salvation as it unfolded in the early centuries of Christianity.

Universal Restoration

I mentioned earlier that the idea of universal salvation spelled trouble for some of the early Christian writers, Origen in particular. Thanks to Origen (or to "Origenism") the word *apokatastasis*, meaning "restoration," from the third century onwards came to be shorthand for *apokatastasis ton panton*, or *universal* restoration. Gregory of Nyssa's sense of the universality of salvation differed from that which was integral to the Origenism condemned at the Fifth Ecumenical Council; nonetheless it caused a stir, as can be sensed from several incidental sources. In one example, the great sixth-century elder Barsanuphius found himself questioned by a monk who was distressed to find the Origenist or Evagrian teaching of *apokatastasis* in Gregory of Nyssa, albeit not in its worst form. The elder could only reply that even the saints are not perfect and without error, for "we know only in part" (1 Cor 13:9).[6] In the following century, Gregory fared better: St Maximus the Confessor, approached with a similar inquiry, responded that St Gregory espoused an acceptable version of the apocatastasis doctrine.[7]

A teaching of universal restoration or salvation comes to be considered heretical when it threatens to impinge upon divine freedom, i.e. by proclaiming that all *must* be saved, thereby denying God the freedom to condemn those who deserve condemnation. It was also specifically problematic for Origen having to do with his treatment of the question of the human body within human generation and salvation.[8] But there are different ways of framing the notion of universal salvation. Any of these raises issues of fundamental importance to one's understanding of God and the human person. For example, implications are inevitably raised concerning:

- what the human person was created for, and in what salvation consists;
- the nature of divine will, both essential and economic;
- the nature of divine freedom;
- the nature of human freedom (i.e., the freedom to choose perdition);
- the effect (and its endurance) of human sin;
- the nature of punishment (corrective or consequential);
- the meaning of "heaven" and "hell;"
- the corporate nature of humanity.

Each of these issues is dealt with in Gregory of Nyssa's teaching on salvation, particularly as understood from his main thinking[9] on the subject, as represented in the De anima.

Gregory of Nyssa on Human Salvation

For St Gregory of Nyssa, salvation was nothing other than the restoration of humanity to its original, essential state, "*he eis to arkhaion tes fuseos hemon apokatastasis.*"[10] Although Gregory can speak here in sequential terms, (i.e., of a "return to a previous state"), he does not give any temporal sense to notion—there was no "time" when humans existed in this "original state." He is talking about the divinely foreordained state for humanity, in which the human person reveals purely the image of God, the God with whom he communes freely in love. This state, which is also that to which we "return" in the resurrection, is one in which we have no passions (*thumos*—zeal/anger, or *epithumia*—desire/lust), for these are only of use to us in the fallen world as our desire and zeal for life with God,[11] neither do we have anything that is related to the space- and time-bound condition of the world.[12] We do have our bodies, although, as Gregory says, "not indeed with [their] present coarse and heavy texture, but with the thread respun into something subtler and lighter."[13]

Salvation, as the restoration to God's intended state, the restoration to the divine image, is the natural course for humanity (and thus for any human person) to follow. Indeed, for Gregory it is not a question as to *whether* one will be saved, but only how difficult or painful the process of salvation will be for any given person. Salvation is a matter of the removal of evil, and therefore the more sinful the person, the more painful will be the process of his purgation from evil. It follows that the more purified a person is, the closer he is to God-likeness, the less arduous will be the transition to the more radical God-likeness of the resurrection. Gregory is clear that this is not a matter of punishment but of natural consequence:

> It is not out of hatred or vengeance for an evil life, in my opinion, that God brings painful conditions upon sinners . . . the painful condition necessarily happens as an incidental consequence to the one who is drawn. So the divine judgment . . . operates

only by separating good from evil and pulling the soul towards the fellowship of blessedness. It is the tearing apart of what has grown together which brings pain to the one who is being pulled.[14]

It therefore behooves us

either to keep our soul altogether pure and free from fellowship with evil, or, if this is utterly impossible because of our passionate nature, to limit our failures in virtue as much as possible to moderate lapses which are easily cured.[15]

Before discussing the purification gone through on the way to salvation, the same treatise *On the Soul and Resurrection* addresses the reality of Hades, or hell. In one passage, the idea that hell might be some kind of "place" is neither supported nor refuted, "as long as [it] does not disturb the principal doctrine concerning the existence of souls after the life in the flesh."[16] Further on, the parable of the rich man and Lazarus (Lk 16:19–31) is discussed for its lessons on the "gulf" between Hades and the bosom of Abraham. That gulf or chasm is nothing other than the gulf we created for ourselves through our own freely willed decisions:

This gulf, in my opinion, does not come from the opening of the earth but is made by the decisions of human lives divided towards opposite choices. He who has definitively pursued pleasure for this life and has not cured his misguided choice by repentance makes the land of the good inaccessible to him hereafter. He digs for himself this impassible necessity, like an immense pit that cannot be crossed.[17]

But is clear that the parable is being interpreted not as a lesson about the life hereafter, but as a cautionary tale for us here and now. The uncrossable nature of the gulf does not pertain to the life hereafter, "for what trouble would it be for the bodiless and intellectual soul to fly across a chasm, however great the distance might be, since that which is intellectual by nature goes instantaneously wherever it wishes?"[18]

Let us look at what Gregory's salvation doctrine has to say about freedom, divine and human. Humans effectively are free to decide their fate, one that will involve more or less purification after death. Human sin thus has an enduring but not limitless effect on our life and salvation, for sin and evil will ultimately fall away. (For Gregory, evil in itself does not even exist, other than as an absence of good, an absence of "being.")[19] Divine freedom is ultimately wrapped up in divine love, and the divine intention for all humankind. Purification therefore is nothing other than God's love, freely and universally offered, and it culminates in the return to the state willed by God in the first place for humanity: free, loving communion with Himself that is ever-deepening, ever growing "from glory to glory."

Does the human person have the freedom to choose perdition? Gregory's teaching rests soundly on the premise that the natural desire of any soul, once it is stripped of evil, is towards God. Moreover, while decisions made in the earthly life are binding, potentially creating uncrossable chasms, these bonds are loosed in the heavenly life. So someone can choose evil as much as he/she wants in the earthly life and believe he/she is choosing perdition, only to be faced with the reality of things in the life hereafter, wherein he/she will realize that all he/she was choosing for himself/herself was a greater degree of pain at the inevitable separation of the evil from the good.

Yet, significantly, Gregory of Nyssa is not perfectly consistent with himself in the total universality of salvation. On the one hand, his system would imply the absolute inevitability of eventual purification from all evil, and hence universal participation in the good things to come. As he says, "Evil must altogether be removed in every way from being, [in the sense that] which does not really exist must cease to exist at all. Since evil does not exist by nature outside of free choice, when all choice is in God, evil will suffer a complete annihilation because no receptacle remains for it."[20] On the other hand, there are veiled implications in the same treatise that there are those for whom the fire of purification will "last as long as the age,"[21] as well as "those who are released from evil."[22]

It is of some interest to note that, as set out in the *De anima*, Gregory's doctrine of salvation has little to say about the role of Christ in salvation, not to mention that of the Church and her sacraments. This has to do with the nature and intention of the text of the *De anima* and not with the overall theology of Gregory of Nyssa, however. The purpose of the *De anima* is to set out as clearly as possible the context and character of the resurrected life. The context lies in its being a "return" to the image-bearing state for which humanity was created, and the character of the resurrected life is psycho-somatic, bereft not only of all evil but also of the instruments given us in this life to struggle towards God. Purely for the purposes of the *De anima*, Gregory takes for granted the central role of Christ as the One through whom and in whom we return to original perfection. The centrality of Christ—the incarnate Logos, born for our sake, truly tempted, put to death, and raised from the dead—in Gregory's understanding of redemption and salvation is more than apparent elsewhere, particularly through his sermons and his polemical treatises against Eunomius and Apollinarius.

I will comment further below on the relationship between Gregory of Nyssa's teaching on salvation and that of other of the Fathers. But I would now like to turn to what I, a neophyte but respectful student of the Wesleys, could uncover in their writings which corresponds in some way to what Gregory taught.

The Wesleys on Redemption and Salvation

> Finish then thy new creation,
>   Pure and spotless let us be;
> Let us see thy great salvation
>   Perfectly restored in thee;
> Changed from glory to glory,
>   Till in heaven we take our place,
> Till we cast our crowns before thee,
>   Lost in wonder, love and praise.[23]

It is stanzas such as this one that led me inexorably to take up what became the topic of this paper, for it is hard to overlook the characteristically Nyssan themes that shine forth from it— themes of salvation as restoration, and as change and movement from glory to glory. The Wesleys do not have a teaching or a *system* on salvation in the same sense as Gregory can be said to have. But they share with their fourth-century predecessor several concerns and convictions regarding God, Christ, the human person, and his salvation.

Restoration to the divine image

Like Gregory of Nyssa, the Wesleys had an acute sense of the human person's creation in the image of God, the image that in this age is tarnished through sin. Common to both Nyssa and the Wesleys was the notion that salvation therefore consisted in a restoration to that image-bearing state.

> I shall fully be restored
> To the image of my Lord.[24]

"What is it to be sanctified?" John Wesley is asked. "To be renewed in the image of God" is his answer.[25] He elaborates:

> This great gift of God, the salvation of our souls, is no other than the image of God fresh stamped on our hearts. It is *a renewal in the spirit of our minds, after the likeness of him that created them.*[26]

Universality

In addition to seeing salvation as restoration to the divine image, the Wesleys clearly possess, or are possessed by, the conviction that all *can* be saved, and a desire that all *would* be saved. Guided by a scriptural conviction that ultimately every knee would bow at the name of Jesus (Phil 2:10),[27] they were sure that what was rendered in Christ was rendered *for all*.

> [The Saviour's] dying love hath left behind
> Eternal life for *all mankind.*[28]

This sense echoes through countless hymns.

> On all mankind forgiven
>   Empower them still to call,
> And tell each creature under heaven
>   That thou hast died for all.[29]

Surely the Wesleyan conviction that salvation was intended for all came in part as a reaction to the Calvinistic leanings of many of their contemporaries, including the "Calvinistic Methodists" headed by George Whitefield. The idea of predestination was deplorable to John Wesley from early on: he was influenced (or at least supported) in this regard at the age of twenty-two, when he had a letter from his mother, who expounded at length and with precision against the "abhorrence" of a rigid Calvinistic doctrine of predestination.[30]

In his sermon some fifty years later *On Predestination,* John was careful to distinguish God's foreknowledge from any existential determinism. Knowledge of events does not cause them, and therefore we are free to believe or not, to sin or not, as if God did not know about it at all.[31] Thus the "predestination" of Romans 8:29–30 is merely an extension of foreknowledge, one that does not determine outcomes. Indeed, if one is to put a fine point on it, "foreknowledge" or "afterknowledge" is a misnomer when one considers the One who "knows from everlasting to everlasting all that is, that was, and that is to come, through one eternal now, [for whom] nothing is either past or future, but all things equally present."[32]

While the Wesleys believe that redemption in Christ is universal, they also believe that humans must strive for holiness, and are justified by faith.[33] In this there is the presupposition that the universality of redemption does not lead necessarily to the universality of salvation. While it can be said that the decisive thrust within the entire Wesleyan corpus, at least as far as I can sense, is on things positive—on the pursuit of holiness, on joy in God and striving towards greater union with Him, on the gifts of the Holy Spirit—there is the implied but sure sense that not all are saved.

The Wesleys can be said to share something of Gregory of Nyssa's universalism: they went out of their way to distinguish themselves from their contemporaries within the non-conformist Christianity of their day in seeing salvation, that restoration to the intended state for the human person, as open to all, here and now and in the next world. Yet they diverge significantly from Nyssen in that they did not espouse a system wherein all *would* be saved as a matter of the divinely ordained nature of things, and as a result of the ultimate non-reality of evil. They did not dwell on the alternative to salvation, but they saw it as a very real potentiality. To say otherwise would for them have been an impossibility.

Going back a step, when we ask what "salvation" actually meant to the Wesleys, it soon becomes clear that they ascribed two levels to the concept: salvation here and now, and salvation in the life hereafter. In some senses, they gave the priority to the former. In the important sermon, *The Scripture Way of Salvation,* John Wesley asks, "What is salvation?" His reply is dictated by the text being preached on—Ephesians 2:8 ("ye are saved through faith"):

> The salvation that is here spoken of is not what is frequently understood by that word, the going to heaven, eternal happiness. It is not the soul's going to paradise, . . . it is not a blessing which lies on the other side of death. . . . The very words of the text itself put this beyond all question. "Ye *are* saved." It is not something at a distance: it is a present thing a blessing which, through the free mercy of God, ye are now in possession of.[34]

Through justification—God's pardon of our sin—and the process of sanctification—God's work in us, with our cooperation, towards holiness, salvation is a reality here and now. Yet at the same time, the Wesleys are aware of an incompleteness to the salvation experienced in this age. This tension between the "already" and the "not yet" in salvation finds a necessarily close parallel in Wesleyan teaching on human perfection, to which I now turn.

Perfection and salvation

Christ's death was a redeeming death for all. Yet there is no salvation without our response. For the Wesleys that response consisted in the pursuit of holiness, or perfection. "Without holiness, no man shall see the Lord" says John, drawing on Hebrews 12:14, "not one of all that innumerable company who was not *sanctified* before he was *glorified*. By holiness he was prepared for glory."[35]

The Wesleyan conviction that salvation was a matter of *this* world found reflection in an acute sense that perfection was not only to be striven for in this world, but also was attainable. This was not an easy doctrine for John Wesley to maintain, particularly as he was liable at times to overstate the matter, and he saw the need to defend and explain himself in the hastily-assembled treatise *A Plain Account of Christian Perfection*. Even there, he insists at one point that sinlessness is possible, and that the scriptural statement, "There is no man that sins not," referred only to the time before the gospel was given.[36] At the same time, both in this treatise and elsewhere, he provides qualifying statements about what is not yet possible in this world, to the point of saying that there is no *absolute* perfection on earth,[37] nor indeed has Wesley ever met a person who has attained all the marks of sanctification, and believes there can in fact be none such in the world.[38]

Still, Wesley's clarifications are often difficult to reconcile with other statements that did imply something of the possibility of absolute perfection. But, what could surely be said about him and his concept of perfection was that he had a powerfully eschatological concept of the Christian life—a characteristic that is found of course in Gregory of Nyssa, but also throughout the patristic tradition.

The Wesleyan ideal of perfection and its living out in the world paid a degree of homage to the concept of the "Christian sage" (or the Christian "true gnostic") of the late-second-century Clement of Alexandria.[39] At the same time it is more powerfully reflected in, and perhaps was influenced by, the practical theology John Wesley found in the Macarian homilies. Here is his rendition of part of Homily 4 (Wesley's numbering), as recorded in his *Christian Library*, the compendium of texts he assembled and published for Christian readership:

> [True Christians] have their heart and mind constantly taken up with the thoughts of heaven; and, through the presence and participation of the Holy Spirit do behold, as in a glass, the good things which are eternal, being born of God from above, and thought worthy to become the children of God in truth and power; and being arrived, through many conflicts and labours, to a settled and fixed state, to an exemption from trouble, to perfect rest, are never sifted more by unsettled and vain thoughts. Herein are they greater and better than the world; their mind and the desire of their soul are in the peace of Christ, and the love of the Spirit; "they have passed from death to life."

The Macarian influence can be said to be explicit—Wesley indicated its importance by singling it out for publication.[40] But while the Wesleys probably did not read much of Gregory of Nyssa's work, their concept of perfection finds reflection also in much of what is categorized as his ascetical writing. Within the large body of work dealing with many of the same issues, Gregory of Nyssa also devotes an entire treatise to the subject of perfection (*De perfectione*, or *peri teleiotetos*), in fact a meditation on the imitation of Christ, at times found with the subtitle "On What It is Necessary for a Christian to be." In addition to the ascetical corpus are three lengthy exegetical works (*On the Psalms, On the Life of Moses*, and *On the Song of Songs*), which are also guides and exhortations to attaining the highest goals of Christian life.

Returning now to the relationship between perfection and salvation, the Wesleyan pursuit of perfection is ultimately not altogether different from Gregory of Nyssa's teaching that the more we have achieved purification in this world, the closer we are to the reality of the next. Wesleyan perfection, in its most Orthodox (or orthodox) sense, is finally to be seen as perfection in love, something that is initiated by the Holy Spirit in us and needs cultivation by us, something dynamic, proceeding from glory to glory in this world and, in a more radical way, from glory to glory in the next. Wesley on occasion might have reached beyond what is felt to be the limits of the perfection attainable in the fallen world, yet the same eschatological yearning, the sense that heaven can be anticipated here and now, can be suggested even by Gregory of Nyssa at times in ways as radical as Wesley did. This discussion's leading quotation ends by suggesting that there are some who will pass into the life of the resurrection "who never needed purification at all."

Finally on this question of "inaugurated eschatology," it is interesting to note within Wesleyan reflection on the Lord's Supper, that this sacrament can be seen as an anticipation of the Kingdom of Heaven:

> We need not now go up to Heaven
>   to bring the long-sought Saviour down
> Thou art to all already given:
>   Thou dost ev'n now thy banquet crown,
> To every faithful soul appear,
> And shew thy real presence here.[41]

Of course, as Frank Whaling is right to point out in his introduction to *The Classics of Western Spirituality* collection, the words "real presence" are not used in any polemical or doctrinal sense.[42] What is clear from this verse, together with several other *Hymns on the Lord's Supper*,[43] is a sense that in the Eucharist, all is given, the whole Christ is there, heaven has been brought to earth.

Conclusions: "Placing" Gregory and the Wesleys

Any sound doctrine of salvation will consist both in the sense that in Christ, in his incarnation, life, passion and death for us, all creation is changed—redemption is

effected, as well as in the responsibility of the human person to work out his own salvation through a life lived in response to God. Salvation, in other words, is both gift
and calling. Nyssan and Wesleyan concepts of salvation address both of these poles. It
could be said that the Wesleys maximized the latter aspect, that of calling—not in the
"Pelagian" sense that perfection and salvation was in the hands of humans, for they
knew that it was before anything else the work of God—but in the degree of holiness
they believed was achievable here in this world. But Gregory can well be said to have
maximized the "givenness" of salvation. At least as he has it in the *De anima*, it is the
all but inevitable outcome, the *telos* (in the sense of consummation), for all. The "calling" is for him the summons to return to nature, to the extent possible here and now,
as this is better done now than in the life hereafter.

Gregory of Nyssa's universalism, however it might be tempered in places, is based
on both anthropological and ontological convictions. He is convinced that the course
of humanity is to return to its intended state, and while he places great stress on the
faculty of human free choice, human capacity to choose evil cannot ultimately prevail
over what Gregory sees as the inevitable triumph of "being" and the ceasing to exist
of non-being, which is what evil ultimately is. Wesleyan universalism—and that is
surely a misnomer—is in a way more orthodox than Gregory's, in that their conviction of the universality of redemption (an important step for them to have taken in
their day) did not lead to a necessarily universal salvation. Thus, human free choice to
turn away from God was capable of ultimately prevailing through eternity.

Gregory's idea of inevitable purgation can be seen as running counter to an
orthodoxy which insists on the possibility of hell, of the finality of human (or angelic)
decisions not to respond to the redemption that is offered to all. Like the Wesleys, then,
he too was reaching somewhat beyond his contemporaries to put forth what is ultimately an extremely hopeful and all-encompassing doctrine of salvation. Yet Gregory
is not a loner within the tradition of the Church; there are strong points of connection between Gregory's version of the apocatastasis doctrine and at least one of the
more universally accepted patristic currents having to do with salvation. I have in
mind the perception shared by many Church Fathers of heaven and hell as one reality, that fire of divine love which is experienced as joyous light by some, and tor-
menting flame by others. As Gregory's brother St Basil the Great had it,

> "The voice of the Lord divides the flame of fire" (Ps 29:7) . . . . I believe that the fire
> prepared in punishment for the devil and his angels is divided by the voice of the
> Lord. Thus, since there are two capacities in fire, one of burning and the other of illu-
> minating, the fierce and punitive property of the fire may await those who deserve to
> burn, while its illuminating and radiant part may be reserved for the enjoyment of
> those who are rejoicing.[44]

Later on, the seventh-century Isaac of Nineveh would write,

> I also maintain that those who are punished in Gehenna are scourged by the scourge
> of love. Nay, what is so bitter and vehement as the torment of love? . . . For the sor-
> row caused in the heart by sin against love is more piercing than any torment. . . . The

power of love works in two ways: it torments sinners, even as happens here when a friend suffers from a friend; but it becomes a source of joy for those who have observed its duties. According to my understanding this is the torment of Gehenna: bitter regret. But love inebriates the souls of the sons of Heaven by its delectability.[45]

These authors are testifying to an interpretation of heaven and hell, of salvation and perdition, that has a clear prominence within patristic thought, and at the same time is not far from Gregory's ideas about the nature of the purificatory fire, which is God's love.

There are other questions involved in the consideration of human salvation, questions that can be posed to both St Gregory of Nyssa and the Wesleys. These would include the relationship between personal and corporate salvation, between salvation and the Church, together with her sacraments. I have gone into some detail on a few key issues in the hope that some kind of light might be shed on aspects of the patristic legacy that can be found in the Wesleys, whatever be the means of that transmission. I will leave the last words to John Wesley and St Gregory of Nyssa:

Having this hope, that they shall see God as he is, they purify themselves ever as he is pure, and are holy, as he that has called them is holy, in all manner of conversation. Not that they have already attained all that they shall attain, either are already (in this sense) perfect. But they daily go on from strength to strength; beholding now, as in a glass, the glory of the Lord, they are changed into the same image, from glory to glory, by the spirit of the Lord.[46]

Changing in everything for the better, let him exchange glory for glory, becoming greater through daily increase, ever perfecting himself, and never arriving too quickly at the limit of perfection. For this is truly perfection: never to stop growing towards what is better and never placing any limit on perfection.[47]

Endnotes

[1] *Oratio catechetica magna* 26, in W. Jaeger, ed., et al., *Gregorii Nysseni Opera*, III.iv, 67.

[2] Cf., e.g., Ted A. Campbell, *John Wesley and Christian Antiquity: Religious Vision and Cultural Change* (Nashville, TN: Kingswood/Abingdon, 1991).

[3] *A Plain Account of Genuine Christianity* 11, in F. Whaling, ed., *John and Charles Wesley: Selected Writings and Hymns*, The Classics of Western Spirituality (New York: Paulist, 1981), 132 f.

[4] One must draw attention here to the work of Nicolas Lossky on the seventeenth-century Anglican divine, Lancelot Andrewes, who certainly represented, if not pioneered, a patristic renewal in the Anglican church. Cf. N. Lossky, *Lancelot Andrewes, The Preacher (1555–1626): The Origins of the Mystical Theology of the Church of England* (Oxford: Oxford University Press, 1991), being the English translation of the original French monograph of 1986.

[5] Henceforth cited as *De anima*.

[6] Letter 604. Cf. L. Regnault, P. Lemaire, ed., *Barsanuphe et Jean de Gaza: Correspondance* (Abbaye Saint-Pierre de Solesmes, 1971), 395–398. This conversation is cited, and somewhat misinterpreted, in Jean Daniélou's "L'apocatastase chez Grégoire de Nysse," *Recherches de Science Religieuse* 30 (1940), 328–347, cf. 334; 341.

[7]J.P. Migne, *Patriologia Graeca* 90, 795B, also cited in Daniélou, see note 5. *Patrialogia Graeca* is henceforth cited as PG.

[8]The condemnation of Origenism in the Fifth Ecumenical Council (AD 553) linked his doctrine of the preexistence of souls with that of the universal restoration, wherein we would be restored to a state of bodiless "pure intellects" (*katharous noas*). Origen's teaching on the resurrection body was in fact not fully consistent. But Gregory's doctrine of apocatastasis was seen as acceptable by the authors cited above due to the fact that he taught that the resurrection and restoration would be bodily.

[9]I say "main thinking" both because it is the major treatise devoted to the subject, but also because it represents "thinking" on the subject rather than a cut-and-dried doctrine. This is largely why Gregory sets out the treatise as a dialogue between himself and his sister Macrina, and why many of the statements are couched with the qualifier "in my opinion" *(kata ge ton emon logon)*.

[10]*De anima et resurrectione,* PG 46, 148A; cf. Also 149D; 156C. (All references to the *De anima et resurrectione,* cited throughout as *De anima,* are taken from PG 46.)

[11]89C.

[12]148C.

[13]108A. See also Peter Bouteneff, "Essential or Existential: The Problem of the Human Body in the Anthropology of St Gregory of Nyssa," in H. Drobner and A. Viciano, ed., *Gregory of Nyssa: Homilies on the Beatitudes,* Proceedings of the Eighth International Colloquium on Gregory of Nyssa (Leiden: Brill, 1999).

[14]97C–100B. Cf. Catharine P. Roth, trans., *St Gregory of Nyssa: On the Soul and the Resurrection* (Crestwood, NY: St Vladimir's Seminary Press, 1993), 83 f.

[15]101B.

[16]69B.

[17]84B. Cf. Roth, *St Gregory of Nyssa,* 71 f.

[18]80CD. Cf. Roth, *St Gregory of Nyssa,* 70.

[19]101A.

[20]Ibid.

[21]101B.

[22]104A.

[23]Hymn 374, in *A Collection of Hymns for the Use of the People Called Methodists.* See A. C. Outler, ed., *The Works of John Wesley,* The Bicentennial Edition of the Works of John Wesley (Nashville: Abingdon, Press, 1980–89), (henceforth cited as *Works*), 7:547; see also Frank Whaling, *John and Charles Wesley, Selected Writings and Hymns,* The Classics of Western Spirituality (New York: Paulist Press, 1981), 228.

[24]Hymn 345, *Works* 7:509.

[25]*A Plain Account of Christian Perfection,* 16 in Whaling, *John and Charles Wesley,* 319.

[26]§13 in Whaling, *John and Charles Wesley,* 310; emphasis original.

[27]Cf., e.g., Hymn 132, *Works* 7:244; Hymn 432, *Works* 7:609. The Philippians verse also inspired (or supported) Gregory of Nyssa's doctrine of salvation; cf. *De anima* (see 69C; 136A).

[28]John and Charles Wesley, *Hymns on the Lord's Supper,* (Bristol: Farley, 1745; reprinted in a facsimile edition, Madison, NJ: The Charles Wesley Society, 1995), Hymn 1, p. 2; henceforth cited as HLS; emphasis added.

[29]1876 *Hymnbook,* 745 in Whaling, *John and Charles Wesley,* 288.

[30]*Works* 25:1796.

[31]§5 *Works* 2:417.

[32]§15 *Works* 2:420. As it happens, John Wesley's argument against crude predestination is precisely that of Symeon the New Theologian as set out in his *Ethical Discourse* II, I; see A. Golitzin, trans., *St Symeon the New Theologian On the Mystical Life,* vol. 1: *The Church and the Last Things* (Crestwood, NY: St Vladimir's Seminary Press, 1995), 83 ff.

[33]The Wesleys tend to strike and maintain a delicate balance between a doctrine of justification by faith alone and emphasis on the importance of holy living—i.e., between the importance of faith and works.

[34]§I,i *Works,* 2:156.

[35]Sermon 58 "On Predestination," 11, emphasis original, in *Works* 2:419.

[36]§12 in Whaling, *John and Charles Wesley,* 307.

[37]Ibid.

[38]Ibid., §19 in Whaling, *John and Charles Wesley,* 335.

[39]The Wesleys give explicit homage in the poem "On Clemens Alexandrinus's *Description of a Perfect Christian*" published in *Hymns and Sacred Poems* (London: Strahan, 1739), 37.

[40]Wesley adopts a remarkably similar approach, and even similar phrasing. See, for example, the citation from *A Plain Account of Christian Perfection* at the end of this essay.

[41]*Hymns on the Lord's Supper*, Hymn 99, p. 116.

[42]Whaling, *John and Charles Wesley*, 30.

[43]Section III of the *Hymns on the Lord's Supper* is dedicated to the theme, "The Sacrament as a Pledge of Heaven."

[44]*Homily* 348 (on Psalm 28) §6 (PG 29, 297AC).

[45]*Homily* 28. Cf. *The Ascetical Homilies of Saint Isaac the Syrian* (Boston: Holy Transfiguration Monastery, 1984), 141.

[46]*A Plain Account of Christian Perfection* in Whaling, *John and Charles Wesley*, 310 f.

[47]*De Perfectione* (*Gregorii Nysseni Opera*, vol. viii.i, 213 f.).

Other Eastern Sources and Charles Wesley

11

The Missiology of Charles Wesley and Its Links to the Eastern Church

Tore Meistad[1]

The purpose of this presentation is to discuss Charles Wesley's contributions to the theology of missions in light of their theological roots,[2] compared to basic ideas in the Eastern Orthodox theology.[3]

The singing of hymns was a major distinctive to the early Methodist movement of the eighteenth century. Charles Wesley's hymns popularized Methodist ideas and probably spread them more widely than the preaching did. For this reason his hymns should be regarded as a primary source of Methodist spirituality in its original form.

Ideas of Mission in Charles Wesley's Hymns

John R. Tyson estimates the total number of Charles Wesley's hymns and poems to around 9,000.[4] Wesley's poetry is so voluminous and covers such a range of themes that it is not possible in this presentation to cover all he produced in order to make a comprehensive evaluation of his ideas. On the other hand, a few theological themes are recurrent in his hymns. In his journal he declares, "Universal Redemption and Christian Perfection as the two great truths of the everlasting Gospel."[5] I will demonstrate that these doctrines are equally important to the Wesleyan and Orthodox tradition, and that they in both traditions aim at a missionary outreach of the church.

The creating, atoning, life-giving Triune God incarnated

Charles Wesley has a trinitarian image of God.[6] His hymns are crowded with references to all three persons in the godhead in a way that emphasizes the plurality rather than the unity in the persons of God. He even describes God in the plural form of the verb "to be"; commenting God's revelation, "God *were* manifested there."[7] and, "Who have so great a God as ours, / A God that *are* so near!"[8] This understanding of the Trinity is basic to all his hymnals, for instance, his collection *Hymns for the Nativity of Our Lord.*[9] These hymns all focus on "Th'incarnate Deity."[10] Christ is God, one of the three, the eternal source of divine life, as expressed in creation and salvation. As the incarnation of God, Jesus Christ reveals not only the human person, but also the fullness of God.

The attributes of God are not discussed philosophically, but elaborated as they are revealed through the Incarnation: "GOD on high ... GOD comes down";[11] "God, the invisible, *appears*, / God, the blest, the great I AM"; "Their Maker and their King"; "the eternal Son of God [...] Lord of earth and skies"; "The Prince of peace . . . Jesus is our brother now."[12] The image of God implied is the creating and saving God who is ceaselessly active in assisting humanity in need. The reference to the God who called Moses—and who took the name "I AM" (Ex 3:14) at Sinai[13]—is illuminating; God at this point is revealed as the Creator who cares like a loving parent, and who interferes in the human history to liberate persons and peoples. The meaning of the Incarnation is that the invisible God has become "our brother." The child Jesus, Mary's and Joseph's child,[14] is the eternal God: "Incarnate see / The Deity / The infinite Creator!"[15] "The Prince of peace" points back to the Hebrew prophecies of the messianic age, in which fallen creation will be restored to its original state by the offering of this peace to everybody: "Apply to every Heart his Peace, / And bring his Kingdom in!"[16]

Because Christ is the Creator of the world, he also has the power to re-create humanity. This is actually the essential purpose for his Incarnation: "Save us Thou, our New-Creator."[17] As often as Charles Wesley refers to the Spirit's role in the first creation, he also conceives salvation as a new creation. For instance, in his hymn for Whitsunday, "Eternal PARACLETE, descend," he describes the re-creating work of the Spirit in salvation by alluding to the first creation.[18]

In the Easter hymn, "Jesus shew us thy Salvation", the last stanza begins: "By the Coming of thy Spirit / As a mighty rushing Wind, / Save us into all thy Merit."[19] Charles Wesley here implies that, from a soteriological point of view, Christ's atoning sacrifice was not completed until Pentecost. He clearly indicates that the forensic focus of Western theology is too limited to comprehend salvation in its fullness. Creation, atonement, and re-creation belong together. God's wrath of sin and judgment are not emphasized but rather "GOD the giver" of new life, "Peace and love."[20] In the Wesleyan perspective salvation is conceived within the context of creation, and the perspective of creation is teleological.[21]

One word, which is frequently used in the hymns quoted in this article, is "feel." It is important to understand that this has not to do so much with emotions as with experience.[22] This emphasis adds to the focus on the present realization of salvation as implied in the inaugurated eschatology of the Wesleys.

Comparison

God's Incarnation as human is a focal point in the Wesleyan theology. This event is more than a historical event, it opens up for the experience of God's kingdom on earth. Rather than pointing back to the remission of the human guilt caused by Adam's sin, it points to the future redemption of all creation. Likewise, the Orthodox tradition affirms that:

> The Incarnation . . . is God's supreme act of deliverance, restoring us to communion with himself.
>
> The Incarnation of Christ . . . effects more than a reversal of the fall, more than a restoration of man to his original state in Paradise. When God's becomes man, this marks the beginning of an essential new stage in the history of man . . . Only in Jesus

Christ do we see revealed the full possibilities of our human nature . . . The Incarnation . . . is an essential stage upon man's journey from the divine image to the divine
likeness.[23]

Charles Wesley's trinitarian theology emphasizes the plurality rather than the unity in
the persons of God. This indicates that he is dependent on the Byzantine conceptions
of God as a multifaceted and an interventionist God who unceasingly is in action for
the redemption of humanity.[24] Ware[25] emphasizes that the Orthodox image of God is
dynamic and not static. He also affirms that, "There is in God genuine diversity as well
as true unity. The Christian God is not just a union, not just unity but community."[26]
Vassiliadis,[27] too, focuses on the significance of God's "I AM" for the Christian image
of God.

While Wesley scholars used to focus on the Christological emphasis of the Wesleyan theology, contemporary scholars rather point to its pneumatological—or,
essentially, its trinitarian—character. Whether God's work is characterized as creation
or salvation, the Holy Spirit is in action. Likewise, the Orthodox spirituality has a
pneumatological character.[28] Salvation is conceived as a filling with the Spirit. Concerning the Eucharist St Symeon the New Theologian affirms, "It is the Spirit Who
really purifies us and makes us partake worthily of the body of the Lord."[29] In his presentation of Orthodox missions Bria[30] emphasizes that the significance of the Spirit as
Creator, Life-giver, and Perfector is the basis of the Orthodox theology of missions:
"Thus Christian mission is the action of the body of Christ in the history of
humankind—a continuation of Pentecost."[31] Bria conceives the rich liturgy of the
Orthodox tradition in exactly the same way, as "the continuation of Pentecost."[32]

Charles Wesley's strong pneumatology suggests that his soteriology is dependent
more on the Eastern than the Western tradition. The Orthodox bishop Ware affirms
his idea that the incarnation of Christ is leading toward Pentecost: "Pentecost forms
the aim and completion of the Incarnation."[33]

Universal redemption

God's grace is universal. Contrary to the Augustinian and Calvinist idea that God's ini-
tiative implies God's mysterious choice of which persons are saved and which are
not,[34] the Wesleys argue for the position that the grace is free and open to every human
person. Because the human guilt is universal,[35] so is God's grace.

The concept of "universal redemption" means that God's grace is universal. Salvation, however, is not. A tension exists in the theology of the Wesleys between the
universal call of the gospel and the redemption of a limited number of persons only.[36]
Their insistence on a universal redemption does not imply a universalism indicating
that all persons will be saved in the end, but rather that all persons without exception
are atoned for by Christ's sacrifice and surrounded by God's prevenient grace.[37] God's
grace is instantly poured out on humanity: "And Streams of Grace eternal roll / O'er
all the Earth below";[38] and: "And tak'st of his Atoning Blood / To sprinkle all
Mankind."[39] This is a recurrent theme in the sermons of John Wesley as well as in the
hymns of Charles Wesley.[40] It is also an important missionary motif. In the messianic

age a fundamental change in the history of salvation has taken place. Now is the time for missions.[41]

The expectation of Christ's immediate return gave the early church a sense of urgency, which characterized its missions. The same was true to the first Methodists, their messianic hope and experience of the fulfillment of its promises sent them out anew every day. The salvation was ready for everybody; the table of the heavenly banquet was set.

The universality of grace is a characteristic to the Wesleyan theology. Charles writes of an "all sufficient grace"[42] and "all atoning Lamb."[43] For this reason the prevenient grace should not be restricted to a revivalist scheme of the sinner's awakening prior to conversion, it rather conceives the unlimited scope of God's salvation.

Barclay concludes his discussion of the Wesleyan heritage by stating that, "The missionary character of the Methodist movement was a natural and almost inevitable outgrowth of its fundamental doctrine of universal redemption."[44] As indicated, this conclusion can be drawn on the basis of Charles Wesley's hymns no less than from John Wesley's sermons.

Comparison

One of the most distinctive premises of the Wesleyan theology is that God's grace is universal, and that Christ's atonement has cosmological effects. These distinctions have obvious roots in the Orthodox spirituality, whose representatives affirm that, for instance, "it is wrong to imagine that sinners in hell are cut off from the love of God."[45] This theological tradition emphasizes that, in the process of salvation, the exclusive foundation is God's grace. But because grace is resistible, the synergy between God's grace and the human will is therefore required. This synergy is evangelical and not Pelagian, however, because the human will is restored by the antecedent grace of God.[46] This indicates that the grace has a universal character and the offer of salvation is universal.[47] Bria affirms that, "God is the creator of the whole universe and [...] he has not left himself without witness at any time or any place. The Spirit of God is constantly at work in ways that pass human understanding and in places that to us are least expected."[48]

The sense that the mission of the church is urgent, is apparent in the Eastern Orthodoxy no less than in early Methodism. Bishop Ware asserts that, "We are to have in our hearts a sense of urgency."[49]

The person in a corporate perspective

The goal of Christ's incarnation is the restoration of all humankind. In the Christmas hymn, "Angels speak, let Man give Ear," Charles Wesley establishes that Christ is "Born his Creatures to restore," and that the news of salvation is for "Every Tongue and Nation."[50] He is "An universal Saviour," the "Lord of all creation," and "The Joy of every nation."[51] It is evident that Christ's incarnation as well as his atonement has significance far beyond the individual and personal level. Because Christ is the Savior of nations and not only persons, the Wesleyan soteriology has a social dimension as well.[52]

Consequently, there is no contradiction in the Wesleyan soteriology between social and corporate perspectives on the one hand, and the focus on the person on the other: "The PROMISE to our Fallen Head / To every Child of *Adam* made, / Is now pour'd out on all Mankind."[53] On the contrary, they are interwoven. Persons, society, and nature are included in salvation as the new creation. The focus on the conversion of the individual has therefore nothing to do with either individualism or subjectivism.[54] As demonstrated in the following stanza, the personal emphasis in this soteriology is conceived within a corporate or actually universal context:

> 4. O might we Each receive the Grace
>   By Thee to call the Saviour *mine!*
> Come, *Holy Ghost*, to all our Race,
>   Bring in the Righteousness Divine,
> Inspire the Sense of Sins Forgiven,
> And give our Earth a Taste of Heaven."[55]

Comparison

The corporate perspectives are manifest in Orthodox spirituality and probably far more so than in contemporary Methodism.[56] Corporate perspectives are implied in the Orthodox ecclesiology, for instance, in the practice of penance.[57] Over and over again Orthodox writers aver that, the salvation of Christ is not for humanity alone; it includes the restoration of the entire creation; "the Incarnation, death, and resurrection of Christ have affected all of creation!"[58] Consequently, the church is conceived "as an eschatological community, a pilgrim people."[59]

Eschatology: salvation conceived as the new creation

What makes everything new, is the presence of God in the midst of human history.[60] The incarnation of Christ means that "God comes down" to the earth as the great "Giver," making it possible that "Peace and love / From above / Reign on earth forever."[61] In the experience of the Wesleys and the early Methodists, this is not only an expression of hope but also an actual experience; the heavenly happiness can be experienced here and now.[62] As "The Lord of all creation" and "The joy of every nation" Christ is "An universal Saviour," whose goal it is to "make us all divine; / And we the life of God shall know, / For God is manifest below."[63]

The expression "make us all divine" refers to 2 Peter 1:4 and Hebrews 3:14, which clarify that the process of deification actually is to make persons "partakers of the divine nature";[64] "For we are made partakers of Christ."[65] The Wesleys affirm that this is a free gift of God's grace to everybody who asks for it.[66]

According to the Wesleyan theology the divine nature is love. The concept of "Christian perfection" implies perfection in love and not a perfection of human nature. The process of sanctification is the process of participating, more and more in God's nature, which is love.[67] Or, as stated in the Orthodox tradition, the believer participates in the energies of God but not in God's essence.[68] Discussing the nature of

God, as it is revealed in the incident when Jacob the patriarch wrestles with the Lord (cf. Gen 32:24–32), Charles Wesley's main point is that God's nature is love.[69] Charles Wesley is positive that "God and Love are One";[70] God is "pure, universal love."[71] The foundation of God's universal grace is God's universal love.

Precisely because the Christians are partakers of the divine nature and not actually made gods, it is hardly possible to speak of a total union with God but rather of a mysterious communion in which the human and divine are united. This is particularly emphasized by Charles Wesley in his *Hymns on the Lord's Supper*, for instance, "We here thy Nature shall retrieve, / And all thy heavenly Image bear."[72]

Charles Wesley firmly believes that from a personal perspective, salvation implies the restoration of God's image in the human soul and a rehabilitation of the sinner, as he or she is penetrated with God's love.[73] This is the beginning of the eschatological transformation of the entire creation. God's love in Christ is "all-victorious."[74] Tyson observes that the hymns of Charles Wesley celebrate these transforming effects of love;[75] for instance,

> Love, that makes us creatures new,
> Only love can keep us true,
> Perfect love that casts out sin,
> Perfect love is God within.[76]

It is demonstrated that in Charles Wesley's theology, the theme of re-creation is basic to his conception of redemption. The concept of "recapitulation" is alluded to, as well as expressed explicitly. St Paul in Romans 5:12–21 (cf. 1 Cor 15:22–23) interprets salvation in light of the discussion of Adam-Christ. Christ is here interpreted typologically as a second or new Adam,[77] who returns to humanity everything which was lost in the fall of the first Adam.[78] Conceived as restoration the salvation implies that Christ becomes "head," not only of the person[79] and of the church (Eph 1:21–22; 4:15; 5:23; Col 1:18) but of the universal powers and authorities as well (Col 2:10). The Creator has reclaimed the creation, we are the Creator's possessions as well as co-workers in the struggle against the evil powers of the world. From this perspective, missions is our response to God's kingdom, which is universal in extent but not yet in its actuality. To be in mission is to participate in God's restoration of the cosmos. It implies, first, to accept God's restoration of ourselves as persons, and secondly, to do whatever we possibly can in presenting other persons and societies to God's transforming love, and thus assist the nature to recover from the human exploitation of it.

Comparison

The Wesleyan and the Orthodox traditions share the idea that, in the Christian church and missions, the *eschaton* is inaugurated. Consequences, God's mission as well as the mission of the church should be understood in the eschatological perspective.[80]

The frequently mentioned idea of the human participation in God's nature in Charles Wesley's hymns resembles the Byzantine Fathers' saying that, "God became human that human become divine."[81] Because of his revivalist context he probably affirms stronger than the Eastern tradition that this is a free gift to everybody who asks for it. However, Eastern fathers affirm that, "it [this deification] is open to all who believe."[82]

The Wesleyan concepts of holiness and sanctification clearly resemble the Eastern Orthodox concept of *theosis* rather than the Western tendency to understand sanctification as a perfect fulfillment of God's will as prescribed in the law. In the Wesleyan understanding, God's sanctifying grace works an actual transformation of the human person as s/he is penetrated by fresh, divine life. The metaphors of living by the power of Christ's resurrection (Philippians 3:10), experiencing the restoration of heaven and earth, and the perfect renewal of love, all express the experience of this transformation due to God's re-creation of the sinner. The Wesleyan notion of Christian perfection resembles almost word for word, St Symeon the New Theologian's elaboration of *theosis*.[83]

Rather than speaking of the believer's union with God, Charles Wesley's focus is on the believer's mystical experience of being in communion with God.[84] There are more arenas for this communion, however, than in the sacraments as well as in the other means of grace. The goal is no less than living the entire human life in communion with God. This is also the emphasis of St Symeon the New Theologian in his affirmation that, "The Lord's commandments are not instructions in morality but . . . instead 'sacramental' in nature, i.e., in observing them we are led to communion with Him 'Who is hidden within His divine commandments.'"[85] In their positive attitudes to God's law, the Wesleys affirm neither Luther's position that the only use of the law in the spiritual kingdom is to promote repentance, nor Calvin's idea that the law is a formal pattern for acquiring sanctification, but the Eastern idea of the law as a means of communion with God as well as of communicating the divine life to the world.

The emphasis on recapitulation is closely connected to the teleological orientation of the Wesleyan concept of Christian perfection. While Protestant theology traditionally is centered around the doctrine of justification by faith, the experience of forgiveness and restoration to be a child of God according to Wesleyan theology marks only the beginning of the way of salvation. Justification is conceived as the door to the house of Christian religion, whose goal is sanctification understood as participation with God. Based in the Greek *teleios* rather than the Latin *perfectus*, perfection is goal-oriented and does not describe a final phase of spiritual development. The emphasis is on the wholeness of a person and points to the growth towards this wholeness, which is based in a perfect relation or communion with God; "holiness" is synonymous with "wholeness."[86] Consequently, the goals of the Wesleyan soteriology transcend the person and point to the salvation of all creation. This is in harmony with the conception of creation in the Orthodox tradition, affirming that, "Creation is not an event in the past, but a relationship in the present."[87]

Because the Wesleyan soteriology begins in the creation and ends in the new creation, the transformation of the person becomes a part of the transformation of the entire cosmos (cf. Col 1:15–23; cf. Rom 8:33–39). The theme of salvation conceived as a new creation is elaborated in the hymn, "Then the whole earth again shall rest"[88] which is written for the celebration of Pentecost. Although it is obvious that the justification of the sinner to Charles Wesley marks the initiation of the Christian life and the beginning of the lifelong way of salvation, both justification and sanctification of the believer are conceived to be one element in the restoration of the cosmos. They are eschatological events on the basis of Christ's incarnation at Christmas, his atoning death and resurrection at Easter, and the outpouring of the Spirit at Pentecost. The kingdom, which is actually present in the lives of the believers, is a kingdom of love.

In his discussion of Charles Wesley's theology of salvation, Tyson makes the point that his Pentecostal hymns do more than recount the story of Pentecost, they actually "re-create the event in the lives of the contemporary Christians. The singers of these hymns pray for their own Pentecost."[89] This observation is basic to the interpretation of the role of his hymns within the context of the Wesleyan revival. In it the way is extremely short from the initial experience of salvation to the active engagement in the mission of the movement. Its eschatology can never—no less than in the Byzantine theology[90]—be reduced to a separate chapter of Wesleyan theology, it rather qualifies the theology as a whole. Charles Wesley's conception of salvation as "heaven below" resembles St Symeon the New Theologian's insistence that the Christians "are already in heaven"[91] and that, "Heaven . . . is a fact, already here."[92]

Retrieving his initial experience of assurance of faith, which happened on the day of Pentecost, May 21, 1738, Charles Wesley interprets his experience as being transferred from darkness to light (cf. Jn 8:12). This understanding of the Christian life as a life in the light is a recurrent theme in his hymns. In this perspective it is interesting to learn about St Symeon the New Theologian's reports of his spiritual experiences as an experience of the light of God.[93]

Finally, Charles and John Wesley both conceive grace as a transforming and not only as a forgiving power. To be encountered by the grace of God is to be embraced and penetrated by it. Their emphasis on the energizing of the Spirit is apparent.[94] Similar to the Orthodox tradition, whose emphasis also is in the transforming effects of the divine grace, they interpret their experiences of the Spirit as "heaven below," or a "heaven on earth."[95]

Love as a manifestation of God's presence

To the Wesleys, the true mark of Christianity is love, which makes love the key concept in their theology. No word is more characteristic of their soteriology; they actually are using it as an apt summation of the gospel.[96] God is love. Love is also the power, which binds God to the creation.[97] This love is a manifestation of the kingdom of God that implies two aspects, first, the believer's experience of transformation to God's image (loving God with all one's heart), and, secondly, the ethical consequences (loving the neighbor). This has more to do with ethics than with emotions. In Charles Wesley's discussion of love in his hymn, "Come, thou holy God and true!"[98] he suggests that love is where God is, love is the evidence of God's presence. God is brought to the widow, the orphan, those without shelter, and the poor, by persons who themselves are transformed by God's love. The outpouring of God's love makes the Christian invincible, and no problem is so big that it cannot be solved by the power of love: "So shall my pure obedience prove / All things are possible to love."[99]

The goal of the Christian religion is to be filled with "the Life Divine"[100] which implies the perfection in love.[101] As Charles Wesley interprets salvation, the outpouring of this divine love in persons should lead to the renewal of God's righteousness[102] in the way this concept is interpreted by the Hebrew prophets, who envisage the restoration of God's will for the nature and society as well as for persons. For this reason love is not conceived in emotional terms but as an experience of transformation to God's image. In this way the perfection in love is supposed to direct the lives of Christians on this earth,[103] making them "Servants" who are first given "Pardon, Holiness, and Heaven" (Wesley 1746b:28) for nothing, and who then are expected to practice the same in the world.[104] The life of restored persons is characterized by the fruits of the Spirit (Gal 5:22–23) to be exercised on the global, more than on the personal, level. The double commandment of love (Mt 22:37–39) is well focused in the Wesleyan spirituality, and although the second part of it focuses on personal recipients of Christian love, the concept of neighbor is extended to include all humankind rather than limited to individual persons. Charles Wesley prays, "I want the Spirit of power within . . . Of love to thee and all mankind."[105]

Because of a necessary interconnection between faith and works, as the fruits of faith, the love of neighbor by necessity comes out of the experience of God's love. Dealing with mutual assistance, this neighborly love is highly practical.[106] The dynamics of the Wesleyan spirituality are focused on the reception of God's grace, the transformation of the person, and the transmitting of this grace to others. This is evident from the hymn, "Jesus, the gift divine I know."[107]

In 1757 Charles Wesley wrote a poem in the memory of the Methodist, Mrs Mary Naylor. In this poem he described an ideal Methodist, a true imitator of Christ, whose character was formed by God's justice and love. The way the concept "justice" is used, it clearly resembles that of the Hebrew prophets, for instance, Amos.[108] In the Wesleyan tradition, then, justice is conceived in the context of God's love.

Comparison

Love is no less fundamental to the Orthodox spirituality.[109] For instance, St Symeon the New Theologian declares that love is "not merely an attribute of God, but the substantial presence of God."[110] St Isaac the Syrian affirms: "Love is the kingdom which the Lord mystically promised to the disciples."[111] As I have pointed out, this is a Wesleyan position as well.

The messianic kingdom and the year of the Jubilee

Charles Wesley's eschatology is dependent on the Hebrew prophecies of the messianic kingdom that announce the coming reign of justice and peace.[112] Besides the dependence on prophecies of the messianic age, for instance, Isaiah 61,[113] his eschatology is also inspired by the Hebrew idea of the year of the Jubilee, the year of restoration for nature and societies as well as persons.[114] In the Sabbatical year (Lev 25:1–7) the soil is to be given opportunity for rest to regain its fertility. But in the Year of the Jubilee (Lev 25:8–55) justice in the social order is to be reestablished. People, who have lost their property due to debt, would return to their property, and slaves would gain their freedom. This was the reason why the first Christians shared their economic resources as well as distributing their surplus to the poor (Acts 2:45; 4:34–5:11). Consequently, the first Methodists, who intended to revive the life of the original Christian church, made a just distribution of economic, educational, and medical resources their top priority. This is evident in John Wesley's sermons, as well as in Charles's hymns.

Over and over again the Wesleys are using Jesus' teaching of the judgment (Matthew 25:31–48) in the way they develop their understanding of how a genuine Christian life should be. This makes their concerns for the poor the center of their image of discipleship, as in the hymn, "Your duty let the apostle show."[115] The last stanza refers to the motif of the Christian as a steward of God's possessions, which is particularly typical to John's theology and ethics; "our" possessions are no more than loans from God and should be administered according to God's will and love.[116] This resembles the idea of the Jubilee.

The popular hymn among Methodists, "O for a thousand tongues to sing,"[117] placed first in *A Collection of Hymns for the use of the People called Methodists* (1780), enhances further our understanding of the messianic reign and the Wesleyan tradition. The date of its composition is significant, May 21, 1739, which is the first anniversary for Charles Wesley's experience of assurance of faith on the Day of Pentecost, 1738. The original poem, published in *Hymns and Sacred Poems* (1740), had eighteen stanzas. The version published in the 1780 *Collection* included only original stanzas 7–10, 12–14, and 17–18.[118]

The outline of the hymn may be sketched in the following way:[119]

Stanza 1: First doxology

> Glory to God, and praise and love
> Be ever, ever given,
> By saints below and saints above,
> The church in earth and heaven.

The hymn opens with a doxology to God, and the context is universal, including heaven as well as earth. The experience of salvation as sanctification ("love" / "saints below") leads to a natural desire to glorify God. As a messianic people the Methodists are a part of the church universal.

Stanzas 2–6: The author's personal experience of salvation, understood as the experience of forgiveness of sins

The following stanzas report Charles Wesley's decisive spiritual experience:

> 2. On this glad day the glorious Sun
> Of Righteousness arose;
> On my benighted soul He shone
> And filled it with repose.

"This day" is referring to the day of Pentecost, May 21, 1738, when he experienced assurance of faith for the first time; he obviously is feeling a need to glorify God on this first anniversary. He interprets his experience as being transferred from darkness to light.

> 3. Sudden expired the legal strife,
> 'Twas then I ceased to grieve;
> My second, real, living life
> I then began to live.

Classical Reformation rhetoric ("legal strife") is alluded to as the basis of his experience, which is presented as being transferred from death to life (references: Rom 3:21; 1 Jn 3:14). The emphasis is, however, different, because it relates to the sudden and total transformation of the forgiven sinner.

> 4. Then with my heart I first believed,
> Believed with faith divine,
> Power with the Holy Ghost received
> To call the Saviour mine.

This stanza defines the experience of May 21 as a deep personal experience of faith ("To call the Savior mine") as well as an experience of empowerment by the Spirit (reference: Rom 8:14–16).

> 5. I felt my Lord's atoning blood
> Close to my soul applied;
> Me, me He loved, the Son of God,
> For me, for me He died!

Christ's atoning death was experienced as applied to him personally (reference: Rom 5:8, 18);[120] the concept of "feeling" relates to experience rather than emotion.

> 6. I found and owned His promise true,
> Ascertained of my part,
> My pardon passed in heaven I knew
> When written on my heart.

The stanza interprets the experience of May 21, as an experience of assurance (reference: Rom 8:16); the concept of "knowing" relates to an intimate personal experience rather than to knowledge as a cognitive phenomenon.

Stanza 7: Second doxology

> 7. O for a thousand tongues to sing
> My great Redeemer's praise,
> The glories of my God and King,
> The triumphs of His grace!

God, whose gracious salvation the Methodist people have experienced, is praised (references: Ps 119:172; 145:1). The language ("a thousand tongues") is universal as well as pneumatological (cf. Acts 2:3), indicating that God's salvation is for the world and not for the Methodists alone, and that salvation, the Spirit, and mission, belong together.

Stanzas 8–9: Calling the Methodists to mission

As a natural response to their experience of salvation, the Methodist people are admonished to proclaim God's grace around the world (references: Mt 9:31; Ps 66:2).

> 8. My gracious Master and my God,
>   Assist me to proclaim,
> To spread through all the earth abroad
>   The honors of Thy name.

The command for mission is pronounced explicitly, however, as more of a promise of empowerment, for which the singer is praying.

> 9. Jesus! the name that charms our fears,
>   That bids our sorrows cease;
> 'Tis music in the sinner's ears,
>   'Tis life, and health, and peace.

The great Christological hymn of St Paul (Phil 2:5–12) is probably alluded to, indicating that the exalted God still is the humble servant, who cares for people. This allusion serves to strengthen the universal tone of the hymn.

Stanzas 10–12: Salvation elaborated theologically

The salvation, which they have experienced, is elaborated in detail. The biblical framework is the Hebrew prophecies of liberation of the captives, to be expected in the messianic age. Now the Messiah has come in Jesus Christ, and the dawn of his kingdom is experienced in the lives of the Methodists. The contents of this experience are,

> 10. He breaks the power of cancelled sin,
>   He sets the prisoner free;
> His blood can make the foulest clean,
>   His blood availed for me.

Wesley stresses liberation from personal sin as well as social evils (references: Is 61:1; 1:18; Gal 2:20). In contrast to the continental reformers, he insists that salvation removes the power of sin and not the guilt of sin only.

> 11. He speaks, and listening to His voice
> New life the dead receive,
> The mournful, broken hearts rejoice,
> The humble poor believe.

Renewal comes through the experience of fresh, divine life (references: Jn 11:24; 3:14; Mt 5:3–4).

> 12. Hear Him, ye deaf; His praise, ye dumb,
> Your loosened tongues employ;
> Ye blind, behold your Saviour come,
> And leap, ye lame, for joy.

Healing is a part of God's re-creation of the world (references: Mt 11:4–5; Mk 7:37; Is 35:5–6; Acts 3:8); an over-spiritualized interpretation, indicating that spiritually dead and blind are referred to, risks missing the significant message of restoration.

Stanzas 13–16: The Methodist message for mission elaborated

The rest of the hymn, which was included in the 1780 edition, is a summary of the Wesleyan message in poetic form. It essentially avers that the proclamation of salvation affirms God's salvation is for everybody; no one is excluded from God's grace:

> 13. Look unto Him, ye nations, own
> Your God, ye fallen race;
> Look, and be saved through faith alone,
> Be justified by grace.

Universal emphasis: All nations are offered salvation, which is free for everybody through God's grace and the sinner's faith (references: Is 45:22; Eph 2:8).

> 14. See all your sins on Jesus laid:
> The Lamb of God was slain,
> His soul was once an offering made
> For every soul of man.

Personal emphasis: Christ's atoning death is for every person on earth (references: Is 53:6; Jn 1:29; Rev 5:6; Is 53:10).

> 15. Harlots and publicans and thieves
> In holy triumph join!
> Saved is the sinner that believes
> From crimes as great as mine.

All the outcasts of this world are included in the offer of God's salvation. In affirming that he himself is no better than "Harlots and publicans," Charles Wesley establishes that a basic solidarity in sin exists among all human persons. The solidarity in the light of God's grace is equally important (reference: Mt 21:31).

> 16. Murderers and all ye hellish crew
> Ye sons of lust and pride,
> Believe the Saviour died for you;
> For me the Saviour died.

Not even murderers and people condemned to hell are excluded from Christ's offer of salvation; he died for every person.

Stanza 18: Conclusion

> 18. With me, your chief, you then shall know,
> Shall feel your sins forgiven;
> Anticipate your heaven below,
> And own that love is heaven.

All who experience forgiveness and justification, which is described as "heaven below," should also expect the door to be opened for the experience of love as they are moving towards sanctification (reference: 1 Tim 1:15).

Comparison

I have not been able to find distinctive references to the themes of the messianic kingdom and the Jubilee, as they are elaborated by the Hebrew prophets, in the Orthodox literature explored for this study, though I assume that such references may be found. In contemporary Orthodox missiology mission is defined as "the proclamation of the good news, i.e. of the coming of the kingdom",[121] however, not without social responsibility: "St Paul understood the collection [to the Jerusalem mother church] as the social response of the body of Christ to God's will. For him, and the rest of the Christian community, this act was not simply a social-ethical one but the inevitable response to the kingdom of God inaugurated in Christ."[122] The same ought to be the attitude of Christian missions today.

I have indicated that the spiritual breakthrough for Charles and John Wesley had to do with the nature of assurance in God. After years of reasoning about God, they finally experienced God's self. This is also an emphasis of the Orthodox tradition, which rather than focusing on the process of reasoning, affirms faith in God as "the assurance that someone is there."[123]

The Poor: "Jesus' bosom friends"

With the heavy emphasis there is on the restoration of justice, peace, and love in the soteriology of Charles Wesley, his focus is on the poor.[124] He honors them, calls them

"Jesus' bosom-friends,"[125] and he obviously approves his brother John's statement, "I love the poor."[126]

John and Charles Wesley struggle to reach an understanding of poverty based on social and economic causes; poverty was, as indicated in the hymn referred to above, a matter of "unrighteousness." They therefore threw themselves into a lifelong struggle against poverty. Contrary to the upper classes, which did not actually mingle with the poor, they wanted "to make the poor our friends."[127]

To the Wesleys, therefore, charity is far more than the Christian expression of kindness and philanthropy; it results from and is directed by the transformation of persons in the kingdom of God.[128] Furthermore, their charity has a global perspective, whose ultimate goal is the removal of the causes of poverty.[129]

The Wesleyan attitudes toward the poor were a matter of total identification and a giving up of themselves for them. They applied Christ's word on radical discipleship (Mk 8:34–38) to their relations with the poor, and they made the poor their special responsibility.[130]

Comparison

For St Symeon the New Theologian, as well as for the Wesleys, the attitudes toward the poor are decisive indications of their communion with God. St Symeon implies that Christians who may serve as spiritual mentors for others "are recognized not just by these charisms, but by their manner of life as well. . . . All such men have kept God's commandments unto death. They have sold their belongings and distributed them among the poor. They have followed Christ by enduring temptation. They have lost their own lives in the world for the sake of love for God."[131] For this reason contemporary Christian missions should support the poor. Bria suggests that the poor are subject to "a double injustice: they are victims of the oppression of an unjust economic order or an unjust political distribution of power, and at the same time they are deprived of the knowledge of God's special care for them. . . . Jesus . . . recognized the poor as those who were sinned against, victims of both personal and structural sin. . . . There is no evangelism without solidarity; there is no Christian solidarity that does not involve sharing the knowledge of the kingdom which is God's."[132]

From his readings of Deuteronomy, Petros Vassiliadis observes, "The society promised by God to his people is a society in which 'there shall be no poor' (15:4), and towards that fulfillment, and having that in mind, all people who in the meantime are poor or in need must be helped."[133]

8. The response of salvation: mission in one's own context

Charles Wesley's idea of the growth of the Christian into discipleship is developed in numerous hymns[134] that demonstrate how the Wesleyan theology of redemption is structured in three parts.[135] First, the reconciliation in Christ is due to the victory of God's love over sin and death (received in justification). Secondly, the believer is re-created as God's grace is imparted, or, the Spirit dwells within (received in sanctification). Thirdly, the renewal of the Christian is actualized through discipleship, which is a life in love and in the imitation of Christ; this is worked out through the diaconal and missionary outreach of the church.

The covenant with God gave the Hebrew people responsibilities more than privileges. In the same way the goal of the Christian's experience of redemption is to spread the gospel to "the present age," as expressed by Charles Wesley's hymn, "A charge to keep I have."[136] In it he clarifies that his charge is to glorify God, and he glorifies God by being a servant to his contemporaries. He is not empowered by God for his own sake, but to be engaged in doing the will of his Master. *Everybody* has received "a charge" from God to be a steward, and this charge is always "contemporary and holistic."[137] The genuine Christian is the one who imitates Christ's humility and servanthood.[138]

In the Wesleyan tradition, salvation is not conceived to be a matter of theological ideas but rather a way, a spiritual journey toward God, which the Christian invites her or his neighbor to join. The ultimate goal of its soteriology is the redemption of the Christian's neighbor and not the redemption of the Christian's own soul. For this reason, this soteriology as a whole embodies an implicit theology of mission. That this is a distinctive Wesleyan perspective is evident from a comparison with Pelagian soteriology, as conceived in the Medieval ages. Notice that the following table exclusively deals with soteriologies and not with the overall theological systems; all these theologies to some degree imply an urge for mission. My purpose is to demonstrate how the missionary imperative comes out of the Wesleyan soteriology:[139]

Soteriology	Pelagian	Wesleyan
Goal of MY redemption	MY redemption	YOUR redemption
Instrument for redemption	Merits earned by good works to YOU as my neighbor	God's redemption of ME
Basis of redemption	Human (supported by divine) powers	God's grace in Christ and empowerment by the Spirit
Fundamental question	"How can I be saved?"	"For what purpose am I saved"?

Western soteriologies tend to focus on a fundamental theological issue: "How can I [a sinner, who has transgressed God's law] be saved?" They therefore inevitably will focus on *my* redemption. In the Wesleyan soteriology this question is significant but not primary, it leads to the more basic, "For what purpose am I saved?" This variation leads to a difference in the attitude toward the neighbor in the Wesleyan and Pelagian soteriology (as interpreted in the Medieval ages). While Pelagianism reduces the neighbor to an instrument for *my* redemption, the *neighbor* is the goal of my redemption in Wesleyanism. For this reason a mandate for mission is implicit in Wesleyan soteriology, explaining why its theological contribution was one of several factors that gave birth to the modern missions movement.

Another implicit mandate for mission is the dedication of the life of the Christian to do whatever God's will is. The emphasis on universal redemption in Charles

Wesley's soteriology has obvious consequences for missions. Charles Wesley's hymn, "Thy will, O Lord, whate'er I do,"[140] indicates that if we want to learn what is God's will, we need to look for God's love. And to be guided by God's love means to give oneself entirely to salvation of the world (cf. Jn 3:16). Christ's self-giving love should become "the goal, purpose, and style of our lives."[141]

Comparison

The concept of the Christian religion as a way of life toward God is equally emphasized in the Orthodox and the Wesleyan traditions.[142] In both traditions mission issues from their soteriologies. St John Chrysostom declares, "I do not believe in the salvation of anyone who does not try to save others."[143] According to St Symeon the New Theologian, "all [are] commanded to 'possess the sun of righteousness shining within us' and 'to provide our neighbor with the example of the immaterial day, the new earth and new heaven.'"[144] Both traditions also share holistic ideas of missions:

> Mission cannot be reduced only to the preaching of the gospel – it implies service, i.e., witness through deeds, as well as words.[145]

> God is not found by a mystical escape to a spiritual realm. People know God because he confronts them by his action. . . . Deuteronomy understands salvation in a very concrete way: here salvation primarily concerns liberation from slavery, from all sorts of slavery. That is why Christian mission cannot be limited to evangelizing the world by preaching liberation only from spiritual bonds, leaving aside or scandalously ignoring the political, economical, cultural, ideological oppression of God's creation in his very image of humanity. It was against this background that Christ in his inaugural proclamation of his gospel applied to himself Isaiah's prophesy: "The Spirit of the Lord is upon me, because he has anointed me to bring good news to the poor. He has sent me to proclaim release to the captives . . . to let the oppressed go free" (Luke 4:18).[146]

The Orthodox and the Wesleyan traditions equally affirm mission as the essence of the church, issuing from the theology of salvation. However, precisely at this point, they also depart, namely, when it comes to the issue of ecclesiology. Meyendorff maintains: "But *missions*, in its ultimate theological meaning, is an expression of *the Church* itself. It cannot grow out of a divided Christendom, but only from the one church, and leads to conversion to this one church."[147] The Wesleyan ecclesiology is based on the presupposition that Methodism is a part of the church universal, and that other denominations are genuine parts of the Christian church. For this reason its missions do have not a similar ecclesio-centric character. On the other hand, contemporary Orthodox theologians, like Vassiliadis, seem to have a less ecclesio-centric perspective: "Applied to *mission*, this trinitarian basis has had the tremendous effect of helping the church to avoid imperialistic or confessional attitudes."[148] He quotes Bria:

> The trinitarian theology points to the fact that God's involvement in history aims at drawing humanity and creation in general into his communion with God's very life.

The implications of this assertion for understanding mission are very important: mission does not aim primarily at the propagation or transmission of intellectual convictions, doctrines, moral commands, etc., but at the transmission of the life communion that exists in God.[149]

Explicit mandates for mission

So far, the hymns referred to indicate various implicit motifs for mission. But Charles Wesley's hymns are also crowded with explicit admonitions to be engaged in mission, which the following examples will indicate. Kimbrough[150] makes the point that the hymn, "Ye servants of God,"[151] is a cry against oppression and persecution not unlike the contemporary African-American "We shall overcome." In his *Hymns of Intercession for All Mankind* Charles Wesley also includes a prayer "For the Heathen," which explicitly refers to the need of mission to the gentiles.[152] The title of this hymn indicates an increased awareness of the mission to the gentiles among the Methodists. Considering that this particular idea of missions had been neglected by the church since the church of the apostles until it was revived by the German pietists, particularly Zinzendorf (1700–1760), Wesleyan Methodism should be considered an early exponent of the modern missions movement.

In his hymn, "Blow Ye the Trumpet, Blow"[153] Charles Wesley pulls his primary missional motifs together: Christ's atonement prepares for the year of Jubilee, and the mission of the messianic people and the reestablishment of economic justice are the proper human responses to their liberation.

Because Charles Wesley's theology is conceived within the context of the Jubilee as well as universal redemption, his soteriological and missional perspectives do not know any limits of God's saving grace and love. So should our perspectives be:

> Teach me to cast my net aright,
>   The gospel net of general grace,
> So shall I all to Thee invite,
>   And draw them to their Lord's embrace,
> Within Thine arms of love include,
> And catch a willing multitude.[154]

Charles Wesley himself was an outstanding example to be imitated when it comes to the outreach of the gospel. For years he was an active evangelist of the Methodist revival. In his hymn, "For a preacher of the gospel," he testifies his restless desire to spread the good news in being consumed by God's love:

> I would the precious time redeem
>   And longer live for this alone,
> To spend and to be spent for them
>   Who have not yet my Saviour known:
> Fully on these my mission prove,
> and only breathe to breathe thy love.[155]

Comparison

Just like Charles Wesley's hymns, the Orthodox tradition offers explicit commands for mission. More typical to both traditions, however, are their implied expectations of mission issuing from their soteriology and ecclesiology: "Mission belongs to the very nature of the church, whatever the conditions of its life, for without mission there is no church".[156] Consequently, the Christian church as a whole is expected to respond to the missionary vocation, "all [clergy and laity, young and old, women and men] have an apostolic calling to witness through the quality of their lives to the experience of the risen Christ. The emphasis, therefore, lies on the realization of the vocation of the whole people of God to live as a corporate witnessing community."[157] For this purpose St Symeon the New Theologian conceives the monks as a *ministerium extraordinarium*, raised by God to take care of the apostolic succession in times when the hierarchy of the church has failed.[158] This is exactly the same rationale as given by John Wesley to defend his use of lay preachers in the Methodist mission in Great Britain as well as abroad.[159] Contemporary Orthodox missiology emphasizes the need to recognize the role of the laity in the missions of the church.[160]

Conclusions

Basic to Charles Wesley's hymns is a coherent missiology, which comes out of his soteriology. Answering the universal corruption of humanity by the universal redemption of God's grace and love, they point to the promises, as well as actual experiences of transformation, as the creation is restored and participates in the nature of God. This universal perspective includes every person, independent of gender, race, economic status, and religion. Because the goal of salvation is the redemption of the Christian's neighbor, mission is the essence of the church. The church is a result of mission and should remain in missionary outreach to the surrounding world. This position is shared by the Orthodox tradition.

Church historians often describe the Methodist movement as an English counterpart to the German Pietism. Similar to the theology of mission in Pietism, Wesleyan missiology should be understood as a rejection of the idea that civil governments should take the responsibilities for missions as well. The idea of missions to the gentiles is combined with the idea of winning individual souls, and that this is the responsibility of the church. Different from the Pietist missiology, however, the Wesleys are anxious to avoid the Pietist subjectivism by conceiving the redemption of the soul in a cosmic and holistic perspective. Although they are speaking of "souls" the whole person is always implied, and the restoration of salvation includes the created world and social structures no less than human persons.

In my opinion, the main reason for this deviation from the Pietist theology is that the Wesleyan theology is much more deeply rooted in the Eastern Christian tradition than is Pietism. Although there are differences in form of expression, depending on the deep liturgical spirituality of the Orthodox tradition and the revivalism of the Wesleyan tradition, their common heritage is apparent. Or rather: The Wesleyan theology comes out of Eastern Orthodoxy and not only the Western tradition. The connecting link is the Anglican theological training of John and Charles Wesley. This training has always included more thorough studies of the Greek Fathers than that of any other Protestant tradition. In addition, the Wesleys continued their studies of the Greek Fathers, also after their ordination. The soteriological and missiological ideas basic to their communication of the good news of the gospel are deeply rooted in Christian antiquity, and in the Greek fathers more than in the Latin fathers.

Endnotes

[1]The late Tore Meistad was Associate Professor, Institute of Theology and Philosophy, Department of Humanities, Agder College, Kristiansand, Norway.

[2]Certain parts of this article have been read previously at the meeting of The Charles Wesley Society, Drew University, Madison, NJ, November 6, 1998.

[3]Within Wesleyan scholarship there is an ongoing discussion on the issue of which theological traditions have been formative to the basically eclectic theology of John and Charles Wesley. Early scholarship used to focus on the roots in Western theology, particularly Luther (for instance, Franz Hildebrandt, *From Luther to Wesley* (London: Lutterworth Press, 1951); Colin W. Williams, *John Wesley's Theology Today* (London, Epworth Press, 1962) and Calvin (for instance, George Croft Cell, *The Rediscovery of John Wesley* (New York: Henry Holt and Company, 1935). In my estimation this emphasis was caused by a need of the early scholars to legitimize the Wesleys by connecting them to the Reformation. More in-depth studies focused on the obvious fact that the Wesleys first and foremost were deeply rooted in the Anglican theological soil (A.M. Allchin, ed., *We Belong to One Another: Methodist Anglican and Orthodox Essays* (London: Epworth Press, 1965); O. Borgen, *John Wesley on the Sacraments: A Theological Study* (Nashville, Tenn.: Abingdon Press, 1972). This observation pointed in the direction of an Eastern emphasis as well as a Western (Tore Meistad, *Martin Luther and John Wesley on the Sermon on the Mount* (Lanham, Maryland: Scarecrow Press, 1999). Several scholars have found that the Greek Fathers actually were more formative to the Wesley brothers than were the Latin Fathers (for instance, Steve K. McCormick, "Faith Filled with the Energy of Love: A Forgotten Strand of Theosis in Chrysostom, Recovered by Wesley [unpublished paper presented to the Wesley Studies Group, American Academy of Religion, 1989]); Randy Maddox, "John Wesley—Practical Theologian," *Wesley Theological Journal* 23(1988): 122–147; Maddox, *Responsible Grace: John Wesley's Practical Theology* (Nashville: Kingswood Books, 1994). Ted Campbell (*John Wesley and Christian Antiquity: Religious Vision and Cultural Change* (Nashville, Tenn.: Kingswood Books, 1991) argues, however, that the significance of the Latin Fathers should not be neglected in the Wesleyan scholarship. As late as in a lecture to the American Academy of Religion, 1998, Mark Ellingsen indicated that contemporary Wesleyan scholars tend to underestimate the significance of the Calvinist theology in the making of the Methodist tradition. My own position is that, John and Charles Wesley are rooted in the Western as well as the Eastern Christian traditions, however, their soteriology and cosmology reveal that their deepest roots are in the Eastern soil.

[4]John R. Tyson, "Charles Wesley's Theology of the Cross: An Examination of the Theology and Method of Charles Wesley as seen in his Doctrine of the Atonement," Ph.D. dissertation (Madison, NJ: Drew University, 1983) 58–66. Tyson's estimate is based on the work of Frank Baker.

[5]*The Journal of the Rev. Charles Wesley, M.A.* ed. Thomas Jackson, 2 vols. (London: Wesleyan-Methodist Book Room, 1849; reprinted Grand Rapids: Baker Book House, 1948), 1:286, henceforth cited as *Journal CW* followed by volume and page number.

[6]Charles Wesley, *Hymns on the Trinity* (Bristol: Felix Farley, 1767; facsimile reprint Madison, NJ: The Charles Wesley Society, 1998); preface by S T Kimbrough, Jr., introduction by Wilma J. Quantrille. See. Wilma J. Quantrille, "The Triune God in the Hymns of Charles Wesley," Ph.D. dissertation (Madison, NJ: Drew University, 1989), 15.

[7]*Hymns on the Trinity*, 60, Charles Wesley's emphasis.

[8]*Hymns on the Trinity*, 61, Charles Wesley's emphasis.

[9]*Hymns for the Nativity of our Lord* (London: William Strahan, 1745; facsimile reprint Madison, NJ: The Charles Wesley Society, 1991), introduction and notes by Frank Baker.

[10]*Hymns for the Nativity of our Lord*, 12.

[11]*Hymns for the Nativity of our Lord*, 8.

[12]*Hymns for the Nativity of our Lord*, 10. In a eucharistic hymn Christ is called "our Elder Brother" (John & Charles Wesley, *Hymns on the Lord's Supper* [Bristol: Felix Farley, 1745; facsimile reprint Madison, NJ: The Charles Wesley Society, 1995], introduction by Geoffrey Wainwright, 113).

[13]Cf., "The Lord of Hosts is He, / The Omnipresent I AM" (*Hymns for Ascension-Day* [Bristol: Felix Farley, 1746]; facsimile reprint with *Hymns for Whitsunday* [Madison, NJ: The Charles Wesley Society, 1994]), introduction and notes by S T Kimbrough, Jr. This idea is crucial to John Wesley as well (*The Works of John Wesley* began as "The Oxford Edition of the Works of John Wesley" [Oxford: Clarendon Press, 1975–1983]; continued as "The Bicentennial Edition of the Works of John Wesley" [Nashville: Abingdon Press, 1984]; 15 of 35 volumes published to date, 1:470, 580–581; abbreviated *Works*).

[14]My expression, "Mary's and Joseph's child," implies a sociological observation intending to emphasize the extent of God's incarnation. The purpose is not to deny the reality of the virgin birth.

[15]*Hymns for the Nativity of our Lord*, 16.

[16]*Hymns for Whitsunday* [original title: *Hymns of Petition and Thanksgiving for the Promise of the Father*], co-published with John Wesley, (Bristol: Felix Farley, 1746; facsimile reprint Madison, NJ: The Charles Wesley Society, 1994), introduction and notes by Oliver A. Beckerlegge; published with *Hymns for Ascension-Day*, introduction and notes by S T Kimbrough, Jr., 27.

[17]*Hymns for Whitsunday*, 12.

[18]*Hymns for Whitsunday*, 20.

[19]Charles Wesley, *Hymns for Our Lord's Resurrection* (London: William Strahan, 1746; facsimile reprint Madison, NJ: The Charles Wesley Society, 1992), introduction and notes by Oliver A. Beckerlegge, 14.

[20]*Hymns for the Nativity of our Lord*, 8.

[21]John Meyendorff, *Byzantine Theology: Historical Trends and Doctrinal Themes* (New York: Fordham University Press, 1974), 219.

[22]Cf. H. A. Hodges & A. M. Allchin, *A Rapture of Praise* (London: Hodder and Stoughton, 1966), 16.

[23]Bishop Kallistos Ware, *The Orthodox Way* (Crestwood, NY: St Vladimir's Seminary Press, 1998), 70–71.

[24]"Thy ceaseless, unexhausted love, / Unmerited and free, / Delights our evil to remove, / And help our misery" (*Works*, 7:382; *The Poetical Works of John and Charles Wesley*, ed. George Osborn, 13 vols. [London: Wesleyan-Methodist Conference, 1868–72], 9:55; henceforth cited as *Poet. Works* followed by volume and page number); cf. Meyendorff, *Byzantine Theology*, 188–189.

Quantrille (*The Triune God in the Hymns of Charles Wesley*, 106–108, 131) observes that Charles Wesley is using metaphors of God emphasizing the trinitarian plurality as well as the trinitarian unity of God. The plurality model is expressed by, "Elohim," "Eternal Persons Three," "Joint-Authors," "Holy Triad," "Tri-une God," and "Three-One." The unity model is expressed by, "Jehovah." "Godhead," "Adoring One," "One Eternal Deity," "Unity Divine," "Lord," and "Very God." The fact that he maintains the distinction between unity and plurality in the triune God indicates that the persons of God are unique at the same time as they are indwelling in each other, thus allowing God to act according to various needs.

Since the 1960s, but particularly the last decade, Wesleyan scholars have increasingly focused on the influence that the Byzantine tradition had on the Wesleys (for instance, Outler, Allchin, McCormick, Maddox).

[25]Ware, *The Orthodox Way*, 29.

[26]Ware, *The Orthodox Way*, 27.

[27]Petros Vassiliadis, *Eucharist and Witness: Orthodox Perspectives on the Unity and Mission of the Church*. WCC Publications, (Geneva: World Council of Churches, 1996; Brookline, Massachusetts: Holy Cross Orthodox Press, 1996), 39.

[28]A Monk of the Eastern Church, *Orthodox Spirituality: An Outline of the Orthodox Ascetical and Mystical Tradition*, second edition (Crestwood, NY: St Vladimir's Seminary Press, 1996), 62–81.

[29]Alexander Golitzin, *St Symeon the New Theologian: On the Mystical Life: The Ethical Discourses*, vol. 3: *Life, Times and Theology* (Crestwood, NY: St Vladimir's Seminary Press, 1997), 13.

[30]Ion Bria, ed., *Go Forth in Peace: Orthodox Perspectives on Mission, WCC Mission Series*, vol. 7

(Geneva: World Council of Churches, 1986), 6–7, 42.

[31]Bria, *Go Forth in Peace,* 79.

[32]Bria, *Go Forth in Peace,* 19.

[33]Ware, *The Orthodox Way,* 93.

[34]John Lawson, *The Wesley Hymns as a Guide to Scriptural Teaching* (Grand Rapids, Michigan: Francis Asbury Press, 1987), 93.

[35]*Hymns on the Lord's Supper,* 3.

[36]At least this was true from their high ideals of Christian discipleship: "The few that truly call Thee Lord, / And wait Thy sanctifying word" (*Works,* 7:101).

[37]The Wesleyan universalism does not neglect the necessity to respond to God's grace: "Thy Promise made to All, and me, / Thy Followers who thy Steps pursue, / And dare believe that God is true" (*Hymns for Whitsunday,* 9).

[38]*Hymns for Whitsunday,* 8.

[39]*Hymns for Whitsunday,* 26. Another example is: "Do we not all from Thee receive / The dreadful power to seek, or leave? / The dreadful power through grace I use, / And chose of God, my God I choose" (*Poet. Works,* 9:203).

[40]The editors of the new edition of *A Collection of Hymns for the use of the People Called Methodists* (1780; *Works,* vol. 7) have identified a great number of references to universal redemption (*Works,* 7:847).

[41]*Hymns for Whitsunday,* 14.

[42]*Poet. Works,* 5:12.

[43]*Poet. Works,* 12:311.

[44]Wade Crawford Barclay, *Missionary Motivation and Expansion,* vol. 1 in, *Early American Methodism: 1769–1844* (New York: The Board of Missions and Church Extension of the Methodist Church, 1949), xli.

[45]St Isaac the Syrian, according to Ware, *The Orthodox Way,* 136.

[46]A Monk of the Eastern Church, *Orthodox Spirituality,* 24.

[47]Golitzin, *St Symeon the New Theologian,* 104, 139.

[48]Bria, *Go Forth in Peace,* 90.

[49]Ware, *The Orthodox Way,* 134.

[50]*Hymns for the Nativity of our Lord,* 6.

[51]*Hymns for the Nativity of our Lord,* 14.

[52]*Works,* 7:81–82.

[53]*Hymns for Whitsunday,* 3.

[54]After years of service to the Wesleyan connection the Irish Methodist lay preacher, Laurence Coughlan, who actually brought Methodism to Newfoundland in 1766, was rejected by John Wesley because of excessive subjectivism (Hans Rollmann, "Early Methodism in Newfoundland," 1998, http://www.mun.ca/rels/meth/texts/ origins/). After his successful revival in Newfoundland he was still rejected when he attempted to be readmitted to the Wesleyan connection (*The Letters of the Rev. John Wesley, A.M.,* ed. John Telford, 8 vols. [London: Epworth Press, 1931], 5:101–103, abbreviated *Letters*). This case is an indication that the Methodist rejection of enthusiasm and subjectivism limited the acceptance of persons with any kind of missionary zeal.

[55]*Hymns for Whitsunday,* 24.

[56]Cf. Vassiliadis, *Eucharist and Witness.*

[57]A Monk of the Eastern Church, *Orthodox Spirituality,* 46.

[58]Golitzin, *St Symeon the New Theologian,* 142, cf. 159.

[59]Bria, *Go Forth in Peace,* 11.

[60]*Hymns for the Nativity of our Lord,* 40.

[61]*Hymns for the Nativity of our Lord,* 8.

[62]*Hymns on the Lord's Supper,* 83.

[63]*Hymns for the Nativity of our Lord,* 14.

[64]John Wesley: *Explanatory Notes Upon the New Testament,* 3rd corrected edition (Bristol: Graham and Pine, 1760–62; reprinted, London: Epworth Press, 1976), 890; cited henceforth as *NT-Notes.*

[65]*NT-Notes,* 818.

[66]*Hymns for the Nativity of our Lord,* 22; *Hymns for Whitsunday,* 12.

[67]Cf. Charles Wesley's hymn, "Love divine, all love excelling / Joy of heaven, to earth come down; / Fix

in us thy humble dwelling, / All thy faithful mercies crown" (*Works*, 7:545; *UMC Hymnal*, no. 384). God is conceived as love, as well as the ultimate source of love, filling the human hearts and lives.

Another hymn uses the metaphor of God as the great potter (cf. Jer 18:1–11), who molds the Christian according to the new divine nature which is given: "My Potter from above, / Clay in Thy hands I am, / Mould me into the form of love, / And stamp with Thy new name: / Thy name is holiness; / Now on this heart of mine / The mark indelible impress, / The purity Divine" (*Poet. Works*, 9:461).

[68]Cf. Ware, *The Orthodox Way*, 22–23.

[69]*Works*, 7:251; cf. *UMC Hymnal*, no. 386.

[70]*Hymns on the Lord's Supper*, 23.

[71]*Works*, 7:251; cf. *UMC Hymnal*, no. 386.

[72]*Hymns on the Lord's Supper*, 27.

[73]*Hymns on the Lord's Supper*, 27, 28, 30.

[74]*UMC Hymnal*, no. 422.

[75]John R. Tyson, *Charles Wesley on Sanctification: A Biographical and Theological Study*, (Grand Rapids, MI: Francis Asbury Press, 1986), 162.

[76]*Poet. Works*, 6:404; cf. 7:235, 236, 355; 10:114; 13:167.

[77]Numerous examples could be cited, for instance: "No condemnation now I dread; / Jesus, and all in him, is mine; / alive in him, my living Head; / and clothed in righteousness divine, / bold I approach th'eternal throne, / and claim the crown, through Christ my own" (*UMC Hymnal*, no. 363). "Meek, simple followers of the Lamb, / They lived, and spake, and thought the same! / Brake the commemorative bread, / And drank the Spirit of their Head" (John R. Tyson, ed. *Charles Wesley: A Reader* [New York: Oxford University Press, 1989], 185; notice the significant editorial change of John Wesley's 1780 version in the last two phrases: "They joyfully conspired to raise / Their ceaseless sacrifice of praise"; *Works*, 7:99!). Other examples are, *Hymns on the Lord's Supper*, 11, 17, 25.

Examples which are taken from hymns quoted in this manuscript are: "He hath been seen, our Living Head" [Charles Wesley, *Hymns for Our Lord's Resurrection* (London: Strahan, 1746), 17; facsimile reprint (Madison, NJ: Charles Wesley Society, 1992)]; "In Christ your Head, you then shall know, / Shall feel your sins forgiven "(*Works*, 7:80; *UMC Hymnal*, no. 57); "Up into thee, our living Head, / let us in all things grow" (S T Kimbrough, Jr., gen. ed., *Songs for the Poor: Hymns by Charles Wesley*, Singer's Edition [New York: General Board of Global Ministries, The United Methodist Church, 1993], no. 2).

[78]Charles Wesley refers to Adam as the "fallen head" of the human race: "The Promise to our Fallen Head / To every Child of *Adam* made, / Is now pour'd out on all Mankind" (*Hymns for Whitsunday*, 3).

[79]"Heavenly Adam (*Works*, 7:552 renders "Father"), Life divine, / Change my nature into thine; / Move and spread throughout my soul, / Actuate and fill the whole; / Be it I no longer now / Living in the flesh, but thou" (after A. M. Allchin, *Participation in God: A Forgotten Strand in Anglican Tradition* [London: Darton, Longman and Todd, 1988], 33.

[80]Cf. Vassiliadis, *Eucharist and Witness*, 52.

[81]Vladimir Lossky, *In the Image and Likeness of God*, ed. John H. Erickson & Thomas E. Bird, with an introduction by John Meyendorff (New York: St Vladimir's Seminary Press, 1974), 103. A. M. Allchin (*Participation in God: A Forgotten Strand in Anglican Tradition*, 27) demonstrates that Charles Wesley belongs to the significant tradition of Anglican divines who emphasize the co-inherence of human and divine; to him, the meaning of the Incarnation was humanity's participation in God.

[82]Golitzin, *St Symeon the New Theologian*, 104.

[83]Golitzin, *St Symeon the New Theologian*, 81.

[84]Another example is, "3. Eager for thee I ask and pant, / So strong the principle divine / Carries me out with sweet constraint, / Till all my hallowed soul is thine; / Plunged in the Godhead's deepest sea, / And lost in thy immensity" (*Works*, 7:532).

[85]Golitzin, *St Symeon the New Theologian*, 109.

[86]Similar to the Byzantine Fathers, the Wesleyan soteriology is conceived as healing. Based on the following stanza, Tyson affirms that, "Charles Wesley knew no limit to love's curative power" (*Charles Wesley on Sanctification*, 304): "Nature's impatient condition / Feels my paralytic soul / Finds in Christ a kind Physician; / By the word of faith made whole" (*Charles Wesley on Sanctification*, 305).

[87]Ware, *The Orthodox Way*, 45.

[88]*Hymns for Whitsunday*, 25.

[89]Tyson, *Charles Wesley on Sanctification*, 193–194.

[90]John Meyendorff, "The Orthodox Church and Mission: Past and Present Perspectives," in Gerald H. Anderson and Thomas F. Stransky, C.S.P., eds., *Mission Trends No. 1: Crucial Issues in Mission Today* (New York: Paulist Press, 1974), 219.

[91]Golitzin, *St Symeon the New Theologian*, 155.

[92]Golitzin, *St Symeon the New Theologian*, 159.

[93]Golitzin, *St Symeon the New Theologian*, 81–85.

[94]*Hymns for Whitsunday.*

[95]Ware, *The Orthodox Way*, 9.

[96]Tyson (*Charles Wesley on Sanctification*, 158) states that Charles Wesley uses the word "love" very frequently in his later published hymns.

[97]"Steadfast let us cleave to thee; / Love the mystic union be; / Union to the world unknown! / Joined to God, in spirit one" (*Poet. Works*, 1:356).

[98]Kimbrough, *Songs for the Poor: Hymns by Charles Wesley*, no. 1.

[99]S T Kimbrough, Jr., *Lost in Wonder: Charles Wesley: The Meaning of His Hymns Today* (Nashville, TN: The Upper Room, 1987), 137.

[100]Charles Wesley, *Hymns for Our Lord's Resurrection*, (London: William Strahan, 1746; facsimile reprint Madison, NJ: The Charles Wesley Society, Madison, NJ, 1992), introduction and notes by Oliver A. Beckerlegge, 9.

[101]*Hymns for Our Lord's Resurrection*, 7.

[102]*Hymns for Ascension-Day*, 6.

[103]*Hymns for Whitsunday*, 5.

[104]In his Eucharistic hymn, "Author of Life Divine" (*Hymns on the Lord's Supper*, 30), Charles Wesley indicates that sanctification leads to discipleship.

[105]*Poet. Works*, 1:307. The concepts "all Mankind" or just "Mankind" are among the favorite phrases of Charles Wesley (cf. *Hymns on the Lord's Supper*, 9, 10, 11, 13, 16, 20, 21, 25, 27, 33, etc.)

[106]Kimbrough, *Songs for the Poor*, no. 2.

[107]*Works*, 7:521–522; Kimbrough, *Songs for the Poor*, no. 11.

[108]Kimbrough, *Songs for the Poor*, no. 12.

[109]Ware, *The Orthodox Way*, 27–29.

[110]After Golitzin, *St Symeon the New Theologian*, 77.

[111]According to Ware, *The Orthodox Way*, 40.

[112]Charles Wesley's hymn, "Our earth we now lament to see," was included in *A Collection of Hymns for the Use of the People Called Methodists* (*Works*, 7:607). Originally its title was, "Peace" (*Poet. Works*, 6:112–113).

[113]Charles Wesley actually wrote a hymn over this Scripture: "The Spirit of the Lord our God / (Spirit of power, and health, and love) / The Father hath on Christ bestowed, / And sent him from his throne above; / Prophet, and Priest, and King of peace, / Anointed to declare his will, / To minister his pardoning grace, / And every sin-sick soul to heal" (Laurence Hall Stookey, "Charles Wesley: Mentor and Contributor to Liturgical renewal," in S T Kimbrough, Jr., ed., *Charles Wesley: Poet and Theologian* [Nashville, Tennessee: Kingswood Books, 1992], 137–154, 144).

[114]I have earlier analyzed John Wesley's theology and the activities of the Methodist movement in light of the Jubilee (Tore Meistad, "John Wesley's Theology of Salvation as a Model for Social Change", *ALH-forskning* (Research series, Alta College of Education), 2:1992. Alta: Alta lærerhøgskole (College of Education).

[115]Kimbrough, *Songs for the Poor*, no. 10.

[116]This is indicated by a number of sermons by John Wesley:

1781: Sermon no. 87: "The Danger of Riches" (*Works*, 3:227–246) affirms that riches are not dangerous by themselves, but the desire of riches and the laying up treasures are. The Christian principle of giving should not be neither that of the Jew (giving 10 percent) nor that of the Pharisee (20 percent), but to give all of what is left after the necessities of the family is covered (*Works*, 3:239).

1786: Sermon no. 88: "On Dress" (*Works*, 3:247–261). He admonishes in his conclusion: "I conjure you all who have any regard for *me*, show me before I go that I have not laboured, even in this respect, in vain for near half a century. Let me see, before I die, a Methodist congregation full of as plain dressed as a Quaker congregation" (*Works*, 3:259–260). Why should he want this? Because in his vision of the Methodist movement it fulfills the scriptural evidence of the messianic age, for instance, in Mt 25:31ff. He comments: "Fifthly, the wearing costly array is directly opposite to the being 'adorned with good works'. Nothing can be more evident than this; for the more you lay out your own apparel, the less you have left to clothe the naked, to feed the hungry, to lodge the strangers, to relieve those that are sick and in prison, and to lessen the numberless afflictions to which we are exposed in this vale of tears [. . .] Every shilling which you save from your own apparel you may expend in clothing the naked, and relieving the various necessities of the poor, whom ye 'have always with you'. Therefore every shilling which you needlessly spend on your apparel is in effect stolen from God and the poor" (*Works*, 3:254).

1788: Sermon no. 108, "On Riches" (*Works*, 3:518–528) declares that "it is absolutely impossible, unless by that power to which all things are possible, that a rich man should be a Christian—to have the mind that was in Christ, and to walk as Christ walked" (*Works*, 3:520). The reason is, riches are a hindrance to the loving God as well as the neighbor. On the contrary, atheism and idolatry are flowing from riches.

1789: Sermon no. 122, "Causes of the Inefficacy of Christianity" (*Works*, 4:85–96) actually deals with the inefficacy of the Methodist movement in reforming the land, primarily caused by their unwillingness to share their riches with the poor. Wesley addresses the Methodists: "Ye are the men, some of the chief men, who continually grieve the Holy Spirit of God, and in great measure stop his gracious influence from descending on our assemblies. Many of our brethren, beloved of God, have no food to eat; they have no raiment to put on; they have no place where to lay their head. And why are they thus distressed? Because *you* impiously, unjustly, and cruelly detain from them what your Master and theirs lodges in your hands on purpose to supply *their* wants" (*Works*, 4:91). His despair is evident; "I am distressed. I know not what to do [with you Methodists]" (*Works*, 4:93). He has released a revival which has created a great paradox; his analysis is based in observations parallel to those described by Max Weber on how the Protestant ethic naturally leads to capitalism, but it takes the discussion farther by adding the theological consequences: "The Methodists grow more and more self-indulgent, because they *grow rich*. Although many of them are still deplorably poor [. . .], yet many others, in the space of twenty, thirty, or forty years, are twenty, thirty, yea, a hundred times richer than they were when they first entered the society. And it is an observation, which admits few exceptions that nine in ten of these decreased in grace in the same proportion as they increased in wealth. [. . .] But how astonishing a thing is this! [. . .] For wherever true Christianity spreads it must cause diligence and frugality, which in the natural course of things, must beget riches. And riches naturally beget pride, love of the world, and every temper that is destructive of Christianity. Now if there be no way to prevent this, Christianity is consistent with itself, and of consequence, cannot stand, cannot continue long among any people; since, wherever it generally prevails, it saps its own foundation" (*Works*, 4:95–96).

1790: In sermon no. 131, "The Danger of Increasing Riches" (*Works*, 4:177–186), less than a year prior to Wesley's death, his message to the Methodists is filled with despair: "After having served you between sixty and seventy years; with dim eyes, shaking hands, and tottering feet, I give you one more advice before I sink into the dust" (*Works*, 4:185). The grand mistake of the rich Methodists is that they no more can "afford" the expenses of taking care of the poor. But their riches are not their own, they are simply the stewards of God's property. Their accumulation of fortunes is nothing less than a robbery of God no less than of the poor: "This 'affording' to rob God is the very cant of hell. Do not you know that God *entrusted* you with that money (all above what buys necessaries for your families) to feed the hungry, to clothe the naked, to help the stranger, the widow, the fatherless; and indeed, as far as it will go, to relieve the wants of all mankind" (*Works*, 4:184).

[117] *Works*, 7:79–81. An abbreviated version is placed as hymn no. 1 in many Methodist hymnals.

[118] S T Kimbrough, Jr. *A Heart to Praise My God: Wesley Hymns for Today* (Nashville: Abingdon Press, 1996), 15–17; cf. *Works*, 7:79–81; *UMC Hymnal*, no. 57.

[119] Kimbrough (*A Heart to Praise My God*, 17–27) suggests another outline: "Prologue" (1), "Conversion" (2–8), "Who is Jesus?" (9–11), "What is our response?" (12–18); the last chapter has the following subchapters, "Outreach to the Marginalized," "Universal Outreach to All," and "Outreach to Every Individual." However, similar to my interpretation, he affirms the Christian outreach to the world as a response to God's transforming grace.

[120] This perspective is different from that of Luther, for instance, which insists that the application of the atonement takes place in baptism.

[121] Bria, *Go Forth in Peace*, 11.

[122]Vassiliadis, *Eucharist and Witness*, 45.

[123]Ware, *The Orthodox Way*, 16.

[124]This is well documented by S T Kimbrough, Jr. in his book: *A Song for the Poor: Hymns by Charles Wesley* (New York: General Board of Global Ministries, 1993)

[125]Kimbrough, *Songs for the Poor*, no. 3.

[126]*Letters*, 3:229.

[127]John Wesley's rules for the stewards of the Methodist societies are illuminating for the Wesleyan attitudes toward the poor: "(11) If you cannot relieve, do not grieve, the poor. Give them soft words, if nothing else. Abstain from either sour looks or harsh words. Let them be glad to come, even though they should go empty away. Put yourself in the place of every poor man and deal with *him* as you would God should deal with *you*" (*Works*, 20:176–177; June 4, 1747; Wesley's italics).

[128]John Wesley's rules for the stewards of the Methodist societies includes, "(9) You are continually to pray and endeavour that a holy harmony of soul may in all things subsist among you; that in every step you may keep the unity of the Spirit in the bond of peace" (*Works*, 20:176; June 4, 1747).

[129]Meistad, "John Wesley's Theology of Salvation as a Model for Social Change."

[130]Cf., Theodore W. Jennings, *Good News to the Poor: John Wesley's Evangelical Economics*, (Nashville: Abingdon Press, 1990).

[131]Golitzin, *St Symeon the New Theologian*, 201–202.

[132]Bria, *Go Forth in Peace*, 64–67.

[133]Vassiliadis, *Eucharist and Witness*, 89.

[134]For instance, *Poet. Works*, 13:43.

[135]Cf. Tyson, *Charles Wesley on Sanctification*, 84.

[136]*UMC Hymnal*, no. 413; cf. *Works* 7:465.

[137]Kimbrough, *A Heart to Praise My God*, 31.

[138]*Hymns for the Nativity of our Lord*, 42.

[139]It could be stated—as Justo L. González (*Christian Thought Revisited: Three Types of Theology* [Nashville: Abingdon Press, 1989]) does, that the Lutheran and Calvinist soteriology is answering the same question as that of Medieval Pelagianism. This position does not at all imply that the mission of the church is absent from the theologies of Luther and Calvin. On the contrary, their theologies include a missionary outlook, however, connected to their ideas of creation, predestination, and the inherent power of expansion implied in the preaching of the gospel. Most significantly, their ideas of the responsibility for mission were conceived in the context of the 1500s, namely (particularly in Luther's case), as a shared responsibility between the preaching of the church and the financial support and military protection of the secular authorities. As observed by Scherer: "Whatever God in his sovereign freedom might be doing to advance the kingdom by spreading the gospel throughout the earth by various anonymous agents, in German territories evangelical preaching and teaching was confined to the lands of the Reformation where the *ius reformandi* applied. Under the privilege known as *cuius regio, eius religio*, each ruler had the right to determine the religious allegiance of his subjects. Evangelical churches existed in the form of territorial or regional bodies established by law, defended by military might, and practicing religious conformity. Personal religious freedom, as corollary of justification by faith, could not be implemented until two centuries later when the Enlightenment made the persecution of dissenters no longer tolerable" (J. A. Scherer, ". . . that the Gospel may be sincerely preached throughout the world: A Lutheran perspective on Mission and Evangelism in the 20th Century", Stuttgart: *Luther World Federation Report* no. 11/12 1982, 15). The missionary imperative was recognized by the church as an implication of the commandment of love of neighbor rather than the great commission of Matthew 28, which was considered as fulfilled by the apostles of Christ. For this reason the missions to the gentiles was understood as missions to neighbor countries (Eric Beyreuther, "Evangelische Missionstheologie im 16. und 17. Jahrhundert," *Evangelische Missionszeitschrift*, 1961, no. 1 [1–10], and no. 2 [33–43]. 6–7). On the other hand, the question whether Christ on his return to earth would find faith at all (Lk 18:8) was the predominant concern of the era of the reformation, and not the missions to the gentiles. It would be completely anachronistic to look for the missiologies of the post-Pietist era in the reformers.

[140]S T Kimbrough, Jr., *Lost in Wonder*, 31.

[141]Kimbrough, *Lost in Wonder*, 35.

[142]Cf. Ware, *The Orthodox Way*, 7–8.

[143]After Ion Bria, ed., *Martyria / Mission: The Witness of the Orthodox Churches Today* (Geneva: World Council of Churches / The Commission on World Mission and Evangelism, 1986), 29.

[144]Golitzin, *St Symeon the New Theologian*, 162.

[145]Meyendorff, "The Orthodox Church and Mission," 63.

[146]Vassiliadis, *Eucharist and Witness*, 87. This was also the scripture for John Wesley's first sermon to the poor in the open air, April 2, 1739 (*Works*, 19:46).

[147]Meyendorff, "The Orthodox Church and Mission," 63.

[148]Vassiliadis, *Eucharist and Witness*, 11.

[149]Bria, *Go Forth in Peace*, 3.

[150]S T Kimbrough, Jr., *A Heart to Praise My God*, 193.

[151]Cf. *Hymns for the Nativity of our Lord*, 44; *UMC Hymnal*, no. 181.

[152]*Works*, 7:609; *Poetic Works*, 6:138. John Wesley concluded his tract *Thoughts upon the Slavery* (1774) by quoting the third stanza of Charles's hymn (*The Works of the Rev. John Wesley, M.A.*, ed. Thomas Jackson, 3rd ed., 14 vols. [London: Wesleyan Methodist Book Room, 1872]; reprinted [Grand Rapids: Baker Book House, 1979], 11:79).

In the second stanza the concept "Gentiles" is used in the biblical sense as opposed to "Jews" in order to include all humankind in the salvation of God. The references to heathen idols and the "pagan hearts" of the "dark Americans" in the third stanza seem to be prejudiced to a modern mind, however, this is obviously not Charles Wesley's intention. On the contrary, by the reference to the descendants of Ham, Noah's son, who were supposed to be the African race (cf. Ps. 105:23), his point is simply to affirm that the grace of salvation is offered to the black as well as to the white races.

John Wesley more explicitly criticizes the Western—so-called Christian—civilization in comparison with the so-called heathen nations, for instance: "With regard to most of the commandments of God, whether relating to the heart or life, the heathens of Africa or America stand much on a level with those that are called Christians [...] For instance, the generality of the natives of England, commonly called Christians [. . .] It is not easy to say, when we compare the bulk of the nations in Europe with those (Indian nations) in America, whether the superiority lies on the one side or the other" (*Works*, 1:616). He is even more explicit in this comment: "Yea, what is most dreadful, most to be lamented is at all these Christian churches!—churches [. . .] that bear the name of Christ, the Prince of Peace, and wage continual war with each other!" (*Works*, 1:508).

[153]*UMC Hymnal*, no. 379.

[154]*Poet. Works*, 5:126.

[155]After T. Crichton Mitchell, *Charles Wesley: Man with the Dancing Heart* (Kansas City, Missouri: Beacon Hill Press of Kansas City, 1994), 87–88.

[156]Bria, *Go Forth in Peace*, 11.

[157]Bria, *Go Forth in Peace*, 13.

[158]Golitzin, *St Symeon the New Theologian*, 41–42.

[159]Albert Outler, *John Wesley* (New York: Oxford University Press, 1964), 174.

[160]Vassiliadis, *Eucharist and Witness*, 67–76.

12

Charles Wesley and the Orthodox Hesychast Tradition

Ioann Ekonomtsev

One of the main problems of Christianity has to do with the opportunity of a human being to know God, an opportunity that is not abstract or imagined but a real meeting with God face to face. Christianity itself was born when God, becoming incarnate on earth, came into direct contact with humankind. So it is not accidental that all rationalistic teachings directly or indirectly challenged the teachings of the church on this essential issue. For example, in elementary Euclid geometry, the crossing of parallel lines is considered to be impossible. This concept is based on elementary logic, and the thought of the possibility of uniting the finite and infinite, eternity and death, in one is unbearable.

The era of pre-Renaissance and then of the Renaissance, which stimulated the interest in rationalistic views of the ancient world, encouraged this problem. It was in the fourteenth century, in the epoch of global European spiritual, ideological, ecclesiastical and political crisis, during the weakening of social-governmental structures, that only small territories remained from the mighty Eastern Roman Empire—Constantinople and part of Peloponnesus—and the proud name "Romans." In Italy the trade republics were prospering—primarily, Venice and Genoa. But they were tiny states, and they prospered only because nobody threatened them. Germany was all divided. England and France were involved in the meaningless One Hundred Years War. Abinion's captivity of Popes ruined their authority and the influence of the Roman Empire. Russia was divided and only gathered its strength for the battle against the Tartar yoke. Serbia and Bulgaria were tired of their struggle for the control of the Balkan Peninsula. Neither they nor Byzantium seemed to notice the danger from the Turks—a predator ready to jump into Europe.

The fourteenth century was the century of the black plague, which destroyed a third of the European population. In an economic sense it was a catastrophe, which enhanced the meaning of being human, and ruined the medieval economic system with all the consequences of cultural and spiritual life. For those who survived this tragedy an interest was strengthened in mystical studies in the East and West. This was an epoch of instability and terrible contrasts. On the one hand, it created a tendency to "catch the moment," to rush for material values, and on the other, it showed the absence of any meaning in these material values.

This was the time of spiritual tension, unique envisioning, hallucinations, penetrating logic and black magic, heroic deeds and terrible orgies, holiness and moral decline. Human personality emerged against the background of the instability of social-governmental structure.

The fourteenth century was anthropocentric. Its representatives cannot be divided into humanists and nonhumanists. At that time everyone was a humanist— those who left the secular world for the desert, and those who were declining into a depth of sin and crime in the midst of philosophical conversation on beauty and morality. But the humanism of these groups was different.

Barlaam

During these times in the first part of the fourteenth century a Calabrian monk, Barlaam, came from Italy to Constantinople in order to get acquainted with Byzantine wisdom. The Emperor's court and intellectual elite of the most educated country of the world warmly welcomed him at that time. Barlaam was very excited. Then he came to Athos and met the monks there. He was shocked that they dared to make statements that they received grace from God and had personal contact with the Creator of the whole universe! "This is clear madness—God is incomprehensible!" Barlaam acclaimed in a loud voice. This resulted in the "hesychasm" controversy, the role of which is not given proper attention in European history.

The Calabrian monk did not reject the possibility of knowing God, but he was under the strong influence of ancient formal logic and was full of deep skepticism regarding the possibility of a mortal coming closer to the mystery of the Three-One God. "All proved phenomena," he argued, "are connected with the causes and axioms on which basis they are proved; at the same time there is neither specific nor axiomatic comprehension by people, of what happens within the Trinity. Therefore, everything, that transpires within the Trinity cannot be proved." It is from this perspective that Barlaam criticized not only the Athonite monks but also Thomas Aquinas.

Accepting the limitations of the cataphatic theology, Barlaam was alien to apophatic method as well. He quoted Dionysius, the Areopagite, with great pleasure. He did it not because he saw in his method a different, negative way of knowing God, but because Dionysius' statements seemed to him to be one more proof of a weakness of the human mind before the mystery of God.

Barlaam considered it possible to speak about the experiential revelation of knowing God, but it is limited by intellectual enlightenment, which helps to understand the church dogmas and the law of human thinking, and such enlightenment is possible only for the church fathers and philosophers. Barlaam is filled with anger at the thought that the Athonite monks could pretend to have such revelations. According to him they are mentally deficient, controversial, ignorant, and have stupid opinions.

The only basis of faith for Barlaam is the books of the Holy Scripture and the church fathers, but he does not believe in their adequate interpretation and does not accept the literal meaning of them. The more Barlaam is filled with skepticism, the more he limits himself by the conservative traditions. Faith and mind are separated. Barlaam consciously draws a line of demarcation between them, accepting as possible and viable both the dogmas of faith and contradictions. All this coexists in individual personality, in society, and in art. Here we have the controversial features of the Western Renaissance, and Barlaam became its spiritual father. The most surprising thing was that nobody was concerned about these controversies. For Renaissance personality and society, thesis and antithesis go together. They rival each other, easily and artistically, but without tension, as if they were presented on a theatrical stage clothed in a robe and in a Roman toga. By the way, the friendly meetings and discussions of the Byzantine humanists/intellectuals were called "theater." To exchange thesis and antithesis in such theater was as easy as changing clothing.

St Gregory Palamas

Barlaam's opponent was a future Archbishop of Thessalonica, St Gregory Palamas, who was acting on behalf of the monk's party. Their points of departure seem to be the same. Like Barlaam, Gregory Palamas accepted the absolute incomprehension of the Divine Essence. He expressed this thought even in a more sharp and categorical form than the Calabrian thinker:

> Every Nature is utterly remote and absolutely estranged from the divine nature. For if God is nature, other things are not nature, but if each of the other things is nature, he is not nature; just as he is not a being if others are beings; and if he is a being, the others are not beings.[1]

How can we speak about knowing God, if God is so transcendent? "We can," responds Gregory Palamas. The essence of God is unknowable but God is not identical to Divine Essence, since God exists not only in the divine self, but also *ad extra*. And God's existence, addressed from within is nothing other than the Divine Will or the Divine Energy.

Being different from the essence, the energy is inseparable from it, and in all its revelation God, united and undivided, is present. This "crazy," paradoxical concept, which comes from the depth of antinomous Christian teaching, is the only possibility of explaining God's existence from the standpoint of transcendence, without falling into pantheism. We know God's creativity, theophany, incarnation of Logos, and the activity of the Holy Spirit. If it were not so, it would be impossible to speak about God at all. St Gregory, with his keen insight, says: "If the substance does not possess an energy distinct from itself, it will be completely without actual subsistence and will be only a concept in the mind."[2] Thus, in contrast to Barlaam and later to Kant, the Archbishop of Thessalonica theoretically proves the principal possibility of an encounter of mortals with God and their knowing of the unknowable God.

As for the relationship of the energy to the Divine Persons, Gregory Palamas speaks about its belonging to all three Persons of the Trinity. This is obvious, because otherwise, the unity of the Divine Will would be destroyed. The energy is the same for all three persons, but the character of the relationship to the energy is different. The one Divine Will appears in the primary source, the Father; it comes through the Son, and shows itself in the Holy Spirit. That is why there is a special meaning of the third person of the Trinity in revealing Divine Energy. That is why St Gregory, in many cases, calls the energies of the Triune God the energies of the Holy Spirit. In the Spirit—*ruah*—there is an energetic source. The great Cappadocians were very sensitive to it. It is the fire" (Mt 3:11, Acts 2:3), says Gregory the Theologian. It is the Spirit of creativity (Job 33:4), creative in the baptism (Titus 3:5) and in the resurrection (Rom 8:1). It is the Spirit, which knows all (1 Cor 2:11), teaches all, and breathes at will; this is the teaching Spirit, the Giver of Revelations and light, but better said—the light itself and the life itself. The Spirit makes me a temple and creates everything that God provides. It separates tongues in the fire, and shares the gifts, creates apostles, prophets, preachers, and teachers.

The second person—the Divine Logos—apart from the mysterious revelation of the mission *ad extra* of the Holy Spirit—emerges from the Three-Person-Closeness; and, like the Holy Spirit, expresses the united Divine Will. This is revealed in the reality of the Logos incarnation, the direct entry of God into the history of humankind.

The great achievement of St Gregory Palamas is his creative development of the holy Fathers' teaching of God the Creator of the world. The problem of creativity becomes the core element of his anthropology, in which the teaching about humankind coincides with the teaching about God. First of all, the Archbishop of Thessalonica sees the image of God in a person's ability to create. This ability was stressed by other church fathers, like the Pheodorite of Kir and St Photi, the Patriarch of Constantinople, but nobody before St Gregory Palamas ever attached such importance to it. The gift of creativity, according to the deep conviction of the Archbishop of Thessalonica, gives mortals a special status in the whole universe.

> In company with many others you might say that also the threefold character of our knowledge shows us to be more in the image of God than the angels, not only because it is threefold but also because it encompasses every form of knowledge. For we alone of all creatures possess also a faculty of sense perception in addition to those of intellection and reason. This faculty is naturally joined to that of reason and has discovered a varied multitude of arts, sciences and forms of knowledge: farming and building, bringing forth from nothing, though not from absolute non-being (for this belongs to God), he gave to man alone. Scarcely anything at all effected by God comes into being and falls into corruption but rather, when one thing is mixed with another among the things in our sphere, it takes another form. Furthermore, God granted to me alone that not only could the invisible word of the mind be subject to the sense of hearing when joined to the air, but also that it could be put down in writing and seen with and through the body. Thereby God leads us to a clear faith in the visitation and manifestation of the supreme word through the flesh in which the angels have no part.[3]

For the epoch of St Gregory Palamas, his notion that human creativity is a creativity out of nothing is unique. Real creativity is a creativity of a new quality, which has never existed before in nature. It is not related to other qualities and cannot appear out of quantitative manipulations, which are fruitless in themselves. This is an absolute addition to what has already existed in the universe. This is a cosmic act, the continuation of the Divine creation of the world.

What is natural for God, however, creates a high tension of spiritual and physical strengths among mortals. It is easier for them, limited by physical, biological, and other laws, to remain inert, rather than try to leap into another existence. Creativity for humankind is *kenosis*, it is sacrifice, it is climbing up Golgotha. That is why the temptation to reject following God, to immure one's lonely existence, is so strong. People use drugs, psychosomatic methods of achieving *nirvana,* the industry of mass hypnosis—computer games, videos—in order to stop their lonely suffering with fruitless dreams and illusions. But this is the way to the degradation of the human personality, to the beast-like image of those, who, because of their belonging formerly to the angels, cannot create, but only make mirages that lead humankind to its end.

Called by God to creativity, mortals cannot commit creative acts by themselves without God's help. The confessions of our great artists reveal that. They speak about inspiration, about an unexplainable force, which is beyond the mind; or like Gaidn, they pray to the Lord for the gift of the Holy Spirit. If, according to Dostoyevsky, creative work is a very hard labor without God's help, then with inspiration and with the help of the Holy Spirit the creative process is fulfilled more quickly and easily, so that the creators themselves are surprised by the results, and they cannot believe their own work. This is understandable, because the creative ecstatic condition is the divine state, for it is God who creates, not mere human beings.

Does inspiration depend on humankind? How can we force the Spirit of freedom by our will, if the Spirit breathes "where it wills"? To some people, says St Gregory Palamas, grace comes forth immediately and engages them fully, a taste of promised blessings, and to others grace waits for the end of their heroic deeds, preparing crowns for them for their patience. So the Archbishop of Thessalonica argues that grace does not depend on human efforts, though he is sure that the efforts of those who are seeking it are not fruitless. Grain grows in prepared soil. On the one hand, the soil is ready to accept grain and to nurture it, and on the other, hard work is needed for its cultivation and fertilization.

Gregory Palamas rejects the Messalian temptation to think that receiving grace depends on human will, nevertheless, he finds quite alien the notion of pessimistic fatalism, which issues from predestination by divine choice. In this regard St Gregory stands in the tradition of the holy Fathers' concept of *synergia*—the interaction between divine grace and the free will of human beings. God does not specify the amount of grace given. Out of God's immeasurable mercy, God gives to all persons more than they can receive. According to his teaching, which is in sharp contrast to the teaching of St Augustine, people differ by a variety of charismatic gifts, talents, and by the ability and readiness to accept Divine grace. "Those who preach," he says, "those who heal, those who learn, and in general those who receive the grace of the Holy Spirit, have more or less a charismatic gift in their own spheres." Thus, the Apostle Paul thanks God for the gift of tongues (1 Cor 14:18), but those who have less gifts, also have a gift from God. In reality "… star differs from star in glory" (1 Cor 15:41), but not one is deprived of light. Every person is worthy and receives the great gift of the Holy Spirit in a different manner. But even those who have little and lack clarity, are involved in a relationship to the Divine light.

Eighteenth-Century England

Now we can turn to another epoch and another Christian culture. The British Empire of the eighteenth century represents a clear antithesis to dying Byzantium. In the four-teenth century there were only small remains of Byzantium but in the eighteenth cen-tury the British Empire was ascending. Its possessions grew in Africa and Asia. In America the significant part of French and Spanish colonies became a part of the British Empire. The scientific and industrial potential of England grew, and it became the leading economic Empire of the world. The level of its culture, especially of phi-losophy and literature, was very high, and it was an antithesis to Byzantium. An atten-tive look cannot miss, however, the similar deep processes at work. The same feature, which was the strongest and most characteristic of the English culture, namely, rationalism, slowly but truly ruined it. The providence of God, faith, and morality were moved to the periphery of life. Hobbes, Adam Smith, and Darwin did not stress the love bequeathed to us by Christ, rather the battle—the battle of all against all. This relates to politics, competition in economics, and the battle of species in the world of animals. The morals of society were in decline, as well as the level of religion in peo-ple. In British Parliament only five to six members of the House of Commons attended the Sunday liturgy. Nobody paid attention to the lower classes, and rebellion grew, especially among the industrial workers. Considering the number of the Eng-lish working class, there could have been more terrible consequences than those of the French revolution.

In England the voice of the Wesley brothers was raised against rationalism and a passionate call was made for unity with God. In his *Journal* John Wesley described the feelings which he experienced on that great day, May 24, 1738, when he felt that special warmth in his heart during the meeting of the Society in Aldersgate Street in London and realized not in his mind but in his heart, with all of his being, the gift of the divine grace. Such a phenomenon cannot transpire merely through abstract thoughts and philosophical speculations. It may be only the result of a true religious experience, which was a goal of the Athonite monks. They were finding in the glory of the light of Tabor the higher happiness and the higher meaning of life. So, it was very natural for Wesley to comprehend the possibility of salvation not only through the grace of the Holy Spirit but also as a result of a direct personal encounter with God. Such comprehension, nat-urally, meant the exclusion of the idea of predestination and, thus, entry of humankind into the Kingdom of freedom and immersion into a depth of religious life.

Charles Wesley, who had a similar religious experience three days before his brother John, described its enlightenment in his multiple hymns in a very penetrat-ing form. These hymns are surprisingly close in their content and spirit to the poetry of Symeon the New Theologian, who is the forerunner of the hesychast tradition in the East. For the Wesley brothers and for St Symeon the New Theologian, (and also for the succeeding representatives of the hesychast tradition) the relationships with the church hierarchy were not easy. The statements of Symeon the New Theologian, on this matter are well known. The relationships of St Gregory Palamas and the influ-ential hesychast party with the patriarch, John Calekas, were also very complicated.

The quick and impressive social-political resonance of the Wesleys' preaching was similar to one of the hesychast teachings in the East. Gelyan Prokhorov argues that we may speak of "political" hesychasm, and one may agree with him. The Wesleys' preaching found a living response in the lower classes of a society, changed the moral atmosphere and social situation in England, and we can say that it saved England from terrible social tribulations.

Hesychasm did not stop the fall and decline of Byzantium, if we mean Constantinople and the Southern part of Peloponnesus under it. But the leaders of hesychasm were thinking in broader terms. They thought not only about conservation of important pieces of Byzantium, but about the whole Byzantium commonwealth which included Greece, the Near East, Slavic and Balkan countries, Caucasus, and Russia, particularly the young, dynamic, and great Moscow principality.

It is characteristic that during the siege of Constantinople in the fourteenth century by Genoa the Emperor and Patriarch were busy with the problems of the Moscow metropolis. From this point of view, the activity of hesychast teachers was in the same way as effective and successful as the activity of the Wesley brothers.

Sometimes one hears that the Puritanism of the Wesley brothers had a negative influence on English, and somewhat later, on American art. The critical comments of John Wesley about theater are well known. But theater, in this instance, is a private matter. The appeal of John Wesley to divine grace, the source of the creative inspiration, however, seems to stimulate the development of real art. We do not speak of its surrogate, which is made for consumption by corrupted interests and evil passions. The glowing example of such art is the poetry of Charles Wesley illustrated here by two stanzas of his poem, "Jesus, Lover of my soul," originally published in *Hymns and Sacred Poems* (1740):

> Jesus, Lover of my soul,
>> let me to thy bosom fly,
> while the nearer waters roll,
>> while the tempest still is high.
> Hide me, O my Savior, hide
>> till the storm of life is passed.
> Safe into the haven guide,
>> O receive my soul at last.

> Other refuge have I none,
>> hangs my helpless soul on thee;
> leave, ah, leave me not alone,
>> still support and comfort me.
> All my hope on thee is stayed,
>> all my help from thee I bring;
> cover my defenseless head
>> with the shadow of thy wing.

We should not forget this specific kind of creativity, which was also characteristic of ascetic hesychasts: one seeks human perfection in the image of God.

Returning to the present, one should stress the great importance of the Wesley phenomenon as a spiritual bridge between the two related Christian cultures of the East and West. There is no necessity to speak about the importance of a dialogue and mutual understanding between them. The twentieth century came to its end, full of dramatic events and tribulations. Nothing gives us an opportunity to assume that the twenty-first century will be less tragic. Secularization grows. The old and new anti-God teachings challenge Christianity and the fundamentals of society. That is why it is so important to recognize the 2000-year-path traveled by Christianity, and to recognize the religious experience of the East and West, which, as the Wesley phenomenon shows us, have important common features.

Endnotes

[1]Robert E. Sinkewicz, ed. & trans., *Saint Gregory Palamas: The One Hundred and Fifty Chapters* (Toronto: Pontifical Institute of Medieval Studies, 1988), chapter 78.

[2]Ibid., chapter 136.

[3]Ibid., chapter 63.

13

Ephrem the Syrian:
A Theologian of the Presence of God[1]

Kathleen E. McVey

Ephrem the Syrian and his importance for history and theology

Ephrem the Syrian, the foremost writer in the Syriac tradition of Christianity, was born in Nisibis near the beginning of the fourth century, C.E., and spent his early life there, teaching and writing hymns, homilies and commentaries, with the approval of a succession of Orthodox bishops. When the Romans lost ground in their ongoing wars with Persia in 363, he was forced to abandon his native city and to move a little to the west in order to remain within the Roman Empire. He continued to write at Edessa, where he is said to have established a school of biblical and theological studies and women's choirs to sing his hymns. Ordained to the diaconate there, he died while ministering to victims of famine in 373 C.E.[2]

Ephrem's importance for the history of Syriac literature and for the history of Christianity in the Syriac-speaking context is immense. His hymns, incorporated early into the liturgy, have exerted a strong influence on both the East and West Syrian liturgical traditions. The literary and hymnic forms that he used, some of which he may have invented, became the standard forms of all subsequent Syriac literature and hymnography. The success of his hymns helped to make hymnody a central teaching method of his church from his own time down to the present. Although his works incorporate many of the themes found in the Jewish-Christian or Gnostic writings of the earliest Syriac Christianity, Ephrem's commitment to Nicene orthodoxy set the subsequent direction of the Syriac Church. He lived almost exactly the same years as Athanasius, and in his own way Ephrem was just as dedicated to the Nicene *homoousion* as Athanasius. In his own lifetime and for a half-century thereafter, his method of biblical interpretation was the sole standard among Syriac writers. Even after the formal introduction of Greek hermeneutic methods in the fifth century, Ephrem's interpretations continued to be studied and held in esteem. Despite uncertainty over the precise lines of his contact with Greek culture, not only a concept of orthodoxy but also many philosophical presuppositions and literary forms analogous to those of Greek Christian theological literature are to be found in his work, and through him they descend into the Syriac heritage.[3]

Appreciation of Ephrem's hymns was not limited to those who spoke Syriac. Writing within decades of his death, Jerome attests to his fame in the Latin church. The fifth-century monastic historian, Palladius, and his contemporaries, the church historians Sozomen and Theodoret, portray him as a model of the ascetic life and extol his extraordinary poetic gift. Both Jerome and the Greek writers assert that even in translation they were able to appreciate his eloquence. The translation of his works into Greek had begun even during his lifetime, and in the following centuries they were translated into virtually every language known to Christianity.[4] Although study of the nature and extent of his influence on later Western Christianity is still in a fairly rudimentary stage, it is clear that he played a significant role in the development of both Byzantine hymnography and Western medieval religious drama.[5]

The extant writings attributed to Ephrem in Greek, Coptic, Ethiopic, Armenian, Georgian, Arabic, Latin, and Slavonic constitute a rich and significant body of materials. But the problem of sorting out his legacy to the universal church is complicated by the fact that his authentic writings in Syriac are scarcely represented in the vast body of writings ascribed to him in most of these other languages. There is a nearly complete mismatch between the texts considered by Syriac scholars to be authentic and those that survive in various other languages under Ephrem's name. The latter body of literature is interesting in itself and well deserves the attention it is just beginning to receive from scholars. It will probably not, however, tell us much about Ephrem himself and about the ways in which the "Ahistorical Ephrem," so to speak, may have influenced Christians beyond the confines of the Syriac-speaking world. That actual influence is more likely to be found through the study of the theological themes and imagery traced through the homilists and hymnographers who postdate him in all these varied linguistic traditions. One aspect of his thought that is of enduring interest and continuous importance for all the Orthodox traditions as well as for Western Christian spirituality is the presence of God in the world.

Ephrem's theology of the presence of God in the world

Ephrem's world is permeated by the Divine presence. His poetry is based upon a vision of the created order as a vast system of symbols or mysteries.[6] No person, thing or event in the world exists without a mysterious relation to the whole. History and nature constitute the warp and woof of reality. To divorce an individual person, event or thing from its context in either direction would destroy the handiwork of God in time and space. Each moment of life is governed by the Lord of Life and is an opportunity to see oneself and the community in relation to that Lord. So not only the events described in Scripture, but all historical events must have profound religious significance.

Nature, too, is replete with intimations of the presence of God. In creating the world, God deliberately presented us not only with examples of beauty and order but also with symbols that allude more richly to the identity of their Creator:

> In every place, if you look, His symbol is there,
> and when you read, you will find His prototypes.
> For by Him were created all creatures,
> and he imprinted His symbols upon His possessions.
> When He created the world,

> He gazed at it and adorned it with His images.
> Streams of His symbols opened, flowed and poured forth
> His symbols on its members.
>
> *Hymns on Virginity* 20.12

At the center of all is Jesus Christ, the Incarnate Word, who is at once the apex of history and the metaphysical Mediator between the ineffable Creator and the creation. Ephrem sets forth this notion most succinctly in the *Hymns on Virginity* 28–30, where he speaks of the three harps of God:

> The Word of the Most High came down and put on
> a weak body with hands,
> and He took two harps [Old and New Testaments]
> in His right and left hands.
> The third [Nature] He set before Himself
> to be a witness to the [other] two,
> for the middle harp taught
> that their Lord is playing them.
>
> *Hymns on Virginity* 29.1

This strophe shows clearly not only that Scripture and Nature play complementary roles in Ephrem's theology but also that the lynchpin of his theological system is the Incarnate Word of God, through Whom God has revealed the relation of the two Testaments to one another and to nature.

In examining his theology of the divine presence, we will begin with his understanding of the Incarnation and proceed to the closely related notions of spiritual progress and sanctification, or *theosis* (divinization). Next we will turn to God's presence in history, first considering Scripture as the record of salvation history, especially as understood through typological exegesis, and then addressing the sacred dimension of the rest of history, specifically the events which Ephrem himself witnessed and contemplated. Finally, we will consider nature as God's domain, first in human beings created in the divine image, then in the sacraments and finally in the rest of the creation.

The Incarnation, lynchpin of Ephrem's theology

A central theme of Ephrem's *Hymns on the Nativity* is the wonder of the Incarnation, conceived as a paradoxical entry of the ineffable, infinite, and omnipotent God into the limitations of human life. It is a theological concept that evokes profound questions: How can the Ruler of the Universe, whom the entire created order is unable to contain, have been contained in a single, small human womb?

> The Power that governs all dwelt in a small womb.
> While dwelling there, He was holding the reins of the universe.

His Parent was ready for His will to be fulfilled.
The heavens and all the creation were filled by Him.
The Sun entered the womb, and in the height and depth
His rays were dwelling.

Hymns on the Nativity 21.6

Not only the bare fact of the Incarnation but also its specific circumstances are miraculous and paradoxical: "[God] deprived the married womb; He made fruitful the virgin womb" (*Hymns on the Nativity* 21.17). Far from showing a weakness, these apparent contradictions show the majesty of the Creator, the "Lord of natures."

Yet these are not pointless displays of might; instead they are the concessions of a loving God to human frailty:

God had seen that we worshiped creatures.
He put on a created body to catch us by our habit.
Behold by this fashioned one our Fashioner healed us,
and by this creature our Creator revived us.

Hymns on the Nativity 21.12

Thus this miraculous and paradoxical self-abasement of God is clearly motivated by love for humankind. Ephrem often associates the language and imagery of divine compassion, mercy, and maternal love with the Incarnation. Among his many epithets for Christ is *Hnonoyo*, the Compassionate One, a title that he applies in virtually every moment in the life of Christ. The feast of the Incarnation, the Nativity, is the day on which "the Compassionate One came out to sinners" (*Hymns on the Nativity* 4.5). Even before his birth, "He dwelt [in Mary's womb] because of His compassion" (*Hymns on the Nativity* 21.8). The Compassionate One, he says, put on the garment of the body to rescue Adam:

He [was] wrapped [in] swaddling clothes in baseness,
but they offered him gifts.
He put on the garments of youth, and helps emerged from them.
He put on the water of baptism, and rays flashed out from it.
He put on linen garments in death, and triumphs were shown by them.
With his humiliations [came] his exaltations.
Blessed is He Who joins His glory to our suffering!

All these [garments] are changes
that the Compassionate One first shed and then put on again
when He contrived to put on Adam the glory that he had shed.
He entwined swaddling clothes with [Adam's] figleaves,
and he put on garments in place of his skins.
He was baptized for [Adam's] wrongdoing and embalmed for his death.
He rose and raised him up in glory.
Blessed is He Who came down, put on [a body] and ascended!

Hymns on the Nativity 23.12–13

"Thanks to the Compassionate One Who bore our pain" (*Hymns on the Nativity* 3.2). "He endured spitting and scourging, thorns and nails for our sake" (*Hymns on the Nativity* 18.35). Out of compassion and mercy, Christ freed human beings and all creation from the slavery of idolatry (*Hymns on the Nativity* 22.4–7). Ephrem relates this theme to the Roman tradition of temporarily releasing slaves for the *Saturnalia*:

> The mercy of the High One was revealed,
> and he came down to free His creation.
> In this blessed month in which manumission takes place,
> the Lord came to slavery to call the slaves to freedom.
> Blessed is He Who brought manumission!
>
> *Hymns on the Nativity* 22.5

Finally, Christians are expected to imitate the merciful condescension of their redeemer. Addressing Christ in his own voice, Ephrem says:

> O [You] Greater than measure Who became immeasurably small,
> from glorious splendor you humbled Yourself to ignominy.
> Your indwelling mercy inclined You to all this.
> Let Your compassion incline me to become praiseworthy
>   in [spite of] my evil.
>
> *Hymns on the Nativity* 21.13

The same is expected of all Christians since their baptism is a rebirth from the side of Christ, the Compassionate One who came to take up the body that would be struck so that by the opening of His side he might break through the way into Paradise" (*Hymns on the Nativity* 8.4). We are all expected to reciprocate, as Ephrem reminds his congregation once again on the feast of the Nativity:

> On this day on which God came into the presence of sinners,
> let not the just man exalt himself in his mind over the sinner.
> On this day on which the Lord of all came among servants,
> let the lords also bow down to their servants lovingly.
> On this day when the Rich One was made poor for our sake,
> let the rich man also make the poor man a sharer at his table.
> On this day a gift came out to us without our asking for it;
> let us then give alms to those who cry out and beg from us.
> This is the day when the high gate opened to us for our prayers;
> let us also open the gates to the seekers who have strayed but sought
>   [forgiveness].
>
> *Hymns on the Nativity* 1.92–96

Finally, Ephrem explicitly binds this imitation of Christ, the Compassionate One, to nonviolent behavior:

> Glorious is the Compassionate One
> Who did not use violence, and without force, by wisdom,
> He was victorious. He gave a type to human beings
> that by power and wisdom they might conquer discerningly.
>> *Hymns on the Nativity* 8.5

The divine condescension to humankind in the Incarnation has brought about a permanent change in the relationship between human beings and their Creator:

> . . . the Deity imprinted Itself on humanity,
> so that humanity might also be cut into the seal of the Deity.
>> *Hymns on the Nativity* 1.99

In addition to this language of seals and stamps, which he shares with the *Logos* theology of Greek Christianity, Ephrem expresses the intimate union of divine and human with the language of painting, likening it to the artist's blending of pigments:

> Glorious is the Wise One Who allied and joined
> Divinity with humanity,
> One from the height and the other from below.
> He mingled the natures like pigments,
> and an image came into being: the God-man!
>> *Hymns on the Nativity* 8.2

The similarity of Ephrem's thought here to Athanasius' dictum, "The Word of God became human so that we might become divine" has been noted.[7] But the difference in Ephrem's view needs also to be stressed. For him the Incarnation not only opens up the way to *theosis* but it also brings a humanization of God. He explores the dimensions of that humanization of God especially through images of birth and suckling. In the Incarnation:

> Christ entered [Mary's] womb a mighty warrior
> and inside her womb He put on fear.
> He entered Nourisher of all
> and He acquired hunger.
> He entered the One who gives drink to all
> and He acquired thirst.
> Stripped and laid bare, He emerged from [her womb]
> the One who clothes all.
>> *Hymns on the Nativity* 11.8.

The image of the suckling child provides a radical image of divine love for humankind. To the infant Christ Ephrem says:

> it is as if your love hungers for human beings

> ... what moves you so to bestow yourself
> upon each who has seen you? ...
> Whence did it come to you so to hunger for human beings?
> *Hymns on the Nativity* 13.12–14

On the one hand, the Son freely chose to become incarnate. "By His will He clothed himself with a body" (*Hymns on the Nativity* 3.5). Yet this choice is clearly prompted by love, and it has the result that He became truly needy by this mingling of divinity with humanity:

> Glory to Him Who never needs us to thank Him.
> Yet He [became] needy for He loves us, and He thirsted for He cherishes us.
> And He asks us to give to Him so that He may give us even more.
> His Fruit was mingled with our human nature
> to draw us out toward Him Who bent down to us.
> By the Fruit of the Root He will graft us onto His Tree.
> *Hymns on the Nativity* 3.17

Perhaps the strongest image of the reciprocity which results from God's condescension to us occurs in a context not of the Incarnation but rather in its figurative equivalent, God's willingness to be clothed in human language, that is to say, the existence of revealed Scripture.[8] In this regard, Ephrem characterizes the Deity as like a nursing mother or wet nurse:

> Attuned to us is the Deity like a nursing mother to an infant,
> watching the time for his benefits, knowing the time for weaning him,
> both when to rear him on milk and when to feed him with solid food,
> weighing and offering benefits according to the measure of his maturity.
> *Hymns on the Church* 25.18[9]

This image of the Triune God pondering the right moment to move each human being from milk to solid food provides the perfect transition from Ephrem's understanding of the Incarnation as a singular historical event, the culmination of the history of salvation, to his notion that it is an ongoing reality accessible to each human being according to the level of his or her spiritual advancement.

The ongoing, individualized presence of God to each human being

Although God's grand concession to human frailty took place uniquely in the Incarnation, it also continues to take place in every time and place for each human being. God is revealed to each according to his or her capacity to perceive.

> He was cheerful among the infants as a baby;
> awesome was He among the Watchers[10] as a commander.

Too awesome was He for John to loosen His sandals;
accessible was He for sinners who kissed His feet.
The Watchers as Watchers saw Him;
according to the degree of his knowledge each person saw Him.
Everyone according to the measure of his discernment
thus perceived Him, that One greater than all.

Hymns on the Nativity 4.197–200

For Ephrem Jesus' encounter with the Samaritan woman at the well is especially symbolic of the individualized relationship God conducts with each human being.

The glorious fount of Him Who was sitting
at the well as Giver of drink to all,
flows to each according to His will:
different springs according to those who drink.
From the well a single undifferentiated drink
came up each time for those who drank.
The Living Fount lets distinct blessings
flow to distinct people.

Hymns on Virginity 23.3

But, not satisfied merely to meet each of us at our present level of spiritual discernment, God leads each of us step by step to higher levels of understanding. Again, the Samaritan woman is paradigmatic of this process:

Because she in her love said, "The Messiah will come,"
He revealed to her with love, "I am He."
That He was a prophet she believed already,
soon after, that He was the Messiah . . .
. . . she is a type of our humanity
that He leads step by step.

Hymns on Virginity 22.21

Most ancient commentators on the story of the Samaritan woman saw her as an immoral woman, one who had been divorced many times or who had simply lived with several men without benefit of marriage. Dipping into the non-canonical books of the Old Testament, Ephrem found another solution to her having had five husbands and a sixth who was not really her husband: Like Sarah in the *Book of Tobit*, she had been unlucky in marriage: all her husbands had died, so no man was brave enough to marry her. Thus her sixth husband did not share her marriage bed. This little detail is not only indicative of Ephrem's style of commentary—one that is narrative, literary, and based on a broad familiarity with Scripture. It is also significant that, having removed the cloud of opprobrium from over her head, Ephrem moves on to portray the Samaritan woman as an apostle, prophet, and type of the *Theotokos*, the Mother of God. He praises her for her readiness to share her insight into Jesus' messianic identity:

> Blessed are you, O woman, for not suppressing
> your judgment about what you discovered.
>> *Hymns on Virginity* 23.1.1–2

Ephrem notes that just as Jesus' love for her led him to meet her need, her love for her neighbors led her to share her news with them:

> The glorious Treasury was Himself present
> for your need because of His love.
> Your love was zealous
> to share your treasure with your city.
> Blessed woman, your discovery became
> the Discoverer of the lost.
>> *Hymns on Virginity* 23.1.3–8

Also laudable is the immediacy of her response to one small sign, to be contrasted with the obstinacy of those who refused to accept even the greater evidence of miracles (*Hymns on Virginity* 23.2)

In her revelation to others of what she had heard, she is like Mary who conceived by her ear and thereby brought the Son to the world:

> [Praise] to you, o woman in whom I see
> a wonder as great as in Mary!
> For she from within her womb
> in Bethlehem brought forth His body as a child,
> but you by your mouth made Him manifest
> as an adult in Shechem, the town of His father's household.
> Blessed are you, woman, who brought forth by your mouth
> light for those in darkness.
>
> Mary, the thirsty land in Nazareth,
> conceived our Lord by her ear.
> You, too, O woman thirsting for water,
> conceived the Son by your hearing.
> Blessed are your ears that drank the source
> that gave drink to the world.
> Mary planted Him in the manger,
> but you [planted him] in the ears of His hearers.
>> *Hymns on Virginity* 23.4–5

> Like the words of the prophets, what she spoke became reality:
> Your word, O woman, became a mirror
> in which He might see your hidden heart.
> "The Messiah," you had said, "will come,
> and when He comes, He will give us everything."

> Behold the Messiah for Whom you waited, modest woman!
> Through your voice ... prophecy was fulfilled.
>
> *Hymns on Virginity* 23.6

She is comparable to the apostles since even before the Twelve were permitted to do so, she preached the good news of salvation to the Gentiles:

> Your voice, O woman, first brought forth fruit,
> even before the apostles [brought fruit] with their preaching.
> The apostles were forbidden to announce Him
> among pagans and Samaritans.
> Blessed is your mouth that He opened and confirmed.
> The Storehouse of life took and gave you to sow.
> [Your] city, dead as Sheol,
> You entered, and you revived your dead [land].
>
> *Hymns on Virginity* 23.7

Spiritual Progress and Sanctification or *Theosis*

Mary, the mother of Jesus, and the Beloved Disciple are also especially significant in Ephrem's understanding of the ongoing process of the Incarnation in sanctification or *theosis*, the full restoration in each human being of the lost *imago dei*. Mary and John see in one another the complementary mysteries of God's condescending love for us and the bold access to Divine love now open to human beings. Through them we, too, may see this twofold mystery of our Savior. John, identified with the "beloved disciple" of the Fourth Gospel, and Mary, the mother of Jesus, are "types" through whom we are able to see Christ as in a mirror while they themselves saw Him in one another. Ephrem begins by evoking the scene at the foot of the cross as it is portrayed in John's Gospel, where Jesus invites Mary and John to regard one another as mother and son:

> Blessed are you, O woman, whose Lord and son
> entrusted you to one fashioned in His image.
> The Son of your womb did not wrong your love,
> but to the son of His bosom He entrusted you.
> Upon your bosom you caressed Him when He was small,
> and upon His bosom He also caressed [John],
> so that when He was crucified
> He repaid all you had advanced to Him,
> the debt of His upbringing.
>
> For, the Crucified repaid debts;
> even yours was repaid by Him.
> He drank from your breast visible milk,

> but [John drank] from His bosom hidden mysteries.
> Confidently He approached your breast;
> confidently [John] approached and lay upon His bosom.
> Since you missed the sound of His voice,
> He gave you his harp
> to be a consolation to you.
>
> *Hymns on Virginity* 25.2–3

The love and care which flowed from Mary to her Son are echoed by the love of Jesus for John and repaid by entrusting her to his care. John shows a special resemblance to Jesus, Ephrem assumes, because he takes His place as Mary's son. But a deeper ethical mystery is contained here: the love of John for his Lord led him to imitate Him, thus bringing into higher relief in him the *imago dei* engraved on each human being:

> The youth who loved our Lord very much,
> who portrayed [and] put Him on and resembled Him,
> was zealous in all these matters to resemble Him:
> in his speech, his aspect and his ways.
> The creature put on his Creator,
> and he resembled Him although indeed he did not resemble what He was.
> It is amazing how much the clay is able to be imprinted
> with the beauty of its sculptor.
>
> *Hymns on Virginity* 25.4

By meditating on the relationship of Jesus to His mother, John was better able to understand the Incarnation:

> The youth in the woman was seeing
> how much that Exalted One was lowered,
> how He entered [and] dwelt in a weak womb
> and emerged [and] was suckled with weak milk . . .
>
> *Hymns on Virginity* 25.8.1–4

Meanwhile, by observing the behavior of the Beloved Disciple, Mary learned about the possibility of spiritual growth and the boldness it encourages:

> The woman also wondered at how much he grew
> that he went up and lay upon the bosom of God.
> The two of them were amazed at one another,
> how much they were able to grow by grace.
> [It is] You, Lord, Whom they saw . . .
> while observing one another:
> Your mother saw You in Your disciple;
> And he saw You in Your mother.
>
> *Hymns on Virginity* 25.8.5–9.4

Nor does the benefit of this insight stop with these two privileged and holy people, it extends to all who are willing to look deeply into their fellow human beings:

> O the seers who at every moment
> see You, Lord, in a mirror
> manifest a type so that we, too, in one another
> may see You, our Savior.
>
> *Hymns on Virginity* 25.9.5–8

For Ephrem, thinking of the story of Martha and Mary, Mary Magdalen exemplifies perfectly the concentration on the inner presence of Christ which leads to the full restoration of the *imago dei*:

> She turned her face away from everything
> to gaze on one beauty alone.
> Blessed is her love that was intoxicated, not sober,
> so that she sat at His feet to gaze at Him.
> Let you also portray the Messiah in your heart
> and love Him in your mind.
>
> *Hymns on Virginity* 24.7.3–8

More broadly speaking, for Ephrem it is the consecrated virgin who has most fully stripped off the old Adam to put on the new at baptism (*Hymns on Virginity* 1.1–8). Her body is clothed in a new garment; it is the Temple of God and His royal Palace.

But however strongly Ephrem admonishes the virgin to preserve her sexual innocence, it is clear that this is not an end in itself, but rather it is symbolic of the full dedication of self to God which is the goal of every Christian life:[11]

> Let chastity be portrayed in your eyes and in your ears the sound of truth.
> Imprint your tongue with the word of life and upon your hands [imprint] all alms.
> Stamp your footsteps with visiting the sick,
> and let the image of your Lord be portrayed in your heart.
> Tablets are honored because of the image of kings.
> How much more will one be honored who has portrayed the Lord in all the senses.
>
> *Hymns on Virginity* 2.15

Biblical symbols and the presence of God in historical events

Among the historical symbols Biblical typology plays the central role. The events in the history of Israel narrated in Hebrew Scripture have religious significance for all people. Like most early Christian writers, however, Ephrem saw the Hebrew Scripture as preliminary sketches, as shadows, when compared with the realities of the New Testament:

> [Christ's] power perfected the types,
> and His truth the mysteries,
> His interpretation the similes,
> His explanation the sayings,
> and His assurances the difficulties.
>
> By His sacrifice He abolished sacrifices,
> and libations by His incense,
> and the [passover] lambs by His slaughter,
> the unleavened [bread] by His bread,
> and the bitter [herbs] by His Passion.
>
> By His healthy meal
> He weaned [and] took away the milk.
> By His baptism were abolished
> the bathing and sprinkling
> that the elders of the People taught.
> *Hymns on Virginity* 8.8–10

Despite the intrinsic importance of the events and persons of the "Old Testament," they are only "antitypes" which were fulfilled in the "types" of the New Testament. On the one hand, the Passover Lamb is an anticipation of Christ and of the salvation gained through Him. To attempt to understand Christ without knowing about the Passover would be to deprive oneself of the depth and richness of meaning placed in human history by God himself. Yet conversely, in Ephrem's view, to stop with the Passover Lamb rather than interpreting it as a symbol of Christ would mean missing the fullness of God's revelation and accepting a truncated version of the meaning of history.

Ephrem's hymns are permeated with typological exegesis. The central figures of this typology are Jesus and Mary. He presents a rich variety of Old Testament types for Christ. In the second of his *Nativity Hymns*, for example, he systematically presents Jesus as the prophet, priest, and king. His selection of Old Testament figures as forerunners of Christ is similar to many other early Christian writers, but he adds unexpected interpretations as well. For example, Jesus is anticipated not only by Isaac, Melchizedek, Moses, and David, but also by Jacob, who is kicked by Esau but does not retaliate.

Ephrem's Mariology is central to his understanding of the Incarnation. Mary was chosen because she was most pleasing to God (*Hymns on the Nativity* 2.7). Yet she who gave birth to the Son of the Most High was given birth by Him in baptism (*Hymns on the Nativity* 16.9–11). Paradoxically, Mary gave birth to and nourished and cared for the Incarnate One who gave life, nourishment and care to her. In this she represents all humans and indeed all creation:

> By power from Him Mary's womb became able
> to bear the One Who bears all.

From the great treasury of all creation
Mary gave to Him every thing that she gave.
She gave Him milk from what He made exist.
She gave Him food from what He had created.
As God, He gave milk to Mary.
In turn, as man, He was given suck by her.
Hymns on the Nativity 4.182–185

Her theological importance is confirmed by the wealth of Ephrem's typology for Mary. She is not only the second Eve, but she is also a second Sarah, Rachel, and Anna; she is favorably compared and contrasted with Tamar, Ruth, and Rahab (*Hymns on the Nativity* 8.13, 13.2–5, , 9.7–16, 15.8, 16.12). Most unusual is Ephrem's imagery drawn from the Jewish priestly cult to provide a typology for Mary's role. The virginity of Mary and of all the "daughters of the covenant" is the vestment of the High Priest, who is Christ:

May all the evidences of virginity of Your brides
be preserved by You. They are the purple [robes]
and no one may touch them
except our King. For virginity
is like a vestment for You, the High Priest.
Hymns on the Nativity 16.13

Like the Ark of the Covenant, Mary is honored not for herself but for the Divine presence within her:

Joseph rose to serve in the presence of his Lord
Who was within Mary. The priest serves
in the presence of Your Ark because of Your holiness.
Hymns on the Nativity 16.16

The Tablets containing the teachings of the Mosaic Law also constitute an antitype which is fulfilled in Mary:

Moses bore the tablets of stone
that His Lord had written. And Joseph escorted
the pure tablet in whom was dwelling
the Son of the Creator. The tablets were left behind
since the world was filled with Your teaching.
Hymns on the Nativity 16.17

These unusual typologies are all based on the premise that in the Incarnation, Mary became the dwelling place of God on earth.

To grasp more fully the significance for Ephrem of these metaphors one must be aware that in Syriac "virginity" (*bethulutho*) is synonymous with "chastity" (*qad-*

dishutho) which also means "holiness." Behind the coincidence in meanings between "chastity" and "holiness" is ultimately a notion of mysterious power, untouchable sacral presence. Mary as the virgin *par excellence* is uniquely suited to be the holy one in whom—or perhaps better the holy *place* in *which*—God deigns to be present.

The sacred dimension of all of history

Not only the events described in Scripture, but all historical events must have profound religious significance. Ephrem's *Hymns against Julian*, along with the *Nisibene Hymns*, display his kinship with the Jewish prophets. Like them, he contemplates the political and military events of his time in the light of his ethical and theological tenets, looking for evidence of Divine activity, rewards, punishments, and edifying moral lessons. Living as he did in an area at the easternmost edge of the Roman Empire constantly under the pressure of Sassanid Persia, Ephrem was presented with dramatic historical events for his contemplation. When the Persian army besieged his town of Nisibis for the third time and it was spared even after its protecting city wall had been broken down, he composed poetry about salvation and grace:

> [God] saved us without a wall and taught that He is our wall.
> He saved us without a king and made known that He is our king.
> He saved us in all from all and showed He is all.
> He saved us by His grace and again revealed
> that He is freely gracious and life-giving. From each who boasts
> He takes away the boast and gives to him His grace.
>
> *Nisibene Hymns* 2.2

Warnings against idolatry and encouragement in adversity are as prominent in his hymns as in the pronouncements of Jeremiah and Isaiah. When the apostate Roman emperor Julian brought his army into Mesopotamia, ostentatiously offering sacrifice to the old pagan deities, pressuring the Christians of Mesopotamia to join in that worship, but finally dying in battle, Ephrem was not at a loss for words. He elaborated the view that God had made the apostate emperor Julian the representative and symbol of all who hold erroneous views—not only pagans but also heretics and Jews. His defeat was a sign to all nations of the ultimate fate of those who oppose God.

The first of Ephrem's five *Hymns against Julian* stands apart from the rest since it was written prior to the emperor's death in battle. Here the poet offers a message of hope and perseverance to the people of Nisibis, threatened with persecution. The other four hymns reiterate and develop that message in the light of subsequent events. Rather than focusing on the loss of their city to the Persians, a catastrophe caused by Nisibene acquiescence to Julian's reestablishment of paganism there, Ephrem emphasizes that the claims of paganism have been proved false by the fate of the apostate emperor. The political events provide a larger-than-life drama of the cosmic conflict between good and evil. God's partisans, the true members of the Church of Nisibis, with the encouragement of the watching angels, withstood the onslaughts of Satan in the form of imperial persecution and Persian military attacks.

Using a favorite metaphor, the mirror as the instrument of divine ethical lessons, Ephrem takes the apostate emperor as the model of human pride as well as of political promotion of religious error. His policies unmasked the false Christians within the Church; his ignominious death demonstrates the folly of his pride as well as the falsity of his beliefs. The divine purpose in the defeat and death of the Roman Emperor was to present to all people a model of the vanity of idolatry. At the same time the fidelity of Christians has been tested and many have been found wanting during the pagan emperor's brief reign. Weak or false Christians have returned openly to paganism, or they have attacked their Creator in the contentious error of the Arian heresy. The Jewish people, he claims, have also returned to idolatrous worship. On the other hand, the city of Nisibis presents, again as if in a mirror, a model for fidelity to God, its rewards, and the consequences of its lapse. Reinforcing this primary imagery is the symbol of the Church as the true vine, beneficially pruned by the rigors of persecution:

> Rely on the truth, my brothers, and be not afraid
> for our Lord is not so weak as to fail us in the test.
> He is the power on which the world and its inhabitants depend.
> The hope of His Church depends on Him.
> Who is able to sever its heavenly roots?
>
> *Hymns against Julian* 1.1

> Although the branch is living, on it are dead fruits
> blooming only outwardly.
> The wind tried them and cast off the wild grapes.
>
> *Hymns against Julian* 1.5

Several other metaphors serve to teach the same lesson: separation of the wheat from the tares, the purification of gold in the furnace and separation of the curds and whey in cheese-making.[12]

To these symbols current in both Biblical and general Hellenistic contexts, Ephrem adds biblical examples of faithless sovereigns and the consequences of their erroneous ways: Nebuchadnezzar, Jeroboam, Ahab, Jotham, Manasseh, Jezebel, Athaliah, and Saul provide precedents for Julian's errors as well as his fate.[13] The attendant notions of true and false prophecy provide a context for his contention that in this case the Church has followed the course of Daniel, confronting the pagan ruler, whereas the Jewish people have followed the precedent of the Israelites under Jeroboam, worshiping the golden calf.[14] While this general approach, aptly named "prophetic anti-Judaism" by Ruether, is typical of patristic writers,[15] Ephrem pursues his view with tenacious originality, accompanied, one suspects, by a modicum of perverse misrepresentation. In support of the parallel with the Israelite worship of the golden calf, for example, he associates Julian's bull coinage with his attempt to rebuild the Temple in Jerusalem as well as claiming that the music and sacrifice of traditional Jewish worship resemble the raucous pagan worship (*Hymns against Julian* 1.16). Likewise to the established argument that Daniel prophesied the permanent destruction of the Jewish Temple, he adds the claim implicit in Constantine's building program but not generally stated in theological polemics that Christian pilgrimage functions as a substitute for the Jewish cult of Jerusalem (*Hymns against Julian* 4.23–25).

Throughout these hymns, he exploits an extensive variety of animal imagery. The Orphic and broadly Hellenistic notion of a philanthropic shepherd king, already well-established as a model for Christ, is presented as a foil for Julian, the bad king (*Hymns against Julian* 1.1–2). Rather than a good shepherd, he is a wolf in sheep's clothing, or a he-goat, favoring the goats rather than the sheep (*Hymns against Julian* 2.1–4). The latter image has the added punch of alluding to Julian's unpopular beard as well as intimating lasciviousness (*Hymns against Julian* 2.6–9). Ephrem's almost apocalyptic description of the conflict between the forces of good and evil is enhanced by his association of the pagans with vermin, dragons, and the primal chaos as well as with the more mundane insults of association with hogs and filth (*Hymns against Julian* 1.3, 1.5, 2.13)

Finally, Ephrem's symbolic imagination provides several examples of the ironic outcome of Julian's efforts. Considering it suitable that "the punishment should fit the crime," he finds numerous coincidences to confirm this view. For example, the emperor's death near Babylon in conjunction with his "denial" of Daniel's prophecy cements the parallel of Julian with Nebuchadnezzar (*Hymns against Julian* 1.18–20). Moreover, Ephrem spins out in elaborate detail the inherent contradiction of Julian's attempt to use Chaldean religion to defeat Persians, and the paradox that he was misled by the oracles to become himself the sacrificial goat (*Hymns against Julian* 2.4–15, 4.5–14). The coincidental features of his uncle Julian's fate should have astonished the emperor as they did Ephrem (*Hymns against Julian* 4.3). Likewise laden with significance is the similarity of Julian's death by a lance to the death of his sacrificial animals, both of which are implicitly contrasted with the death of the true Lamb, who, being pierced, released humankind from the curse of the lance that barred the gate to Paradise (*Hymns against Julian* 3.14).

After the death of Julian, the Roman army had chosen a new emperor, Jovian, an Orthodox Christian. Seeing no alternative to surrender under the disadvantageous terms offered him by Shapur, Jovian accepted them. These terms included cession to Persia of the city of Nisibis without its inhabitants. The city was, in Ephrem's eyes, the sacrificial lamb that saved the Roman army (*Hymns against Julian* 2.15.6). Unlike Ammianus Marcellinus, however, who portrays the fate of Nisibis in exclusively negative terms, Ephrem stresses that, although the city itself was ceded to Persia, the Persian ruler showed respect for its Christian churches and permitted its citizens to depart for Roman territory rather than executing them, enslaving them or exiling them into the eastern reaches of the Persian Empire, as had been the fate of the inhabitants of other recalcitrant Mesopotamian cities (*Hymns against Julian* 2.22–27). To celebrate his victory and show appropriate disdain for the religion of the Roman army that had attacked his empire, the Persian king was apparently satisfied to destroy the pagan temples associated specifically with Julian (*Hymns against Julian* 2.22). Still the entire Christian population of this fortress city migrated within a short time to the adjacent cities of the Roman Empire. Ephrem was among those who went to first to Amida, then to Edessa, where he would spend his last ten years. Thus the heroic struggle of his native city, a symbol of Rome and of Christianity, against the mighty Persian Empire, a struggle which had occupied most of his adult life, ended in defeat and disgrace. The "constant, unwearying herald" was surrendered to the Persians (*Hymns against Julian* 2.16.6). As he meditates on these events in his *Nisibene Hymns* and in his *Hymns against Julian*, Ephrem again shows himself to be a genuine heir to the Jewish prophetic tradition, interpreting historical events as directed by divine Providence towards the attainment of justice in this world.[16] There must be a reason for God's allowing Nisibis to be taken. For him that reason is clear: the apostasy of the Christian Roman emperor and of those who followed him in reinstating pagan worship:

> Who else has so multiplied altars?
> Who else has so honored all the evil spirits?
> Who else has so pleased all the demons?
> He angered only the One, and he was broken.
> In him was confuted the entire faction of wrong,
> a force unable to support its worshipers!
>
> *Hymns against Julian* 4.6

Human beings in the divine image, and the divine presence in all of nature

Ephrem's emphasis on the Incarnation and his extension of that historical moment into the process of sanctification show clearly that human beings have a special place in the created order.

> Blessed is He Who engraved our soul and adorned and betrothed her to Him[self].
> Blessed is He Who made our body a Tabernacle for His hiddenness.
> Blessed is He Who with our tongue interpreted His secrets.
> Let us give thanks to that Voice Whose praise on our lyre
> and Whose power on our kithara[17] are sung.
>
> *Hymns on the Nativity* 3.7.1–5

> He is He Who Himself constructed the senses of our minds
> so that we might sing on our lyre something that the mouth of the bird
> is unable to sing in its melodies.
> Glory to the One Who saw that we had been pleased
> to resemble the animals in our rage and greed,
> and [so] He descended and became one of us that we might become heavenly.
>
> *Hymns on the Nativity* 3.1.

Although it is clear that human beings, with the *imago dei*, enjoy a unique position in the world, certain material things enjoy a privileged place since they link the world of nature to the world of Scripture. That privileged place is rooted in things of nature, in their physical properties and their names. So oil is symbolic of Christ and the salvation brought by Him, not only because He is literally, "the Anointed One"

who fulfills the roles of priest, prophet and king, but also due to the natural properties of oil: its healing and strengthening properties, its capacity to provide light, its use
with pigments for painting an image, its ability to ease forces in conflict, and even its
property of floating on water, as Jesus walked on the water! (*Hymns on Virginity 4–7*).
All these properties resonate in the baptismal anointing in which the *imago dei* is
restored to us:

> The lamp returned our lost things, and the Anointed also [returned] our treasures.
> The lamp found the coin, and the Anointed [found] the image of Adam.
>   *Hymns on Virginity* 5.8.5–6

The bread and wine of the Eucharist, although they provide a less fertile field for
Ephrem's imagination, play a similar role.[18]

> Blessed is the Shepherd Who became the sheep for our absolution.
> Blessed is the Vineshoot that became the cup of our salvation.
> Blessed also is the Cluster, the source of the medicine of life.
> Blessed also is the Ploughman Who Himself became
> the grain of wheat that was sown and the sheaf that was reaped.
> He is the Master Builder Who became a tower for our refuge.
>   *Hymns on the Nativity* 3.15

Not only the elements of the sacraments, however, but other material things and concepts are symbolic of Christ. So Satan's temptations of Jesus have ironic appropriateness: he tempted with bread the "Sustainer of all," with stones, "the perfect Stone," with
kingship the true King (*Hymns on Virginity* 14). Even things without a symbolic tradition in Scripture may be seen as representative of Christ's altruistic suffering. In the
eleventh of his *Hymns on Virginity* Ephrem considers a series of minerals, plants, and
animals all worked by human craft for our benefit despite the harm done to them. Like
a Buddhist or Manichaean sage, Ephrem notes that they all suffer for our benefit, making them symbolic of Christ:

> The sea belongs to the diver who bursts in and descends in it.
> Its gulf gives space to him; it shows him its treasure;
> it gives and enriches him; it carries [him] and brings him up.

> Cut stone becomes by its suffering
> a bulwark for the human being. In calamity and in battle
> it stands before him and preserves his treasures.

> Wood by means of its harsh treatment resembles the cross:
> it carries in the sea; it bears on dry land;
> it increases by its uses, and enriches by its helps.

> Even strong iron is weak in the fire.

It is malleable and yields to human strength,
and when it has been well-beaten, it repays the one who struck it.

Noble gold is beaten without offense.
To all those who beat it, it gives its sides as a symbol of our Lord.
Its insult is for honor; its suffering is for glory.

Iron and a sharp stake, indeed, pierce the pearl
like that One Who was pierced by nails and on the cross.
It becomes by its suffering an adornment for humankind.

And who will tell the suffering of the grain of wheat?
Indeed, how many scourgings and afflictions it encounters!
By its torments it gives life to its tormentors.

The foot of its crusher also abuses the cluster of grapes.
By its blood [the foot's] filth is washed away; with its must it sweetens him;
and if it ages with him, it makes him merry with its wine.

When a fruit is eaten, by means of its suffering its taste
pours out in the mouth. This is a symbol of that Fruit
that brings to life His eaters when His body is eaten.

When the honey that sweetens all is extracted,
as it is worked, it softens its strength for those who eat it.
It delights health; it nourishes sickness.

Incenses are, like the victors, cast into the fire.
Their scents rise up like their good Lord
Who by means of His death exhaled the scent of His vitality.

So also when the bird beats the air
with its wings as with arms, the back [of the air] is subjected to it,
and like a bride it is carried on high by the power [of the air].

So also the farmer by means of iron
rends and cleaves the earth, but she is not angered by her suffering:
her treasures and her womb she opens by her sufferings.

The sheep in its shame strips off its garment and cloak
and gives all of it to its shearers,
like the Lamb Who divided His garments for His crucifiers.

Great is the symbol of the lamb who is quiet in his life
and sings in his death. His loins are for festivities
and the strings of his lyre for melodies and songs.

> So old is the teaching that its time is not known.
> It dwells in youth although it is scorned along with it.
> It becomes small [and] makes it great to honor it very much.
>
> All these things teach by their symbols:
> they open by their sufferings the treasure of their riches,
> and the suffering of the Son of the Gracious One is the key of His treasures.
> *Hymns on Virginity* 11.4–20

Finally, every beauty of daily life is a tangible reminder of the graciousness of our God:

> But remaining are all those things the Gracious One made in His mercy.
> Let us see those things that He does for us every day!
> How many tastes for the mouth! How many beauties for the eye!
> How many melodies for the ear! How many scents for the nostrils!
> Who can be compared to the goodness of these little things!
> *Hymns on Virginity* 31.16

Selected Bibliography

Recent English translations from Syriac of writings by or about St Ephrem with introductory materials

Ephrem the Syrian, *Hymns on the Nativity, Hymns Against Julian, Hymns on Virginity and on the Symbols of the Lord,* intro., trans. Kathleen E. McVey, Classics of Western Spirituality, New York: Paulist, 1989.

Amar, Joseph, ed., trans. *A Metrical Homily on Holy Mar Ephrem by Mar Jacob of Serugh,* Patrologia Orientalis 47.1 (1995).

Brock, Sebastian, ed., trans., *The Harp of the Spirit: Eighteen Poems of Saint Ephrem,* Studies Supplementary to *Sobornost* 4, 2 ed., London, 1983.

Lieu, Samuel N. C., ed., trans., *The Emperor Julian: Panegyric and Polemic,* Liverpool, 1986; 2 ed. 1989.

St Ephrem, *Hymns on Paradise,* intro., trans. Sebastian P. Brock, Crestwood, NY: St Vladimir's Seminary Press, 1990.

St Ephrem the Syrian, *Selected Prose Works,* intro., trans. Edward G. Mathews, Joseph P. Amar, Fathers of the Church 91, Washington, D.C.: Catholic University of America, 1995.

Studies

Bou Mansour, Tanios, *La Pense symbolique de Saint Ephrem le Syrien,* Bibliothèque de l'Université Saint-Esprit 16, Kaslik, 1988.

Brock, Sebastian, *The Luminous Eye: the Spiritual World Vision of St Ephrem,* rev. ed., Cistercian Studies 124, Kalamazoo, Michigan: Cistercian Publications, 1992.

Griffith, Sidney. *Faith adoring the mystery: reading the Bible with St Ephrem the Syrian,* Milwaukee: Marquette University, 1997.

Hogan, Martin, *The Sermon on the mount in St Ephrem's Commentary on the Diatessaron*, New York: P. Lang, 1999.

Murray, Robert, *Symbols of Church and Kingdom: A Study in Early Syriac Tradition*, Cambridge, England: Cambridge University Press, 1975.

Palmer, Andrew, ed., *The Influence of Saint Ephraim the Syrian*, Hugoye: Journal of Syriac Studies, 1.2 (July 1998) and 2.1 (January 1999) [http://www.acad.cua.edu/syrcom/Hugoye].

Petersen, William, *The Diatessaron and Ephrem Syrus as Sources of Romanos the Melodist*, Corpus Scriptorum Christianorum Orientalium 466, Subsidia 73, Louvain: Peeters, 1986.

Possekel, Ute, *Evidence of Greek Philosophical Concepts in the Writings of Ephrem the Syrian*, Corpus Scriptorum Christianorum Orientalium 580, Subsidia 102, Louvain: Peeters, 1999.

Valavanolickal, Kuriakose A., *The Use of Gospel Parables in the Writings of Aphrahat and Ephrem*, Studies in the Religion and History of Early Christianity 2, New York: P. Lang, 1996.

Yousif, P., *L'Eucharistie chez S. Ephrem de Nisibe*, Orientalia Christiana Analecta 224 (Rome, 1984).

Endnotes

[1]Some segments of this essay have appeared previously in the general introduction, introductions to individual hymns and notes to my book, *Ephrem the Syrian: Hymns*, Classics of Western Spirituality (New York: Paulist, 1989). This essay was first published by Routledge Press in the volume *The Early Christian World*, edited by Philip E. Esler and is reprinted here by permission. It was delivered as a paper at the consultation on "Orthodox and Wesleyan Spirituality" sponsored by the General Board of Global Ministries of The United Methodist Church and St Vladimir's Orthodox Theological Seminary in January, 1998.

[2]In addition to allusions within Ephrem's genuine literary corpus, ancient sources for Ephrem's life include Sozomen, *Church History* 3.16, Palladius, *Lausiac History* 40, Jerome, *On illustrious men* 115, Theodoret, *Church History* 4.26, a Syriac *vita* tradition, and a Syriac homily by Jacob of Serug; for a concise overview of these materials and the recent scholarship, cf. Sebastian Brock, "St Ephrem in the Eyes of Later Syriac Liturgical Tradition" in *Hugoye: Journal of Syriac Studies*, 2.1 (January 1999) [http://www.acad.cua.edu/syrcom/Hugoye].

[3]On Ephrem's use of Greek philosophical concepts, see Ute Possekel, *Evidence of Greek Philosophical Concepts in the Writings of Ephrem the Syrian*, Corpus Scriptorum Christianorum Orientalium 580, Subsidia 102 (Louvain: Peeters, 1999).

[4]On the corpus of translations and their authenticity, see McVey, 4, n. 6. Further, see the excellent collection of conference papers published by Andrew Palmer in *Hugoye* 1,2 (July 1998), and 2.1 (January 1999).

[5]For bibliography on this subject, cf. McVey, 5, n. 7.

[6]On Ephrem's use of symbols, cf. Tanios Bou Mansour, *La Pensée symbolique de Saint Ephrem le Syrien* (Bibliothèque de l'Université Saint-Esprit 16, Kaslik, 1988).

[7]Observed by Sebastian Brock, ed. trans., in St Ephrem the Syrian, *Hymns on Paradise* (Crestwood, NY: St Vladimir's Press, 1990), 72–74, with regard to *Hymns on Faith* 5.17; with regard to *Hymns on the Nativity* 1.99, in McVey, 74, n. 66.

[8]Brock characterizes this as another sort of "Incarnation" of the Word, Brock, 45–49.

[9]The translation is Brock's, in "The Holy Spirit as Feminine in Early Syriac Literature," *After Eve: Women, Theology and the Christian Tradition*, ed. Janet Martin Soskice (London: Marshall Pickering, Collins, 1990), 73–88, esp. 83–84.

[10]On "Watchers," a class of angels often mentioned by Ephrem, cf. McVey, 229, n. 36.

[11]On Ephrem's understanding of virginity and of "singleness" in the context of early Syriac tradition, see Thomas Koonammakkal, "Ephrem's Ideas on Singleness" in *Hugoye: Journal of Syriac Studies* 2.1 (January 1999).

[12]*Hymns against Julian* 1.10–13, 2.10–11; 1.13, 2.24, 4.1; 4.2.

[13] *Hymns against Julian* 1.8, 1.20, 2.2, 4.5, 4.8.

[14] *Hymns against Julian* 1.16–20, 2.2.

[15] Rosemary Ruether, *Faith and Fratricide* (New York: Seabury, 1974), 117–82.

[16] Jouko Martikainen, "Some Remarks about the Carmina Nisibena as a Literary and a Theological Source," *Orientalia Christiana Analecta* 197 (1974), 345–52; Sidney H. Griffith, "Ephraem the Syrian's Hymns 'Against Julian': Meditations on History and Imperial Power," *Vigiliae Christianae* 4 (1987), 238–66.

[17] Or, zither (Syriac *qytr'*).

[18] For example, see *Hymns on Virginity* 16.2.4.5 and 31.13–14. Further on Ephrem's understanding of the Eucharist, see P. Yousif, *L'Eucharistie chez S. Ephrem de Nisibe*, in *Orientalia Christiana Analecta* 224 (Rome, 1984).

14

Kenosis in the Nativity Hymns of Ephrem the Syrian and Charles Wesley

S T Kimbrough, Jr

This is a preliminary inquiry, that requires ongoing research, as the literature of Ephrem the Syrian and Charles Wesley is so extensive. The inquiry will be limited to the views of both poet-priests on divine *kenosis* as expressed in their hymns on the nativity of Christ. While the *Tendschrift* from which they were writing undoubtedly varies, since they were writing some fourteen centuries apart, it will be come clear that both view God's self-emptying, self-limitation, and self-effacement in the Incarnation of Jesus Christ as the foundational foci for Christian spirituality. While there is no concrete evidence that Charles Wesley read the works of Ephrem the Syrian, no doubt he had read his brother John's *A Plain Account of Genuine Christianity* (1753) and was aware of the reference to Ephrem and other church fathers.[1] One finds numerous references throughout Charles Wesley's works to writers from the early period of the growth of the church, though no specific ones to Ephrem have been identified. One thing is very clear from the extensive writing of both authors—they understood the potential value of hymnody as a resource for Christian spirituality and they prepared the way for the deepening of this medium of spiritual nurture.[2]

There are likenesses and differences between Ephrem and Wesley and their literature, and this study will reveal many parallel and complementary ideas in both writers. These take on their full meaning in their developed theologies of the Incarnation. In Ephrem's hymns there is also a developed mariology embedded in a strong anti-Jewish polemic. Neither a mariology nor a strong anti-Jewish polemic is found in Wesley's nativity hymns.[3] Unquestionably Ephrem's mariological perspectives are integral to his understanding of the Incarnation.

The texts of Ephrem the Syrian used for this study are those compiled by Kathleen McVey consisting of the sixteen *Hymns on the Nativity*, which were probably written "for liturgical use at the feast of Christ's birth, and manifestation of the world, celebrated in his time on 6 January."[4] McVey includes the four additional nativity hymns which were added to the collection by a sixth century compiler and adds eight more which brings the total to twenty-eight nativity hymns. Most of the original sixteen hymns are sung by Mary to her son. The hymns reveal that Ephrem was an excellent biblical interpreter and exegete and they are a rich source of highly developed typological exegesis and typology for Mary.

Many of Ephrem's hymns were integrated into the liturgies of the Eastern-rite churches and some are still used in the East and West Syrian liturgies. His extraordinary poetical gifts have been acknowledged by the translation of many of his hymns into numerous languages.

The texts of Charles Wesley used for this study are the eighteen poems which were published in the hymn booklet *Hymns for the Nativity of our Lord* (1745), his most famous nativity hymn "Hark! the herald angels sing,"[5] which John Wesley did not hold in high regard and was originally published in *Hymns and Sacred Poems* (1739), eighteen previously unpublished nativity texts,[6] which have appeared in *The Unpublished Poetry of Charles Wesley*, 3 vols.,[7] and finally ten poems based on the nativity narratives of the Gospels of Matthew and Luke, which are found in *Short Hymns on Select Passages of the Holy Scriptures*, 2 vols. (1762). As Frank Baker suggests, "Charles, far more than his brother John, seems to have been greatly drawn to the festivals of the Church Year, and most especially to Christmas, which he preferred to think of, not in sentimental terms as the birth of the Babe of Bethlehem, but theologically as the Incarnation, the Nativity of our Lord,"[8] Wesley's nativity hymns are primarily doxological affirmations and prayers for the community of faith.

No doubt Wesley wrote nativity hymns for use in connection with Advent and Christmas, both to be read and sung. However, as there was little place for hymn singing in the eighteenth-century Anglican liturgy, the hymns found more use in the Methodist societies than in the official liturgies of the church. When John Wesley initiated singing at the time of the reception of the elements during the Eucharist, some of these hymns may have been used, particularly at the times of Advent and Christmas. Wesley's hymns over the years became more and more integrated into liturgical use by Anglicans and many Protestant denominations. It is interesting to note that the contemporary Roman Catholic hymnal, *Worship III*, published in the USA, contains eleven Charles Wesley hymns. It should be added that, like the hymns of Ephrem the Syrian, many of Wesley's hymns have been translated into numerous languages. Without question one of his most popular hymn texts is one having to do with the Incarnation: "Hark! The herald angels sing."

While Wesley was an astute biblical interpreter and exegete like Ephrem, his nativity hymns reflect little or nothing of the elaborate typological exegesis found in Ephrem's nativity hymns. One does find Wesley practicing rather elaborate typological exegesis in some of his biblical-narrative poems, but these are not among his nativity hymns and, hence, are not included in this discussion. It should be noted, however, that Charles Wesley published a commentary on the entire Bible written in poetry entitled *Short Hymns on Select Passages of the Holy Scriptures*, 2 vols. (Bristol: Farley, 1762). Unquestionably a study of the typological exegesis of Ephrem and Wesley is an important further step in the exploration of the theology of both poet-priests.

It is the intent of this study to point out parallels of thought in Ephrem and Wesley as regards divine *kenosis* in their nativity hymns and to indicate the significance as regards Christian spirituality. In conclusion, it will be shown that the parallels themselves are not the most important matter, rather the way in which both theologians utilize paradox as an important paradigm of spirituality.

Kenosis and Mystery

In discussing "Orthodox and Wesleyan Spirituality" it is vitally important to explore the nativity hymns of Ephrem the Syrian and Charles Wesley, for they are important keys to the understanding of spirituality in the Orthodox and Wesleyan traditions. Above all, the sense in which divine *kenosis* in and through the Incarnation becomes determinative for spirituality is revealed in these texts.

Kenosis is the beginning point for Ephrem the Syrian and Charles Wesley in their understanding of the Incarnation. At the heart of Ephrem's theological understanding in his nativity hymns the emphasis is on the amazing transformation in the Creator's nature, who is unchanging. He writes:

> This Lord of nature today was transformed contrary to his nature.[9]

Charles Wesley responds to this miraculous transformation in a similar manner, yet expressing a deep sense of its mystery:

> Our God contracted to a span,
> incomprehensibly made man.[10]

Ephrem exclaims:

> The Lofty One became like a little child, yet hidden in Him was
> A treasure of Wisdom that suffices for all.
> He was lofty but he sucked Mary's milk,
> And from His blessings all creation sucks.[11]

God deigns to take on the form of a little child. In so doing God becomes accessible to all humankind, but this is incomprehensible, a mystery.

Central to the nativity hymns of Ephrem the Syrian and Charles Wesley is a deep *sense of mystery* with regard to the Incarnation, seen not only as the most important redemptive event in history, but through which God continues to be accessible to all humankind. For both poet-priests the Incarnation is the mystery! It is unfathomable! Ephrem speaks of God's hidden nature as follows:

> If anyone seeks Your hidden nature,
> behold it is in heaven in the great womb
> of Divinity. And if anyone seeks
> Your revealed body, behold it rests and looks out
> from the small womb of Mary![12]

Ephrem is unequivocally convinced of the wonder of the Incarnation which is beyond human comprehension.

> You are utterly a wonder. In every side that we seek You,
> You are near and far, but who is it that reaches You?
> Investigation is not able to stretch it[self] to reach You.
> Wherever it stretches out to reach [You], it is cut off and falls short.

It is too short for Your mountain. Faith reaches [You]—
and love and prayer.[13]

Wesley bids Christ reveal to him the mystery:

> O Christ, my hope, make known to me
> the great, the glorious *mystery*.
>   the hidden life impart,
> come, thou desire of nations, come
> formed in a spotless virgin's womb,
>   a pure, believing heart.[14]

Furthermore, Wesley affirms that the community of faith has a responsibility "to sound the mystery"—to celebrate it, to make the mystery known as mystery!

> See I the infant's face
>   the depths of Deity,
> and labour while ye gaze,
>   to sound the mystery.[15]

Finally, he writes in stanza one of a poem entitled "Christmas Day":

> Stupendous mystery!
>   God in our flesh is *seen*
> (While angels ask, how can it be?)
>   And dwells with sinful men!
>   Our nature He assumes,
>   That we may his retrieve;
> He comes, to our dead world He comes
>   that all thro' Him may live.[16]

Participation in the Divine

Divine *kenosis* has a distinct purpose that has manifold implications for Christian spirituality: human beings become participants in the divine. Therefore, the character and nature of human beings take on the character and nature of the Creator-God. Ephrem eloquently articulates this aspect of the Incarnation:

> Today the Deity imprinted itself on humanity,
> So that humanity might also be cut into the seal of Deity.[17]

Charles Wesley perceives the Incarnation similarly.

> Made flesh for our sake,
> that we might partake

> the nature divine
> and again in his image, his holiness shine.[18]

The spiritual journey with Christ involves being "cut into the seal of Deity" or partaking in the divine nature. All aspects in the development of Christian spirituality, i.e. scriptural interpretation, the grasp of Christian heritage, intellectual discipline, monasticism, liturgical participation, and contemplation—all seek to move the follower of Christ toward participation in the divine nature.

Wesley's strongest statement on *theosis*, that is, *becoming* divine—not becoming *like* the divine or partaking *in* the divine—comes in his nativity hymn #5 in the fourth stanza of which he writes:

> He deigns in flesh t'appear,
> widest extremes to join,
> to bring our vileness near,
> *and make us all divine*;
> and we the life of God shall know,
> for God is manifest below.[19]

Diverse dimensions of God's self-limitation in the Incarnation evoke a sense of awe from both Ephrem and Wesley. In the Incarnation *God's majesty is concealed.* Ephrem exclaims:

> Blessed is the Unlimited who was limited.
> Your majesty is hidden from us;
> your grace is revealed before us.[20]

Similarly Charles Wesley asserts:

> Emptied of his majesty,
> of his dazzling glories shorn,
> beings Source begins to be
> and God himself is born![21]

God is shorn of majesty? Indeed, claims Wesley:

> Lo! He lays his glory by,
> emptied of his majesty!
> See the God who all things made,
> humbly in a manger laid.[22]

And further:

> The everlasting God comes down
> to sojourn with the sons of men;
> without his majesty or crown
> the great Invisible is seen:

of all his dazzling glories shorn
the everlasting God is born.[23]

If human beings become participants in the divine nature through the Incarnation, the perceptions of God received through Scripture, tradition, and experience become determinative for human nature and spirituality. How God is revealed in the Incarnation is decisive for spirituality.

The Revelation of God in the Incarnation

God as a stranger

In the Incarnation God is revealed as a *stranger*. This is a kenotic emphasis of vital importance to Christian spirituality. It is an interesting paradox for One, namely Jesus, who is often spoken of as the "friend of sinners." The Holy One who becomes human is estranged from those to whom the divine comes closer. Ephrem declares:

> He became a servant on earth: He was Lord on high.
> Inheritor of the height and depth, who became a Stranger.
> But the One who was judged wrongly will judge in truth,
> and in whose face they spat, breathed the Spirit into the face.[24]

Charles Wesley comprehends well this dimension of *kenosis*, when he writes:

> Wrapped in swathes the immortal stranger,
> Man with men,
> We have seen
> lying in a manger.[25]

And—

> God see the King of glory,
> discern the heavenly stranger,
> so poor and mean,
> His cradle is a manger.[26]

In hymn 16 Ephrem has Mary reflect upon what she shall call God incarnate and one name she suggests is "stranger":

> What can I call You, a stranger to us,
> Who was from us: Shall I call You Son?
> Shall I call you brother? Shall I call You Bridegroom?
> Shall I call you Lord, O [You] Who brought forth His mother
> [in] another birth out of the water?[27]

Even to *Theotokos*, the Mother of God, the God-child is a potential stranger!

The self-humbling of God

In the Incarnation God is also revealed as a "self-humbling God," who divests self of divine majesty. Ephrem avers:

> He [was] wrapped [in] swaddling clothes in *baseness*,
>   but they offered him gifts.[28]

Divine majesty is revealed in "baseness"? Yes, but such self-humbling of the divine evokes the response of human gift-offering! Wesley similarly emphasizes the self-humbling baseness and poverty of God in the Incarnation.

> Triumph we, the sons of grace,
>   that our God is born so poor,
> doth his majesty abase
>   our salvation to secure.[29]

Wesley expresses his utter amazement at God's self-humbling action in the Incarnation:

> See the eternal Son of God,
>   a mortal son of man,
> dwelling in the earthly clod,
>   whom heaven cannot contain!
>
> Stand amazed ye heavens at this!
>   See the Lord of earth and skies!
> *Humbled to the dust* he is,
>   and in a manger lies.[30]

The immortal becomes mortal and is "humbled to the dust." This is the same God of whom the psalmist writes: "God is clothed in majesty and splendor."

Wesley even goes so far as to speak of God's self-humbling act in the Incarnation as evoking divine helplessness that will be the ultimate help of all humankind.

> Gaze on that *helpless* Object
> Of endless adoration!
>   Those infant hands,
>   shall burst our bands
> and work out our salvation.[31]

The cosmic God

The God, who is revealed as a stranger and as self-humbling is also made known as a cosmic God in the Incarnation. Both Ephrem and Wesley introduce the notion of the cosmic and mysterious significance of the Incarnation. Earth and heaven are encompassed by the Incarnation miracle. Ephrem breaks forth in praise:

> Glory to Him who became *earthly* although
> *heavenly* by his nature.[32]

One can but effervesce with awe, as does Wesley, at this wonder of the God, who is God of the cosmos, joining earth and heaven.

> See the stupendous blessing,
> which God to us hath given!
> A child of man
> in length of span,
> who fills both *earth* and *heaven*.[33]

He picks up this theme in *Short Hymns on Select Passages of the Holy Scriptures* (1762):

> God is in our flesh revealed,
> heaven and earth in *Jesu* join,
> mortal with immortal filled,
> and human with divine.[34]

This acknowledgment of the cosmic unity of earth and heaven in the Incarnation is the cause of the Christian's song:

> Their newly-born King,
> transported they sing,
> and *heaven* and *earth* with triumph doth ring.[35]

The participation in the divine nature through the Incarnation becomes determinative for the holy life. As followers of Christ take on the divine nature, that is, as they seek to be made holy in perfect love, they too must be willing to be self-humbling strangers, divested of majesty, and citizens of earth and heaven who share in God's cosmic mysteries. These are by no means the only aspects of the divine nature which are revealed in Scripture, tradition, and experience, but they are ones which are mutually emphasized by Ephrem and Charles Wesley in their nativity hymns.

The Benefits of the Incarnation

Sanctification

Ephrem affirms, as does Wesley, that the Incarnation is the time for the indwelling of the Spirit and the sanctifying of life.

> On this feast let everyone garland the
> door of his heart. May the
> Holy Spirit desire to enter in its door
> to dwell and *sanctify*. For behold,
> She moves about to all the
> doors [to see] where She may dwell.[36]

It is the Incarnation that enables sanctification, which Wesley understands as the Christian's life-long quest in one's journey with God, others, and all creation.

> Made flesh for our sake,
> that we might partake
> the nature divine
> and again in his image, his *holiness shine.*[37]

God becomes flesh that we may be holy. The Hebrew Scriptures implore us "to be holy for I the Lord your God am holy," but we cannot fully know the nature of God and, hence, cannot expect to be made completely holy in this life. To be holy means to participate in the divine nature by the transformation of our own natures. Yet, Wesley desires that the *full* image of God be shown in us:

> And while we are here,
> our King shall appear
> his Spirit impart,
> and *form his full image of love in our heart.*[38]

The path along which the followers of Jesus move toward the realization of the full image of God in their heart is the path of sanctification. This quest is at the heart of spirituality.

It is therefore no surprise that, while Ephrem and Wesley do not perceive the individual Christian apart from the corporate body of Christ, the church, they stress strongly the presence of the divine within the individual. It is not possible to think of sanctification without this dimension of the relationship to God. Hence, Ephrem writing in reference to the mother Mary says:

> "Blessed is the woman in whose heart
> and mind You are."[39]

He also pens a more general admonition.

> Let you also portray the Messiah in your heart
> and love Him in your mind.[40]

This last quotation from Ephrem is quite similar to Wesley's plea which we have cited previously:

And form his [Christ's] full image of love in our heart.[41]

The sanctified life is one in which the Incarnation comes to dwell within the individual. It is thus that the human and divine are made one, as Wesley asserts.

> Didst thou not in thy Person join
> the natures human and divine,
>   that God and man might be
> henceforth inseparably one?
> Haste then and make thy nature known
>   incarnated in me.
>
> I long thy coming to confess,
> the mystic power of godliness,
>   the life divine to prove:
> the fullness of thy life to know,
> redeemed from all my sins below
>   and perfected in love.
>
> Christ, my hope, make known in me
> the great, the glorious mystery
>   the hidden life impart:
> Come, thou desire of nations, come
> formed in a spotless virgin's womb,
>   a pure believing heart.[42]

In the life lived in Christ "the glorious mystery" of the Incarnation indwells the faithful! They are embodiments of God's mystery.

Victory over darkness and death

The indwelling mystery of the Incarnation is the light of the world and all creation, which obliterates darkness in the lives of all followers of Christ. In Ephrem's hymn number 5 on the nativity he makes this vividly clear:

> Darkness is defeated to signify
> that Satan is defeated, and light conquers
> to shout out that the First-born is victorious.
> The Dark One is defeated with the darkness,
> and our Light conquers with the sun.[43]

Wesley shapes these ideas in the form of a prayer:

> Light of those whose dreary dwelling
>   borders on the shades of death,

> come, and by thy love's revealing,
>   dissipate the clouds beneath:
> the new heaven and earth's Creator,
>   in our deepest darkness rise,
> scattering all the night of nature,
>   pouring eye-sight on our eyes.[44]

Ephrem breaks forth in a hymn that is a litany of thanksgiving praising God for the Light of the Incarnation which shines in the darkness and strips it of its power to conceal evil.

> Glory to that One Who begot His Light in the darkness,
> and [the darkness] was hidden by its vices that concealed its secrets,
> but [the Light] stripped off and took away from us the garment of
>   blemishes.[45]

Hope

God's self-emptying, self-humbling Incarnation, therefore, becomes the hope of the world, indeed all creation. Ephrem expressed the hope in this manner:

> Since human hope was shattered, hope was
>   increased by your birth.
> The heavenly beings announced good
>   hope to human beings.[46]

Ephrem does not aver that humankind was hopeless before the coming of Christ, rather that "hope was shattered." He does not say the Savior's birth fulfills all hope, rather than it "increases hope." This too is a reality of divine *kenosis*.

Charles Wesley also sees the Incarnation as the "hope of all the earth."

> Israel's strength and consolation,
>   hope of all the earth thou art,
> dear desire of every nation
>   joy of every longing heart.[47]

The incarnate "helpless Object" of which Wesley speaks in a previously cited hymn paradoxically becomes the "hope of all the earth."

Peace

For both Ephrem the Syrian and Charles Wesley the Incarnation inaugurates the reign of peace. Ephrem is very specific about the kenotic dimension of non-violence. Peace does not reign through violence. God chooses the limitation of non-violent exercise of divine power to empower the reign of peace.

> Glorious is the Compassionate One Who did not use
> violence, and without force,
> by wisdom He was victorious. He gave a type
> to human beings that by power
> and wisdom they might conquer discerningly.[48]

Wesley describes various aspects of the reign of peace. It is established in mercy; it vanquishes sorrow, anger, hatred, envy, malice, and discord. Because of the Incarnation the alarm of war will no more be sounded and the people of earth shall be joined in amity.

> Come then to thy servants again,
> > who long thy appearing to know,
> thy quiet and peaceable reign
> > in mercy establish below:
> and sorrow before thee shall fly,
> > and anger and hatred be o'er,
> and envy and malice shall die,
> > and discord afflict us no more.
>
> No horrid alarum of war,
> > shall break our eternal repose,
> no sound of the trumpet is there,
> > where Jesus's Spirit o'er flows:
> appeased by the charms of thy grace
> > we all shall in amity join,
> and kindly each other embrace,
> > and love with a passion like thine.[49]

Therefore,

> Glory be to God the giver,
> > peace and love
> > from above
> reign on earth for ever.[50]

The church

The church is a gift of God enabled by the Incarnation, but it is a mystery, indeed a perfect mystery, according to Ephrem.

> Blessed are you, O church, with ten blessings
> that our Lord gave; a perfect mystery.[51]

Ephrem describes the Incarnate One who establishes the church in this way:

> He is from eternity
> and the length of His times is incomprehensible.[52]

While Wesley does not use the word "mystery" in the same manner as Ephrem to describe the church, he expresses the longing to grasp the mystic power of godliness which is revealed through the Incarnation and for God to make known to him "the glorious mystery" or "the hidden life," which is revealed through the church of God.

> I long thy coming to confess,
> the mystic power of godliness.
> . . .
> O Christ, my hope, make known to me
> the great, the glorious mystery.[53]

Wesley is confident, however, that there is an aspect of the mystery related to the church which we must ever keep in view—

> We search the outward church in vain,
>   they cannot him we seek declare,
> they have not found the Son of man,
>   or known the sacred name they bear.[54]

The outward church is not the explanation of the mystery, but in Wesley's view, as in that of Ephrem, it is directly related to the gift of the incarnate Christ.

> Cast we off our needless fear,
> boldly to the church draw near,
> Jesus is our flesh and bone,
> God with us is all our own.[55]

Sharing in the life of the poor

The Incarnation opens hearts to the poor. God becomes incarnate for the rich and poor alike. Ephrem affirms—

> On this day when the Rich One was made poor for our sake,
> let the rich man make the poor man a sharer at his table.[56]

While Ephrem sees the poor as made sharers at the table of the rich, Wesley reverses the equation and states that—

> The Wise men adore,
>   and bring him their store,
> the rich are permitted to follow the poor.[57]

Whereas Ephrem sees the poor as welcomed at the table of the rich. Wesley sees the rich, as a result of the Incarnation, as being "permitted" to follow the poor.

In writing of the Virgin Mary, Ephrem further expands the understanding of sharing in the life of the poor through the Incarnation by shaping the following questions as coming from the lips of Mary.

> "All the chaste daughters of the Hebrews
> and virgin daughters of rulers
> are amazed at me. Because of You, a daughter of the poor
> is envied. Because of You, a daughter of the weak
> is an object of jealousy. Who gave You to me?
> "Son of the Rich One, Who despised the womb
> of rich women, what drew You
> toward the poor? For Joseph is needy,
> and I am impoverished. Your merchants
> brought gold to a house of the poor."[58]

Ephrem has numerous references to the mother Mary throughout his nativity hymns and many of them are addressed directly to her. This "daughter of the poor" interestingly becomes one who is envied and one who is the "object of jealousy." Even Mary queries,

> "Son of the Rich One, Who despised the womb
> of rich women, what drew you
> toward the poor?"[59]

God does not choose a woman of wealth to bear the divine Son Jesus, rather a woman of poverty!

In stressing the paradoxes of divine *kenosis* in the Incarnation, Ephrem uniquely summarizes how God shares in the life of the poor through the birth of Christ.

> The womb of Your mother overthrew the orders:
> The Establisher of all entered a Rich One;
> He emerged poor. He entered her a Lofty One;
> He emerged humble. He entered her a Radiant One,
> and He put on a despised hue and emerged.[60]

And further—

> Women heard that behold a virgin indeed
> would conceive and bring forth. Well-born women hoped
> that He would shine forth from them, and elegant women
> that He would appear from them. Blessed is Your height
> that bent down and shone forth from the poor.[61]

Sharing in the life of Mary

Ephrem stresses the vital role of Mary in the Incarnation, especially as relates to life of the poor. A like emphasis is not found in Wesley, however, the few references to her in Wesley's nativity hymns also reveal an understanding of her indispensable role in the Incarnation. As we share in the incarnate life, we share in her life as well, for the Incarnation does not transpire without her.

In the eighteen poems in Wesley's booklet *Hymns on the Nativity of our Lord* there is only one reference to the Virgin Mary, but it is particularly noteworthy.

> O Christ, my hope, make known to me
> the great, the glorious mystery,
>> the hidden life impart:
> Come, thou desire of nations, come,
> formed in a spotless virgin's womb,
>> a pure believing heart.[62]

There is no question for Wesley that the paradox of the Incarnation is that it is hidden in a glorious mystery, for God's *kenosis* takes its shape in and issues from "a spotless virgin's womb." Hers was a believing heart, even though she did not fully comprehend the mystery. A theme which resonates in Ephrem and Wesley as a model for the community of faith in every age.

In other nativity hymns of Wesley there are a few additional references to Mary. One reference which has become completely lost to the Wesleyan tradition is found in stanza 7 of Wesley's most famous nativity hymn. "Hark! The herald angels sing." I believe it can be said unequivocally that this stanza is retained in no contemporary hymnal of the Wesleyan tradition.

> Come, Desire of Nations, come
> fix in us thy humble home;
> rise, the woman's conquering seed,
> bruise in us the serpent's head.[63]

As in numerous hymns by Ephrem, which emphasize the vital and distinctive role of Mary, mother of Jesus, in the Incarnation, for Wesley it is through this woman that God's victory is enabled. This is the path God chose and no other. Therefore, Wesley shapes a perpetual advent prayer for the community of faith, which these four lines comprise.

In a hitherto unpublished poem Wesley avers that God is made visible through the "fruit of a virgin's womb." Mary fulfills the indispensable role of being the avenue of God's visibility on earth, revealed to all humankind.

> The solemn hour is come
>> for God made visible,
> fruit of a virgin's womb
>> a man with men to dwell,

> The Saviour of the world t'appear
> And found his heavenly kingdom here.[64]

The next stanza of the poem concludes with the provocative couplet:

> His sacred flesh the only shrine
> That holds Immensity Divine.[65]

God chooses Mary's womb to birth "sacred flesh," "Immensity Divine," and yet, nowhere do Scripture and tradition reveal that in so doing God nullified Mary's humanness. Indeed, it is her humanness, her womanly nature which participates directly in the divine Incarnation. Here again Wesley and Ephrem are one in the indispensability of Mary's role in the Incarnation.

Sharing in the contemplative life

There is a Charles Wesley poem included in his MS Luke based on Luke 1:80 ("The child grew, and waxed strong in spirit," and so on), which is vital to a discussion of "Orthodox and Wesleyan Spirituality," for it emphasizes how the Incarnation enables and expects the contemplative life. The way it resonates with the life of the desert fathers is extremely significant. This poem, however, remained unpublished until 1990, when it appeared in volume 2 of *The Unpublished Poetry of Charles Wesley*.

> A preacher should himself conceal,
> sequestered in the desert dwell,
> content for years to fast and pray,
> daily in grace and knowledge grow,
> till strong for God, the Master show
> his messenger in open day:
> dead to the low desires of men
> the anchorite should then be seen:
> yet daily still himself deny,
> simple and bold the truth declare,
> the people for his Lord prepare,
> and Jesus' servant live and die.[66]

Living the Paradox/Living the Mystery:
Implications for the Spiritual Journey and Practice of the Incarnate Life

One thing is very clear from this study of the nativity hymns of Ephrem the Syrian and Charles Wesley: for the Orthodox and Wesleyan traditions Christian spirituality is perceived as Incarnational. One's daily walk with God in Christ is a personification of the Incarnation in the life of the believer. Hence, one assumes the nature and character of the divine in that walk. In Ephrem's words "humanity [is] cut into the seal of Deity," and in Wesley's words one "partakes of the divine," one is "made divine."

Kenosis is itself a pattern for Christian spirituality. Followers of Christ willingly assume the role of incarnating the faith-life revealed in the Incarnation. Though it is beyond human comprehension, they commit their lives to living the mystery. This is itself a kenotic act for it means assuming the limitations of the Incarnation. They seek throughout their lives God's revelation of the "glorious mystery." They know, as Ephrem says, that "investigation is not able to stretch it[self] to reach You [God]," and they dedicate themselves to the lifelong vocation "to sound the mystery" (Wesley).

How are humans to be "cut into the seal of Deity"? How are they to shine in God's holiness? They must be shorn of majesty, as the divine in the Incarnation. Self-divestment is a pre-requisite to participation in the life of holiness. This means that one is willing to become a stranger for God's sake. This is *xeniteia*, one is a stranger on the earth, and in one's spiritual walk with Christ one seeks to emulate the self-emptying of God in Christ for the sake of others. One understands that those with whom one is most familiar may be estranged for the sake of the gospel. One may feel isolated, misjudged, and rejected, as did Jesus.

Just as Jesus was "humbled to the dust," so must be the servant of Christ. There can be no genuine Christian spirituality that is not marked and strengthened by the humbling of self. This is the central life-posture of the follower of Christ.

To what extent does the "cosmic God" provide a pattern for Christian spirituality? One lives the reality that one is a citizen of earth and heaven. One is linked to this world and God's cosmic mysteries through the Incarnation of Christ. It is this linkage, this sharing in the life and creation of God that are the reason for the Christian's song. It is the celebration of God's mystery and mysteries which evokes songs of praise and thanksgiving, indeed worship itself.

The spiritual journey of the Christian is the way of holiness or sanctification through which the full image of God's love is formed in the hearts of the faithful. Human beings participate actively and passively in this lifelong process. Their wills are actively involved in the quest, as the ascetic life would emphasize, and God's grace imbues the lives of the faithful with holiness through prayer, contemplation, study, service, and the sacraments. God's grace anticipates the holy life.

The sanctified life is one in which the Incarnation indwells believers and this involves divine and human will. Knowing that God alone is fully perfected in love, one humbly seeks this perfection and, as one is indwelt by Incarnate Love, one makes incarnate this love among others and amid the whole of God's creation.

Therefore, Christian spirituality is an Incarnation of all dimensions of God's revelation in Christ, which are too numerous to list. Here, however, we have spoken of bringing light where there is darkness, being a personification of hope, being a peacemaker, living the glorious mystery in and through the church, sharing in the life of the poor, and sharing in the contemplative life. These are hallmarks of the journey with God and the path of Christian spirituality.

Perhaps the most central reality in both traditions that is vital to the practice of spirituality is that *one must live the paradox of the Incarnation.* Numerous parallels have been shown here between the thought and theology of the Incarnation found in the nativity hymns of Ephrem and Wesley. As valuable as they are to an understanding of the developed theologies of the Incarnation in these poet-priests, what both of them emphasize that is central to Christian spirituality in the Orthodox and Wesleyan traditions is that individual followers of Christ, and the church as a whole, must *live the paradox of the Incarnation, i.e.* live the mystery! A key to the Christian's walk with God is how one deals with or lives with paradox. This is probably where Ephrem and Charles Wesley inform Christian spirituality the best.

Ephrem dedicates entire poems to the presentation of the paradox(es) of the Incarnation: hymn #4 celebrates the paradox of the Incarnation itself, hymn #11 addresses the paradox that Mary is a virgin and a mother, and hymn #23 affirms that God is hidden and revealed, unlimited and limited, and that divine majesty is hidden and grace revealed in the Incarnation. While Wesley usually does not dedicate entire poems to this theme, he clearly emphasizes the paradox(es) of the Incarnation in his hymns on the nativity. The paradox of all paradoxes for him is that God is born:

> Emptied of his majesty,
> of his dazzling glories shorn,
> Beings Source begins to be
> and God himself is born.[67]

> What moved the Most High so greatly to stoop,
> He comes from the sky our souls to lift up;
> that sinners forgiven, might sinless return
> to God and to heaven; their Maker is born.[68]

The "unborn-ness" or ingenerateness, *agennesia*, of God becomes the "born-ness" or generate-ness, *genesis*, of the divine Child, Jesus.

Here are a few of the paradoxes of the Incarnation emphasized by Ephrem and Wesley:

Ephrem	Wesley
God became earthly though heavenly by nature	A Child of man fills both earth and heaven
human hope is shattered, yet hope is increased in the incarnation	a helpless Object becomes the hope of all
a servant of earth is Lord on High	God is incomprehensibly made man
One who is judged wrongly, judges in truth	depths of Deity are seen in an infant's face
the unchanging God is transformed	the Maker is born, made flesh that we might become divine
the Unlimited is limited	the Invisible appears, or becomes visible

In a poem which is based on Jeremiah 31:22, "A woman shall compass a man," which Charles Wesley construed to have a prophetic reference to the virgin birth and which should be considered a nativity hymn, though he never included it in such a collection or designated it as such, he writes:

> When he did our flesh assume
>> that everlasting Man,
> Mary held him in her womb
>> whom heaven could not contain!
> Who the mystery can believe?
> Incomprehensible thou art:
> Yet we still by faith conceive,
>> and bear thee in our heart.[69]

Here he affirms what Scripture and tradition are ever saying: "The Word became flesh among us" (Jn 1:14). Who can explain the paradox of God's assumption of human flesh in the form of Jesus? Who can explain the paradox of the Virgin Mary's conception of the Holy Child? These mysteries are unfathomable to the human mind. "Who the mystery can believe? / Incomprehensible thou art." Investigation cannot prove the mystery, as Ephrem says. There are realities which transcend human logic and testing. Love's reality resides within. We can *be* love incarnate, though we cannot explain it. We *can communicate incarnate reality in our thoughts, words, emotions, and actions—in who we are.* We incarnate, we personify love's reality. Though we do not fully comprehend it, "Yet we still by faith conceive / and bear thee in our heart."

Ephrem and Wesley learned and experienced that to live the mystery of the Incarnation means to live the paradox of the Incarnation.

> 'Tis mystery all: the Immortal dies!
> Who can explore his strange design?[70]

Ephrem and Wesley emphasize that in living the mystery, living the paradox, questions and confession go together; that to be emptied of everything but love is what it means to serve a God who in Christ was emptied of all but love.

It is precisely on this point of *living the paradox, living the mystery,* in the nativity hymns of Ephrem the Syrian and Charles Wesley that we experience in the art and theology of these two poet-priests the memory of an undivided, common tradition of the church which roots all spirituality in the Incarnation of God in Jesus Christ and we are shown the life-posture for living, worship, and service. "Who [will] explore this strange design?"

Endnotes

[1]"All this may be allowed concerning the primitive Fathers. I mean particularly Clemens Romanus, Ignatius, Polycarp, Justin Martyr, Irenaeus, Origin, Clemens Alexandrinus, Cyprian; to whom I would add Macarius and Ephraim Syrus." (See "A Plain Account of Genuine Christianity," in *John and Charles Wesley: Selected Writings and Hymns* [New York: Paulist Press, 1981], 132.)

[2]Lester Ruth has noted a few of the themes which resonate in Wesley's *Hymns on the Nativity of Our*

Lord and Eastern Christian sources, though without specific references to the latter. See "Where Heaven meets Earth (and East meets West): The Nativity Hymns of Charles Wesley," *Sacramental life,* Advent/Christmas (1998), 170–75.

[3]In the third stanza of a previously unpublished poem based on Luke 2:13, Wesley does say this:

> Let Jews and Greeks as folly deem
> his fancy, his death blaspheme
> (that two-fold rock of human pride,
> a Savior born and crucified.)

This is hardly an anti-Jewish polemic *per se,* but it is by no means a positive statement about the Jews and Greeks. See S T Kimbrough, Jr. and Oliver A. Beckerlegge, *The Unpublished Poetry of Charles Wesley,* 3 vols. (Nashville: Kingswood/Abingdon, 1988, 1990, 1992), 2:80; cited henceforth as *Unpub. Poetry,* followed by the volume and page numbers.

[4]Kathleen E. McVey, *Ephrem the Syrian Hymns,* in the series Classics of Western Spirituality (New York: Paulist Press, 1989), 29. This volume will be cited henceforth by ESH followed by the hymn, stanza, and line numbers of Ephrem's texts, and the page number in the McVey volume, e.g. ESH 5:10,1–5, p. 107.

[5]Wesley's original opening lines read: Hark! How all the welkin rings, / Glory to the King of Kings. This was altered by George Whitefield in 1753 to: Hark! The herald angels sing, / Glory to the newborn King.

[6]See *Unpub. Poetry,* vol. 2.

[7]*Unpub. Poetry,* vol. 2, the two poems based on Matthew 1:21 and 2:3 (2:17–18); the 14 poems based on passages from the Gospel of Luke; two poems entitled "On Christmas Day" and "Christmas Day" (3:106).

[8]Frank Baker, in "Introduction" to *Hymns for the Nativity of Our Lord* (London: William Strahan, 1745), reprinted (Madison, NJ: The Charles Wesley Society, 1991), iii. This volume is henceforth cited as HNL followed by the hymn, stanza, and line numbers.

[9]ESH 1:97, p. 74.

[10]HNL 5:1, 5–6.

[11]ESH 4:148–49, p. 100.

[12]ESH 13:7, 1–6, p. 138.

[13]ESH 21:24, 1–6, p. 178.

[14]HNL 16:7.

[15]HNL 5:3, 1–4.

[16]*Unpub. Poetry,* 3:106.

[17]ESH 1:99, 1–2, p. 74.

[18]HNL 8:5, 104.

[19]HNL 5:5.

[20]ESH 223:2, 5–3, 1, p. 188.

[21]HNL 4:2, 5–8.

[22]HNL 12:2.

[23]HNL 13:2.

[24]ESH 21:14, p. 176.

[25]HNL 3:5.

[26]HNL 6:3.

[27]ESH 16:9, 1–5, p.

[28]ESH 23:12, p. 189.

[29]*Unpub. Poetry* 2:79, poem based on Luke 2:7, stanza 3, lines 1–4.

[30]HNL 4:3.

[31]HNL 6:5.

[32]ESH 23:4, 1, p. 188.

[33]HNL 6:6–10.

[34]*Short Hymns on Select Passages of the Holy Scriptures,* 2 vols. (Bristol: Farley, 1762), 2:6, 5–8. This volume will be cited henceforth as SH followed by the volume, poem, and page numbers, e.g. SH 2:622, 318–319.

[35]HNL 16:9, 1–3.

[36]ESH 5:10, 1–6, p. 107.

[37]HNL 8:5, 1–4.

[38]HNL 8:8.

[39] ESH 17:5, 1–2, p. 154.

[40] ESH 24:7, 7–8, p. 367; from the *Hymns on Virginity.*

[41] HNL 15:8, 4.

[42] HNL 15:4, 6, 7.

[43] ESH 5:15, 1–5, p. 108.

[44] HNL 11:1.

[45] ESH 3:9, 1–3, p. 85.

[46] ESH 23:6, 1–2, p. 188.

[47] HNL 10:1, 5–8.

[48] ESH 8:5, 1–5, p. 10.

[49] HNL 18:4–5.

[50] HNL 3:10.

[51] ESH 25:10, 1–2, p. 202.

[52] ESH 25:11, 3–4, ibid.

[53] HNL 15:6, 1–2 and 7, 1–2.

[54] HNL 17:4.

[55] HNL 12:3.

[56] ESH 1:94, p. 74.

[57] HNL 16:11, 1–3.

[58] ESH 15:2–3, p. 146.

[59] ESH 15:3, 1–3, p. 146.

[60] ESH 11:7, 1–6, p. 132.

[61] ESH 8:20, p. 123.

[62] HNL 15:7.

[63] *Hymns and Sacred Poems* (London: William Strahan, 1739), 207.

[64] *Unpub. Poetry* 2:75, based on Luke 1:26–27: In the sixth month the angel Gabriel was sent from God—to a virgin, and so on.

[65] Ibid.

[66] *Unpub. Poetry,* 2:78. While Charles Wesley's poem can hardly be interpreted as a plea for the vocation of solitary contemplation, for he speaks of "reentry" of the anchorite, nonetheless he makes a case for the importance of contemplation, even for years of fasting and prayer, as an avenue to growth in grace and knowledge. One should read this text, however, alongside of "The Preface" to *Hymns and Sacred Poems* (1739), which was probably mostly the work of John Wesley, though both he and Charles edited the volume. While he reveres those to whom he refers as "Mystick Divines," he clearly opposes a life that is asocial, that is, is lived solely in solitude. He affirms that St Paul teaches clearly—life in Christ is to be lived in community and involves bearing one another's burdens. *Hymns and Sacred Poems* (1739) includes the poem "*On Clemens Alexandrinus's Description of a Perfect Christian*" which opens with these four lines:

> Here from afar the finished height
> of holiness is seen;
> but O what heavy Tracts of Toil,
> what deserts lie between. (p. 37)

While John Wesley no doubt agreed with the spirit of the poem, the entire poem (eight stanzas of four lines each) describes perhaps more accurately the sense of Charles Wesley's approach to the spiritual journey with Christ, or the journey of holiness: it is a long journey of struggle through the deserts of life, sometimes of despair, yet never without hope. John often would have preferred to leap over the "deserts . . . Between," while Charles knew that was impossible.

[67] HNL 4:2, 5–8.

[68] HNL 7:4, 1–4.

[69] SH 2:1231, 32.

[70] *Hymns and Sacred Poems* (1739).